International Marketing Communications

The Marketing Series is one of the most comprehensive collections of books in marketing and sales available from the UK today.

Published by Butterworth-Heinemann on behalf of the Chartered Institute of Marketing, the series is divided into three distinct groups: *Student* (fulfilling the needs of those taking the Institute's certificate and diploma qualifications); *Professional Development* (for those on formal or self-study vocational training programmes); and *Practitioner* (presented in a more informal, motivating and highly practical manner for the busy marketer).

Formed in 1911, the Chartered Institute of Marketing is now the largest professional marketing management body in Europe with over 22,000 members and 25,000 students located worldwide. Its primary objectives are focused on the development of awareness and understanding of marketing throughout UK industry and commerce and in the raising of standards of professionalism in the education, training and practice of this key business discipline.

Titles in the series

International Marketing Communications

Tom Griffin

Published on behalf of the Chartered Institute of Marketing

BUTTERWORTH
HEINEMANN

Butterworth-Heinemann Ltd
Linacre House, Jordan Hill, Oxford OX2 8DP

ℛ A member of the Reed Elsevier group

OXFORD   LONDON   BOSTON
MUNICH   NEW DELHI   SINGAPORE   SYDNEY
TOKYO   TORONTO   WELLINGTON

First published 1993

British Library Cataloguing in Publication Data
Griffin, Tom
  International Marketing Communications
  I. Title
  658.8

ISBN 0 7506 0552 9

Library of Congress Cataloguing in Publication Data
Griffin, Tom, 1928–
  International marketing communications/Tom Griffin.
  p.   cm. – (The Marketing series)
  'Published on behalf of the Chartered Institute of Marketing.'
  Includes bibliographical references and index.
  ISBN 0 7506 0552 9
  1. Communication in export marketing.   2. Advertising media
  planning.   I. Series: Marketing series (London, England)
  HF1416.G75   1993   93–6984
  659.1–dc20   CIP

Printed and bound in Great Britain by
Redwood Books, Trowbridge

To young men and women who have the instincts to pursue a career in international marketing communications and the conviction to follow through.

Contents

Preface

As the first edition of this book goes to press the dynamics of the marketplace are having a major impact on the practice of advertising and promotion.

In June, 1987, an International Advertising and Marketing Congress was held in the Great Hall of the People in Beijing. It was billed as the 'biggest advertising and marketing congress in the world'.

Political changes in Eastern Europe and the USSR have brought about a shift away from central planning and control toward a freer market economy. The International Advertising Association is organizing crash, short-term advertising seminars to be conducted in different Eastern European countries. In the same region, Ogilvy, a unit of the WWP (advertising) Group, was recently assigned the Ford advertising account which 'heralds an aggressive push by Ford into Eastern Europe, particularly Hungary, Yugoslavia, Czechoslovakia, and Poland'.[1]

As Europe moves towards the realization of a single market with a population approaching 400 million it is predicted that business in almost any field will be concentrated in a few super companies and among many small specialized companies...both attempting to communicate with 'increasingly precisely-targeted sub-groups'.[2]

In North America, a Free Trade Agreement has been finalized between the USA and Canada, and another between the USA and Mexico is in the final stages of negotiation. Tariffs and trade restrictions of all types are being lessened. This means increased cooperation and competition, hopefully larger markets for all parties, and greater need for effective communications.

Further to the south, democratic institutions have replaced authoritarian rule. Real economic progress is being made within Latin American countries, and overall regional growth is being stimulated by new initiatives towards freer exchange of goods and services across borders.

Southeast Asia, including South Korea, Taiwan, Hong Kong, Singapore, and Southern China, is emerging as the region of fastest economic growth in the world.

Elsewhere in the world, some countries are fraught with inflation, debt, poverty, and social unrest making them less desirable as marketing targets for both domestic and international firms.

Expenditures of the top fifty advertisers in thirty-eight countries approached 14 billion dollars in 1989. P&G topped the list with worldwide spending of 2.7 billion dollars followed by Philip Morris with 2.5 billion, Unilever and General Motors at 1.7 billion each, and Nestle at 1.1 billion. Expenditures of the top fifty combined represent an increase of 10.5 per cent over 1988.[3]

Despite these and prior increases, promotion budgets of consumer product manufacturers have shifted markedly in the past five to twenty years. Promotion budgets that once saw advertising of a mass communication type account for as much as 80 per cent of the total now find the reverse is true. The term advertising continues to represent many forms of direct and indirect communications that are treated in this text. However, the modern marketer must think, plan, and execute with greater versatility today, selecting from all the available weaponry those tools which will achieve the marketing objectives for the brand in the most cost efficient manner. That's why the title of this work is international marketing communications. Its purpose is to acquaint beginners and refresh practitioners with these tools and their use to enable them to become more effective members and managers of the communications team.

To this end, this text identifies and explains the principles of marketing communications used by producers of consumer and industrial goods and services operating in different parts of the world. These principles will be discussed in the context of varying customer and consumer types, environments, communication techniques, and media options. Examples will be employed to illustrate how various communication techniques are used to reach customers and consumers under different environmental conditions and constraints.

The perspective of this work is more managerial and general than vocational and with specialized content.

Does this text have point of view? Yes. The matters gathered and presented have been processed through the eyes of a person who has been employed on both sides of the business.

It is hoped, however, that enough material has been presented so that the reader will obtain a good grounding in the subject matter and lead to further exploration of this fascinating and complex topic.

While every effort has been made to be comprehensive, it would be presumptuous on the writer's part to think that this work is truly global in nature. There are simply too many facets to the business of marketing communications, and the environments on earth are too many and too complex to pretend the work is complete.

No pretence is made in this work to suggest that all customers and consumers are alike. However, it is probable there is a certain commonality among all people of this world when it comes to basic physical and psychological needs. This commonality is reflected in the purchase of certain brands such as Coca-Cola and Marlboro cigarettes. No doubt it is also possible to find groups of consumers in many of the major cities around the world with similar tastes and preferences for products like Dewars Scotch whisky and Levi jeans. But in a great many cases people's needs are not filled everywhere in the same way with the same product. Take coffee for example. Middle Easterners have a preference for Turkish or Arabic coffee. Southern Europeans prefer a dark-roasted, expresso-type coffee. The Finnish like a strong, full-bodied coffee. US drinkers go for a thinner, blander cup. In other parts of the world there is little if any demand for coffee at all.

Despite the commingling of the tastes and preferences of some 400 million Europeans in a single market, Barry Day describes a byproduct that is emerging. As he explains, 'It's a way of saying OK, I'll smoke your American Marlboros...drink your French Perrier...slip on your Italian Guccis...and slide behind the wheel of your German BMW. I'll do all these things and more because I really *am* a member of the Global Village. But, *mon vieux*, never for a moment forget that underneath all this I am still *me*...I'm French. No, not just French — *Breton*. British. No, English. No, what am I talking about? *Yorkshire*. I am *all* those things and I will choose from all the things now available to me the combination, the programme that says to me (and everyone around me) that I am uniquely *me* and no one else.'[4]

When it comes to industrial products such as commercial aircraft, electronics, and earth-moving equipment, there is, however, much greater homogeneity. Similar technology is employed. Essentially the same needs prevail. Despite product similarity, social, political, economic, cultural and infrastructural differences in various nation states will necessitate different communication techniques.

Nonetheless, opportunities exist for standardization when it comes to planning, implementing and evaluating international communication programmes. Global/local, standardized/non-standardized themes will be explored throughout this book.

As for organization, this text is divided into six parts. Part One consists of four chapters which treat the basic terms and concepts, and the planning, organizing, and information systems needed to conduct international marketing communications. Part Two is comprised of two chapters that picture the conditions and constraints of different country environments and buyer behaviour and decision-making within those environments. Part Three is the heart of the subject matter under investigation and concerns message strategy formulation, message making and evaluation of message effectiveness covered in two chapters. The next four chapters in Part Four deal with the print and broadcast forms of mass media; mail as an alternate targeted media form; and the means by which a media plan is formulated, implemented, and evaluated. In Part Five, sales promotion, public relations and packaging are treated in two chapters as other forms of media for marketing communications. The final part and chapter focuses on current trends and future developments.

Notes

1 Lipman, J. (1991) Advertising. *The Wall Street Journal*, 5 June, B8.

2　Day, B. (1990) 1992 and the U.S. A presentation, Chicago, Lintas Future Day, 2 October, pp. 11, 28.
3　Giges, N. (1990) Global marketing & Media. *Advertising Age*, 19 November, S 1−10.
4　Day, *op. cit.*, pp. 23, 24.

Acknowledgements

I am hesitant to write about acknowledgements because I fear I may not mention my appreciation to one or more of the many sources which have contributed directly or indirectly to this text on international marketing communications. Calling your intention, however, to the many references at the end of each chapter is one way of recognizing the contributions of so many different publications, organizations, and people to whom I am indebted for making this work possible.

Joining the International Advertising Association (IAA) at the outset of the 1980s gave me the opportunity to come in contact with and learn from many experts here and abroad who willingly have shared their time and knowledge, either in person or as luncheon speakers. Staff members at IAA headquarters who were so very helpful at the beginning were Earle Braisted, Sylvan Barnet, Jr. and Marie Scotti. Through this IAA association over the years I have had the chance to meet many people who freely and graciously shared their expertise with me and students who accompanied me on field studies to many different countries in the Western Hemisphere and Europe. In the USA, those people include Gunilla Broadbent, and Erika Engels-Levine; more recently Joan Barry, Jane Personeni, Les Marqulis, David Beattie and at IAA headquarters Norman Vale and Richard Corner. Elsewhere in the world those people who have been most helpful over the years include Jordi Garriga, Albert Wolvesperges, Claude Chauvet, Hector Mendez Puig, Benjamin Fernandez Toca, Antonio Dieste, Giles Hennessy, Mitchell Reed and Wim Bakker.

Toshio Yamaki, Professor of Advertising and Marketing at Tokyo Keizai University, Tatsuo Sekine, President of Tokyo Kikaku Co. and Tom Teglassy, Adjunct Professor at Pace University are three other colleagues I also wish to acknowledge for the helpful information they supplied.

Field studies and conferences have led me, often accompanied by students, to places like Toronto, Mexico City, Guatemala City, San Jose, Caracas, San Juan, Lisbon, Madrid, Barcelona, Lyon, Paris, Strasbourg, Mulhouse, Basle, Stuttgart, Munich, Dusseldorf, Stockholm, Helsinki, Amsterdam, Brussels, London, Dublin, Tokyo, Taipei and Hong Kong. In these business centres we have been received and learned about marketing, advertising, and promotion from many executives in companies like Coca-Cola, Pepsi-Cola, IBM, Colgate, Nabisco, Kelloggs, Heinz, Grupo Quimico, S.C. Johnson, Goya, V. Suarez, J.M. da Fonseca International Vinhos, El Corte Ingles, La Caixa, CPC, Nestle, Caterpillar Tractor, Perrier, Superba, Baco, Sandoz, Timken, Birkel, Henkel, Fokker, Philips, Nielsen, Time, Moet Hennessy, Procter & Gamble, Johnson and Johnson, Pechiney, Bull, Toyota, Shiseido, Mizuno Corporation,

Guerlain, Avon, Kirin Brewery and many others. Similarly, executives in advertising agencies, domestic and international, have been very generous in sharing their insights with us. Names of these agencies include one or more offices of BBDO, Leo Burnett, FCB, Grey, McCann-Erickson, J. Walter Thompson, ARS Publicidad, Grey Daiko, Ogilvy & Mather, Chiat Day, and Anderson & Lembke.

Publications which have been particularly useful in preparing this text include *Advertising Age, Marketing Pocket Book* (UK), The *International Advertiser, Advertising World, International Media Guides,* and *Dentsu Japan Marketing/Advertising Yearbook.*

The scope of this self-assigned task proved to be more formidable than anticipated, requiring an inordinate amount of time, particularly towards the end. In this regard, I wish to thank my wife, Noel, for her tolerance and patience.

In the actual preparation and editing of this text, I am indebted to my colleague, Marc Schienman, for his comments and suggestions on a number of chapters. I also wish to acknowledge the important contributions made by Angelica Gianchandani, Rosa SanFilippo, Theresa Soehnlein, and Manjot Purewal in researching, preparing, and/or reviewing material for this text.

Finally, I want to recognize my assistant, Dinesh Karuthedath, without whose help this work could not have been completed. His expertise in editing, preparing exhibits and tables, and generally formatting all material for computer processing was a tremendous asset. These activities were only surpassed by his marvellous spirit of cooperation and his dedication and perseverance in seeing the job through to completion.

Part One *The Management of International Marketing Communications*

The initial portion of this text introduces the basic terms and concepts of marketing and the role of marketing communications within this function. After treating the basic terms and concepts in Chapter 1, the subjects of planning, organizations and information systems for international marketing communications are explained in context of the overall operations of the firm in Chapters 2, 3 and 4.

1 An introduction: basic terms and concepts

At the beginning of a study of international marketing communications certain groundwork is needed. This groundwork covers the basic terms and concepts that define the function of international marketing communications and relate it to other functions of the firm and the environments in which operations are conducted. That is what this first chapter attempts. On completion it is then possible to move ahead in each chapter to piece together the mosaic called international marketing communications.

Marketing communications is defined as any form of communication other than personal selling, involving message and medium, designed to directly or indirectly stimulate buying behaviour.

Marketing communications is a component of marketing, a major business function. In order to manage this component, it is essential to have an understanding of marketing and its relationship to overall business operations. This understanding begins with a grasp of a fundamental proposition called the 'marketing concept', and knowledge of the following: characteristics of a market, controllable and uncontrollable variables, differences between domestic and international markets, the communication process, marketing communication types and targets, and an understanding of the international marketing communicator's job.

The marketing concept

Peter Drucker[1] described marketing as a '...system of integrating wants, needs, and purchasing power of the consumer with the capacity and resources of production'. J.B. McKitterick[2] explained the main task of marketing management as '...making the business do what suits the interests of the customer', rather than the reverse. These ideas are cornerstones of the marketing concept which underlies modern, rational marketing thought and action. Louis E. Boone and David L. Kurtz and other writers have identified the General Electric Company as one of the first companies to recognize, articulate, and activate the marketing concept.[3] General Electric's 1952 Annual Report described this new approach for conducting their business. It included the following elements:

1   marketing involvement at the beginning, not at the end of the production cycle;

2   marketing determination, through research and analysis, of consumer wants
    in terms of product, price, location, and timing; and
3   marketing authority over production planning, scheduling of production,
    and inventory control in addition to authority over sales, distribution, and
    servicing of the product.[4]

In 1952 and earlier, other progressive companies had been operating under a
similar set of guideposts. For example, the success and leadership of Henkel's
detergent, PERSIL, since the early 1900s was based on a product guarantee,
a continuous programme of innovative research to maintain quality while
improving performance, creative advertising and broad distribution.[5]

Today, companies express their involvement and adherence to the marketing
concept in different ways. Henkel's goal is to organize and operate as close
to the market as possible.[6] Fokker Aircraft (Dutch) emphasizes the use of
marketing research to determine both passenger (consumer) and airline (customer) needs in designing new aircraft.[7] IBM strives for a better understanding of
the customers' perspective and the development of closer working relationships
(partnerships) to sustain product and service leadership.[8]

In the 1990s, the top marketing concerns of European corporate executives
are 'understanding customer needs and satisfying them in a manner superior
to their competitors'.[9]

The Coca-Cola Company's mission statement incorporates the precept that
'...we must recognize that we and our franchisees are fundamentally in the
business of servicing our customers and meeting the needs, real or perceived,
of our consumers.'[10] These are market-driven enterprises — a cornerstone of
the marketing concept.

In the business organization, the role of the marketer is to perform as the
intermediary between the firm and the environment(s) in which the firm
chooses to conduct business. As an intermediary, the marketer performs a
matching function: matching the needs of the market(s) located in one or more
environments with the capabilities and resources of the firm. The Coca-Cola
Company defines its fundamental resources as 'brands, systems, capital, and,
most important, people'.[11]

Environment

In using the word 'environment' in an international marketing context, reference
is normally being made to a country or nation state where, within geographical
boundaries, a group of people often with a common language and culture are
united under a single government. Environment can also refer to a region
comprised of a major part of one country such as the *southeast* USA, two or
more countries such as the European Community, and to the world as a
whole.

Market

Within an environment one or more markets may exist. Geographically, a market signifies a local, regional, national, or international aggregation of buying units. For example, the market for commercial aircraft of the type Airbus and Boeing manufacture would be considered national or international. The market for household detergents could be local, regional, national, or international. The former, in terms of number of customers, is relatively small. In some countries there is only one customer — the national airline. In other countries there are no customers at all. In still others, outside of the USA, the number of customers can be counted on one hand. In contrast, the detergent market is widespread in most countries with users found in most households.

Sometimes a market can be concentrated in a single area such as 'Silicone Valley' in California for electronics manufacturers. Sometimes a market will be limited to a handful of customers scattered among a few countries of the world as in the case of fuel gauges for fork lift trucks. And sometimes a market will be spread among many people in many parts of the world as is the case with Coca-Cola which sells 400 million drinks per day in 160 countries.[12]

For the firm, regardless of product type or markets served, adequate volume potential must exist in terms of order size, number of buyers, and/or frequency of purchase to make the marketing effort worthwhile.

Consumer targets

For consumer products like food, cleaning, and personal care it is customary to think of the buying unit as an individual or a household. If the household is the target, then each family member's influence on purchase and usage should be considered when planning marketing communications. Take, for example, Royal Polos (a fruit-flavoured ice stick sold in Spain) which are made at home in the freezer. Mothers buy; children consume. It is the marketing communication job to determine whether advertising should be directed to mother, child, or both.

Business targets

For most types of industrial or business-to-business products and services the organization is considered to be the buying unit. Several different members of the firm, including representatives from engineering, production, research and development, marketing, and even top management may actively participate in the buying decisions for products and services of any consequence. For this reason, organizations, not people, constitute this market.

Market constraints

When taking into account different markets around the world, a variety of constraints with respect to the ability of a firm to market its products in any given environment may be encountered. There can be political, legal, economic, or cultural barriers which may preclude an opportunity to market. Therefore, *accessibility* is another factor which must be considered when dealing beyond one's own borders.

It is also necessary to take into account *purchasing power* of the buying unit and its *willingness to spend* or exchange purchasing power for goods or services needed.[13] In international markets a great variation will be found in purchasing power among business organizations as well as households and people in general. Needs and wants will vary significantly due to differences in tastes and preferences of consumer units, and the requirements of industrial buying organizations.

Basic market determination factors

In the determination of an international market, then, these elements should be considered:

1 people, households, or organizations
2 accessibility
3 purchasing power
4 willingness to spend

Controllable and uncontrollable variables

Marketing managers must deal with two basic types of variables in matching needs and wants of a market with the capabilities and resources of the firm − those which they can control and those which they cannot.

The principal *uncontrollable* variables in any given environment are listed below. With respect to each variable a number of questions need answers.

Political/legal
What system of government (free enterprises, socialistic, communistic) exists? What is the official policy towards luxury goods as opposed to basic necessities; towards technology transfer? What laws must be adhered to with respect to ingredients in product, packaging, advertising, and other forms of promotion?

Economic

What is the level and trend in per capita income? Is and has the balance of payments been favourable or unfavourable? How much foreign debt has the country incurred? Are interest payments to service foreign debt a burden? Is inflation in check or out of control? Are exchange rates stable? Is the currency convertible?

Cultural

Are there religious barriers? What about education and literacy rate? How about customs, tastes, and preferences of consumers?

Competition

Are there few or many competitors? How formidable are they? What are the relative strengths and weaknesses of the various products offered?

Infrastructure

What energy sources and supply, what transportation and warehousing facilities, what communication, banking, advertising and promotion services are available?

Technology

What is the level of industrial development? Are production systems up-to-date? Is the commercial infrastructure modern or antiquated?

The *controllable* variables are the following.

The product

Products have both tangible and intangible properties. These properties should be evaluated in terms of their ability to deliver consumer satisfaction. Brand name, packaging, warranties, and guarantees as well as physical ingredients and/or inner workings are all parts of a product. A consumer will buy a Mercedes not only for its ability to provide safe, dependable transportation but also for its ability to project the personality and life style of that individual. A Shiseido cream is purchased for its ability to soften skin *and* enhance the beauty of the purchaser. Perrier is consumed for its properties of quenching thirst and because its considered to be the drink of young, modern sophisticates. A Sony Trinitron television set is selected because its name stands for the highest picture quality among all brands on the market.

The distribution channel

This can be viewed as a conduit through which information and products and services flow to bring producer and consumer together. In some instances contact is made directly between producer and consumer. In other instances one or more intermediaries will play a role in the channel of distribution. This role may involve physical movement, storage, and handling; or selling (normally considered a promotion function); or both. Names commonly associated with intermediaries include agents, brokers, importers, distributors, wholesalers, and retailers.

Price

While price is normally considered controllable in dealings between producers and direct buyers, government price controls are found in many parts of the world. These controls limit freedom of action in raising prices and may cause a firm to go out of business.[14] When products are sold across borders, tariffs (taxes on imports) will commonly have to be factored into the pricing equation along with insurance and added freight charges. Another government assessment which results in an increase in the price to buyers in many countries is value added tax (VAT). It is figured as a percentage of the value which a manufacturer or intermediary adds and must be paid each time the product changes hands in the channel of distribution.[15] It should also be recognized that when intermediaries who buy and resell become part of the distribution channel the ultimate consumer price is no longer controlled by the producer. That price will be increased by the mark-up or margin the intermediary(ies) elect to take.

Promotion

These are activities, all involving communications, which are placed behind the product to move it from manufacturer to the ultimate consumer for the purpose of satisfying that person's or organization's needs. Included are personal selling, advertising, sales promotion, product publicity, and public relations.

Research

Research is used to assess market opportunities for product introductions and to evaluate the effectiveness of all controllable variables before and after their use in a marketing programme. Research can aid in the evaluation of product, packaging, competitive offerings, and advertising, sales promotion, publicity, and public relations effectiveness.

The particular combination of controllable variables employed in any given environment is called the 'marketing mix'.

National versus international marketing

To conduct marketing operations within a given country environment the firm draws on its capabilities and resources to develop and carry out a programme of activities involving the controllable marketing variables aimed at its target market(s). These operations are planned and implemented with knowledge of the constraints imposed by the uncontrollable variables of the environment. (See Figure 1.1.)

In considering a given environment, there are few, if any products which have a universal appeal. That is why markets are looked on as clusters of consumers, as Figure 1.1 indicates, some larger than others. Consumer clusters may be formed as a result of geographic concentration; by socioeconomic grouping involving age, income, education, family size, and other related factors; by similarities in life styles, activities, and interests; or by a combination of these characteristics. Different marketing mixes may be used to reach and service different consumer clusters. If sizeable, the company's own sales organization may provide coverage. In other smaller clusters agents or distributors may be retained.

In international marketing, the basic process and principles are essentially the same as national marketing. However, environmental, operational, and organizational differences are usually found. Tastes and preferences of the market may vary. For example, liquid soap for the bath and shower has become widely accepted in Germany, but not in the USA. Cultural differences will influence clothing styles and food preferences. Laws may vary with respect to shopping hours and days. Television advertising opportunities differ in terms of availability. Money-off coupons may be commonplace in one country and banned in another. Retail food outlets may be highly concentrated among a relatively few stores in one country and the opposite condition — many small

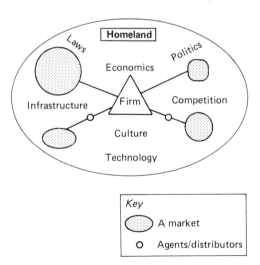

Figure 1.1   *The firm, its markets and the national environment*

stores — may exist in another country. For example, Nielsen reports that hypermarkets and supermarkets accounts for 84 per cent and 83 per cent of total grocery store turnover in the USA and France in contrast to only 12 per cent and 8 per cent in Portugal and South Korea.[16]

An international marketer may elect to sell through a distributor or importer in one country and establish a subsidiary which both manufactures and provides marketing services in the next. Market size, strength of competition, and relative purchasing power are factors which influence these types of business decisions. The types of differences cited above provide the reason for being able to say that international marketing is more complex than national marketing. Figure 1.2 visually portrays an international marketing environment.

Customer clusters (markets) are served in several foreign environments as well as at home. Instead of one set of uncontrollable variables, there are now five. There could be as many as 100 or more. This would depend on the scope of operations of a firm. As previously indicated, Coca-Cola is sold in 160 countries where eighty or more different languages are spoken. Johnson & Johnson has manufacturing subsidiaries in forty-seven countries and sells in most countries of the world.[17]

As environmental and market conditions vary, controllable variables will require adjustment. This may call for product, packaging, pricing, promotion, and distribution changes. In country A, subsidiary operations (manufacturing and marketing) have been established. In country B, a joint venture has been

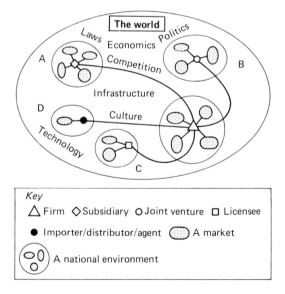

Figure 1.2   *The firm, its markets and the global environment*

created. In country C, product is being marketed by a licensee. And, in country D, product is being exported from the home country; host country sales and distribution are handled by an agent or importer/distributor. Products may require simplification because higher priced, more complex and ornate items may not sell. Packaging may have to change for reasons of language and different labelling requirements. Similarly, advertising and other forms of promotion may require adjustment. For example, a television advertising commercial for Kellogg's cereal in Britain would be banned in Holland because it claims to contain extra vitamins, outlawed in Germany because the wording sounds like a competitive claim, and the child wearing a Kellogg T-shirt would have to be edited out in France because children are forbidden from endorsing products on TV.[18]

The communication process

To understand what international marketing communication is and how it works requires an appreciation of the communication process.[19] Simply stated, it is a process (shown in Figure 1.3) by which information is exchanged between individuals and organizations.

The transmission system by which information is exchanged is comprised of the following elements.

1 An *information source or sender* which can be an individual or organization. Senders are responsible for determining what message is to be sent and

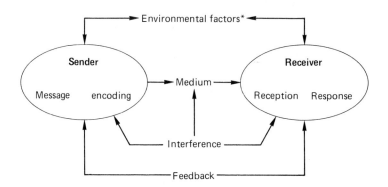

* Differences in culture, politics, laws/regulations, economics, competition, infrastructure and technology

Figure 1.3 *The communication process*

how it should be encoded (translated) in order to reach the intended receiver.

2   A *medium* (or media) which can be personal or impersonal, oral, written, and/or visual.

3   A receiver or audience for whom the message is intended and their response which can be positive, negative, neutral, or nonexistent.

4   *Interference* which can be generated by competitors, media, and reception problems.

5   *Feedback* which may be voluntary or sought by the sender to determine the nature of the receiver's response.

6   *Environmental factors* which will have a bearing on the nature of the message and its translation and transmission.

Internationally, the communication process increases in complexity as the number of borders crossed increase.

Senders of messages can be people, brands, a company, or any combination of the above. A company president or sales representative may speak on the phone, correspond, or visit with customers. Fact sheets, pamphlets, and brochures with brand and company identification are exchanged. Various types of advertisements for brands and companies are prepared for transmission by non-personal means.

The message and its translation (encoding) must be in a form appropriate for the medium selected and understandable to receivers. Voice, other sounds, words, colours, pictures, and actions are used for this purpose. For a US television commercial to be effective in the Republic of Ireland, a 'mid-Atlantic' voice is essential according to one advertising executive. Another practitioner stated that in Belgium (and elsewhere in Europe) when selecting talent for a television commercial, it is necessary to not only select a voice with care but also the facial look, expression, and dress. When language translation is required, a literal interpretation may not convey the intended message. 'Plays on English words are totally impractical in Chinese − and vice versa' according to John Roddy.[20] To illustrate his point, Roddy cited the back translation from Chinese of an English headline for a new Minolta camera − 'maxis are out Minis are in' − as saying something quite different: 'mini cameras are becoming quite popular.'

In situations where the same language is spoken, within a country or across borders, words must be chosen carefully. For example, an English tourist pulls into a US service station and requests the attendant to 'top it up with petrol, wash the windscreen, check under the bonnet, and see if the tyres need air, including the spare in the boot. . . .' What the tourist needs to say is, 'fill the tank with gas, wash the windshield, check under the hood, and see if the tires need air, including the spare in the trunk.'[21]

Actions, or pictures of action in one culture may have no meaning or may not be understood in another culture. A gesture for saying 'goodbye' in a Latin American country could be interpreted for 'come here' in the USA.

Interaction between the message and the medium must be considered. *Encoding* must accommodate the medium or channel through which the message is to be transmitted (and vice versa). For example, if the firm is selling an ingredient type of food product to consumers which can be used in a variety of recipes, the recipe presented in a magazine reaching an upper income, sophisticated audience will not be the same as a recipe presented in a magazine reaching a middle to lower income, family audience.

In preparing and translating messages sight should not be lost of the fact that the communication is always a reflection on and expression of company policy. Whatever is sent — personal letter, brochure, magazine advertisement — should be in keeping with the image which the organization wishes to project.

The medium selected could be a personal letter or telephone call to one or a few receivers, or a radio, loudspeaker, television, magazine, outdoor, or transit advertisement designed to reach many receivers.

Whatever the *medium*, it must be appropriate for the message being delivered and be selected from the choices available in a particular environment. If the message requires considerable explanation, a brochure, magazine or newspaper advertisement are suitable alternatives. If the need to demonstrate is critical, the ideal medium would be personal communication, or, depending on the type of product, television would be appropriate, providing that alternative existed.

Receivers are the intended recipients of the message. They can be members of the marketer's sales force; representatives (agents and distributors); channel members (wholesalers and retailers); editors working for newspapers, magazines, radio and television stations who write or select product information stories for placement in their medium. They can also be customers, prospects, and those who influence purchases by others.

Whether or not *reception* takes place depends on what the message was, how it was translated and transmitted. These are the kinds of questions marketing communicators seek answers for. Was the content of interest? Was the language translation appropriate? Were the right words, pictures, sounds, and actions used? Was something learned? Did an attitude change occur? Was it positive or negative? Did it stimulate some form of action such as sending in for more information or an actual purchase?

Interference may disrupt message transmission in several different ways. The *first* of which is *noise*. It can be generated by competitive activity (advertising and promotion) and the clutter from all other messages being transmitted at the same time. The *second* is media or channel distortion: poor quality reproduction of printed material or inaudible voice communication on the phone or radio. The *third* factor is the appropriateness of the medium itself in terms of audience and editorial compatibility. In selecting magazines for an advertising campaign in one or several foreign markets, was the editorial climate appropriate for the intended receivers? Was the editorial adjacency for an advertisement in a given magazine compatible? An advertisement for a first aid spray should receiver greater readership when placed next to an editorial column on family health than when placed next to an article on how to prepare fillet of sole bon femme. The *fourth* factor relates to the receivers themselves. Were they preoccupied with their own thoughts at the time of message transmission? Were other situational factors present at the time of transmission to cause inattentiveness?

Feedback is sought to determine whether or not the communication objectives were attained.

Where communications involve person-to-person contact, as in the case of personal selling, feedback — answers to questions — can be immediate and continue throughout the presentation in order to evaluate effectiveness in a timely manner and make message adjustments if indicated.

The situation is quite different with non-personal forms of communication such as advertising. Other means, often involving a formal research study, must be employed to determine the nature of response and evaluate the message effectiveness.

For the communication process to function effectively those involved must have a clear understanding of relevant *environmental* factors in the various countries where receivers are clustered. Compelling messages cannot be forged without a sensitivity towards social norms, preconceptions, tastes, preferences, customs, and standards of behaviour which prevail in any given marketplace. Media alternatives and constraints must be known in order to transmit messages efficiently. In acquiring information (feedback) to evaluate receivers' responses, the opportunities for formal and informal research must be ascertained.

Marketing communications: targets and media alternatives

In planning and executing marketing communications programmes, the targets must be identified and defined, and the appropriate media selected. In subsequent chapters detailed explanations on identifying targets and selecting media alternatives will be given. At this juncture it is important to be aware of the targets and alternatives which exist.

Targets

In designing information to be communicated within and across borders there are four basic target classifications:

1   company sales representatives
2   intermediaries: agents, brokers, manufacturers' representatives, distributors,
              wholesalers, and retailers
3   editors (print and broadcast)
4   prospects, users (consumers), and influencers

The firm's sales representatives and intermediaries it elects to work with in the channel of distribution need information about the firm, its policies, products, pricing and the marketing programme being put behind the goods and/or services it produces. The originator of these communications may be either the firm itself or the sales representative of the firm who calls on channel members. Editors are another class of communication recipients. There are two basic types of editors that control and transmit information called publicity which may help stimulate sales.

One type of editor controls information through trade media, e.g., *Modern Packaging* magazine for the packaging industry, or *Aviation Week* for the aircraft industry. The other is engaged in newsworthy information transmission through the general press and broadcast channels, e.g., local and national newspapers, news and special interest magazines, radio and television stations. Firms, with or without the help of public relations counsel, prepare and send stories about their goods or services slanted to the audience of a particular medium or type of media. If the editor who receives the story believes that his/her readers, listeners, or viewers will be interested in and may benefit from the content, then there is the likelihood that the story, all or in part, will be used. When the product information is transmitted in this manner, the firm, often not identified as the sponsor, will benefit from this editorial endorsement, providing the message is favourable.

Customers, prospects and influencers comprise the ultimate target. Types of communication include tangible objects such as samples; incentives such as coupons and rebates; persuasive messages via advertising, direct mail, and telephone; and information about the company and its products disseminated at meetings, shows, and sponsored events such as a marathon or football championship. The purpose of these communication activities is to inform, create goodwill and/or a favourable attitude and stimulate buying action.

Media alternatives

The manner in which media alternatives are classified are by no means uniform from country to country. In the UK and other European countries a distinction is made between 'above-the-line' and 'below-the-line' media. Above-the-line media include advertising activities such as press (magazines and newspapers), television, radio, cinema, and posters for which a commission or fee is paid to a recognized advertising agency. Below-the-line usually include various types of communications designed to promote sales.[22] In Japan, the *Dentsu Marketing/Advertising Yearbook* classifies television, newspapers, magazines, and radio as 'major media'. Outdoor, transit, and movies along with direct mail, flyers, POP, telephone directories, and exhibitions/screen displays are classified under 'sales promotion'.[23]

For the purposes of classification in this text, the alternatives, excluding selling in person or on the phone, have been divided into three basic categories as shown in Exhibit 1.1.

Exhibit 1.1 *Marketing communications media by category*

I *Mass media*	II *Sales support media*	III *Other media*
• Newspapers	• Sales literature	• Mail
• Magazines	• Point-of-sale material	• Publicity
• Outdoor	• Audio visual and films	• Packaging
• Yellow pages	• Exhibitions/trade shows	• Specialized media
• Television	• Meetings and seminars	• New media
• Radio	• Sponsorships	
• Cinema	• Special events	
	• Presentation aids	

As for media alternatives, it is the rule rather than the exception to use a combination in carrying out a marketing plan. A consumer plan may include television, magazines, and yellow pages; trade shows, sales literature, point-of-sale material, and in-person presentation aids; mail, publicity, and packaging. A business-to-business marketer's plan is likely to include (trade) magazines, mail, publicity, trade shows, sales literature, and presentation aids. Other marketers, particularly ones that rely on direct response communications, will limit their activities to a few or possibly a single medium such as mail. Sales literature is very much a part of most mail media campaigns as well as being a sales support medium.

Regardless of target or type of communication activity, there is a need to evaluate effectiveness by means of some form of feedback (step five in the communication process) whenever time, money, and effort is expended. This is accomplished by evaluating unsolicited responses from target groups, and through planned research studies to assess effectiveness.

The job of the international marketing communicator (IMC)

In smaller organizations, the international marketing communication job may be one of several that a marketing manager assumes or one of many that the president of a company assumes. In larger organizations, one person may be designated to manage this function or the person in charge may have a sizeable staff, each staff member performing a specialized task. Regardless of organizational size, the IMC may retain suppliers or consultants to provide package design, advertising, promotion, publicity, and marketing research services.

IMCs conceive, execute, and evaluate programmes in support of predetermined marketing objectives. To perform this function the IMC must have a clear understanding of the firm's short- and long-range goals, policies, and planning systems as well as an intimate knowledge of the products or services being marketed and a good working relationship with all internal personnel who work in the different functional departments such as accounting, product development, production, and distribution.

IMCs must have a working knowledge of all aspects of marketing as well as of the assorted communication techniques and media alternatives. This individual must coordinate with and integrate communication plans into the firm's overall marketing effort...and be accountable for the results achieved.

Preceding the development of communication plans, the IMC has to know and understand the environmental constraints imposed on marketing communications, the channel members with whom the firm must deal, and each target market so that effective communication programmes can be planned and implemented. Once executed, the IMC then becomes responsible for employing appropriate techniques to evaluate communication effectiveness.

In the process of plans development, the IMC must establish a good working relationship with suppliers of communication services so that, whether the service is advertising, promotion, or publicity, the message output is appropriate, strong, clear, unambiguous, and imaginative.

Finally the IMC as an individual should have good oral, written, and visual communication skills; a flare for showmanship; a creative bent; and an ability to evaluate and criticize objectively communication ideas and concepts of co-workers, inside and outside the company. The IMC's role is visualized in Figure 1.4.

For the right person with the will to study; persevere; develop good communication, interpersonal, and planning skills, and deal with the complexities of the global environment, international marketing communications can be a challenging and rewarding job.

In this chapter a number of terms and concepts relating to marketing and the sub-function marketing communications, the subject of this text, have been defined, including the work of the IMC. The stage is now set to explore the principal elements of this subject matter in more depth. The first of these elements is international marketing communication planning.

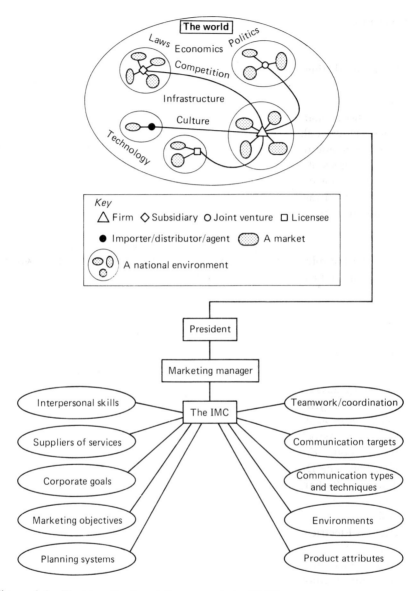

Figure 1.4   *The international marketing communicator (IMC)*

Questions

1 Define marketing communications.
2 What is the role of marketing in a business organization?
3 Describe the meaning of 'environment' and 'market' as they are used in international marketing.
4 What elements should be considered in the determination of a market?
5 List the major uncontrollable variables in any given environment and give examples of each.
6 List the major controllable variables and explain each.
7 Compare/contrast national marketing to international marketing.
8 Could any type of medium be used for communication to markets in any country? Explain why or why not.
9 What is the significance of feedback and how it may be obtained?
10 Describe the role of an international marketing communicator. What are some important qualities that a successful IMC should have?

Notes

1 Drucker, P.F. (1958) Marketing and economic development. *Journal of Marketing*, **XXII**(3), 256.
2 McKitterick, J.B. (1957) What is the marketing management concept? In *The Frontries of Marketing Thought and Science*, (ed. F.M. Bass). American Marketing Association, Chicago, p. 78.
3 Boone, Louis E. and Kurtz, David L. (1977) *Foundations of Marketing*, Hinsdale, The Dryden Press, Illinois, p. 15; McCarthy, E.J. (1975) *Basic Marketing*, Richard D. Irwin, Inc., Homewood, IL, 5th edn, pp. 26—27; Stanton, William J. (1975) *Fundamentals of Marketing*, 4th edn, McGraw-Hill Book Company, New York, p. 13.
4 General Electric Company (1953) *1952 Annual Report*, The Company, New York, p. 21.
5 Notes taken at meetings with personnel from Henkel in Dusseldorf, Germany in May—June 1987.
6 *Ibid.*
7 Notes taken at meetings with Wim Bakker and Jurek Keur at Fokker BV in Amsterdam, May, 1987.
8 Notes taken at meetings with personnel from IBM in Belgium in May—June, 1987.
9 Larrecle, Jean-Claude, Powell, William W. and Ebeling, Hardy Deutz

(1988) Europe's key marketing issues for the '90's. *International Advertiser*, May—June, p. 20.

10 Goizueta, Roberto C. (1989) *Coca-Cola, A Business System Toward 2000: Our Mission in the 1990's*, The Coca-Cola Company, p. 3.

11 *Ibid.*, p. 2.

12 Notes taken at a presentation given by Ralph Cooper, President, The Coca-Cola Company Northwest Europe, London, 7 June 1989.

13 Runyon, Kenneth E. (1984) *Advertising*, 2nd edn, Charles E. Merrill Publishing Company, Columbus, Ohio, p. 78.

14 Terpstra, Vern (1987) *International Marketing*, 4th edn, The Dryden Press, Chicago, pp. 551—553.

15 Onkvisit, Sak and Shaw, John J. (1989) International Marketing, Merrill Publishing Company, Columbus, Ohio, p. 89.

16 Nielsen Marketing Research (1987) *International Food and Drug Store and Trends*, A.C. Nielsen Company, p. 51.

17 Johnson & Johnson (1986) *Annual Report*, p. 39.

18 Terpstra, *op. cit.*, p. 448.

19 See Engel, James F., Warshaw, Martin R. and Kinnear, Thomas (1987) *Promotional Strategy*, 6th edn, Irwin, Homewood, IL, pp. 39—53; Onkvisit, pp. 586—588; Toyne, Brian and Walters, Peter G.P. (1989) *Global Marketing Management*, Allyn and Bacon, Needham, MA, pp. 535—538.

20 Roddy, John (1982) Advertising and marketing in South East Asia — a lesson in give and take. Speech given at a New York Chapter International Advertising Association meeting, New York, June.

21 Mandell, Maurice I. (1984) *Advertising*, 4th edn, Prentice Hall, Englewood Cliffs, NJ, pp. 14—15.

22 Wilmshurst, John (1985) *The Fundamentals of Advertising*, William Heinemann Ltd, London, pp. 95, 96.

23 Publications Department (1989) *Dentsu Japan Marketing/Advertising Yearbook 1990*, Dentsu Inc., Tokyo, p. 133.

2 *International marketing communications planning*

A central concept

International marketing communication planning is a central concept in the body of information which is being treated in this text. By way of introduction, the subject is discussed in terms of what it is or should be and why it has major significance in the operation of a firm's business.

Next, matters which are pertinent but preliminary to the act of planning are reviewed. Then a comprehensive planning system framework is visualized and explained.

Following this, a marketing plan structure is introduced; planners, annual and strategic, are discussed; budgeting, profit planning, and promotional expenditure norms are treated. The last element covered is the flow chart of promotional activities — the centrepiece of a marketing communication plan.

Nature and significance

Communication planning is part of the total marketing planning of a business unit or company. Marketing planning has been described in several different ways. In one instance, it has been called a road map to estimate time, congestion en route, and cost to complete the trip.[1] It also has been described as a 'highly responsive process for guiding firms through the hazards of a rapidly changing environment.'[2] In the final analysis it should be:

- an assembly of all important facts, conclusions, and operating decisions,
- a complete operating guide for internal management and retained suppliers of communication services, and
- a benchmark for judging accomplishments.[3]

To generate the plan, three basic informational inputs are essential from the international marketing information system:

1 Knowledge of the product — its features, benefits, and technology.
2 Knowledge of the market(s) — especially customers, consumers, and competition.
3 Knowledge of the marketing function — including all communication techniques and applications.[4]

With respect to the cost of planning, the benefits must outweigh the costs. However, the costs of planning are relatively small compared to operating costs in foreign markets when working with joint venture partners or subsidiaries. Therefore, a small improvement in effectiveness, or a new opportunity uncovered can easily offset planning costs. Looked at in another way, costs of planning can be equated to costs of errors or missed opportunities.[5]

Preliminary matters

In this section readers are asked to consider a number of considerations preliminary to the act of planning which involve differences within and among any given environment which involve variables inside and outside of the firm's control. (Information in this section is based on a paper presented by Tom Griffin at the Third Bi-Annual World Marketing Congress, Barcelona, Spain, August 1987.)

Inter-environmental considerations

Differences among environments is a major factor in planning international marketing communications. A number of factors must be examined to determine these differences and also attempt to establish any similarities. The factors include social, cultural, political, legal, and economic characteristics; also characteristics of customers, consumers, influencers, and prospects. (These factors are in Part Two, Chapters 5 and 6.)

Global or local marketing

A topic of much debate in recent years has been global marketing and promotion. This debate has centred around thoughts expressed by Levitt[6] on the subject. He envisioned an emerging global market for standardized consumer products on a vast scale. Benefits to the global organization included significant economies of scale in production, distribution, management, marketing, (and communications). In planning advertising, this has become a partial if not a total global reality for more than one consumer product, such as Coca-Cola or Marlboro cigarettes.

The global approach, however, does not have universal acceptance. A study among 120 senior executives revealed this. Those products found to be most appropriate for global brand strategies were high technology products like computer hardware, airline and photographic equipment, heavy machinery and machine tools. Considered much less appropriate were products like sweets, clothing, food, toiletries and household cleaners.[7]

One researcher has concluded that (global) standardization strategies are 'very situation specific'. Factors to be taken into account include the product itself, consumer behaviour, legal, and product use conditions as well as the firm's resources, objectives, and ambitions.[8]

Controllable variable considerations

Domestically or internationally, marketers should recognize the traditional tools of promotion, such as advertising, sales promotion, and publicity are important but not the only factors to be taken into account when planning communication programmes. Other elements with communication value are the product itself, brand name, packaging, pricing, and method of distribution. All of these tools should be evaluated in the context of any given environment. Direct translation seldom works. Host country systems, infrastructure, laws, and regulations often require different approaches and techniques. Possible changes in six key marketing variables are outlined below. As these variables change so will communications. The purpose here is to give the reader an idea of the number a variety of changes that may have to be made in cross-border planning.

Product
The product as well as the package and brand name may need to be changed to make it a suitable offering in a particular foreign environment. For example, different Berol handwriting instruments are marketed in the UK and the US to respond to different consumer preferences in terms of shape and feel.[9] In turn, this will necessitate communications adjustments.

Method of selling
Conditions in the host country may require changes in the selling method and the communications programmes designed to support this effort. At home the firm may use a direct sales force. In the host country a distributor-appointed sales system may be more effective and cost efficient. Infrastructure differences could be another factor that would dictate change. For example, the firm may sell through the mail at home. However, the nature of the postal system in the host country may preclude this method of selling. The non-personal communication support activities will require adjustment in content and form as selling methods change.

Advertising
Adjustments can be called for in both message and medium. The home country message may be couched in an idiomatic expression in a visual setting that cannot nor will not translate due to language and/or cultural differences

in the host country. The principal advertising medium used at home is television. In the host country television time can be insufficient or non-existent. Therefore, media plans must change.

Sales promotion

Differences in effectiveness of techniques and regulations may require sales promotion changes in the host country. At home, for example, trade show participation may be found to be ineffective. In the host country, however, trade shows are considered to be a key activity in order to wage a successful selling effort. The material used at point-of-sale in the home country may not have the same effect or acceptance in the host country. Regulations may preclude the use of coupons and samples in the host country — techniques found to be very successful at home.

Information

Significant differences can exist in the availability, accuracy, and timeliness of secondary data, and in the firm's ability to conduct primary research in the host country. For example, reliable, current industry or competitive information may not be obtainable. This can also hold true for consumer demographics and psychographics. With respect to market research studies, cultural characteristics and infrastructure may inhibit a firm's ability to obtain awareness and attitudinal information about a product and its advertising. For example, cultural constraints may preclude the possibility of conducting personal interviews among women as has been the case in some Middle Eastern countries. Telephone interviewing may not be possible due to the lack of phones in many environments. Varying conditions, then, impose difficulties and generate uncertainties with respect to the normal information needs of a firm in planning communication programmes.

Effect of entry method

The way of doing business in a host country may cause difficulty in planning, executing, and evaluating marketing communication programmes. At home, the organization of the firm is monolithic: there is one management, one chain of command. In the host country, a joint venture may have been formed. Inputs for marketing communications planning and decision making, varying in quality and quantity, emanate from two different managements. What is expected and what is received by home country management may be quite different. Similarly, when working through importers and distributors in a host country market, informational inputs for planning and evaluating the effectiveness of marketing communications programmes may be limited.

Effects of size and scope of operations

The size and scope of operations will have a direct bearing on international marketing communication planning. Larger organizations will normally have greater financial ability to hire and train communication specialists, provide headquarters staff to assist field management develop communication programmes, and retain the services of outside organizations to undertake communications research, and create and implement advertising, promotion, and publicity programmes. Larger organizations are also more apt to use greater sophistication and more variety in the selection of communication techniques to reach customers, prospects, and other communication targets.

Small organizations with limited personnel and financial resources will customarily rely on a single employee to perform a variety of communication tasks, often in combination with other duties. It is also likely that fewer and more ordinary communication techniques will be used. More communication assignments will be carried out in house; outside service organizations that perform specialized communication tasks are less apt to be retained.

Planning complexities and problems related to size

The problems in planning marketing communication programmes in a large multinational firm are quite unlike those encountered in a small firm where management of marketing communications rests in the hands of export department personnel. In the latter case, the principal communication activities would be those in support of the selling effort and oriented toward the achievement of short-term results.

In contrast, the multinational (or global) firm, which may not only have foreign subsidiaries but also an intermingling of product divisions organized in a matrix configuration, poses a planning complexity of a much higher order. Target audiences are likely to be dispersed. Communication planners will be addressing long as well as short-range problems. Multiple product lines will require a commensurate number of creative strategies and media plans.

In the small firm, the chief executive may not perceive a need for marketing planning, including communications. Even if subordinates attempt to plan, without active support and involvement of the chief executive, formalized marketing planning is not likely to work.[10] Another problem faced in smaller companies concerns staff limitations with respect to communication specialists. There may only be the sales manager who concentrates on personal selling and managing the selling activity.[11] Overall, the sophistication and extent of planning marketing communications will be limited.

A different set of problems can be found in the large multinational firm. Planners exist at both the strategic (long-range, company-oriented) level and the operational (short-range, product-oriented) level. The number and type of people involved, the different levels of management, and the physical separations which exist between corporate headquarters and far-flung subsidiaries create problems of understanding, coordination, and internal communication.[12] It has been found, for example, that regardless of physical separation, if a close working relationship does not exist between strategic and operational planners, planning systems have been found to be ineffective.[13]

Regardless of organizational size, strategic planning (which should contain a communication component) can suffer if there is a lack of involvement of line personnel at the divisional and departmental levels.[14] This apparently stems from the fact that many managers don't understand that a relationship exists between planning and the entire management process.

Type of business

The type of business will have an influence in planning marketing communications. Consumer goods producers are apt to produce separate marketing plans for each major product (line). Industrial goods producers are more likely to prepare a general business plan, containing marketing and communication components. Service producers normally take one of two tacks: develop a single marketing plan for all services or include the marketing plan as a part of the overall business plan.[15] Industrial goods producers will also place greater emphasis on personal communications (selling) than on advertising due to the relatively small number of customers, importance of the individual sale, and the technical complexity of the product. The converse will generally hold true in the case of consumer goods producers.

Planning system framework

To plan international marketing operations in a systematic and meaningful way, a framework is needed to conceptualize how the planning process and supportive procedures should work. The structure and process requires understanding on the part of all participants to optimize the contribution of each individual involved and to achieve the results desired. The entire process, normally repeated on an annual basis, is linked to a chain of dynamic, interrelated activities which represents the way in which the firm is managed.[16]

The international marketing planning system (IMPS) connects the internal and external sub-systems of the firm with the environment(s) in which it transacts business. The IMPS is shown in Figure 2.1. One element of the system, the 'world', was introduced in Chapter 1. The international marketing information system (IMIS) will be treated in Chapter 4.

The planning system is pervasive. It encompasses all factors which affect the ability of the firm to market its goods and/or service in various countries around the world.

The process is both continuous and cyclical, though the formal planning process normally is concentrated in a predetermined time period of three to four months. It is continuous with respect to gathering information and generating ideas for improving performance. The cycle for the international marketing plan is usually one year.

The international marketing information system (IMIS) component should operate in a way that it is continually processing relevant information from the firm's global environments where business is being or will be conducted. This input should include both an evaluation of existing programmes and information for future planning purposes. The conduits for this information are both intra-firm constituents — those individuals and organizational departments under direct control of the firm such as field representatives and marketing departments in foreign subsidiaries — and inter-firm constituents — members of communication suppliers and intermediaries. In addition, there should be a capability of obtaining relevant information directly from the environments in which the company operates. This would come from various secondary resources including, in certain cases, syndicated research.

The output from the IMIS is used by planners to develop programmes for markets served, whether direct from the home office, through subsidiary operations, or in concert with a licensee or joint venture partner.

In the process of plans development, suppliers of services such as advertising agencies should be working as partners with their counterparts in the firm. Intermediaries, like foreign distributors, and members in the firm's organization, like field representatives, should be encouraged to participate in the planning process through the contribution of ideas. They should also be used as a sounding board for evaluating different marketing communication approaches.

When marketing plans have been completed they are exposed to a review and approval process by management. This takes time and often requires several revisions. An adequate interval must be provided for this portion of the process.

Once approved, there is a need to produce all elements of the plan — whether it be advertising, product publicity, booklets, brochures, demonstration kits, and other elements — against a predetermined schedule. This involves coordination and proper timing for the completion of the work among those responsible for its production, including suppliers of advertising and promotion services. The process is the same for headquarters staff and subsidiary personnel.

As the planned activities are produced, whether an advertising campaign,

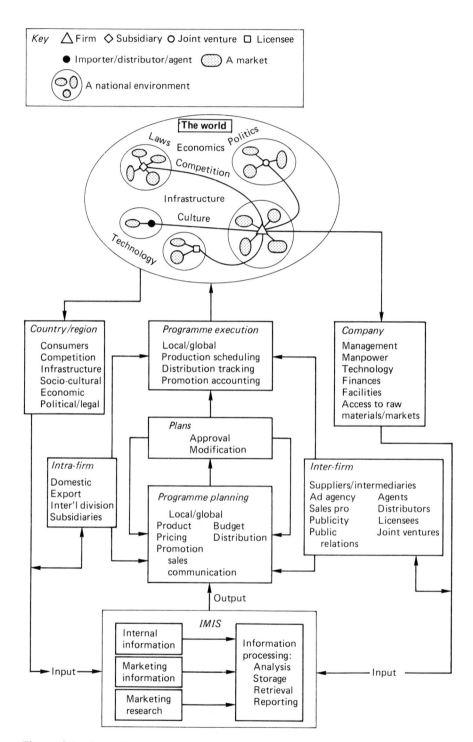

Figure 2.1 *International marketing planning system*

sales promotion event, or participation in a trade show, they must be carried out to the last detail and with precise timing for maximum effectiveness. No tolerance is allowed for sloppy execution.

Throughout the entire execution phase accurate records must be kept on all activities engaged in as well as of all expenses incurred. This information is essential when evaluating programme effectiveness.

Marketing plan structure

The marketing plan can be described as a written document prepared annually and comprised of these nine elements:

1   A *situation analysis* comprised of facts and figures which include market and environmental trends, strengths and weaknesses of the product or service versus competition.
2   A summary based on the *problems* and *opportunities* revealed in the situation analysis.
3   *Objectives* or end results to be achieved during or by the end of the year normally expressed in terms of sales, shares of market, distribution, and profit contribution. See special note below.
4   *Strategies* designed to achieve the objectives involving product, package, price, distribution channel(s), advertising, sales promotion, publicity, public relations, and research projects aimed at target market(s).
5   *Tactics* or the detailed plans involving each element of strategy.
6   A sales forecast.
7   An estimate of income, expense, and profit.
8   A flow chart or schedule of promotional activities to be put behind the product or service.
9   A means to evaluate the overall effectiveness of the plan and each element of strategy.

A special note about objectives, strategies, and tactics
In writing marketing plans, the terms 'objectives', 'strategies', and 'tactics' are used frequently. The latter two terms are easier to define and understand. Strategies are the general means and tactics are the detailed means by which an objective is to be attained. Combined, they answer the question '*how?*'

The term 'objective has' greater complexity. A marketing objective goes beyond the general definition of the word: 'being the object of a course of action'.[17] In marketing, time and change are customarily integral parts of the definition. For example, a marketing objective could be to increase cases sold

8 per cent in 1992 over 1991, or gain distribution in 150 new stores during the period January to June 1992.

While general marketing objectives take on the complexities of time and change, this is not always the case with the sub-functions of marketing. When establishing advertising objectives, quantification and specification in terms of time and change may or may not be parts of the objective statement. Here are two that are:

- To increase brand awareness from 40 to 50 per cent among the target market by the end of the planning year.
- To bring about a change in favourable attitude toward the brand from 20 to 30 per cent among the target market at the conclusion of the advertising campaign.

Note. For objectives of this type, before and after research is needed for measurement purposes.

Under other circumstances, time and change is not specified, and quantification is less precise, for example:

- To reach large families with special emphasis on young children ages five to ten.
- To concentrate the greatest weight of advertising in metropolitan areas.
- To place extra weight of advertising immediately prior to the two peak selling seasons in April and September.

(Readers will observe that the first set of examples involved the advertising message, and the second set concerned its placement or the media in which the advertising message is to run.)

An ideal way to communicate objectives and strategies in a marketing plan is to set them up, side-by-side on a spreadsheet. On the left, list each objective one-by-one. Then, on the right, match up one or more strategies for each objective. Do not make the mistake, as so many writers do, of combining objectives and strategies in a single statement. The side-by-side format will readily demonstrate to the reader what is to be accomplished and how it will be done. Also remember: to be an objective, there has to be a way to measure its attainment.

Theory and practice

The marketing plan structure outlined is a synthesized version of plans outlines of six authorities on the subject.[18] This model was the focal point in two different studies conducted by this writer. They were both surveys, one among forty advertising agency executives located in twenty-seven countries outside the USA, and the other among seventy-nine advertising executives in the USA and nineteen other countries. More than one-half of the respondents in each study indicated the plan model was 'very similar' to the one they or their clients used.

The differences and similarities worthy of note are reported under these headings:

Situation analysis
Among larger firms there is an indication of a more detailed and structured format and content than outlined in the model.

Strategies
Despite the absence of comments about strategy formulation, it was thought likely that this key topic is given careful consideration in the annual planning process.

Tactics
Both studies pointed to weak tactical sections with lack of specific detail and timing as to how strategies would be implemented.

Evaluation
This section appeared to be the weakest section of all in both studies. In some cases there was a completed void when it came to plans evaluation.

With respect to elements missing in the plan model, findings indicated that certain advertising respondents included a set of *assumptions* and also an *opportunity/risk assessment*. Both of these are worthwhile additions to the second section of the plan which, in effect, is a summary of the situation analysis. When dealing across borders and facing varying environmental conditions, a set of assumptions can help put the problems and opportunities in the proper perspective.

Plan model differences were also reported in terms of the type of business: consumer, industrial, or service. Here are several key observations:

- Consumer product planning is more thorough, detailed, and sophisticated than industrial product or service planning
- The role of packaging, advertising, sales promotion, and publicity is more important in consumer plans
- The emphasis in industrial product planning is significantly different from either product or service planning
- Analysis of end user needs in consumer plans will cover more 'subjective' and 'impulse' issues
- Industrial market data is 'rougher'

Planners and approvers

The person with the responsibility for annual planning is a line manager. In the consumer product company this person's title would be product or brand manager. In industrial firms, this person's title is more likely to be marketing manager. Group planning is prevalent among service organizations as well as industrial producers. Among smaller firms the planner is apt to be the general manager or even the president.

Those who approve annual plans, as expected, would be at one or two levels above the annual planner, at least in the larger organizations where there are several layers of management. In many instances a group will be involved in the decision-approval process, more so in industrial firms than in either consumer or service companies.

Strategic planning and planners

While certain studies conducted in the UK and the USA in the early 1980s have indicated a lack of strategic planning in many of the companies questioned, this writer's survey[19] indicated that more than four out of five firms contacted prepared strategic (long-range) plans. The most common time frames were three or five years, with small and service companies preferring the shorter time frame, and consumer, industrial, and larger firms preferring the longer period.

Strategic planners and annual planners with respect to titles were one and the same in about 50 per cent of all firms. Where different, they appeared for the most part to be line managers at one level or more above the annual planner.

Differences exist between the annual and strategic plan; however, among some organizations little distinction is made between the two plans though the latter tends to be less detailed but covers more topics. For example, the strategic plan is apt to include information on acquisitions, investments, physical resources, business spin-offs, and diversification. It can be said, then, that strategic planning is more company centred than product centred, dealing with all available resources and alternatives.

Profit arithmetic and budgeting

In the course of the marketing planning process, the planner in charge is responsible for preparing an estimate of sales, costs, expenses, and profit contribution. It is often called the profit and loss statement or simply the P and L. An example of what this statement looks like for a particular brand is shown in Exhibit 2.1.

The planner who shall be called product manager, has overall responsibility for the performance of the brand and is also cast in the role of the marketing communicator. This means that the product manager must complete every entry on the P and L statement with or without the help of others. Help, if needed, normally comes from members of other departments such as production for cost of goods; finance for discounts, allowances, and certain standard costs such as transportation, warehousing, and selling; and various outside suppliers for advertising, sales promotion, publicity, public relations (not normally a brand expense), and marketing research. All of the above items are listed in Exhibit 2.1 including the main categories for marketing communication expenses. Note that the statement has columns for previous, current, and new year entries along with 'percentage of sales' columns for each to facilitate comparison. Once the P and L has been approved and the new year begins, the finance department will issue a monthly P and L for the brand which will show actual versus estimate and previous year by month and year-to-date. The form would be set up as shown below.

P and L for: Brand: _____ Country: _____ Year: _____ Month: _____

	Current month				Year-to-date			
	Previous year (1)	*Estimate* (2)	*Actual* (3)	*Variance* (3−2)	*Previous year* (4)	*Estimate* (5)	*Actual* (6)	*Variance* (6−5)
Unit SP Unit Sales etc.								

Focusing on the marketing communication budget portion of the P and L, the product manager will need to prepare an expense estimate for each element in the advertising, sales promotion, product publicity, and marketing research plans where costs will be incurred. These expenses are summarized in an attachment to the P and L and the totals for advertising, etc. are carried forward to the P and L itself. An example of a budget summary attachment is shown in Exhibit 2.2.

Exhibit 2.1 *Profit and loss statement: Brand* _____, *Country* _____

	Previous year	Percentage of sales	Current year	Percentage of sales	New year	Percentage of sales
Unit selling price						
Unit sales total						
Gross sales ($)						
Cash discount						
Returns/allowances						
Total deductions						
Net sales						
Cost of goods (including transportation and warehousing)						
Gross margin						
Marketing expenses:						
Selling						
Advertising						
media						
production						
Sales promotion						
consumer						
trade						
Incentives						
trade incentives						
promotion materials						
Product publicity						
Marketing research						
Contingency						
Total marketing expense						
Contributing margin						

Exhibit 2.2 *Promotion budget summary sheet*

Advertising 1 Consumer magazine	Cost/pg 4-colour	Insertions	Total/ magazine	Total cost	% of total
Goodhousekeeping	$95,000	6	$570,000		
Ladies Home-Journal	72,000	5	360,000		
McCalls	89,000	6	534,000	$1,464,000	19.4

2 *Spot television*: 15 high potential markets, 18% of total US households, combining day (40 GRPs/wk @ $697) and Fringe (40 GRPs/wk @ $919) time, total 80 GRPs/wk in 28-wk flights, one winter, one fall. . . . .

				1,034,000	13.7

3 Production: Magazines —			90,000		
TV commercial —			150,000	240,000	3.2

Sales promotion

1 Consumer incentives:
- 40c store coupon in March magazines — $473,000
- 30c in-pack coupon, 2 months' supply — 505,000
- Buy 3 get 1 free on pack rebate offer, 2½ months supply — 425,000 → 1,403,000 — 18.6

2 Trade incentives:
- $2.00/case advertising allowance plus $3.00/case off-invoice — $1,051,000
- $2.50/case stocking allowance — 876,000
- $1.5/case display allowance plus 1 case free with 5 — 936,000 → 2,863,000 — 37.9

3 Promotion material (POS, brochures, etc.). — 185,000 — 2.4

Product publicity: 3 magazine feature stories, 2 TV kits, 5 general news stories. . . — 145,000 — 1.9

Marketing research: focus group testing, syndicated research, attitude and awareness study. . . — 220,000 — 2.9

Total annual budget				$7,554,000	100.0

Budget determination

A problem that every product manager faces is budget determination. How much should be spent on the various activities under that person's control which is represented by the elements listed in Exhibit 2.2?

Introductory promotion costs are always greater when launching a product new to any given market. Companies in the consumer product field, in particular, may be willing to lose money by investment spending in the first or second year after introduction. This is in anticipation that over time the well established product will generate a greater income steam than a new product launch with less market penetration due to lack of introductory promotion vigour.

Key factors to take into account are the marketing objectives for sales, share of market, and corporate profit expectations along with industry growth potential and the competitive situation. (How unique is the product versus alternatives available in the marketplace?)

There is no single method that will provide an answer to the budget question in terms of total spending or spending on any given element. Techniques which should be included in the determination are the following.

Per cent of sales
It is customary to consider what per cent of sales advertising and promotion has represented in prior years for established products, or if new to a market, what per cent has that been on the part of similar offerings and/or what has that per cent been in other markets where offered. The advertising to sales ratio and advertising (and promotion) to sales ratio are commonly called the 'A/S' (or 'A&P to S') ratio. If the A/S last year was 8 per cent, this becomes a departure point for establishing a spending level in the year ahead.

Amount of money spent per sales unit
Spending can also be based on a per unit basis. This is, in effect, another way of expressing the A&P/S ratio. For example, if 200,000 cases were sold last year and $600,000 was spent on advertising and promotions, the A&P expenditure per case was $3.00.

Share of advertising (voice) to share of market
If competitive advertising and share of market figures are available, another good departure point is the share of advertising to share of market comparison. If a brand enjoys a 20 per cent share of market, under normal conditions it would be expected to spend 20 per cent of the total advertising in its category.

Objective or task method
This is related to what is to be accomplished not only in terms of sales and share of market but also in terms of communication end results. If a brand

objective is to increase the level of awareness from 50 to 60 per cent of the target market, it becomes a question of the amount of advertising it will take to accomplish this task. Or, if a brand objective is to reach a given percentage of the target audience with a certain frequency in a given time period, it becomes a matter of determining what media spending will be necessary to attain this goals.

In the promotion area, if the objective is to have a certain number of retailers provide low price features on the brand, sufficient funds will have to be allocated to get this job accomplished.

Budgeting, in the final analysis, requires the use of a combination of the techniques mentioned above along with a realistic appraisal of the market, strength and weaknesses of the product versus competition and the probable resources that the firm is willing to commit.

Promotional budget norms

Information collected here and abroad will give the reader an idea of both trends and norms with respect to current promotional spending practices.

Major shifts in consumer manufacturer spending on advertising, consumer promotion, and trade promotion have taken place in the USA over the past ten to twenty years. Donnelley Marketing has been tracking these developments since 1976 as can be observed in Figure 2.2.

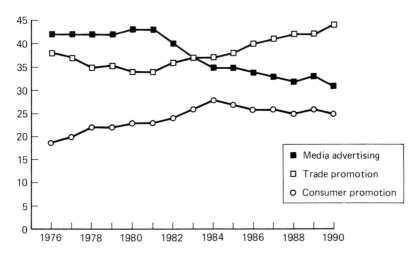

Figure 2.2 *Percentage of total promotion ($) allocated to advertising, trade and consumer promotion.* Source: *Donnelly Marketing Annual Surveys of Promotional Practices 1976–1990*

The figures show a steadily increasing trend for consumer promotion from 1976 to a peak in 1984, and subsequently a moderate decline to the 1988 figure of 25 per cent. Media advertising remained on a plateau between 1976 and 1981 but has been falling ever since to the latest low of 31 per cent. Trade promotion dropped from a high of 39 per cent in 1976 to a low of 34 per cent in 1980–1981 but has been rising steadily since then to a current high of 44 per cent. These changes have been documented as well by personal interviews of the writer and recent articles in *Business Week* and *Advertising Age*. For example, Hershey Foods Corp. is reported to have spent $245 million out of a total of $342 million on sales promotion in 1988; that is 71 per cent of the total compared with $97 million or 29 per cent allocated to advertising.[20]

Do such trends exist outside of the USA? The answer is yes. Wilmshurst reported such a trend had taken place in the UK dating back to the 1970s.[21] A study by this writer conducted in 1987 also revealed that the trend was not confined to the USA.[22] Information was obtained from nineteen well-known consumer goods manufacturers, twelve of which were located in Europe and elsewhere throughout the world. For comparative purposes, Donnelley's figures for consumer and trade promotion were combined under a single 'sales promotion' heading. Both studies showed a trend away from advertising to sales promotion over the five-year period 1983 to 1987 when the figures were averaged. However, advertising still commanded more than half of the total advertising and sales promotion budget in this study, whereas Donnelley's figures showed a drop for advertising to less than one-third of the total advertising and sales promotion budget. Another factor to take into account is that in Griffin's study the trend to sales promotion among companies in his sample was not uniform; eight of nineteen companies reported increases in their advertising appropriation over the five-year period. Therefore, while it can be said there are definite indications of a global trend away from advertising to sales promotion among consumer product companies, the trend is by no means uniform. Individual country–company situations must be examined to establish the true picture.

From the same study by this writer, it is possible to establish norms for spending among the principal promotion activities for industrial as well as consumer firms. The separation is needed because of the well-known importance of personal selling among industrial producers. (In addition to nineteen consumer companies in the sample there were twenty-eight industrial companies, all but two of which were located in the USA.) In Figure 2.3 it can be observed that personal selling in industrial firms approaches two-thirds of the total marketing expenditures and has grown marginally in importance as compared with five years ago. Advertising accounts for approximately one-eighth of the total budget and has declined three percentage points (19 per cent). Sales promotion expenditures have remained about the same, accounting for 10 per cent of the total. Marketing research has increased nearly one-half

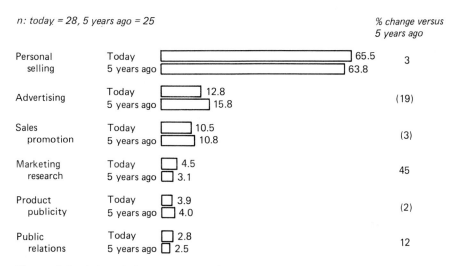

Figure 2.3 *Industrial firms: percentage of budget spent on various marketing activities today versus five years ago*

though the base is relatively low. Product publicity has remained virtually the same while the expenditures on public relations has risen moderately.

This same breakout of marketing expenditures is reported in Figure 2.4 for consumer firms. As previously noted, two-thirds of these firms were foreign. Advertising, the most important weapon, accounting for one-third of the total

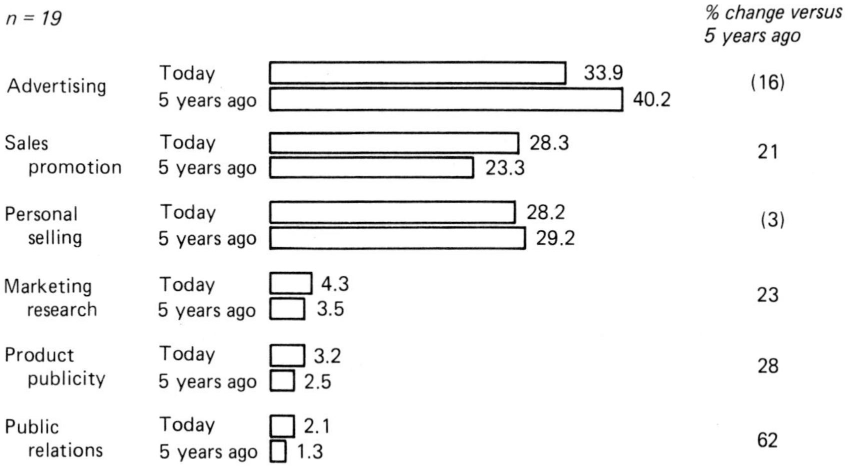

Figure 2.4 *Consumer firms: percentage of budget spent on various marketing activities today versus five years ago*

expenditures, shows a decline of over six percentage points (16 per cent). Sales promotion, the second most important activity (fractionally ahead of personal selling), shows an increase of five percentage points (21 per cent). Personal selling's importance declined slightly. Combined, marketing research, product publicity, and public relations accounted for less than one-tenth of the total marketing expenditures. The percentage changes, particularly with respect to public relations, were relatively large as against five years ago.

The figures just reviewed should be useful to planners of marketing promotional activities both in the industrial and consumer firm.

Scheduling promotional activities

The centrepiece of any marketing plan is the annual schedule or flow chart of promotional activities. An entire year's programme showing all advertising and promotional activities and their coordination from a timing point of view is summarized in this one spreadsheet. In the span of a few minutes, planners and managers can visualize how funds have been allocated to the various promotional activities in order to achieve predetermined marketing objectives. An example of such a flow chart is shown in Exhibit 2.3. The activities budgeted in Exhibit 2.2 are scheduled over the year in Exhibit 2.3.

Summary

Marketing planning is an indispensable activity of large and small firms alike. It provides direction for the mobilization of human and physical resources in the firm in coordination with suppliers of raw materials and services and intermediaries who form the conduit to the marketplaces of the world. It establishes goals against which progress can be measured. Planners must be knowledgeable of all aspects of the environments where business is conducted, of the capabilities and resources of the firm, their suppliers, and members in the channels of distribution. Planners must know how to combine the controllable variables of the marketing mix in the best alternate combination to combat foes in the marketplace in order to achieve predetermined objectives. Planners are required to develop budgets and P&Ls, and prepare the overall schedule of activities to take place during the planning period. It is their responsibility to put all elements of the marketing plan together in a concise, cohesive, and understandable fashion, to work their plan, and ultimately to evaluate their performance, including every element of strategy, in preparation for the ensuing planning cycle.

Exhibit 2.3 *Schedule of promotional activities: Brand _____ , Country _____ , Year _____*

	Jan	Feb	Mar	Apr	May	June	July	Aug	Sept	Oct	Nov	Dec	Year
Advertising													
Consumer magazines													
Good Housekeeping													
Ladies Home Journal													
McCalls													
Spot TV (15 markets)													
Daytime (16 weeks)		8 weeks							8 weeks				
Fringe (10 weeks)													
Sales promotion													
Consumer:													
50¢ magazine coupon													
30¢ in-pack coupon													
On-pack rebate													
Trade													
$2/cs. ad allowance +													
$3/cs. off-invoice													
$2.50/cs. stocking allowance													
$1.50/cs. display allowance + 1 with 5													
Publicity: as occurring													

Questions

1 What basic informational inputs are needed in developing a marketing plan?
2 Explain what effect changes in the controllable variables will have on marketing communication plans.
3 Identify and give reasons why international marketing communication planning may be different in large and small firms.
4 Visualize and briefly describe the international marketing planning system.
5 List the nine elements of a marketing plan.
6 Distinguish the difference between objectives and strategies. Include in your answer two examples of each.
7 In what ways may a marketing plan differ in practice from the nine-step model you identified in Question 4?
8 Does the strategic plan contain the same elements as an annual marketing plan? Give reasons for your answer.
9 Explain the significance of a profit and loss statement.
10 What techniques should be used in budgeting marketing communications?
11 Describe the promotional expenditure trends which have taken place in the USA and elsewhere. In so doing, distinguish the difference in marketing activity spending between consumer and industrial organizations.

Notes

1 Roth, Robert F. (1982) *International Marketing Communications*, Crain Books, Chicago, 1982, p. 33.
2 Majaro, Simon (1982) *International Marketing*, George Allen & Unwin, London, p. 181.
3 Runyon, Kenneth E. (1984) *Advertising*, 2nd end, Charles E. Merrill Publishing Company, Columbus, Ohio, p. 88.
4 Keegan, Warren J. (1989) *Global Marketing Management*, 4th edn, Prentice Hall, Englewood Cliffs, NJ, p. 602.
5 Dunn, Watson S. and Lorimor, E.S. (1979) *International Advertising and Marketing*, Grid Publishing, Inc., Columbus, Ohio, pp. 3–4.
6 Levitt, Theodore (1983) The globalization of markets. *Harvard Business Review*, May–June, 92.
7 Peterson Blyth Cato Associates and Cheskin & Masten (1985) *Survey on Global Brands and Global Marketing*, New York.
8 Walters, Peter G.P. (1986) International marketing policy: a discussion of the standardization construct and its relevance for corporate policy. *Journal*

    of International Business Studies, Summer, 67.

9   Pelch, Andrew, Export Manager, Berol, USA Inc., Personal Interview, July 1987.

10 McDonald, Malcolm H.B. (1982) International marketing planning. *European Journal of Marketing*, **16**, (2), p. 23.

11 *Ibid*, p. 25.

12 Hulbert, James M., Brandt, William K. and Richers, Raimar (1980) Marketing planning in the multinational subsidiary: practices and problems. *Journal of Marketing*, Summer, p. 13.

13 McDonald, *op. cit.*, p. 28.

14 Steiner, G.A. and Schollhammer, H. (1983) In *The Truth about Corporate Planning* (Hussy D.) Pergamon Press, Oxford, England, p. 395.

15 Hopkins, David S. (1981) *The Marketing Plan*, report no. 801, The Conference Board, New York, pp. 4, 12, 84−109.

16 Majaro, *op. cit.*, pp. 183−184.

17 Morris, William (1969) *The American Heritage Dictionary*, Houghton Mifflin Company, Boston, p. 905.

18 Griffin, Tom (1989) Marketing planning: observations on current practices and recent studies. *European Journal of Marketing*, **23**, (12), 12/89.

19 Information from Griffin's paper on marketing planning (1989) *European Marketing Journal*, **23**, (12).

20 Erickson, Julie Liesse and Dagnoli, Judann (1989) The party's over. *Advertising Age*, 27 February, 1.

21 Wilmshurst, John (1985) *The Fundamentals of Advertising*, William Heinemann Ltd, London, p. 10.

22 Griffin, Tom (1990) Promotional expenditure trends here and abroad: implication for the 1990s. In *International Academy of Management & Marketing 1990 Conference Proceedings*, Dallas, Texas, **II**, pp. 215−225.

3 *Organizing the international marketing communication function*

Introduction

This chapter examines the subject of organizational structure from a marketing communication perspective in the international firm and its principal supplier of communication services, the advertising agency.

The chapter sets forth basic organizational configurations of advertisers including the marketing communication function and variations within it. It also looks at the organization and inner workings of an advertising agency and concludes with an explanation of how an advertising agency and advertiser interface.

Before focusing on specific types of organizational structures, several basic factors relating to the role and importance of the marketing communication function are considered. These factors include type of product or service, product mix, number and nature of markets served, and method of doing business. Management style, which has a bearing on the organization of the firm itself, is also examined.

Type of product of service

Producers may be classified as one of the three general types. The first type involves products sold by the one business to another such as raw materials, parts and components, industrial cleaners, fork lift trucks, and packaging. In reference to this first type, the term *business marketing* is used. The second category takes into account manufacturers that market products to consumers (individuals and family members). The term *consumer marketing* is associated with this second category. The term *service marketing* is related to the third type of producer involving banking, insurance, nursing homes, restaurants, hotels, and airlines and many other services.

In business marketing the emphasis is on personal communication as opposed to non-personal forms. More money and manpower will be placed behind personal selling than advertising, sales promotion, and publicity. The converse is generally true in consumer product marketing, though exceptions are noted as in the case of INO Food Corporation discussed later in this chapter. Some service producers, such as airlines often concentrate communication activities on corporate advertising campaigns because their 'products' all stem from a central (transportation) theme e.g. United Airlines: 'Fly the friendly skies of United.' Insurance companies tend to emphasize a combination of corporate identity (mass communications) and personal selling.

Product mix

The breadth and depth of product lines will have a bearing on the complexity of marketing communication organization and operations. For example, Pepsico, Inc. (USA) operates in three business categories: soft drinks, snacks, and restaurants.[1] Sandoz (Switzerland) markets pharmaceuticals, chemicals, plant protection agents and seeds, and food products.[2] Philips (Netherlands) has five product sectors: lighting, consumer electronics, domestic appliances, professional products and systems such as telecommunications, and (electronic) components.[3] Within the product lines of Pepsico, Sandoz, and Philips there would be a considerable divergence in number of items offered. Many of the lines involve separate and distinct channels of distribution, customers, and consumers. Each would require its own unique marketing communication programme.

Markets – number and nature

Some companies only operate across a single border, for example, between the USA and Canada. Other companies operate on a multinational or global scale. Henkel, for instance, conducts business in 166 countries.[4] Johnson & Johnson operates 160 companies in fifty-five countries.[5] Philips has facilities in over sixty countries.[6] Company structure and the location of marketing communications within this structure will differ depending on the number of markets served; also on the relative importance and nature of the market. For example, Fiji represents a very different market situation from China, and China's market situation would bear little resemblance to Germany's.

Method of doing business

Another important consideration in establishing differences in organizational structure, including the way in which marketing communication fits into the structure, is to look at international operations in terms of the method used to conduct business, not just at the moment of entry but over time. Exporting is the first method examined. This is followed by licensing, joint ventures, acquisitions, and subsidiaries.

Exporting

While exporting is often thought of as only the start-up method of doing business internationally, to be followed by alternate forms involving increasingly greater commitments of human and physical resources beyond home-country borders at a future date, this is not necessarily the case. Take, for example, the Boeing Company of Seattle, Washington, one of the foremost commercial aircraft manufacturers in the world. It assembles aircraft at one central location and then exports them from this central location to all parts of the globe. Its marketing communications department consists of only three managers despite a large advertising budget to support the sale of aircraft throughout the world. To conduct marketing communication operations, the managers rely heavily on the company's network of sales consultants for information gathering purposes, and work closely with their global network of advertising and public relations agencies to plan and implement communication programmes.[7]

Like Boeing, Harris Graphics Corp., a manufacturer of printing equipment, relies on the export method to market its products worldwide. Advertising schedules are run in seventeen countries to support its selling effort. Compared with Boeing, however, its advertising budget of $100,000 would be considered minute. The challenge of communicating on such a broad scale with such a small budget is shared by the merchandising manager at Harris Graphic's headquarters in Westerly, Rhode Island and its advertising agency, Griswold-Eshleman in Cleveland, Ohio, along with Harris's French affiliate and its Belgian advertising agency.[8]

For a company like INO Food Corporation, a producer of speciality cheeses under the Rondele label which got its start in Europe by exporting from its plant in Wisconsin, the principal marketing activity is sales. This function is handled in Europe by a master distributor who covers 200 supermarkets and other large retailers. The non-personal communication programme in Europe does not include consumer advertising. Point-of-sale material (modifications of the type used in the USA) and promotional brochures for the trade are the main vehicles.[9] Based on the foregoing facts, it is hypothesized that the responsibility for preparation of these vehicles lies at INO's marketing subsidiary in Paris with approval of INO's sales vice-president at headquarters in the USA. The (advertising) messages on point-of-sale materials and brochures would be written and translated with the help of people at the master distributor organization. Design and production would be handled by outside service organizations who specialize in this work.

In other situations involving exports, a company in one country may determine that a certain product made in another country would add value to its product line. Either party may initiate the arrangement. The result is an export opportunity for the producer, and an addition to an existing line and new profit opportunity for the marketer. An example of this concerns Oy

Gustav Paulig Ab of Helsinki, Finland, a leading processor and marketer of coffees, teas, spices, and frozen foods. In 1956 it began to import Melitta coffee filters and filtering equipment from Germany for household and catering use. In recent years it has enjoyed as much as 60 per cent of the filter paper business and 15 per cent of the equipment business with its imported Melitta line. Here is another Paulig example. In 1983 it began to import Jubilee concentrated chocolate extract and Jubilee individual portion hot chocolate machines from Food Producers International, a US company.[10] Under these circumstances, the exporters of the coffee and hot chocolate products can rely on their importer, Paulig, to perform marketing communication activities as well as the overall marketing function.

Licensing

Internationally, some licensing agreements involve patents and processes; others involve trademarks such as Mickey Mouse; and still others involve manufacturing and marketing including communications. To illustrate, C.A. Venezolana de Pinturas, a Grupo Quimico company, is a manufacturer and distributor of coatings for the household, industrial, and automotive markets. In Venezuela besides manufacturing products of its own, it also operates under technology licences from Sherwin-Williams Co. (USA), the Glidden Company (USA), Cook Paint and Varnish Co. (USA), Bitumes Speciaux (France), and Basf (USA−Germany).[11] No doubt, this company has to comply with guidelines from the licensors when it comes to matters involving trademarks on packaging and in promotional communications as well as conform with patent and process specifications. Other than that, it is most likely that all other marketing communications would be the responsibility of the licensee.

Fast foods, auto, and soft drink franchisees, a type of licensing, are normally bound by a broader set of guidelines for marketing communications. Not only would the use of brand and/or corporate name be specified but also decorations, signage, point-of-sale material, and all forms of advertising, often being supplied by the franchisor, would be rigidly controlled in most instances. The amount to be spent on advertising and promotion can also be a condition of the franchise agreement.

With respect to organizational structure, the licensee that can largely control the marketing communication function is free to establish whatever structure seems to best suit the firm. In situations involving franchises of the type introduced above where communications budgets are large and marketing territories are extensive, the organizational structure on the part of the franchisee as well as the franchisor can be complex. Specialists in advertising, sales promotion, and publicity would be needed in both organizations.

Joint ventures

Joint ventures are entered into between home and host country firms on the expectation that a synergistic arrangement will evolve from such a partnership. This should make it possible for both organizations to realize a greater return from a given business venture than if either one tried to operate independently. Each contributes an expertise that the other does not possess. The customary contribution is product and process (technical) expertise from the home country organization and marketing expertise from the host country firm. Frequently, the licensing of a brand will accompany the partnership arrangement. In these instances, rigid process and quality control standards are established in manufacturing the product as well as specific instructions for use of brand name on packages and in advertising with respect to colours, letter style, and design.

In the industrial field, an example of such an arrangement is INTESIKA, C.A., a company formed in 1981 by Corporation Grupo Quimico and Sika Finanza, a Swiss company, to manufacture speciality chemicals for the construction and petroleum industries in Venezuela and countries in the Americas. Sika Finanza's participation included equity and technology; Grupo Quimico's input was manufacturing and marketing.[12] From a marketing communication perspective, the burden would be on Grupo Quimico; the Swiss company's primary concern would be product (quality and uniformity) and brand name usage.

In the consumer field, one example of a company which has been extensively committed to joint ventures is Heineken. Historically, it has had limited home market opportunities due to country size. Its first participation dates back to 1930 when a joint venture was formed with Malaysian Breweries in Singapore. This was followed by a joint venture with a brewery in Indonesia. Today, Heineken has joint ventures with companies in Europe, the Caribbean Basin, Africa, and Asia/Oceania. Financial participation is, in nearly all cases, combined with technical services and often with the licensing of one or more Heineken brands.[13] Heineken would have an active interest in the use of its brand marks; otherwise the host country partner would have responsibility for marketing communications.

In an industry such as soft drinks, where franchising has been the norm rather than the exception, in certain country markets changes have occurred in the marketing channel. Instead of licensing a number of franchises in a particular country, a single joint venture partnership is established. For example, in the mid-1980s Coca-Cola replaced its six franchised bottlers with a distribution and sales system concentrated in a single, dominant UK organization, Cadbury Schweppes. Even though there has been a considerable amount of consolidation occurring in the franchise system in Europe, Coca-Cola is strongly committed to this system.[14]

Acquisitions

For many companies, particularly the large, well-financed ones, acquisitions are an attractive means by which growth in sales and profits can be achieved in foreign countries as well as at home. As Dr Uwe Specht pointed, out, 'It is (often) better to acquire good, old brands and add your technology than to try to penetrate a market with your own brand.'[15] For example, in 1984 Henkel Chemicals of Great Britain acquired the corporate group Monarch Adhesives Ltd and Alfred Adams Ltd. Henkel Corporation, Minneapolis, took over the Industrial Cleaners Division of Pennwalt Corporation, USA.[16] Nestlé made a major US acquisition in 1985 with its takeover of the Carnation Company, an organization with several well-known brands including Coffeemate, Contadina, and Friskies.[17] In 1988 the Campbell Soup Company made two major European acquisitions: the Freshbake Foods Group PLC, a leading UK marketer of frozen convenience foods and Beeck-Feinkost GmbH, a leading refrigerated foods manufacturer in Germany.[18]

With respect to the organizational structure for marketing communications when companies are acquired, this is a matter to be resolved between the two parties when the acquisition agreement is made. In some instances the acquired company is permitted to continue to operate as it always has, at least at the outset. This is more likely to occur in countries where the surviving (parent) company has had no prior operations. It also would also be true in instances where the acquired company is large. Take the Carnation–Nestlé merger in 1985. Carnation's 1985 sales amounted to over eight billion Swiss francs, or 19 per cent of Nestlé's total sales, while, between 1984 and 1985 the Group's factories increased in number from 292 to 362 mainly due to Carnation's contribution.[19]

In other cases where both organizations are operating in the same environment, a consolidation and concurrent reduction in staff may result along with a new organizational structure, including, of course, the marketing communications function. If the acquired company is engaged in business marketing, chances are the number of marketing communication people involved will be relatively few, possibly just one individual. If the company is in the consumer field and operates on a national scale in the USA, for example, a number of marketing communication workers could be found to be redundant as well as suppliers of marketing communication services.

Subsidiaries

Apart from acquisitions, control can be maximized when firms set up marketing and/or marketing subsidiaries, sometimes called affiliates or operating companies. This implies 100 per cent ownership by the headquarter's firm.

(This condition is typical among the large multinationals, including Unilever, Nestlé, Henkel, CPC, Philip Morris, IBM, etc.) Under these circumstances, top management has the option of developing a highly centralized form of organization with tight controls, or placing the job of management squarely in the hands of its subsidiaries, thus operating in a decentralized manner. In the latter case, the subsidiary, in effect, is an autonomous operating unit. Under these circumstances, the subsidiary would be responsible for planning, implementing, and evaluating the effectiveness of its own operations, including marketing communications, normally with guidance and overall direction from the headquarters company.

Having discussed organizational structure and the job of marketing communications under different methods of conducting international business in general terms, attention will now be focused on management style. Following this, a series of organizational structures will be introduced that locate the function of marketing communications under different operating conditions.

Management style

Management style has a relationship with organizational structure including marketing and marketing communications. Majaro's explanation of management style, which will be looked at from an organizational viewpoint, is helpful in understanding certain differences found in large international firms. No doubt some of these characteristics are also present in smaller firms.[20]

Majaro's classification of international firms calls for three basic organizational types: 'macropyramid', 'interglomerate', and 'umbrella'. In linking the headquarters of an organization with its field units, three decision levels are identified: *strategic* (top of the pyramid) where corporate objectives and strategies are determined; *management* (mid-section of the pyramid) where corporate objectives are translated into business unit objectives; and *operational* (base of the pyramid) where responsibility rests for performing the tasks to achieve the business unit objectives. These organizational arrangements are shown in Figure 3.1.

The macropyramid form of organization calls for centralized authority and planning, maximum marketing standardization, and rigid performance standards on the part of local managers. This will not only include marketing but also the communication sub-function.

In contrast, the interglomerate organizational style places major importance on the financial dimension of the business. Management at the country or regional level may conduct their business, including marketing communications, as they see fit so long as the profits and overall financial progress at this level meets the requirements of headquarters' strategic management.

The umbrella management style is unlike the other two systems just described.

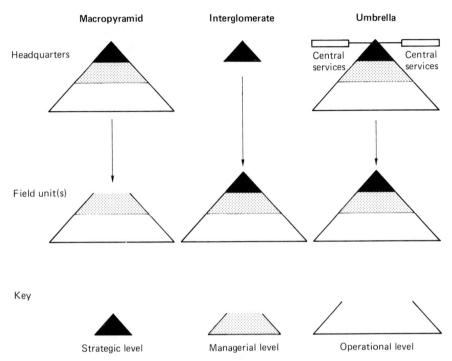

Figure 3.1 *Management style and organization.* Source: *Majaro, Simon,* International Marketing, *Routledge*

Headquarters curbs its control over its outposts. One key responsibility is to form broad corporate objectives. Another is to provide assistance, advice, and support to its outposts pertaining to the various functional areas of the business including marketing communications. Headquarters personnel, specializing in advertising, promotion, and market research would be available to aid local level management in planning communication programmes and transfering knowledge and successful techniques from one outpost to the next.

What Majaro has so clearly identified are two forms of centralized organization (macropyramid and interglomerate), each with very different orientations, and one decentralized form (umbrella) of organization with support from headquarters staff. Which style is the best? Strategic management may take their pick. It seems obvious, however, that most managers working at the middle and operational levels would prefer the umbrella organization.

Basic organizational configurations

The organizational structure of companies involves the division of authority and responsibility in four basic ways: function, product, markets served (geography), and matrix. In large and more complex organizations involving a number of products and a number of markets, the structure is often hierarchical. In certain cases the first level is product, the second is geographic, and the third or bottom level is function. In other situations the first level is geographic rather than product. In Figure 3.2 the basic configurations mentioned above can be observed.

In the large organization structure in Figure 3.2, geographic groupings are shown by regions (for simplicity sake). Many firms are organized and operated on a country-by-country basis, then grouped regionally. The regional offices that report to world headquarters are intermediate headquarters for groupings of individual countries. In instances where country markets are relatively small, as in the case of Central America, one subsidiary organization may serve several markets. A case in point is Colgate-Palmolive with offices in

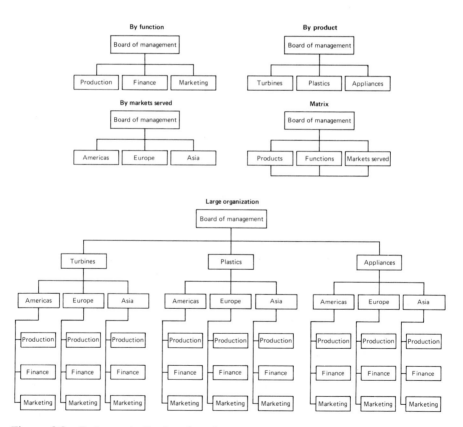

Figure 3.2 *Basic organizational configuration*

Guatemala City which serve Guatemala, Honduras, and El Salvador; countries which possess 9.1, 4.3, and 6.4 million inhabitants respectively.

Equipped with a basic understanding of the different organizational configurations and a sensitivity towards the principal variables which influence those configurations, it is possible to use prior examples cited and others to infer what structural form would be appropriate.

Location of the marketing communication function

Among the exporting firms discussed, it is possible to conclude that most would have a functional form of organization. Marketing communications would be managed centrally with input from sales agents for Harris Graphics and INO Foods, and from field sales consultants, advertising agencies, and public relations firms for Boeing.

Where licensing and joint ventures are concerned, the nature of the agreements would have to be reviewed to determine the location of the marketing communications function. In cases where the licence or joint venture involves technology (production or process), the responsibility would normally rest in the licensee's or foreign joint venture partner's hands. In other instances, the licensor or home country joint venture partner may remain involved with branding, advertising, and promotion so that the organizational structure would reflect their marketing communication interests.

As for acquisitions, it is largely a matter for the surviving parent company to determine. If the parent decides to permit the acquired firm to run autonomously, the marketing communication function would remain as if the merger had not taken place. In many instances, the acquired firm is left to operate on its own for a period of time so that the parent company management can gain a better understanding of the acquisition's operations. Subsequently a determination is made as to whether or not the two staffs should be merged for more efficient operations. In the case of the Carnation Co. merger into Nestlé, the former's structure would be comparable to the large, complex organizational structure pictured in Figure 3.2 with numerous plant locations and many markets to serve. If the consolidation of marketing communications and other functions were to take place between the two organizations, it would be a project to be carried out over time, due to the many manpower, organizational and operational problems it would pose.

Some form of marketing communication activity would exist at the subsidiary level in large, complex organizations. The precise nature would depend on the type of products offered, the size of the market served, and the style of management. For business products where the emphasis is on sales activities, the non-personal forms of marketing communications might be handled by sales management. (It is possible that a 'marketing department' simply would not exist.) For large consumer marketers where marketing communications would encompass all key activities including advertising, sales promotion, and public relations, one or more advertising agencies would likely be retained. In small markets, only the sales activity would be managed and performed in the subsidiary. Other communication activities would be supplied by the regional office or from headquarters. In instances where the style of management calls for centralized control, the marketing communication activity in the subsidiary would be concerned with implementation, not planning. If decentralized, the activity would involve planning and evaluation as well as implementation.

Domestic versus foreign sales

One variable implied in organizational structuring but not made explicit is the relative importance of domestic versus international sales. Companies with a relatively small percentage of total sales derived from foreign markets will have a different structure than those with larger percentages. Given a small volume of sales from cross border business, it is likely that this business will be handled by an export department. Organizationally it would appear on the chart just like another regional office in the home country. The export department would have to work through a domestic advertising and promotion department for marketing communication elements and programmes. Where overseas sales volume is significant a company is apt to have formed an international division. This division will have equal status with the other main functional departments. In this case, the marketing communication sub-function will have an international focus and should be better equipped to fill the communication needs of its international representatives, customers, and consumers. See Figure 3.3 for these two organizational configurations.

Variations within the marketing function

Job assignments within the marketing communication function will differ markedly among organizations. In smaller consumer and in many business-to-business marketing organizations with one or a few product lines, the responsibility for all non-personal forms of marketing communications may rest in the hands of a single individual. That one person will be called on to direct the activities outside suppliers (if used) of communication services — advertising, sales promotion, and publicity — as well as plan, implement, and evaluate the assortment of marketing communication activities conducted throughout the year.

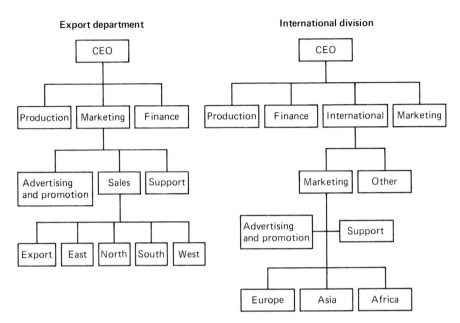

Figure 3.3 *Export department and international division*

Product management

In cases where there are multiple product lines, it is common to find a product management system in place. Individual product managers are assigned to manage one or more brands or product lines. The extent to which they are granted responsibility and authority will depend on the individual organization. In the most complete sense, they can be thought of as general managers with sales and profit responsibility in addition to all aspects of the marketing and promotion mix. When carrying out these responsibilities, product managers must work with other internal departments such as sales, sales promotion, and public relations. In some cases, product managers supervise the work of their advertising agencies. In others, they work through the company's advertising department to obtain advertising support for their brands. Where product managers essentially control the advertising function, an advertising services department will normally exist to prepare and consolidate media budgets and schedules, and follow up to make sure that the advertising ran as planned for all product groups. This system of organization is depicted in Figure 3.4.

Staff assistance in complex organizations

In large, complex decentralized organizational structures of the 'umbrella' type, headquarters staff specialists are in place to transfer functional and

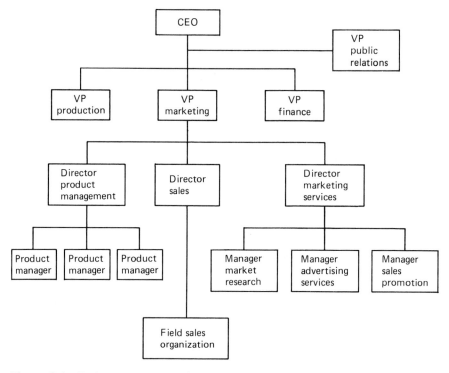

Figure 3.4 *Product management marketing organization*

products expertise to regional offices, and through them, to country subsidiaries. The purpose of this functional and product knowledge transfer is to help improve the efficiency, effectiveness, and overall performance of the geographic business units. Figure 3.5 shows this organizational linkage at the three levels. As Keegan states, 'The relationship of staff organizations can become a source of tension and conflict in an organization if top management does not create a climate that encourages organizational integration.'[21]

International advertising agency overview

The pattern of growth of international advertising agencies has been varied. Historically, the normal pattern was for advertising agencies to follow their clients overseas. Take for example, McCann-Erickson Worldwide that went international to serve a major client, Exxon, and follow another, Coca-Cola, as

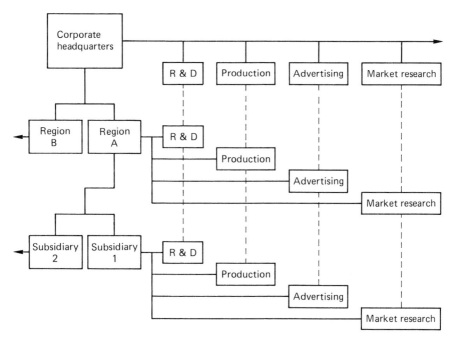

Figure 3.5 *Staff specialists' linkage with operating units.*
Adapted from Keegan, Warren J. (1984) Multinational Marketing Management *(3rd edn),*
p. 579. © *Prentice-Hall Inc. 1984. Reproduced by permission of Prentice-Hall Inc., Englewood*
Cliffs, NJ

it penetrated world markets. Similarly, when Ford Motor Co. entered overseas
markets, J. Walter Thompson Co. was close behind.[22]

The Japanese have been slow in establishing their own network of international agencies because Japanese advertisers have used local or international
agencies outside the home country. A reason given is that the Japanese
agencies are not knowledgeable about many foreign markets.[23] To overcome
this difficulty, some Japanese agencies formed joint ventures overseas. Two of
these ventures in the USA were DYR (Dentsu, Japan, and Young & Rubicam,
USA) and Hokuhodo (Japan) and Lintas (USA). In both cases, due to client
conflicts, they were terminated. HDM, a relatively new venture between
Dentsu, Young & Rubicam, and France's Eurocom which handled accounts
such as Japan Air Lines, Colgate-Palmolive, Henkel, Peugeot, and Kentucky
Fried Chicken has also failed.

In recent years, mergers and acquisitions have been one of the most sensational trends in the agency business. Internationally, that was looked on as a
way of developing global networks to compete with the large, already established
multinational agencies. For others, it was looked on as a smart international

business expansion move in terms of sales and profits. Examples of this include the alliance formed between Foote, Cone & Belding Communications, Chicago and Publicis, France which is called FCB-Publicis, and the recent acquisitions by the WPP Group (UK) of J. Walter Thompson and Ogilvy & Mather, agency giants in their own right.

For an idea of the size of some of the largest advertising agency networks, see Table 3.1. It shows name of organization, worldwide gross income, number of offices, and number of countries in which the offices are located.[24]

Table 3.1

Company	Income ($ million)	Offices	Countries
Young & Rubicam	758	127	44
Saatchi & Saatchi Worldwide	740	138	61
McCann-Erickson Worldwide	657	144	67
Ogilvy & Mather Worldwide	635	275	51
BBDO Worldwide	587	121	50
Lintas: Worldwide	538	135	48

Despite the size and scope of the large multinational advertising agencies, small and medium agencies will be found to be healthy in most countries of the world. In fact, a number of clients, including large, international firms, are often inclined to retain smaller, independent agencies for their creative talents, and because of the feeling that there is less chance for leakage of information about their businesses to competitors.

Advertising agency organization

While it is true that certain advertising agencies provide limited services (creative and media only, for example), and other organizations specialize in only one type of service such as sales promotion, in this chapter the organization for a full service agency will be examined. Structures for those firms that provide single or limited services would simply be a truncated version of the full service organization. The structure shown in Figure 3.6 identifies the principal divisions of work within the full service agency.

Account service provides the day-to-day liaison with the client. *Account planners* are the link between the target market and the creative group and provide an in-depth interpretation of consumer needs and wants to those who actually do the creative work. *Creative* is comprised of copywriters and artists who are

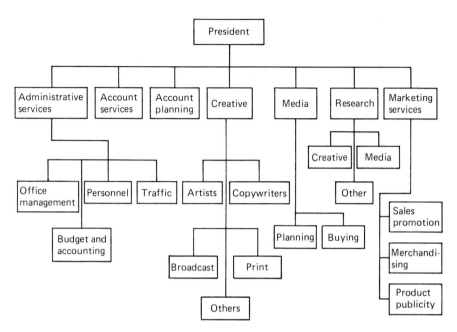

Figure 3.6 *Organization of the full service advertising agency*

assigned as a team to develop the creative strategy by working together with account service and/or account planners, then turn this strategy into advertising by visual and verbal means. When creative executions are approved by the client, the production department takes over to complete the job under the watchful eyes of the creative team.

Media performs a dual function. First a plan is developed to indicate where, when, with what frequency, and at what cost the creative message will be transmitted. Once approved, media buyers arrange for the actual placement of the advertisements according to the plan at the most favourable cost.

The work of the *research* department is to supply input for planning and evaluating the effectiveness of communications as well as help define the overall marketing problem. Therefore, it contributes to the work of account planning, creating, and placing advertisements.

Marketing services deal with communications and marketing problems other than advertising. *Sales promotion* prepares plans aimed at customers in the channel of distribution and at consumers. *Product publicity* creates and implements publicity programmes directed toward pre-selected targets. *Merchandising* involves people who are experts on channels of distribution and means by which cooperation can be obtained from channel members. (Note should be made here that some advertising agencies form separate organizations to provide the services mentioned above.)

The *administrative services* department is comprised of staff to support the activities of the operating departments...personnel, office management, budgeting and accounting, and traffic. Members of the traffic department are assigned to the various clients of the agency and perform a function of seeing that each job which comes into the agency is produced on schedule and according to specifications.

The agency work group

Each client account is assigned personnel from the various departments of the agency according to need. Some accounts may require only creative and media services while others may want all in-house communication services...advertising, sales promotion, publicity, and merchandising. The work group can be visualized as a diamond as shown in Figure 3.7.

Account service, account planning, and creative, with support from traffic, formulate strategy, develop the creative concept, and establish the position for the product, sometimes with and sometimes without assistance from other departments in the agency. When the basic requirements of the job have been reviewed and approved by the client, the work is produced with the help of all agency departments involved.

The advertiser/advertising agency relationship

The advertising agency is retained by the advertiser (client) to perform certain specified services. These services customarily include the preparation and placement of advertising and other communication services which may also

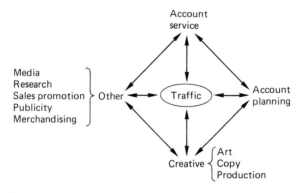

Figure 3.7 *The agency work group*

include marketing research, sales promotion, package design, direct mail, and product publicity.

Even though either organization would have the power to terminate the relationship in a relatively short period of time (usually ninety days), in establishing such an association, both parties should view it as a long-term proposition...as a partnership where confidentialities are exchanged, not withheld. Key agency personnel working on an account should know as much about the client's business as does the client. This knowledge is needed to optimize the services which the agency has been asked to provide.

On a day-to-day basis, it is the agency's account executive who would interact with his or her counterpart, often the product or marketing manager depending on the type of client organization. The main purpose of account work is to understand and interpret the client's communication problems so that the best possible solutions can be generated within the agency.

Subject to the precise nature of the job at hand, creative, media, promotion, and/or marketing research specialists often complement the account executive in meetings with the client. At the time of the year when product or marketing managers are called on to develop the annual marketing plan, the account executive and other agency members assigned to the account should be ready to participate in any and all phases of the marketing plans preparation.

Periodically, a communication service review will be called for by the client. At those sessions, higher management, often including the presidents of the respective organizations, participate. In between, it is also common to find higher management in both organizations keeping in touch on a regular basis, often over lunch, to find out how things are going on the account and address any problems which might occur.

Many client—agency relationships extend over decades. The reason for this is the fact that the agency has continued to deliver a superior communication product(s) and fill the client's marketing communication needs based on a close, open, and interactive partnership relationship.

Summary

It is important to recognize that the type of product or service, product mix, number and nature of markets served, and method of conducting international marketing operations will all have a bearing on the organization of the international marketing communications function and the overall marketing structure within the firm.

Styles of management may vary from close control of all business functions to the absence of control other than for financial performance in the large multinational firm with subsidiaries located in different countries around the world. In the case of the former, a highly centralized structure will exist along with closely monitored management systems allowing little freedom for those in charge of subsidiary operations. In the latter case, a tight-knit, financially oriented management group will sit at corporate headquarters allowing considerable autonomy at the subsidiary level providing financial performance is satisfactory.

An alternative to these schemes is a central management system which sets broad policy and basic objectives while allowing its outposts considerable management autonomy and providing support and staff assistance from headquarters.

Regardless of company size, it is management's responsibility to determine how domestic and international operations will be related; whether a functional, product, or geographic structure will best serve its business goals. Within the structure selected it is management's decision to determine the set-up for marketing and marketing communications along with the extent to which, if any, internal staff assistance is needed.

As for suppliers of services, it is necessary for management to determine precisely what services are needed and whether they should be provided by one multinational advertising agency, many domestic agencies, or combination of the two. Another decision for management is to determine whether all communication services should be provided by a single, full-service advertising agency or if different services (e.g. creative, media, sales promotion) should be provided by different suppliers. To obtain the maximum performance from any supplier, it is important to know how it operates internally as well as how the advertiser and agency should interface. In this way the needs of both organizations can best be served.

Questions

1   Explain why type of product or service, product mix, and number and nature of markets served have a bearing on organizational structure.
2   Identify the five different methods of doing business internationally. Briefly describe the principal characteristics of each method.
3   Majaro discussed three types of management styles. Identify each style and give a brief explanation of each style.
4   Discuss the need for a product management system in a marketing organization.
5   Why are staff specialists needed in complex organizations?
6   Some companies offer multiple product lines within the business. Many of the lines will involve separate channels of distribution, customers, and consumers. Give an example of a company that operates in three or more

categories and explain how each category will require its own unique marketing communication programme.

7   The organizational structure of companies involves the division of authority and responsibility in four basic ways. Discuss their basic differences.

8   Explain the functions that a full service advertising agency would be able to provide.

9   Illustrate how the agency work group can be organized. Describe the function of each member of the agency work group.

10   You are part of Company X and you are currently in charge of advertising. Company X has decided to hire 'Bob's Ad Agency' to handle all of your company's advertising needs. As a client of 'Bob's Ad Agency' explain your expectation of the type of relationship your company would develop with the agency.

Notes

1   Pepsico, Inc. (1988) *1988 Annual Report*, Purchase, NY, pp. 8−32 and inside back cover.

2   Sandoz Ltd., Sandoz *A products brochure*, Basle, Switzerland.

3   Philips, *Philips − A Versatile Company*, pp. 7−11.

4   Henkel KGaA (1984) *Henkel Annual Report*, Dusseldorf, p. 47.

5   Foster, Lawrence G. (1986) *Johnson & Johnson One Hundred Year Illustrated History*, Johnson & Johnson, New Brunswick, NJ, p. 5.

6   Philips, *op. cit.*, p. 3.

7   Gething, Tom (1985) Boeing sells big planes overseas by stressing specific features. *International Advertiser*, October, 17.

8   Cudlipp, Edythe (1983) Reaching the international market on $100,000. *Advertising World*, October/November, 6.

9   Terpstra, Vern (1987) Selling American cheese to Europe. In *International Marketing*, 4th edn, The Dryden Press, Chicago, pp. 171−2.

10   Oy Gustav Paulig Ab (1986) *High Quality Imported Products*, Helsinki.

11   Corporacion Grupo Quimico, C.A., A Brochure on Grupo Quimico, Advertising and Public Relations Department, obtained in January 1989, p. 9.

12   *Ibid.*, pp. 26, 27.

13   Heineken, N.V. (1987) *Heineken* (a brochure prepared by the company), Amsterdam, received in June, p. 11.

14   Cooper, Ralph, notes taken during a presentation to a Pace University study group at Coca-Cola Northwest European Division Headquarters, London, 7 June 1989.

15 Specht, Uwe Dr, personal interview, Henkel KGaA, Dusseldorf, 2 June 1986.
16 Henkel, *op. cit.*, p. 29.
17 Nestlé S.A. (1985) *Annual Report*, pp. 7, 19, 23, 35.
18 Campbell Soup Company (1988) *Annual Report*, Camden, NJ, p. 11.
19 Nestlé, *op. cit.*, pp. 7, 47.
20 Majaro, Simon (1982) *International Marketing*, Routledge, London, Chapter 2.
21 Keegan, Warren J. (1989) *Global Marketing Management*, 4th edn, Prentice-Hall, Englewood Cliffs, NJ, p. 639.
22 Hill, Julie Skur (1989) World brands. *Advertising Age*, 11 September, p. 77.
23 *Ibid.*
24 Key global clients of multinational shops. *Advertising Age*, 11 September 1989, pp. 78−87.

4 *Information for international marketing communications*

Introduction

Correct assessment of market potential, tastes, preferences, and appropriate communication techniques are absolutely essential for the profitable operation of firms large and small that attempt to penetrate foreign markets. Even the most sophisticated marketers have made costly mistakes by the inept assessment of foreign market needs and norms. A case in point concerns the Procter & Gamble Co. which lost $200 million over sixteen years from 1971 to 1987 in learning that Japan is unlike the USA. Now they have finally turned their business mistakes into successes by using worldwide technology but tailoring it in a way to meet the needs of the Japanese market. For example, had Procter & Gamble better understood market needs, they might have introduced a thinner, better fitting disposable nappy (diaper); featured their company name prominently as well as the brand name in their product advertising, and used an indirect instead of a direct approach in demonstrating a special feature of their product...all of which Procter & Gamble does now. The result: a major recovery in market share for a major brand.[1] (The indirect approach in advertising referred to above involved a talking nappy which promised that the product wouldn't leak or cause nappy rash. The direct (US) approach would be to pour a cup of liquid onto the nappy and show how all the liquid was absorbed.)

When considering the world as a whole or just a few specific environments within a global context, marketing and communications problems become more complex than when focusing on a single country environment. It is for this reason that communication information gathering activities must have a specific focus; otherwise the process of assembling and classifying information could become endless without providing meaningful input for the solution of marketing and marketing communication problems. This matter of focus should be of concern in an organization of any size, but it becomes more acute as the organization diminishes in size and fewer people are assigned to do this type of work. This points to the need to designate one person to be placed in charge of the information gathering and processing activities for whom a clear job description has been written.

To operate a successful information programme the most important requirements are: a system, a knowledge of its applications, and a basic understanding of the techniques available. These subjects along with a discussion of certain problems and pitfalls, will be addressed in the text which follows.

The system

Information for international marketing communications is obtained by means of the international marketing information system (IMIS). The IMIS is an enlarged domestic system and a part of the overall international marketing planning system (IMPS) as discussed in Chapter 2. Inputs for the IMIS come from within the company, from its field representatives, channel members (intermediaries), and from the environments in which it operates. Outputs from the system are used to plan and evaluate marketing and marketing communication programmes. There are four parts to the system which is shown in Figure 4.1.

Internal information

Internal information, whether it is obtained from company headquarters or local subsidiary offices if they exist, comes from sales records, costs and examples of advertising, promotion, and publicity activities, and information supplied by various staff members. Sales records are particularly useful because they reveal who's buying what items, in what quantities and how often. Heavy and light purchasers can be identified by products bought and geographic location. This becomes a means by which your existing customer target market can be defined and categorized. By examining prior advertising, promotion, and publicity activities, and obtaining input from key internal executives as to the effectiveness of the material and programmes as well as suggestions for future efforts, a departure point can be established for the preparation of new campaigns.

To facilitate this process Roth[2] suggests an internal information audit. This is a formal assessment of a company's strengths and weaknesses. It includes a survey of the company's organizational structure, its products, markets, sales and distribution methods, advertising, merchandising, public relations, and

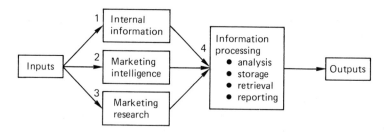

Figure 4.1   *The international marketing information system*

marketing research activities. It should be undertaken periodically, comparing present programmes with past efforts at headquarters and among subsidiaries if they exist, and always put in writing.

Marketing intelligence

Marketing intelligence involves two basic kinds of information: field information obtained from sales representatives, brokers, importers, distributors, and, in some cases, suppliers; and information from an assortment of published sources and syndicated research services, customarily called secondary research. Field information of importance to marketers include competitive price, advertising and promotion reports, and any changes in the channel of distribution which will have an effect on the business. Trade journals report on industry trends and events of news to marketers. Syndicated research includes demographic and psychographic information, share of market and distribution trends and advertising expenditure reports.

Marketing research

Marketing research is a general term used to describe different types of research of a primary nature. Marketing research is used when it is determined that neither internal nor marketing intelligence information will provide the appropriate input for the solution of a marketing communication problem... and when adequate funds are available. Runyon[3] describes marketing research as 'data originated in view of a specific need'. In most organizations, even large ones, the projects are normally directed from within but the actual work is performed by outside suppliers. Roth[4] gives a listing of some of the largest research organizations that operate internationally and identifies several directories including *Market Research Organizations Worldwide* published by the US Department of Commerce, and the *International Directory of Marketing Research Houses and Services* published by the New York chapter of the American Marketing Association.

As for different types of research, the following distinctions have been made by Wells:[5]

1 *Marketing research* — research that investigates all the elements of the marketing mix, i.e. identifies consumer needs, evaluates pricing levels, tests the effectiveness of various promotional strategies.
2 *Market research* — research that gathers information about specific markets.
3 *Consumer research* — research that focuses on how consumers think, feel, decide, and behave.

Research of all the above types can be either *qualitative* or *quantitative*. Qualitative research involves small numbers, is usually exploratory or diagnostic in nature, and is impressionistic rather than definitive; no hard and fast conclusions are drawn.[6] Quantitative research concerns the assembly of large amounts of commercial data, advertising expenditures, purchases, and the like; the results of which are expressed numerically.[7] Specific qualitative and quantitative research techniques will be discussed in another section in this chapter.

Information processing

Information processing deals with the coding, classification, tabulation, storage, retrieval, and organization of information for presentation purposes. If the information is of the quantitative type, various statistical treatments may be performed. Depending on the degree of sophistication and funds allocated for this purpose, the capabilities of an information processing unit will vary considerably, they will range from simple hand tabulations, ratios, percentages, manually stored and retrieved information to complex, computer manipulated statistical treatments with fully automated storage and retrieval of data and the capability to print and visualize numbers in tables, charts, and graphs.

IMIS application

Having described the IMIS, the system will be examined to see how it can be applied in both small and large organizations to help plan and develop marketing communications. One might argue that the IMIS is only suitable for big, multinational firms. But this is not the case. The scale of the IMIS can be tailored to the size of the organization and be bound by a predetermined research budget. With respect to budget, findings from a recent study of fifty-two consumer, service, and industrial companies within and outside the USA indicated that approximately 5 per cent of companies' total marketing expenditures were spent on marketing research. Of the total of the marketing research budget, about 20 per cent of that was spent on advertising research in consumer and service companies. The majority of industrial firms reported no expenditures on advertising research.[8]

In the small export firm internal information of the type mentioned earlier should be readily available. If not, one of the first steps in developing an IMIS involves the orderly assembly and classification of that material. Marketing intelligence can be gathered from secondary sources and through representatives appointed in other countries. The extent to which marketing research activities would be engaged in are determined by the funds available for this purpose.

However, with cooperation from foreign sales representatives, home country government's foreign commercial offices, and the commercial offices of foreign governments in the home country, it is possible to develop a list of customers and prospects to whom questionnaires can be sent to ascertain interest and potential for the product or service offering.

In the USA, the Foreign Commercial Service of the US Department of Commerce will either undertake market research surveys for an exporter in selected countries or develop a customized export mailing list of foreign companies operating in a particular industry in one or more foreign environments for direct contact by the US firm. These and other services are available at a minimum charge.[9]

For exporters wanting to travel abroad to make first-hand contact with customers and prospects, the US Department of Commerce regularly schedules participations in various trade shows and sends industry missions to different foreign environments. For example, in September 1988 a mission was organized and sent to Chile, Colombia, Peru, and Venezuela to present US safety, fire, and security equipment. Costs of participation are reasonable. This permits an opportunity to expose company products and literature, and obtain information for future marketing and communication programmes as well as attempt on-the-spot sales.[10]

Large firms which operate through international divisions and have marketing and manufacturing facilities abroad are apt to have managers overseeing IMIS activities and marketing research specialists in their headquarters and subsidiary marketing department organizations. With more staff and the likelihood of larger budgets which permit greater use of suppliers of research services, it is reasonable to expect that research needs will be fulfilled to a greater extent than in the case of the smaller company. It is also true, however, that, as the scale of international operations increase, headquarters' funds available will have to be prioritized and spread among a greater variety of research projects, calling for good communications and close coordination between the home office and its outlying operating units. This is an opportune time to examine in greater detail the various types of information needed to manager the international marketing communication function and relate these needs to the IMIS.

Marketing communication information needs and techniques

In developing communications aimed at any target whether it be a sales representative or end user the information system should have as one of its principal focuses the answer to the question: *what to say?* In other words, what should be communicated? This holds true in the preparation of a sales fact sheet or flyer as well as for a four-page magazine advertising insert prepared by the advertising agency. These information needs will be examined by various subjects for investigation and will be related to the appropriate IMIS component(s).

The product

The very essence of knowing what to say stems from a thorough understanding of the product and its attributes. As Reva Korda, one of advertising's most respected writers once said, 'I go right to the merchandise: feel it, wear it, eat it, know it.'[11] The Internal Information System component is the place to begin this investigation. The quest for understanding should be engaged in by both members of the client organization and the advertising agency. Bill Bernbach attributes a visit to the Volkswagen factory in Wurzburg, Germany for giving inspiration to the now famous Volkswagen 'Lemon' print advertisement. It was a story about quality control based on a factory inspector's rejection of a paint job because he observed a scratch through his magnifying glass, not observable by the naked eye.[12]

The search for ideas on what to say should be *a continuous* one. Take the case of Arm and Hammer Baking Soda, a 135-year-old product. It was given a new life cycle about twenty-five years ago when someone discovered that the product could absorb refrigerator odours as well as be an effective antacid. Rather than sit in the medicine cabinet year-in, year-out waiting for the occasional usage, now a new package is recommended every three months to help keep refrigerators odour-free.

Product evaluation is also undertaken by means of marketing research to help identify those attributes of greatest interest to potential customers. Sometimes testing is done on a monadic basis (by itself) and at other times on a comparative basis with other product(s), normally the category leader. Respondents are asked to rate product(s) on specific characteristics (e.g. sweetness, sourness), their likes and dislikes, and by their intentions to buy. Testing is not only undertaken to reveal new advertising claims but also to determine product performance versus competition. This approach is equally valid for earthmoving equipment as it is for instant coffee.

Sales and share of market

From records of sales it can be determined who is buying what items, in what quantities and how often. Analysis of this information can identify heavy, medium, and light purchasers for the purpose of establishing the frequency of which non-personal as well as personal communication contact should be made. Established customer lists can be matched up with lists of known prospects drawn from intelligence sources for the purpose of identifying different target groups so that the appropriate promotional programmes can be developed for each target group.

Share of market information can be pieced together in an informal way by having representatives question customers, or data can be obtained formally by using a syndicated service such as Nielsen (see next paragraph). This information, gathered by means of marketing intelligence, '. . . is often a key factor in influencing the kind of advertising to be used'.[13] In a host country environment, where comparative advertising is permitted, a little known brand may benefit by comparing its qualities to one of the leading brands. A note of caution: if a brand has a high market share, it is wise to avoid this approach because a comparison with a slower selling item would place it in an unfavourable light.

Nielsen Marketing Research, a company of the Dun & Bradstreet Corporation, audits a variety of consumer package and durable goods such as foods, beverages, health and beauty aids, and household products in principal retail outlets in twenty-seven countries. This syndicated service provides share-of-market information along with retailers' purchases and inventory, pricing, deals, and distribution statistics. By subscribing to this service, clients can not only obtain the above types of information but also monitor responses to various marketing activities including advertising campaigns, new product launches, pricing and promotion strategies.[14]

Exploratory research

Exploratory research, not to be confused with marketing research, has also been called 'pre-research' or 'up-front' research. It is used for problem definition and idea development.[15] It is often undertaken at a time when an advertising agency gets a new account or assignment. Internal information and marketing intelligence components of the IMIS can come into play when exploratory research is undertaken. The process begins by reading reports, memos, and articles about the product, company, and industry. Sales records, annual reports, complaint letters, and trade journal information are scrutinized. During this phase, sales representatives, distributors, and retailers are interviewed. The outcome of this exploratory work are specific thoughts on what should be said in marketing communications and/or recommendations for formal marketing research studies to explore alternatives more fully.

Content and format analysis

Prior to the development of any new communications, be it advertising or promotional material, it is customary to undertake an analysis of the communications previously produced in comparison to the competitive material. In this respect, within any organization's IMIS there should be a complete file of past advertising and promotion material produced by the firm and its principal competitors. Content and format analysis consists of a systematic review of each visual and/or verbal element.[16] In the case of print advertising, these elements should be contrasted:

- headline
- illustration
- claims or appeals
- support for the claims
  (visual and verbal)
- package illustration
- signature line

(Note that content and format analysis should be applied to all communication types.)

Consumer information

Consumer information that will be useful in determining what to say in advertising and promotion can be first approached by reviewing articles, reports, and surveys published in trade journals and other magazines such as (in the USA) *Advertising Age*, *Beverage World*, *Automotive News*, *Business Week*, and *Fortune*. From time to time newspapers like the *Wall Street Journal* and *New York Times* will carry stories on products and industry categories. Similar magazines and press are available in other countries, a number of which have international editions like *The Economist*, and *Financial Times*, and *Marketing Week* in the UK; *Paris Match* and *International Herald Tribune* in France; *Handelsblatt* and *Capital* in Germany; and the *Nihon Keizai Shimbun* in Japan. However, the likelihood that this kind of information will provide more than general background material and possibly some 'thought starters' is quite remote. Much more specific in nature are the syndicated research services like Simmons and MRI found in the USA. These services give share of usage, demographic, magazine readership, and television viewing information by brand and category for many different consumer durable and non-durable products including autos, appliances, food, beverages, and household supplies (see Chapter 12).

In addition to these sources just mentioned, informal questioning of product users by client and agency personnel is a good way to obtain insight on what to say in marketing communications.

Marketing research

If budget permits and questions persist as to message content, formal marketing research is the best means of gathering helpful information. Whether the investigation will be a small-scale qualitative study or of a quantitative nature, there should be a written research proposal so that the work to be performed and the expected outcome are clearly understood in advance. Without the discipline of sitting down and clearly writing out what is needed, much time and money can be wasted on meaningless research. Included in this proposal should be these elements:

1 statement of purpose
2 review of related research, indicating why this particular study is needed
3 research method
4 means of measurement (statistical treatment if appropriate)
5 analysis of data
6 written report which would cover above topics plus findings, conclusions and implications

While a detailed explanation of the variety of research methods is outside the scope of this work, the principal techniques used in planning, developing and evaluating marketing communications will be introduced. (A number of good texts are available on marketing research including: Luck, David and Rubin, Ronald S. (1987) *Marketing Research*, Prentice-Hall; Kinnear, Thomas C., and Taylor, James R. (1983) *Marketing Research: An Applied Approach*, McGraw-Hill, and Zikmund, William G. (1988) *Exploring Marketing*, Dryden Press.) Research design beyond the exploratory stage is a matter for experts. In practice, competent internal or external research counsel should be obtained to plan and implement such studies.

Focus groups

Probably the most frequently employed research technique in advertising and marketing communications is the focus group. It can serve as a relatively inexpensive and rapid means of evaluating advertising themes, visual treatments, promotional literature, package designs, and exhibit ideas in either a very rough conceptual stage or at any stage of development.

The groups selected, comprised of no more than ten to twelve people at most, should be representative with respect to the subject matter to be explored.[17] The group should be led by an experienced moderator. The moderator's role is to make sure that a preset list of topics are covered, all participants are given the opportunity to express what they think and feel, and that the major points brought out during the session are sufficiently probed.[18]

While the focus group technique has potential for use nearly anywhere, the manner in which it is conducted may have to vary by environment. For example, in the Middle East, the moderator must establish rapport at the outset, be sure to give a clear explanation of the purpose of the meeting at the beginning, and allow for side discussion.[19] In Africa, the researcher may have to work with two groups of three to five members rather than one large group. Since the span of attention may be relatively short, frequent breaks for food/ drink may be needed, and because of less familiarity with the abstract, it is necessary for participants to see real ads and hold real packages.[20]

The focus group technique is not always used for just obtaining preliminary ideas and 'thought starters'. For example, in developing a new advertising approach, an account planner at a major advertising agency in New York was reported to have conducted 200 focus group sessions to confirm a hypothesis.

Depth interviews

Depth interviews are another qualitative technique where trained interviewers meet and talk with typical members of a target group at length to probe feelings, attitudes, and behaviour towards different brands in a given category or some other marketing subject. While responses by individuals cannot be projected to a larger group of people, the insights derived can be instructive in shedding light on how a member of a target audience views some research question.[21] This technique, however, is time-consuming and costly. The results, to a large degree, are dependent on the skills of the interviewer.

Survey research

In contrast to focus groups and depth interviews, survey research is considered to be a quantitative technique. But the number of respondents used, even though comprised of several hundred people, often preclude the findings to be representative of the entire group under consideration. The key elements in the design of a survey include several factors. One is the selection of the people to be interviewed (the sample) to be sure they are members of the target group of interest.

Another element involves the development of the research instrument or questionnaire to be employed in the survey. Questions are normally of the structured type as presented in the omnibus research instrument shown in the appendix to Chapter 5. (Some unstructured (open-ended) questions can be useful also depending on the nature of the survey.) In preparing the questionnaire, two issues arise. One concerns the instrument's reliability: will the same or similar results be obtained when the instrument is reused? In other words, will the instrument provide stable, dependable, predictable results?[22] That is why questionnaires should be pre-tested among a small, representative group before use among the full sample. The other issue involves the instrument's validity. A simple test for this is an answer to the question: Are we measuring what we think we are measuring?[23] A way to ensure that a questionnaire is valid is to select a panel of six to eight experts, explain the purpose of the survey, and review the questions with them for their approval.

Problems and pitfalls

To put the subject of survey research in an international perspective, some of the experiences of several experts will be recounted. Regarding demographics, recognition of wide discrepancies of various characteristics among countries must be factored into the planning process. For example:

- The gross domestic product per capita in the Philippines is $600 compared with $15,000 in Switzerland.
- Rapid changes in inflation rate occur in certain countries. A 1981 management report on Argentina indicated the peso had risen to 8,250 pesos to the dollar, a 11 per cent increase from two weeks earlier.
- Unlike the USA and Canada, about two-thirds of the Mexican and Brazilian population is aged between four and thirty-four.[24]

Language meaning can be another headache for researchers. A number of 'English' words were used by participants in an Australian focus group session, including 'Sheilas' and 'tarty' which a US Levi Strauss analyst could not interpret.[25]

In Finland, a lot of Mothercare brand jeans were thought to have been sold in children's shops. After a careful investigation it was discovered that the jeans were actually being made at home by mothers.[26]

When doing research in several countries it should not be assumed that the product has a similar appeal and enjoys the same usage. For example, in Sierra Leone, Guinness Stout does not compete with beer...it is used as a blood tonic.[27]

Qualitative data only has value when you know what it refers to. When 87 per cent of Nigerians say they take a bath twice a day, you may assume they're jumping into a bath tub or taking a shower. Not so. Most would be sponging down with soap and one, maybe two buckets of water.[28]

These kinds of problems and pitfalls suggest a number of careful steps which should be taken into account when conducting international surveys. William Wilson has suggested these guidelines:[29]

1   Use experienced interviewers.
2   Spell out all instructions in detail and in writing.
3   Know the language capabilities and limitations of the people you deal with.
4   Don't assume your terminology like 'open-ended codes', 'clean cards', 'verification', 'editing' is understood. Make sure.
5   Write out the concept for every question; verbatim translations don't work.
6   Back translate every question using separate people.
7   Keep questions and instructions as simple as possible.
8   Allow long lead times, keep communications open, and stay on top of the field work.
9   Don't depend on simultaneous multinational reporting; don't let completion of work in one country hold up work in others.
10 Plan on higher, not lower costs for international research work.

Information for message development

Thus far, the discussion has centred on message preparation or 'what to say' information. Now attention will be focused on message development or 'how to say it' information. Wells calls this diagnostic research.[30] In the early stages, alternate rough advertising concepts such as slogans, headlines, and layouts can be shown to co-workers, individuals and groups in the target market to obtain feedback on the relative strength of the ideas shown or discussed. This type of exploration is designed to eliminate the weaker concepts so that added effort can be concentrated on those that are believed to be the most promising. When the ideas are more fully developed, and headlines, words, and illustrations are brought together in a unified whole, though still in an unfinished stage, they can be shown again to co-workers, individuals, and focus groups for further comment and suggestion. (This topic is treated more fully in Chapter 8.)

Focus group problems

In considering the use of a technique such as the focus group, certain weaknesses should be recognized. For example, a focus group may be dominated by one or two individuals who are sufficiently persuasive to sway other participants to their point of view. In some situations, those who will use the information to be obtained will attend the sessions as observers; then only extract and put to use information which supports their own preconceived notions.[31] (In advertising agencies, the use of account planners (discussed in Chapter 7) is designed to eliminate this problem.)

Underlying the entire focus group process is the ability of the moderator to know what to look for, how to manage the participants, and how to extract the most useful information in guiding further creative work.

One-on-one diagnostics

In an attempt to overcome the negatives of group explorations, some advertisers and their agencies conduct individual interviews to show, discuss, and obtain feedback to aid in the creative development process. These interviews are often carried out in high traffic locations such as a shopping centre where the class of goods in question are actually sold. In addition to individuals' ideas about creative concepts, the interviewer will normally obtain information on demographics, usage habits, and information about other products of the type being investigated.[32]

Psychological tests

One test of advertising effectiveness is the ability of the advertisement to attract attention. (This relates to selective perception which will be discussed in Chapter 6 on buying behaviour.) If the message is screened out mentally, the advertising effort has been in vain. For this reason, researchers have invented methods to measure attention. Psychological testing is being used for this purpose. The approach is liked by many researchers because of its objectivity: involuntary responses are recorded. This means they cannot be distorted as in the case of attitudinal testing.[33]

The techniques include the eye camera test which records the movement of the eyes over an advertisement and the time spent on the various elements of the ad — headline, illustration, etc.

Another approach is to measure the amount of pupil dilation as the subject looks over an ad; more dilation indicates a positive response; less dilation a negative response. A third approach is measurement of brain wave activity while the subject views an ad. The thought is that activity on the left side of the brain indicates cognitive mental process (learning), and right side activity indicates an emotional or attitudinal response. Measuring activity in the two halves of the brain, then, indicates how an ad is being processed.[34]

These approaches, however, are not without their shortcomings. The people who agree to this type of testing may not be representative of the target group. The setting for the test is unnatural...asking subjects to sit in front of and become attached to a strange machine. Another difficulty is relating the physical response to the attitude, learning, or behaviour change. These shortcomings along with the relatively high cost, limit the acceptance of this approach among advertisers.[35]

Other diagnostic problems

Any preliminary creative evaluation process creates problems. These include the possible lack of important detail which will detract from the impact of the advertisement due to the preliminary nature of the advertising concepts presented. Also, though effort is made to select participants that represent prime prospects for the product under investigation, this may not be possible. A further problem is the unrealistic setting in which subjects are placed when evaluating the concepts. This will have an effect on the quality and value of the input.[36]

Despite the shortcomings mentioned about message preparation and developmental information gathering techniques, greater recognition is being given to the value of preliminary input as an aid in guiding the creative process. This is evidenced by the trend which started in the UK a number of years ago to include account planners (discussed in Chapter 7) as key members of the creative work group. They have as their principal responsibility the interpretation of the needs, wants, knowledge, attitudes, beliefs, and behaviour of the target group to those who have the direct responsibility for the creation and production of marketing communications.

Information topics for future treatment

There are two remaining information topics which will be treated at subsequent points in the text. The first involves the evaluation of marketing communication effectiveness after the communication programme has been implemented. The second is concerned with planning and evaluating the effectiveness of the media programme.

Summary

Regardless of size, a company that seeks growth and prosperity in the international arena over time is more likely to achieve its objectives if it has a smooth functioning system for gathering, analysing, and interpreting information. The system described in this chapter can be used for this purpose. It provides a framework for managing a company's information needs for conducting international communication operations.

Determining 'what to say' (the subject of Chapter 7) is possibly the communicator's most important assignment. A number of suggestions were made in this chapter on how to go about gathering information which can aid this critical task.

Regardless of the information gathering assignment, as explained, the information needed must be clearly defined before a decision is reached on the best alternate techniques, also discussed, to be used to gather it.

For those who are engaged in managing, planning, and implementing information gathering programmes across borders, it is best to be aware, as pointed out, of the kind of problems that may be encountered and be prepared to cope with them in advance.

The techniques for testing advertising messages being developed and after they are produced are explained in Chapter 8, while media planning and evaluation research are covered in Chapter 12.

Questions

1 Identify the principal parts of the international marketing information system.
2 Describe the difference among internal information, marketing intelligence, and marketing research.
3 As a marketing manager of an organization that manufactures and markets personal computers sold through distributors and retailers, discuss how you would develop and apply an information system in your organization.
4 How does an international marketing information system differ between a small and large firm?
5 What is meant by content and format analysis?
6 Explain the advantages and disadvantages of focus groups? List ten sample questions that could be asked in launching a detergent product.
7 Indicate five ways in which pitfalls in doing international marketing research can be avoided.

8 What research methods would be appropriate in the following situation and why?

- Coca-cola launching a new cola product.
- Tuition fee increase in your school.
- Procter & Gamble introducing a disposable nappy.

9 What is your evaluation of the psychological testing method?

Notes

1 P&G goes global by acting like a local (1989) *Business Week*, 28 August, 58.
2 Roth, Robert F. (1982) *International Marketing Communications*, Crain Books, Chicago, pp. 11−21.
3 Runyon, Kenneth E. (1984) *Advertising*, 2nd edn, Charles E. Merrill Publishing Company, Columbus, Ohio, p. 130.
4 Roth, *op. cit.*, pp. 29−32.
5 Wells, William, Burnett, John and Moriarity, Sandra (1989) *Advertising Principles and Practices*, Prentice-Hall, Englewood Cliffs, NJ, p. 145.
6 Sampson, Peter, from quotation in Mandell, M.I. (1984) *Advertising*, 4th edn, Prentice-Hall, Englewood Cliffs, NJ, 273.
7 Wells, *op. cit.*, p. 145.
8 Griffin, Tom (1987) Unpublished research study.
9 US Department of Commerce, *Business America*, Special Report Edition, Superintendent of Documents, US Government Printing Office, Washington, DC, 26.
10 US Department of Commerce (1988) *Business America*, 20 June, 22.
11 Korda, Reva (1977) Starts in Your Eyes. *Wall Street Journal*, reprint, Creative leaders, 1977−1987.
12 Bernbach, Bill, in video taped interview with John Crichton, American Association of Advertising Agencies, New York.
13 Runyon, *op. cit.*, p. 118.
14 Nielsen Marketing Research (1986) *The Worldwide Services of Nielsen Marketing Research*, Northbrook, IL, 4−5.
15 Wells, *op. cit.*, pp. 146−7.
16 Runyon, *op. cit.*, p. 122.
17 Sciglimpaglia, Donald (1983) *Applied Marketing Research*, The Dryden Press, Chicago, p. 69.
18 Wells, *op. cit.*, p. 155.
19 Sabbagh, Tony (1982) A presentation on marketing research in the Middle East, American Marketing Association Conference, New York, May.

20 Goodyear, Mary (1982) The trials, tribulations, and successes in doing qualitative research in the developing world. *Marketing Review*, **37**, (5), 21−25.

21 Wells, *op. cit.*, p. 154.

22 Kerlinger, Fred N. (1973) *Foundations of Behavioral Research*, 2nd edn, Holt, Rinehart and Winston, Inc., New York, p. 443.

23 *Ibid.*, p. 457.

24 Misrack, Joan (1982) Sleuthing abroad: what the text books never told you. Presentation at an American Marketing Association Conference, New York, p. 3.

25 *Ibid.*, p. 4.

26 *Ibid.*

27 Goodyear, *op. cit.*, pp. 21−5.

28 *Ibid.*

29 Wilson, William J. (1982) Pitfalls in international research. *Marketing Review*, **37**, (4), 17−20.

30 Wells, *op. cit.*, p. 157.

31 *Ibid.*, p. 158.

32 *Ibid.*, pp. 158−9.

33 Berkman, Harold W. and Christopher Gilson (1987) *Advertising*, 2nd edn, Random House, New York, p. 421.

34 *Ibid.*, p. 422.

35 *Ibid.*, p. 421.

36 Wells, *op. cit.*, pp. 158−9.

Part Two   *The International Environment*

An understanding of environmental conditions and constraints, and buyer behaviour and decision making within the context of different environments are essential in planning marketing communications programmes. These are the subjects under investigation in Chapters 5 and 6.

5 *Environmental conditions and constraints*

Introduction

This chapter focuses on three types of environmental information which is essential in planning international marketing communications. One type of information communicators need to possess is a thorough grasp of the characteristics of message recipients. To acquaint readers with the diverse characteristics of different groups of message recipients, the first part of this chapter treats the subject of cultural sensitivity; not to give answers, but to heighten the level of awareness of the similarities and differences among the diverse societies who inhabit this earth. The second part of this chapter involves the use of global demographic, economic, and infrastructural information for planning purposes. Part Three is designed to provide enough information about advertising and promotion laws and regulations in various countries of the world to alert communicators of the need to know first hand, or through suppliers of services, how these restrictions may impinge on marketing communication programmes. Finally, to aid communicators in the efficient assembly of all three types of published information, the fourth part of this chapter discusses the organization and maintenance of an environmental fact file.

Cultural sensitivity

To produce compelling marketing communication programmes in one or many social settings requires a special sensitivity towards the group(s) for whom the message is intended. This group, call it the target market, is influenced by individuals within the group, as well as norms and standards of behaviour and beliefs established by the group as a whole.

As with other environmental factors, the marketing communicator needs to acquire a general cultural sensitivity with respect to different environments. In places where communication programmes are planned and conducted, special cultural knowledge is required. In this chapter, cross-border cultural implications will be explored in general terms. In the next chapter on buyer behaviour, the subject will be given closer scrutiny with respect to individual and group behaviour.

Culture is multidimensional. Cateora[1] defines culture as the human made part of the human environment − 'the sum total of knowledge, beliefs, art, morals, laws, customs, and many other capabilities and habits acquired by humans as members of society'.

High/low context communications

Before taking a look at different dimensions of culture in various foreign environments, Edward T. Hall's dichotomous concept of high and low context as a means of understanding different cultural orientations should be examined. According to Hall,[2] a high context communication contains little explicit information; the context lies within the setting of the message, and the internalized experiences of the receiver. Low context communication is just the opposite; most is explicit. Cultures can be classified by context type when it comes to communication. Keegan has drawn on Hall's work to distinguish between certain cultural types. This typology can be observed in Exhibit 5.1.

Exhibit 5.1   *High and low context cultures*

Factors/dimensions	High context: Japan, Middle East	Low context: USA, Northern Europe
Lawyers	Less important	Very important
A person's word	Is his or her bond	Is not to be relied on: 'get it in writing'
Responsibility for organizational error	Taken by highest level	Pushed to lowest level
Space	People breathe on each other	People carry a bubble of private space around them and resent intrusions
Time	Polychronic — everything in life must be dealt with in terms of its own time	Monochronic — time is money. Linear — one thing at a time
Negotiations	Are lengthy — a major purpose is to allow the parties to get to know each other	Proceed quickly
Competitive bidding	Infrequent	Common

Source: Keegan, Warren, J. (1989) *Global Marketing Management* (4th edn), p. 117. © Prentice-Hall Inc. 1989. Reproduced by permission of Prentice-Hall Inc., Englewood Cliffs, NJ.

Self-reference

The self-reference stigma should be avoided. While the experienced communicator will have been conditioned to evaluate any foreign market in terms of its unique human characteristics, the less experienced might be tempted to evaluate those characteristics, unconscientiously, in terms of his or her own indigenous culture experiences. This type of interpretation, described by Lee[3] as the 'self-reference criterion' (SRC), is in direct violation of the marketing concept and opposite of the approach a communications specialist should always take: thinking of the message from the receiver's perspective; having empathy with the target audience.

Relevant cultural dimensions

Cultural dimensions of particular relevance to the IMC include language and communication, aesthetics, education, religion, attitudes and values, and social organization. As Terpstra[4] points out, '. . . language defines a culture', so that in any given country there could be two or more cultural divisions as in the case of Canada with French and English and its two cultural groups and also in the case of Belgium where Flemish is spoken in the North and French in the South. In these regions, differences in political and social thought can be found as well as differences in tastes and preferences for such diverse products as cars and coffee.

Silent versus spoken language

Hall[5] has identified two main components of language: that which is spoken, and that which is not. The latter involves a person's posture and use of gestures, sometimes called 'body language', which was noted in Chapter 1 in regard to 'hello, goodbye' hand gestures. The head gesture for 'yes' in the Philippines is a movement upward, while the gesture for 'no' is a movement downward.[6] This is in contrast to an up and down head movement versus a side-to-side movement for 'yes' and 'no' in the USA.

The ability of a spoken language to convey meaning is influenced by both natural and man-made phenomena. For example, there are thirty-two words to describe the winds of Provence, France.[7] Less industrialized societies are apt to have limited vocabularies for commercial and industrial activities in contrast to English spoken in the UK and USA where such vocabularies would be extensive.[8] (It was surprising to this writer to find that in Barcelona, Spain, the word for marketing in Spanish was 'marketing'.)

Because of the diversity of languages and dialects spoken in some countries – as many as 203 in India – a limited number of hybrid languages (lingua francas) are used for communication between groups.[9] In Zimbabwe, to reach the black population with an advertising message, it is necessary to not only use English, the official language, but also to use two 'vernacular' languages, Shona and Ndebele, which are comprised of various ethnic group dialects.[10]

Language translation

Language translation for all forms of communication is a precarious matter. Literal translation seldom works. General Motors made that mistake when attempting to use the slogan 'Body by Fisher' in Flemish language advertising in Belgium. It translated into 'Corpse by Fisher' instead.[11] Ford avoided a translation problem when introducing a car into Mexico which is called 'Sable' in the USA. In colloquial Spanish 'sable' means 'sponging'. So the name, 'Taurus', another Ford product not sold in Mexico, was used instead.

Even working with the same language in different countries can cause major problems. For example, in Mexico 'tortilla' is the word for a griddlecake made of unleavened cornmeal, whereas in Spain, 'tortilla' is an omelette. In the UK 'chips' are what a US citizen would call 'french-fries'; 'crisps' are potato chips. In Zimbabwe an auto horn (USA) is a 'hooter'; traffic lights are called 'robots'.[12]

Aesthetics

Aesthetics, as a reflection of a culture, is expressed by means of design, colour, music, and dance. Product, packaging and advertisements must be aesthetically pleasing to win acceptance in any given environment. Attitudes towards modern, as well as traditional designs, require understanding. Calligraphy is considered the supreme art form in the Arab world; it is the principal source of embellishment for architecture, metal work, ceramics, glass and textiles.[13] See Exhibit 5.2 for recommended calligraphic-style logo for the front of a food package. While effective in the Middle East, this design approach would probably win little favour elsewhere.

Colours must be treated with care depending on the particular country where communications are being conducted. The colour of flowers can be used to illustrate this point. Purple flowers are associated with death and unhappiness in Brazil. White lilies have this association in Canada, Great Britain, and Sweden; white and yellow lilies in Taiwan; and yellow lilies in Mexico. Yellow flowers stand for infidelity in France, and disrespect for a woman in the Soviet Union. As for products themselves, Parker's white pens won little acceptance in China where white is the colour of mourning. And in India, Parker's green pens met with a similar fate because green is associated with bad luck.[14]

Even though the music of rock groups and popular singers has acceptance

Exhibit 5.2 *Calligraphic-style logo for front of food package*

in many different environments, indigenous music and musical instruments will have special significance also in many parts of the world. Take, for example, the Scottish and Irish bagpipers and the Calypso steel bands of the Caribbean. In Zimbabwe, it was recommended that drums instead of a guitar be used for the song in a commercial message.[15]

Wide variations in preference and appropriateness exist when it comes to instruments, sounds, and rhythms. Just think of the alternatives: martial music, Dixieland jazz, rock and roll, calypso . . . steel drums, tubas, violins . . . soft and sentimental, fast and loud. Use of music in communications, whether an oboe solo in a television commercial or the employment of a brass band for a new store opening, should fit the occasion and the audience.

Education

Education, according to Terpstra,[16] is a cultural process involving the transmission of traditions, ideas, attitudes, and skills as well as training in academic disciplines such as mathematics and the sciences. Education has been used for various purposes, including the improvement of agricultural techniques (and yields) and the containment of population growth in India; also for the transmission of manual skills of masonry, plumbing, and carpentry to inhabitants of former British Caribbean possessions.

With respect to marketing, there is a relationship between its controllable elements and level of education. The level will have an effect on product complexity/simplicity and the nature of the information used to communicate the product's benefits, features, specifications, and operational instructions. Level of education of a particular culture will also affect advertising, packaging, and sales promotion in terms of the balance between verbal and visual elements and the complexity/simplicity of the message. The ability to conduct marketing research studies will also be affected by the level of education.

Religion

Marked differences can be found in religious teachings and beliefs. In the predominantly Christian western world, it can be argued that the Catholic Church has attempted to have a greater hold on its followers than in the case of most other Christian religions in terms of worship, religious observance, marriage and divorce, fasting and abortion.

In the Hindu religion in India,[17] there is an adherence to a caste system where each member in a caste has a specific occupational and social role, and where the ultimate goal is cessation of any craving and release from suffering. This dogma is quite the opposite of other religions which accept and encourage the accumulation of wealth.

In the Islamic world, with some 800 million (Muslim) adherents, the Koran is the ultimate guide. Strict rules of conduct must be observed, particularly by women. Veils must be worn in public in most Islamic cultures. Women in Saudi Arabia cannot board an airline flight without written permission from a male family member or check into a hotel without written permission from a male relative or official sponsor.[18] In Pakistan, women are said to 'defer to men and boys, to give them the best morsels of food, to abide by their decisions'.[19] With respect to the consumption of foodstuffs, Muslims are prohibited from eating pork and drinking alcohol, beef is a taboo for Hindus, as are pork and shellfish for Jews.[20]

Holidays

Holidays are influenced by religion as well as people and events of significance to a nation state. Non-religious holidays around the world have names such as Constitution Day (South Korea), Queen's Birthday (Solomon Islands), J.J. Robert's birthday (Liberia), Fêtes des Forces Armées (Mauritania), and Liberation Day (The Netherlands). From a religious standpoint, probably the greatest constraints imposed on business and communications can be found in the Islamic countries. In Saudi Arabia, for example, the period of 29 April– 27 May 1987 was Ramadan, a month of fasting during which Muslims refrain from eating, drinking or smoking from sunrise to sunset. Business activity slows down considerably during this month. For about one month before and after the August pilgrimage holiday (Id-Al Adha – 4–9 August 1987), over one million foreign pilgrims enter Saudi Arabia to perform the pilgrimage to Makkah. Government and business attention is focused on the pilgrimage. Visits by foreign businessmen are discouraged and visas are hard to obtain during this period.'[21]

In other parts of the world, businessmen can be fooled by observing only the religious holidays of the countries in which they resided. Certain Christian religious holidays are observed in some countries and regions, and not elsewhere. For example, Epiphany (6 January), Ascension Day (the fortieth day after Easter), Whit Monday (Monday following Whit Sunday or Pentecost, seven Sundays after Easter), and Corpus Christi (the Thursday after Trinity Sunday). In the Caribbean region, and most likely elsewhere, many types of businesses are all but closed as people celebrate and take time off between Christmas Eve and the Epiphany (in some places called Three Kings Day).

Attitudes and values

The attitudes and values of a society in many instances stem from religious teachings. For example, in a Buddhist or Hindu society 'wantlessness' is the ideal; therefore people do not have the same motivation to produce and consume as in most Western societies.[22]

Whether stemming from religious beliefs or not, it should not be assumed that people in other societies hold similar attitudes and values. In Asia, people are not individualists...individualism is suspect and at odds with society. It is far more important to be in harmony with others. 'For this reason, as Roddy explains, the most popular products tend to remain the most popular products.'[23]

With respect to personal selling, Asian people don't like it; it is considered to be almost an invasion of privacy. That is why there is a basic weakness at the retail level, and why advertising has such strength in Asian markets.[24]

As for distinct values of different cultures, negative stereotypes should be avoided in communications and positive values emphasized. In Asia, this would mean emphasizing loyalty, harmony, modesty, a strong work ethic, sense of obligation, oneness with nature, and human dignity. In the Arab world, emphasis should be placed on hospitality, personal dignity, continuity, stability, and psychological and emotional strength. In Africa, positive values would be continuity, respect for elders, story-telling, memory, oneness with nature, interdependence, community, cooperation, and harmony. In Latin America, emphasis should be placed on patience, interdependence, cooperation, and survivability under adversity.[25]

Social organization

Social organization involves various types of groupings of people including families, social class, age and women.[26] In the USA, for example, the family is considered to be father, mother and the unmarried children. In other nations, particularly among the less developed, the family is large and extended. Brothers in Zaire would be cousins and uncles in the USA. In these extended families resources may be pooled; consumption decision making takes place in a larger unit.[27]

Among the Chinese, the family and close relatives comprise the essential unit; nearly everyone else is a stranger. This means that putting yourself in someone else's position is not easy for any Asian to do (an important law of good advertising).[28]

Every society has a social class structure, some more rigid than others. Even in the USA where the perception of an open, classless society exists, classes are defined on an upper to lower basis, each described with considerable accuracy. Determinants of social class include income, wealth, education, occupation, family prestige, value of home and neighbourhood. Since a wide variance will be experienced from society to society, census data (if available) and marketing research studies are needed to identify the social structure of any given environment.[29]

As for the role of women, there have been many changes in the USA and elsewhere in recent history. Over one-half of the adult women (eighteen+) in the USA are working. This has implications for broadcast advertising, purchasing habits and the consumption of many different types of goods. Increasing numbers of women in the workplace can be found in most societies of the world today as women continue to gain greater equality with men in all facets of life.

Even in the most restrictive of societies, the role of women is changing. Here is a description of the Arab housewife of today:

> When it comes to the household, (the Arab housewife) is the decision maker, even if sometimes it is by 'remote control'. Despite the outwardly male-oriented nature of Arab society, Mideast advertisers see women 'exercising real power within Arab families'. This contradicts the stereotyped view of the Arab woman 'cloistered at home and totally subservient to her husband'.
>
> In Saudi, women generally stay at home and much of the grocery shopping is

done by the male members of the household; however, it is the woman who chooses the products (often by brand) to be purchased. In Kuwait, Bahrain, and the UAE, women are less restricted; the new generation of women are more likely to appear in public unveiled, to shop unescorted, and to drive.[30]

With respect to social grouping by age, many countries of the world are facing an upward age shift in their population with declines in the population under fifteen years old. This phenomenon can be observed in Table 5.1. Marketers will have to factor the consequences of these changes into their plans.

Table 5.1 *Population trends by age category, selected countries*

Country	Year	Per cent of population Under 15	15–64	65+	Total
China	1960	38.9	56.3	4.8	100.0
	1985*	29.7	65.0	5.3	100.0
	2010*	21.4	70.3	8.2	99.9
Japan	1960	30.2	64.1	5.7	100.0
	1985*	21.8	68.2	10.0	100.0
	2010*	18.9	63.1	18.0	100.0
South Korea	1960	41.9	54.7	3.3	99.9
	1985*	31.2	64.7	4.0	99.9
	2010*	22.4	70.0	7.6	100.0
Sweden	1960	22.0	66.0	12.0	100.0
	1985*	18.2	64.8	16.9	99.9
	2010*	15.1	66.2	18.7	100.0
UK	1960	23.3	65.1	11.7	100.1
	1985*	19.5	65.4	15.1	100.1
	2010*	18.0	66.3	15.7	100.0
USA	1960	31.0	59.7	9.2	99.9
	1985*	21.9	66.4	11.7	100.0
	2010*	20.6	67.1	12.3	100.0
West Germany	1960	21.3	67.8	10.9	100.0
	1985*	15.4	70.2	14.5	100.1
	2010*	14.5	65.4	20.0	99.9

* Estimated. Note: Due to rounding, totals vary slightly from 100 per cent in some cases.

Source: *World Monitor,* June 1989, 45 (United Nations Statistics).

Cultural sensitivity among business people

Special note should be taken of cross-cultural dealings and among business people. As indicated earlier, time and space have different meanings to business people in different environments. This is true of other factors also. By knowing some of the differences in business etiquette in various countries, travellers abroad should be prepared to expect variances in business customs in all host country environments.

With respect to time, a business person may wait two hours or more after the pre-designated time for the appointment to take place in a Latin American country. As for deadlines for the completion of work, in the USA a deadline signifies the degree of urgency. In the Middle East an attempt to impose a deadline may be cause for cessation of work. In Japan, a delay of even years may mean that the customer is building up to something, not losing interest. As for space, negotiations in the USA may be carried on at a distance of three to eight feet, while in the Middle East negotiations may be conducted at a distance of two to three inches.[31]

In Germany it is wise to make appointments well in advance, and to be on time. In that country also, until a real friendship has been established, use of first name and casual invitations on the foreigner's part are not advisable...it could mean losing instead of winning friends and business. In business negotiations, Germans want facts and figures to support any claims made, not superlatives![32]

There are other variations in business customs depending on the country. For example, you must argue to win to be taken seriously in Italy. In Switzerland, you must speak with precision because you will be taken literally. In the Orient, points must be made without winning arguments so the other party doesn't lose face.[33]

A business person from the USA with something to sell in Japan should not attempt to start at the top. After initial introductions are made at the prospect's office, it is necessary to find out who is working in the area in which the US business person has an interest. It is probably a twenty-eight-year-old staff member. After this contact is made, socializing with an invitation for lunch or dinner comes before business. Following this, the business appointment is made and the proposition is explained. In the course of meetings, which may be several, to fully explain the proposition, it is then appropriate to ask if a presentation can be made to the 'higher ups'.[34] When engaged in dealing with Japanese, a period of silence is not considered awkward but rather is to be enjoyed. 'No' is a word to be avoided because it can regarded as losing face. When it comes time to sign the contract, don't pull out a Bic: Japanese do not sign important documents with disposable pens.[35]

The foregoing examples indicate how different business customs can be in different environments of the world. For communicators preparing material to be transmitted, knowledge of these differences can be extremely important.

Laws and regulations

Laws and regulations governing marketing activities are of prime concern to marketers. They must be known and observed in all countries where marketing activities are planned or being conducted since, '. . . a foreign business operates as a guest and at the convenience of its host'.[36] Laws and regulations can apply to ingredients, packaging, retail price ceilings, margins and markup limitations, distribution, and various types of advertising and sales promotion.[37] Of greatest concern to marketing communicators are the last two categories. J.J. Boddewyn has written a number of publications under the auspices of the International Advertising Association on these subjects, including:

- *Advertising to Children* A 1984 study of regulations and voluntary guidelines for TV, radio, print, and direct mail in forty countries.
- *Comparison Advertising* Two studies on regulation and legislation, use of the practice, and problems related to naming of competitors in advertisements, 1983 and 1978, fifty-five countries.
- *Foreign Languages, Materials, Trade and Investment in Advertising: Regulation and Self-Regulation in Forty-six Countries* Covers overall use of foreign languages and materials as well as regulatory status of restrictions; sanctions applied to foreign-produced ads which violate local laws; restrictions on international movement of advertising materials; foreign control of advertising agencies; and tax treatment of advertising expenditures abroad, 1985.
- *Medicine Advertising Regulation and Self-Regulation in Forty-six Countries* Regulations and self-regulations for prescription and non-prescription medicine advertising; claim substantiation, wording, warnings, and advertising to children, 1985.
- *Tobacco Advertising Bans and Consumption in Sixteen Countries* 1986.
- *Food Advertising Regulation and Self-Regulation* A thirty-five-country study of regulations concerning descriptive, nutritional, and health-related words and expressions in food advertising; pre-clearance of radio and TV commercials, 1982.
- *Outdoor/Billboard Advertising Regulation* A thirty-eight-country study on major rules, regulations, taxes, and restrictions, 1979.
- *Premiums, Gifts and Competitions* Information on laws and regulations for premiums, sampling, contests, sweepstakes, couponing, price-off promotions, refunds, and continuity programmes in thirty-eight countries, 1978.

Other recent publications of a similar nature sponsored by the IAA include the following:

- *International Restrictions on Advertising by Media and Selected Products* (by James P. Neelankavil)   Covers the availability of television, radio, newspapers, magazines, cinema, and outdoor media for advertising; the advertising restrictions by medium; advertising restrictions for alcohol, children's products, food, health and beauty aids, pharmaceutical, and tobacco; and taxation on advertising. This is a four-volume series published in 1985 and 1986.
- *Worldwide Restrictions on Advertising: An Outline of Principles, Problems and Solutions* (by Robert Bruce, Bruce P. Keller, and Jeffrey Cunard)   Examines the legal framework for advertising, especially in the European Community and the United Nations, published in 1986.*

For advertisers who have a special interest in advertising laws and restrictions in Europe, The European Advertising Association publishes a *Redbook* which is billed as the 'single answer to all those questions on advertising regulations across Europe'.[38]

The comprehensive nature and scope of these publications should give the reader an idea of the importance of laws and regulations pertaining to advertising and promotion on a global scale. As James P. Neelankavil has stated,[39] 'We find a worldwide increase in restrictions being imposed over the last ten years. Many nations have established stringent truth-in-advertising rules. More restrictions are springing up in the aftermath of the political, religious and cultural upheavals around the world.' Supernational organizations as well as national governments are very much involved in the regulatory process. This includes agencies of the European Community, UNESCO (The United Nations Education, Scientific and Cultural Organization), and WHO (World Health Organization).

To indicate the far-reaching nature of the laws and regulations dealing with advertising and promotion, several examples are cited.

In the case of advertising to children, restrictions are extensive but by no means uniform. The extent and variety of these restrictions are shown in Exhibit 5.3 which lists thirteen different types of advertising and promotion practices and gives the 'do's' and 'don'ts' for the ten different countries.

In Hispanic America, recent developments include a new law in Mexico which prohibits advertising for cigarettes at parks, stadiums, sport centres, theatres, and near schools; also prohibits advertising on TV for cigarettes before 9.30pm and alcohol before 10.00pm.[40]

---

* The above list of publications along with the brief explanations has been reproduced with the permission of the International Advertising Association.

Exhibit 5.3 *Restrictions on promotion to children*

Question: Keeping in mind that there are maybe some government or voluntary restrictions applying to the following practices, can advertising to children do the following?

Practice	Argentina	Australia	France	Japan	Malaysia	Norway	Turkey	USA	Zimbabwe	Brazil
1 Offer premiums	No	Yes	Yes	Yes	Yes	No	No	Yes	No	Yes
2 Offer gifts	No	Yes	Yes	Yes	Yes	No	No	Yes	No	Yes
3 Offer participation in competitions	Yes	Yes	Yes	Yes	Yes	No	No	Yes	No	Yes
4 Invite to order by mail/phone	No	Yes	No	Yes	No	No	No	Yes	Yes	No
5 Compare brands	No	Yes	No	Yes	No	Yes	No	Yes	Yes	Yes
6 Use well-known personalities, characters, puppets, heroes	Yes	No	No	Yes	Yes	Yes	No	Yes	Yes	Yes
7 Use children as endorsers	Yes	No	No	Yes	Yes	Yes	No	Yes	Yes	Yes
8 Use children as presenters or commentators when not knowledgeable about products	Yes	No	No	Yes	No	Yes	No	No	No	Yes

(*continued overleaf*)

Exhibit 5.3 (continued)

Question: Keeping in mind that there are maybe some government or voluntary restrictions applying to the following practices, can advertising to children do the following?

Practice	Argentina	Australia	France	Japan	Malaysia	Norway	Turkey	USA	Zimbabwe	Brazil
9 Have no adults present in children's ads	Yes	Yes	Yes	Yes	Yes	Yes	No	Yes	Yes	Yes
10 Direct requests to children to purchase or use	Yes	No	Yes	Yes	Yes	Yes	No	No	Yes	No
11 Direct requests by or to children to induce or lead others to buy	Yes	Yes	No	Yes	No	Yes	No	No	Yes	No
12 Indicate approximate price of toy	No	No	Yes	No	No	No	No	No	No	No
13 Indicate absence of necessary parts	No	Yes	No	No	No	Yes	No	Yes	No	No

Source: Boddewyn, J.J. (1984) Advertising to children: regulation and self-regulation in 40 countries, International Advertising Association, 21–24. Reproduced by permission of the International Advertising Association. New York, pp.

Elsewhere, the Peruvian Government decreed that all advertising must be produced locally; in Chile, the Association of Film Producers forced the Government to enforce a long-standing law which prohibits all TV spots produced outside the country from airing on Chilean TV.[41]

Pharmaceutical advertising is coming under attack in many countries. Recently, it was reported that twenty-four countries require some type of prior approval. In Great Britain, spending on ethical drug advertising in the trade press is now limited to 10 per cent of sales.[42]

Changes made are not always more restrictive. The Thai Consumer Protection Board, after a ten-month controversy over a print ad for Colgate, ruled in favour of comparative advertising. This followed recommended guidelines for comparative advertising by the Advertising Association of Thailand. Colgate claimed greater effectiveness than Darkie and Close-up toothpastes in fighting cavities due to its special formulation.[43] In fact, unlike earlier reports, J.J. Boddewyn has reported a trend toward fewer restrictions after completing an expanded update of a 1985, forty-six-country report.[44]

Based on the above discussion of laws and regulations, the implications for marketing communicators are clear; it is essential to know and keep abreast of changes in the restrictions on advertising and promotion on a country-by-country basis. This is equally true of supranational developments which are occurring in the European Community. For example, the European Commission submitted a proposal for a directive to coordinate various national measures associated with broadcasting, including the amount of air time allowed for advertising, separation of advertising from programmes, and advanced checking of advertisements.[45] These matters are of prime interest to many advertisers and must be followed closely.

Advertising taxation

In recent times, taxes on advertising have been commonplace in Europe and non-existent in most other regions of the world. In Europe, according to John Furniss, most countries have adopted the value added tax (VAT) but the tax rate varies from country to country, and also by medium. In West Germany, all media is subject to a 14 per cent VAT. In Spain, there is a 4 per cent tax on all media plus a 5 per cent tax on radio and television.[46] In some European countries, foreign advertisers are exempt from paying the VAT, while in others, foreign advertisers are not.[47] Though VAT is the most common form of taxation, it is by no means the only method. In Greece, for example, there is a special 3.6 per cent stamp tax on advertising invoices and a 10 per cent turnover tax. Belgium levies a national tax of 4 per cent on cinema advertising in addition to a uniform 19 per cent VAT.[48]

International Media Guide summarizes the advertising tax requirements on a country-by-country basis by region. In contrast to the widespread adoption of the VAT in Europe, among twenty countries in the Asia/Pacific region, only South Korea is shown as having a tax − 10 per cent VAT. In Latin America, among twenty-nine countries, only five are shown as having advertising taxes.[49]

As with other types of regulations, advertising taxation is a matter which must be closely monitored in many countries. Organizing and maintaining a fact file for ready reference when dealing with a number of foreign environments can be time consuming and unproductive. This means that each communicator must determine the nature and extent of the basic information needed to be informed properly as a member of the marketing team and the manager of the communications function.

Relevant secondary sources

A selection of relevant secondary sources for general environmental conditions and trends is shown in Exhibit 5.4. It would be useful to have these references readily available in the company or nearby public library but not in an IMC's fact file unless that person has the support of a number of staff personnel. A workable alternative would be to have a small collection of key general references if the budget permits. One such reference is the *Europa Yearbook*. Despite the fact that many of the economic and demographic statistics are dated (a general problem for information of this kind), it does provide a broad base of information on most countries of the world. Each country survey begins with a recent history of political, economic, and social conditions. This includes population, economic activities, finance, balance of payments, and external trade statistics and trends. Also included is a directory of political organizations, embassies, judicial systems, religious organizations, media availabilities (dailies, periodicals, radio and TV stations), banks, and various trade organizations such as Chambers of Commerce. All of this information is contained in two volumes.

Similar works published annually in two volumes but containing a greater breadth and depth of statistical information on business and marketing are Euromonitor's *European and International Marketing and Data Statistics*. In addition to European country reports, the International Edition 1988/1989 included 153 countries grouped in fifteen regions. Both editions cover twenty-four subject areas ranging from statistics and trends on demography to consumer expenditure patterns on food, clothing, beverages and housing; advertising patterns and media access; telecommunications; automotive production and registrations.

Another group of references which should be considered for inclusion in the

Exhibit 5.4 *Sources of information on general environmental conditions and trends*

United Nations Publications

- *World Economic Survey* (annual) — current trends
- *Demographic Yearbook* — statistics for almost 250 entities
- *Statistical Yearbook* — industrial production, trade, financial, development assistance, health, education and technology data
- *Survey of Economic Conditions in Africa* (annual)
- *Economic Survey of Europe* (annual)
- *Economic Survey of Latin America* (annual)
- *Yearbook of International Trade Statistics* — export and import statistics for 139 countries

Organization For Economic Cooperation and Development (OECD)

- *OECD Economic Survey* — annual review of recent trends, economic policy, future prospects for twenty-four member countries including economic statistics

US Government Printing Office

- *International Economic Indicators* (quarterly) — charts and statistics on the US and seven other major industrialized nations

International Monetary Fund (IMF)

- *Direction of Trade* (monthly) *Yearbook* (annual) — statistics on value of exports and imports in US dollars

World Bank

- *World Development Report* (annual) — reviews economic and demographic developments, discusses economic outlook and provides maps and statistics on public and private socioeconomic indicators

Far Eastern Economic Review

- *Asia Yearbook* — country-by-country brief on social, political, economic conditions and foreign relations

Interamerican Development Bank

- *Economic and Social Progress in Latin America* — annual survey on Latin American economy usually emphasizing one sector

---

Source: Reiman, Eva L. (1984) *International Trade Sources*, Mortola Library, Pace University, Pleasantville, NY, July.

international marketing communication fact file for English readers include *Business America, Overseas Business Reports (OBRs)*, and *Foreign Economic Trends (FETs)*, all published by the US Department of Commerce. *Business America* regularly features the trade outlook in different countries and covers such topics as copyrights, commercial holidays, special industry reports (e.g. service industries and telecommunications), and trade fairs, missions, and promotions taking place in various business centres around the world.

The OBRs and FETs are country specific. In looking at these reports for Costa Rica, it appears the FET is updated annually and the OBR is revised every six years. The FET contains key economic indicators such as population, gross domestic product (in total and per capita), unemployment figures, balance of payment statistics, government finances, and US − Costa Rican trade information. These indicators are followed by a six-page explanation of their meaning along with monetary and fiscal policy, and external finance information.

The OBR is a marketing-oriented report. Its contents include the best opportunities for US exporters along with a commentary on key host country industry trends. The remainder of the report covers information useful in the conduct of business with Costa Rica such as sales and distribution channels, free trade zones, advertising media, agents and distributors, patent and trademark protection, import procedures, export controls, and helpful information for business travellers.

To access general economic and business conditions in a number of environments, an alternative to the published information already mentioned is the use of a software product such as Global Data Manager of the US Department of Commerce. This is a database programme containing 160 variables for nearly every country in the world on population, economics, communications, education, etc.

For those operating in the UK, the Advertising Association's *Marketing Pocket Book* has a wealth of information on economic and demographic conditions, consumers, distribution, marketing expenditures, media and selected European statistics. The Dentsu Japan Advertising/Marketing Year Book contains similar information with in-depth treatment. Also in Japan, the Keizai Koho Center recently began publishing a similar pocket book packed with similar information (domestic and international) but without the emphasis on marketing and media expenditures. The first edition (*Japan 1991 − an International Comparison*) was published in October 1990. Major advertising agencies operating in countries around the world are an alternative source of marketing and advertising information.

To keep abreast of current developments, certain publications concerning the international business scene should be on the marketing communicator's regular reading list. High on that list should be the *Economist*. Other selections, dependent on the focus of interest, include the *Financial Times, South*, the *Asia-Pacific Review, Business Week, Fortune*, and the *Herald Tribune*.

Another means of keeping abreast of business conditions in markets in different countries is through affiliation with local business organizations. For example, the *Europa Yearbook* lists both state-sponsored and private organizations representing trade and industry groups that include producers of agricultural and manufactured goods, export promotion, and chambers of commerce. Membership in one or more of these organizations may be advantageous, particularly when a change in government takes place and economic problems exist.

A case in point concerns the austerity programme imposed by the Perez Administration in Venezuela when it took over the reins of government in early 1989. The serious riots, civil unrest, and extend of economic dislocations were not expected. To be current with the rapidly changing picture from a business perspective membership in the Venezuelan American Chamber of Commerce (VenAmCham) could have been very helpful. Information was obtainable through personal contact with other members and through the VenAmCham's monthly *Business Brief*. The *Brief* reports on economic developments of the nation as a whole on a business sector-by-sector basis, and through periodic polls of its members with respect to future developments. The VenAmCham is just one of the US Chambers of Commerce located in forty-nine countries around the world, all affiliated with the US Chamber of Commerce.

Summary

After reading this chapter on environmental conditions and constraints, it should become apparent that a great deal of information is needed in order to plan marketing communication programmes to reach target groups in different parts of the world.

Relevant sources of secondary information must be comingled with intelligence provided by the field sales organization and/or members of the distribution channel as well as primary research studies when operating on a multinational basis.

A perspective of the global environment

In Chapter 1, the elements to be considered in the determination of a market included people, purchasing power, accessibility, and a willingness to spend. To demonstrate how demographic (population statistics), economic (gross national product), and infrastructural (media availability) information can be used to evaluate the existence and prospects for one global market, the major portion of a paper presented at 1986 Annual Conference of the European Marketing Academy is reproduced in the pages which follow. The purpose of its inclusion is to demonstrate how readily available secondary data can be pieced together to evaluate a hypothesis and draw certain conclusions. (The following is an abridged version of a paper presented by Tom Griffin at the Annual Conference of the European Marketing Academy, Helsinki, Finland, June 1986.)

The world as a single market

Hypothesis

Some would have us believe that because of rapidly converging activity, interest, preference, and demographic characteristics, the world is evolving or will evolve into one or several large, homogeneous, logistically compatible, and readily accessible market groupings.

Market — an operational definition

In this paper three criteria will be used to define 'market' and evaluate the hypothesis above. They are:

1 People — their numbers, location, concentration, and education.
2 Purchasing power — as evidenced by gross national product.
3 Accessibility — in terms of the ability to deliver a 'global' advertising message.

A look at global statistics

While the concept of convergence does have validity for certain groupings of people in some parts of the world, a look at selected statistics will demonstrate the gulf that exists among many groups of people in many different locations around the globe.

This examination was undertaken by grouping countries geographically, largely along continental and subcontinental lines, into fourteen regional divisions as shown in Table 5.1. It will be noted that several countries, due to their location and special characteristics, did not lend themselves to regional grouping. (Eastern European countries, the USSR, the Democratic Republic of Korea and Mongolia were not included in this analysis due to the absence

Table 5.1 *Selected demographic characteristics by region, ranked by the index of GNP to population*

Region Category	1 Per cent of total population	2 Per cent of total GNP	3 Index col 2 col 1	4 Urban pop per cent of total pop	5 # in secondary school as a % of total in
North America	6.1	31.3	513	77	95
Japan	2.8	11.1	395	78	92
Oceania	0.5	1.8	360	87(a)	84(a)
Western Europe	9.1	32.1	353	68	86
Middle East	2.5	3.1	124	61	51
South Africa	0.7	0.8	114	50	NA
South America	6.0	5.5	92	66	46
Rep of Korea and Hong Kong	1.1	1.0	91	76	75
Caribbean and Middle East	2.9	2.0	69	46	27
Northern Africa	2.8	1.3	46	45	41
Eastern South- Asia	8.8	2.0	23	34	41
Central Africa	8.6	1.5	17	23	15
Middle South- Asia	23.8	3.6	15	21	24
China	24.3	2.9	12	21	44

Notes (a) Excludes Papua New Guinea with per cents of 17 and 13 for cols 4, 5.
(b) These statistics were derived from the *World Developments Report* (1984), The World Bank, Oxford University Press, New York, pp. 218, 219, 260, 261, 266, 267.

of data on gross national product (GNP). Several other small political units were excluded because they were not reported in the statistics used.)

Regional dissimilarities

Looking at Table 5.1 reveals marked dissimilarities among regions on all four characteristics included in the Table: per cent of total population, per cent of total GNP, urban population as a per cent of total population, and number in secondary schools as a per cent of total population in that category.

Relationship between population and GNP

In respect to the relationship between per cent of total population (column 1) and per cent of total GNP (column 2), the contrast among regions becomes more striking when the latter (GNP) is indexed to the former (population) as shown in column 3. The ranking of regions follows this indexing. The highest ranked region, North America, has an index of 513. The lowest, China, has an index of twelve. This signifies a forty-three-fold difference.

To simplify the analysis of this data, the fourteen regions were compressed into three categories according to the indexing and ranking described above and observed in Table 5.1. This produced the information shown in Table 5.2 which provides the per cent of population and per cent of GNP divided into high, medium, and low categories.

The figures in Table 5.2 show that the regions in category I with less than one-fifth (19 per cent) of the world's population, located on four different continents, share more than three-quarters (77 per cent) of the world's GNP. The relatively small category II has a GNP which roughly parallels population. The acute difference lies in category III where 68 per cent of the world's population enjoy a meagre 11 per cent of the world's GNP.

From the disparity in GNP... equated to purchasing power... which these figures indicate, it is difficult to conceive of a (global) market developing in category III regions for many of the goods and services which are currently mass produced and promoted in category I regions, or for that matter, in category II as well.

Urbanization and education

Returning to Table 5.1 to examine the last two characteristics — urban population as a per cent of total population (column 4) and number in secondary schools as a per cent of the total people in that age bracket (column 5) — these observations can be made. The concentration of people in urban centres is related to their accessibility in terms of advertising message delivery. It should be noted that the regions with relatively high indices of GNP to population also possess relatively high per cents of urban concentration. It would be reasonable to expect, then, that both people and purchasing power would be more easily reached by advertising media available in the regions at the upper end of the list as shown in Table 5.1. At the lower end of the list are the regions and countries with the greatest numbers of people, the lowest economic indices and the lowest concentration of population in urban centres. Reaching people with purchasing power in these regions would surely be difficult and cost-inefficient.

In regard to the numbers in secondary schools as a per cent of total people

Table 5.2 *Per cent of population and Gross National Product (GNP) by high, Medium, and low GNP/population categories*

	Per cent of total population	*Per cent of total GNP*	*Per cent of total GNP to per cent of total population*
Category I (high) North America, Japan, Oceania, and Western Europe	19	77	4.1 to 1
Category II (medium) Middle East, South Africa, South America, Rep of Korea, Hong Kong, Caribbean and Middle America	13	12	0.9 to 1
Category III (low) Northern Africa, Eastern South Asia, Central Africa, Middle South Asia, and China	68	11	0.2 to 1

in that age bracket, the higher per cents, with one or two exceptions, also relate to regions with higher indices of GNP to population. It is reasoned, then, that the ability to read and comprehend advertising messages would diminish as the percentages shown in column 5 become smaller and smaller. This would be most acute in regions such as Central Africa and Middle South Asia.

To offset the literacy problem, the greater use of pictures and images in advertising would be appropriate. This, in turn, points to television as the most appropriate medium. In the next section of this paper the availability of television and other media will be examined.

Communication alternatives

In looking at the world, 'global' marketers of mass-produced goods, of necessity, must concern themselves with the capability of transmitting messages about their offerings by means of mass communication. Both broadcast and print are alternatives. Television, however, is acknowledged as the most powerful selling vehicle and is more appropriate than print or radio in regions or countries where educational levels are low.

The availability of television, radio, and telephones

This gives rise to an examination of the incidence of television sets, radio sets, and telephones as shown in Table 5.3. It will be observed that the data is organized and presented by the same three categories used in Table 5.2. Even though this information (the latest) is three to five years old, the sharp contrast in the availability of communication receivers most likely exists today and will continue to prevail in the foreseeable future.

While no attempt has been made to average data within the three categories, marked differences can readily be observed in the incidence of television sets,

Table 5.3 *Television, radio, and telephone availability by high, medium, and low GNP/ population categories*

	TV sets per 1,000	Radio sets per 1,000	Telephones per 100
Category I (high)			
North America	560	1630	74
Japan	551	668	48
Oceania	333	1001	52
Western Europe	311	459	44
Category II (medium)			
Rep of Korea, Taiwan and Hong Kong	222	431	12
Middle East	175	290	14
South America	96	354	6
Caribbean and Middle America	93	201	5
South Africa	70	275	12
Category III (low)			
Eastern South Asia	47	141	7
Northern Africa	40	149	2
Middle South Asia	14	85	1
Central Africa	5	63	2
China	5	60	(a)

Notes (a)   Less than 0.5/100.

(b)   In categories I and II, and category III, East Asia and N. Africa, data was included for all or most of the countries. In the remaining category III regions, data were available and included for five of eight Middle South Asian countries and only five of thirty-two Central African countries.

(c)   Source of information: *Statistical Abstract of the United States* (1985) US Department of Commerce, Bureau of Census, Washington, December 1984, p. 849.

radio sets, and telephones, particularly between categories I and III. In the former, when it involves broadcast media (television and radio), there is the potential for delivery of an advertising message to nearly all homes. In the USA, for example, there is upwards of 98 per cent penetration of homes in respect to both television and radio (Bates 1982). Even in a Western European country like Spain where there are 254 television sets per 1,000 population, there is a 93 per cent household penetration (*Stern* 1985).

This potential diminishes in moving from top to bottom regions in category II.

In category III the penetration of broadcast media, notably in respect to television, where sets per 1,000 range from forty-seven down to five, contrasts sharply with regions in category I. The ability to deliver a message to large groups on television and also radio diminishes sharply when sets in use are compared between these two categories. For example, in Indonesia it was reported (Curtis 1981) that television is limited to 3 per cent and radio is limited to 24 per cent household penetration.

The incidence of telephones per 100 population produces an even more striking contrast in regions in both category II and category III as compared with category I. For one thing, the dearth of telephones virtually eliminates the opportunity to do research by phone in categories II and III. In another respect, the growth trend in telemarketing in category I countries, for example, has little if any potential in category II and category III regions.

The ability to advertise on television

A recent front page article by John Hillkirk (1985) in *USA Today* reported on the linkage of viewers in fifty-five nations to view a four-day conference of evangelism and discipleship. The telecast originated from four continents, used every available satellite in the free world, and travelled to ninety cities around the globe. This indicates the global potential for transmission of advertising messages.

But religious programming is one thing. The reality of delivering a commercial advertising message is quite different. When it comes to transnational television broadcasting and advertising, the closest existing entity is the pan-European, eleven-country Sky Channel. It, according to an article in *International Advertiser* (1985), now reaches about 3 per cent of Europe's 100 million households and is expected to reach 7 per cent by 1986. Current and potential reach, however, is not considered to be a large pan-European audience. Carolyn Hulse (1984), writing on the same subject, points to nationalism, cultural insularity, and cultural sovereignty as inhibiting the growth of pan-regional television advertising. One example she cites concerns Canada. On the one hand, eleven of the top thirteen television programmes are US imports.

On the other hand, the federally financed Canadian broadcasting system is committed to reducing US programming to three hours per day or less.

Along the same lines, Jack Burton (1984) described the stringent new television regulations set down in a forty-one-page advertising code by the Malaysian Government. It is designed to 'protect its largely Islamic population from the excesses of Western advertising and marketing'.

William Lynn (1984), Corporate Media Director, Coca-Cola Co., described the dilemma of buying television time in Germany. Television is that company's principal media the world over. In Germany they are limited to only three commercials a month.

For Lynn's organization and all others that rely on television to deliver their advertising message, the ultimate obstacle is encountered in countries like Denmark, Norway, and Sweden where no radio or television advertising is permitted (*Stern* 1985).

Global print possibilities

In the USA, until *USA Today* started publishing a few years ago, newspapers were largely considered a local medium. On the other hand, magazines were largely considered to deliver a national audience and be purchased on that basis. In other regions of the world, notably Europe, newspapers as well as magazines have long-standing reputations for delivering a national audience.

Outside of the home country or region, the ability of most print vehicles to deliver an advertising message has been limited. When it comes to a general audience, *Reader's Digest* can be considered an exception (Lachlan 1984) which appears in seventeen languages and forty-one editions.

There are, of course, exceptions when it concerns the delivery of a specialized audience such as business, finance or science, and as discussed further at a later stage in this paper.

Trade and industrial publications are another classification of print media. These publications enjoy a global following in respect to the specialized nature of the topics they cover. These magazines and newspapers, however, are not treated at greater length in this report because they do not deliver a general or consumer-oriented audience.

To take a closer look at those 'global' print media which are designed to deliver the kind of audience just mentioned, attention of the reader is directed to Table 5.4. This table presents the findings of a study *Advertising Age* conducted among top media, advertiser, and ad agency executives. They were asked to identify the leading 'global' publications they felt met certain criteria such as 'mass' circulation on at least three continents and global editorial content.

In perusing Table 5.4, please note that the final two columns refer to the number and per cent of copies which the publication delivers outside its home

Table 5.4 Leading global print alternatives: figures shown are paid circulation (000s)

Publication prime	North America	Europe	Middle East/Africa	Asia Pacific	Latin America	Total	Outside area #	%
Dailies								
Financial Times	6	202	5	3	(c)	216	14	6
International Herald Tribune	2	120	11	24	–	157	37	24
Wall Street Journal	1960	25	–	27	–	2,012	52	3
Weeklies								
Business Week	775	41	–	21	17	854	79	9
The Economist	101	115	13	20	4	253	138	55
Guardian Weekly	25	17	5	12	1	60	35	58
Newsweek	3,037	303	(a)	208	46	3,594	557	15
Time	4,993	525	(a)	383	100	6,001	1,008	17
Monthlies								
International	–	70	35	30	30	165	95	58
Management	9,018	684	(a)	377	90	10,169	1,151	12
National Geographic	19,535	7,302	(a)	2,181	1,265	30,283	10,748	36
Reader's Digest	555	66	5	22	6	654	99	15
Scientific American	8	13	28	14	11	74	46	62
South	–	26	120(b)	301	309	756	447	59
Worldpaper								
Other								
Fortune	617	55	–	30	(c)	702	85	12
Harvard Business Review	213	12	3	8	4	240	27	11

Notes (a) Europe figures include Middle East and Africa.
(b) All of this circulation is in the Middle East.
(c) Less than 500 circulation or included in 'other'.
(d) Source of information, *Advertising Age, International Survey*, 3 December 1984, p. 51.

territory. For example, the *Financial Times'* home territory is considered to be Europe. Therefore, 14,000 or 6 per cent of its circulation is delivered outside of Europe.

Examination of the circulation figures bears out what was mentioned earlier. Only *Reader's Digest*, with a circulation of ten million plus, delivers large numbers away from its North American base. If it had three readers per copy, in North America it would reach approximately 23 per cent of the population. In the remainder of the world, it would reach less than 1 per cent of the total population.

Other publications which just begin to approach the *Reader's Digest*'s magnitude of global circulation are the *National Geographic* and *Time*. Each have circulations outside North America of approximately one million copies.

The remaining publications listed in Table 5.4, for the most part, would appear to deliver specialized target audiences, no doubt in relatively large numbers. Instead of consumers, these audiences would more likely be business and financial executives, scholars, scientists, politicians, and also public and private libraries. But, as *Advertising Age* reported (1984, 3 December, p. 50), 'US global advertisers say global publications (shown in Table 5.4) are at the fringe — not the heart — of their media buying plans.'

Conclusions and implications

Has the global era of marketing arrived? Is it just over the horizon? From the way some educators, practitioners, and companies have expressed themselves in the past year or two the answer would be yes. Selling has been described as the art of exaggeration. It is possible that this age-old technique is being used to attempt to influence some individuals' or organizations' potential clients.

In a different sense, the impression could be left that certain marketing and advertising experts, opinion leaders, and organizations are practising a certain form of imperialism of their own. At least, it appears that they may be seeing the world through their own set of specially tinted glasses.

This paper called on its readers to focus on two basic quantitative measures and their relationship in considering the world, or parts of it, as a market. These measures involved people and purchasing power. To facilitate the analysis, the world was divided into fourteen regions, then grouped into three categories to reflect a high, medium, and low relationship between GNP (purchasing power) and population. As one might predict, the 80−20 principle was again discovered. Roughly 20 per cent of the world's population accounts for 80 per cent of its GNP. This simple analysis points to the great dichotomy which confronts advertisers in attempting to identify global market opportunities. If the same analysis is made on a region-by-region basis, the differences are that much greater.

Other basic measures included urbanization and education. In respect to the former, it was found that the more affluent regions had greater concentrations of population in urban centres. This should simplify and reduce the cost of distribution and promotion. Alternatively, lower concentrations of population in urban centres, found in lesser affluent regions, would tend to increase costs of distribution and promotion...and bring about higher prices for goods and services.

As for education, the less affluent regions of the world revealed lower percentages of young people in school at the secondary level. This measure was included to evaluate the extent of education provided in different regions of the world. Though literacy rate would have been a better measure, it can be reasoned that in regions where less educational opportunity exists there is less likelihood of a (advertising) message to be understood. This, thereby, would reduce the accessibility of those regions (markets) to advertisers.

Accessibility was also evaluated in terms of communication alternatives in delivering an advertising message on a global basis. As pointed out in the body of the paper, the availability of broadcast media and telephones varies greatly by category and region. The availability of phones was two per hundred or less in most category III regions, and the availability of television sets was fourteen per thousand or less in the most heavily populated regions of the world.

Not only are there physical limitations on broadcast media but also many countries in all three categories limit the amount of time, nature of the programme and advertising message. And in the extreme, and countries in category I and elsewhere do not permit any advertising on either radio or television.

When it comes to print, outside of one or two alternatives, such as the *Reader's Digest*, the ability to deliver a 'global' advertising message to a consumer, as opposed to a specialized audience, is not a reality.

To conclude, the findings presented in this paper suggest that a true global market for advertisers of mass-produced goods does not nor will exist in the foreseeable future. Advertisers would be best advised to think globally and to act locally to give consumers what they want in order to improve the quality of life (Haueter 1983).

References

Advertising Age (1984), quotation, 3 December.
Chase, Dennis (1985) In *Advertising Age*, April, p. 50.
Bates, Ted (1982) *Instant Media Guide*, Media Department, New York.

Burton, Jack (1984) Malaysia clamps down on TV advertising. *Advertising Age*, 6 September, 26.

Earle, Richard M. (1984) Success stories will turn on brand management. *Marketing News*, 11 May, 7.

Haueter, Eric (1983) Speech on modular marketing, Pace University, New York, 3 May.

Hillkirk, John (1985) TV satellites to link viewers in 55 nations. *USA Today*, 27 December, Section B, 1.

Hulse, Carolyn (1984) Pan-European TV: its time may never come. *Advertising Age*, 12 March.

International Advertising Association (1984) *Global Marketing — From Now to the Twenty-First Century*, IAA, New York.

International Advertiser (1985) 'How Pan-European is Europe?', 8 September.

Kimbrell, Wendy (1984) In *Advertising Age*, 29 October, 52.

Lachlan, E.C. (1984) *Reader's Digest* spans the globe. *Advertising World*, 18 September.

Levitt, Theodore (1983) The globalization of markets. *Harvard Business Review*, May—June, 92—102.

Lynch, Mitchell (1984) Harvard's Levitt called global marketing 'Guru'. *Advertising Age*, 25 June, 49.

Lynn, William (1984) In a round table: Global TV: wave of the future or industry pipe dream? *Advertising Age*, 3 December, 49.

Michaels, Julia (1985) In *Advertising Age*, 7 October, 50.

Mussey, Dagmar (1984) In *Advertising Age*, 3 September, 4.

Reinhard, Keith (1985) In *Advertising Age*, 15 April, 46.

Runyon, Kenneth (1984) *Advertising*, Charles E. Merrill, Columbus, Ohio, pp. 7, 12.

Saatchi & Saatchi Compton Worldwide (1984) Advertisement, *New York Times*, 3 June.

Stern Advertising Department (1985) *The Media Scene in Europe 2*. Gruner & Jahr, Hamburg.

Questions

1   What is meant by high and low context cultures? Give examples to support your answer.
2   Why should the self-reference criterion be avoided?
3   Identify the various cultural factors that have to be taken into account in international marketing communication planning. Explain why these factors have to be taken into account.
4   Does business culture pose the same concern to marketers as does consumer

culture? Why or why not?

5 Based on your reading of this chapter how extensive are laws and regulations that affect marketing communications?

6 What goods or services are subjected to the most stringent limitations?

7 Give examples of four recent restrictions on marketing communications.

8 What are conditions concerning advertising taxation that are found in different parts of the world?

9 If you were asked to provide five sources on environmental conditions and constraints, what names would be on your list?

Notes

1 Cateora, Philip R. (1987) *International Marketing*, 6th edn, Irwin, Homewood, IL, p. 95.

2 Hall, Edward T. (1976) *Beyond Culture*, Anchor Press/Doubleday, Garden City, New York, pp. 79, 88–89.

3 Lee, James A. (1966) Cultural analysis in overseas operations. *Harvard Business Review*, March–April, 106–114.

4 Terpstra, *International Marketing*, 4th edn, The Dryden Press, Chicago, p. 88.

5 Hall, Edward T. (1959) *The Silent Language*, Anchor/Doubleday, New York.

6 Harris, Philip R. and Moran, Robert T. (1989) In *Global Marketing Management*, (Toyne, B. and Walters, P.) Allyn and Bacon, Needham, MA, p. 168.

7 Delbanco, Nicholas (1989) A sentimental journey. *Michigan Today*, The University of Michigan, **21**, (3), 3.

8 Terpstra, *op. cit.*, p. 87.

9 *Ibid.*, p. 89.

10 Hamadziridi, Jessica (1989) Unpublished marketing paper, Pace University, May.

11 Ricks, David A. (1981) *Wall Street Journal*, 31 March.

12 Hamadziridi, *op. cit.*

13 Halaby, Ghida (1989) Unpublished Middle East Marketing Communication Plan, Pace University, May.

14 Onkvisit, Sak and Shaw, John J. (1989) *International Marketing*, Merrill Publishing Company, Columbus, Ohio, pp. 240–241.

15 Hamadziridi, *op. cit.*

16 Terpstra, *op. cit.*, p. 94

17 Terpstra, *op. cit.*, p. 98

18 Alirez, Marianne (1987) Women of Saudi Arabia. *National Geographic*,

October, 452.
19 Crossette, Barbara (1989) In Pakistan women seek basic rights. *The New York Times*, 26 March, L9.
20 Onkvisit and Shaw, *op. cit.*, p. 238.
21 US Department of Commerce (1987) *Business America*, Washington, DC, 5 January, p. 34.
22 Terpstra, *op. cit.*, p. 105.
23 Roddy, John (1982) Address on advertising and marketing to Southeast Asia delivered to the New York chapter of the International Advertising Association, 8 June.
24 *Ibid.*
25 Fouke, Carole J. (1989) Sensitivity to culture builds foreign markets. *Marketing News*, 19 June, 9.
26 Terpstra, 106−7.
27 *Ibid.*, 106.
28 Roddy, *op. cit.*
29 Wells, William, Burnett, John, and Moriarty, Sandra (1989) *Advertising Principles and Practice*, Prentice-Hall, Englewood Cliffs, New Jersey, pp. 119−120.
30 Halaby, *op. cit.*
31 Hall, E.T. (1960) The silent language in overseas business. *Harvard Business Review*, May−June, 87−96.
32 Hall, E.T. (1983) Doing business with Germans: everything communicates. *Advertising World*, June/July, 8, 10.
33 Cateora, Philip R. and Hess, A. (1983) *International Marketing*, 5th edn, Irwin, Homewood, IL.
34 Notes taken at lecture delivered by Tadao Fujimatsu at Pace University, White Plains, New York, 17 October 1986.
35 O'Connor, Matt (1986) Japan, where 'maybe' maybe way to go. *Chicago Tribune*, 18 November, Business, 1, 11.
36 Cateora, *op. cit.*, p. 162.
37 Terpstra, *op. cit.*, pp. 136−140.
38 European Advertising Association Advertisement (1989) *International Advertiser*, March−April, 5.
39 Neelankavil, James P. (1986) *Restrictions on Advertising by Media and Selected Products in 14 Countries of Asia*, The International Advertising Association, New York, April, 1.
40 Baldwin, Lettia (1984) New Mexican law restricts liquor and cigarette advertising. *Advertising Age*, 9 April, International Section.
41 Michaels, Julia (1986) Foreign spots under fire in Latin America. *Advertising Age*, 10 February, p. 46.
42 Lachlan, E.C. (1983) Regulations direct ad traffic differently around the world. *Advertising World*, April−May, 39.

43 McKinney, Mary (1984) Thai officials give okay to comparative advertising. *Advertising Age*, 9 April, International Section.

44 Boddewyn, J.J. (1989) Barriers to advertising a glimpse of hope. *International Advertiser*, May/June, 21.

45 Commission of the European Communities (1986) *Television and the Audio-Visual Sector: Towards a European Policy*, Brussels, August/September, 6, 7.

46 Furniss, John D. (1984) How to find your way through Europe's tax maze. *Advertising World*, October, 24, 26.

47 Hook, Michael (1979) The value added tax in Europe: latest developments. *Advertising World*, Summer, 22.

48 Furniss, *op. cit.*, pp. 24, 26.

49 *International Media Guide*.

6 Target audience behaviour and decision making

Introduction

An understanding of buyer behaviour and the decision-making process is needed in order to be able to formulate successful marketing communication programmes. In Chapter 5, factors that influence buyer behaviour were considered from a broad societal point of view. Various aspects of culture, such as language, aesthetics, religion and business etiquette were considered. In addition, environmental constraints involving geography, population, and income dispersion and concentration, and communication infrastructure found in different country groupings around the world were examined. In this chapter, the focus will be on the behaviour of citizens and members of organizations with respect to the buying decision process.

Buyers

Buyers are considered to be basically one of two types. Citizens are one type. They are individuals who buy for themselves and/or family members. Members of organizations are the other type. They buy for the benefit of the organization as a whole as well as for the various functional areas of the business.

Influencers

In both instances, it is possible for the buyer to be influenced by others when making a purchase. In the case of a citizen, influencers can be other family members and reference groups. Recall the difference between the nuclear family in the USA and the extended family in many lesser developed countries. In the USA, the husband, wife, or even the children may exert the strongest influence.[1] In the extended family, influencer patterns can be quite different. In situations where age is revered, the eldest may exert the greatest influence over the majority of family purchases. Regardless of environment, marketing communicators need to know who the key family influencers are and what characteristics they possess before attempting to create marketing communications programmes.

Reference groups

A reference group has been defined as 'a group of people that an individual uses as a guide for behaviour in specific situations'.[2] They can include religious groups, ethnic and social organizations, celebrities, fellow workers, or a person who lives on the same street who is considered an expert on a particular subject such as cooking. An understanding of reference group influence has led many advertisers to select certain personalities to be seen in their advertisements. An example of this was Coca-Cola's 'Mean Joe Green' television commercial. (Mean Joe was a famous US football player who gives a boy fan his jersey after the boy offers Mean Joe his Coke.) This same commercial was adapted for use in other countries including Spain and Thailand where the hero (referent) in each country became one of the local soccer/football stars.

A referent can also be an authoritative source of information found in books and periodicals. For instance, a well-known cook book specifies a certain type of rice for use in a particular recipe (e.g. converted rice). A magazine such as *Consumer Report*, which has gained a reputation for rating different consumer products, publishes a story on the advantages and disadvantages of branded TV sets. Or a food technology journal publishes an article on asceptic canning. In each case, the publication becomes the referent for at least some of its readers.

Organizational buying

In the case of organizations, the buyer is normally identified as the purchasing manager or agent. The decision to purchase many different types of items, as with citizens, is a shared one. The family in this instance, however, is comprised of other organizational members. Depending on the nature of the impending purchase, the decision can rest solely in the hands of the purchasing agent or many different organizational members may participate. Take, for example, the introduction of a new package for a consumer product. This will involve packaging machinery, package and label design, consumer acceptance, and capital budgeting. Representatives from production, quality control, purchasing, graphic design, marketing and top management would likely participate. Added to this list would be the firm's technical director. With today's emphasis on low-cost production (robotics) and quality (zero defects), technical directors have been described as those who control purchasing decisions.[3] The special interests of each participant in the buying process must be known if effective communications are to be developed.

In some circumstances organizational buying may involve participants outside as well as inside the buying organization. An example of this situation is

drawn from an account of the Boeing Company's marketing programme for its
767 aircraft to Nippon Airways of Japan. As a part of Boeing's communication
campaign for its multimillion dollar aircraft, there were five distinct targets:
airline management, industry and government leaders, the travelling public,
and travel agents. They were targets for media advertising. Other identified
influencers included technical people, senior bank and other financial managers.[4]

Involvement and risk in decision making

The extent to which the purchaser will seek support and participation from
referents in decision making will depend on the perceived risk. This holds true
for citizens and members of organizations. Perceived risk can be economic or
psychosocial in origin. Economic risk is associated with incorrect product
choice involving performance problems, physical safety, and time, money, and
convenience loss. Psychosocial risk is related to either psychological or social
discrepancies between the product's benefit and the buyer's personal or social
self-image, the latter being caused by reference group disapproval.[5]

When neither economic nor psychosocial risk is perceived by the buyer, the
decision is described as *low involvement*. This would normally include such
products as aspirin, beer, carbonated beverages, convenience foods and routinely
purchased industrial products.

When there is a perception of economic or psychosocial risk or both, the
purchase decision is described as *high involvement*. Products in this category can
include homes, cars, stereos, fashion items, insurance, vacations, and a variety
of industrial machinery, equipment, and processes.[6]

The decision process

The actual process of purchase decision-making has been broken down into
five steps by Wells.[7]

1 *Need recognition* is the first stage and occurs when the consumer recognizes
   or is informed of a need. The need in the case of a citizen may emerge
   when an advertisement is read in a magazine, a billboard is seen from
   the window of a car, or during a casual conversation with a friend or
   co-worker. In an organizational buying situation, it is most likely that the
   spontaneity of citizen need arousal will not exist. On regularly consumed
   items, a system of automatic replenishment will probably be in place. The

purchasing agent will be automatically informed of the need for repurchase through a daily or weekly inventory report system. When supplies are exhausted in various functional areas of the business purchase orders will be issued and sent to the purchasing agent.

On major items such as new production equipment, the need may be recognized by the technical director during his or her attendance at a trade show. In marketing, the need arousal may stem from competitive activities.

2 *Information search*, the second stage, can be instantaneous as in the case of impulse items found in supermarkets such as sweets and chewing gum. As for frequently purchased items, the search is casual: a check of the pantry cupboard to see which brand was purchased last, or in the case of a purchasing agent, a look at the files will reveal who the most recent supplier was. These are low involvement situations. Where the perceived risk is considerable (high involvement), the information search would be extensive and include obtaining information from a variety of sources of an authoritative nature: literature, experts, outside consultants.

3 *Evaluation and comparison*, stage number three, often includes referents depending on the nature of the involvement, high or low. Advertising and 'spec sheets' (detailed facts about performance features, benefits, installation, and applications) will be perused. Trade journals and consumer reports may be consulted, depending on the nature of the purchase. Alternate products will be examined. Trial runs and performance testing may be engaged in.

4 *Outlet (or vendor) and product purchase decision* is stage number four. For citizens it means the specific product offering and type of shop in which the item will be purchased...department, variety, chemist, or discount shop. Packaging, point-of-sale material, and special incentives such as coupons or price reductions will play a role at this decision-making stage. For organizational buyers, the choice of vendor, relative product qualities, guarantees, installation requirements, and servicing arrangements as well as delivery time will all play a role in the decision process. (These factors must be addressed by marketers when communicating with potential customers.)

5 *Post-purchase evaluation* is the fifth and final step. Does the product live up to expectations? Is the performance and service satisfactory? Many consumers, after the purchase is made, continue to read information and seek approval of others in support of their purchase. This is particularly true of high-involvement type products. Advertising and editorials as well as reference groups are consulted. The citizen or the purchasing agent is attempting to reduce any anxiety which may have developed as a result of the purchase. In psychological terms this condition where anxiety reduction is sought, is called post-purchase dissonance.

From unawareness to purchase

The process of decision making outlined in the previous section has some elements which are akin to several well-known 'hierarchy of effects' models used to describe the influence of advertising (and other forms of communication) on consumer behaviour. These are step-by-step models which lead buyers from a state of unawareness through to purchase. Delozier[8] developed a synthesized version of the Lavidge-Steiner, DAGMAR, and Maguire models. It is shown below:

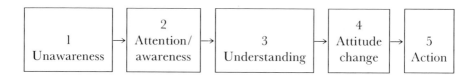

As Ray[9] has pointed out, all hierarchy of effects models have two common features:

1   All contain three basic states

- *cognitive*: attention, awareness, comprehension, learning, belief
- *affective*: interest, feeling, evaluation, conviction, yielding
- *conative*: intention, trial, action, adoption, behaviour

2   All models assume that the steps are sequential: cognitive reactions come first, then affective, then conative. Ray agrees with the first premise, but disagrees with the second. In addition, he puts the basic states into more commonly understood terms: learn, feel, do. As for variation in sequencing, a number of useful concepts for planning marketing communications can be developed from three basic hierarchies which Ray introduced. They are discussed below.

The learn—feel—do sequence
Two basic conditions must be met for this sequencing, which is like Delozier's synthesized model, to exist: first, for the audience to be *involved* in the topic of the communication campaign, and second, where there are clear differences between the topic and other alternatives. (Note that perceived risk and level of involvement play a role in this sequence.) This sequencing, as Ray[10] states, is appropriate when 'there is audience involvement, product differentiation, and

emphasis on mass media in communication in which the product is in the early stages of the life cycle.' Examples given included L'egg's tights and the Hewlett-Packard hand-held calculator.

The do—feel—learn sequence

Two theories are associated with this sequence which places behaviour first and learning last. The first is concerned with dissonance reduction, similar to 'post-purchase dissonance' reduction discussed earlier in this chapter. The idea behind this theory is that 'people are very often put in a situation where they are forced to make a choice between two alternatives that appear to be very close in quality but are complex and have many hidden or unknown attributes.'[11] With high involvement items, cars for example, after the choice is made, people seek out information to strengthen their convictions about their choice, and reduce dissonance. Theorists argue that marketing communications planners must target and aim messages at those who have already purchased for positive reinforcement purposes (as well as at prospective customers).

The second theory is based on the thought that 'people determine that they have attitudes by perceiving their own behaviour'...and that 'they will tend to develop information that will support the attitudes.'[12]

In situations where the *do—feel—learn* sequence applies, these conditions will be present: 'involvement; low differentiation for complex alternatives; non mass media, personal sources important; mature stage of life cycles.'[13] Types of products where research has been done to support these theories are cars, major appliances, and home entertainment equipment.

Proponents of this type of sequencing argue that the principal mass media effect is to reduce dissonance or provide information to bolster self-perception after behaviour and attitude change.

The learn—do—feel sequence

This sequence (derived from television audience research by Krugman) is based on the premise that 'most television viewers are not involved with either the advertising or the topics'.[14] Television, after considerable repetition, is thought to aid learning (cognition). As a result of enhancement of recall of brand name or idea, then, when a person(viewer) is in a purchasing mode the product is bought. After experience with the product attributes, feelings change. Conditions favouring the *learn—do—feel* sequence include low involvement and differentiation, the importance of mass media, and a mature stage of the life cycle. As expected, this type of sequencing will apply to many but not all low-priced consumer goods, and also, according to Ray,[15] to part of the insurance purchasing process and to many industrial purchasing decisions by purchasing agents.

Implications for the marketing communication mix

To optimize the marketing communication programme, the tools (advertising, publicity, sampling, etc.) should be matched up with the appropriate sequencing pattern.[16]

In the *learn—do—feel* (low involvement) sequence, advertising should be selected as the main tool. Attitude development is not an important concern. But the product should be of high quality relative to alternatives in order to deliver product satisfaction after purchase. Advertising should be complemented with point-of-purchase activities, product sampling, and price promotions to induce trial.

In the *learn—feel—do* sequence, mass media advertising is effective along with publicity. The combination can create comprehension and attitude change. In the case of business products, advertising can be used to create awareness, general comprehension, and interest.

Where a *do—feel—learn* sequence exists, personal selling, sampling, and promotions should be used to produce the action response. Information and attitudinal material should be introduced to support the choice that current users have already made.

In the case of any of these models, the 'compensation principle' may apply. This refers to a communication technique that has a strong effect on one element of the sequence and the opposite effect on another element. For example, the effect of great fear may increase attention and awareness (learning) but decrease the attitudinal effect because high fear is felt to be unreasonable. In instances like this where high awareness and a negative attitude is brought about by advertising, other communication vehicles such as personal selling and promotion should be introduced to turn the negative into a positive effect.

An understanding of how learning takes place and feelings are developed will be of value to the person attempting to develop compelling marketing communications. As previously noted, learning is associated with cognition and feeling is associated with affects or emotions. To develop this understanding it is necessary to examine all those psychological factors described by Wells[17] which are believed to exert a strong influence on individuals' response to advertising (and other forms of marketing communication). They are motives and needs, perception, learning, and psychographics.

Motives and needs

As discussed in Chapter 1, the essence of the marketing concept is filling needs. Identified as the first step in the decision process earlier in this chapter, 'needs are the basic forces that motivate you to do something.'[18] Some are physical; others are psychological, such as affection, association, recognition, respect and appreciation. Runyon[19] calls these central or basic needs as opposed to peripheral needs; the latter 'consist of the preferences one has for alternate means of satisfying central needs.' A central need could be enough liquid for survival, while the peripheral need would be the particular drink(s) to satisfy the central need. Water, fruit juice, beer, a carbonated beverage, etc. are all (peripheral) possibilities. The order of preference, including brand choice, is up to the individual. Consumers look on products and services as different ways of satisfying peripheral needs. Marketers seek ways to develop products and communication programmes which will be preferred over competitive offerings in satisfying these needs.

Perception

Through the five senses − sight, sound, smell, taste, and touch − people select some information and assign meaning to it, while other information is ignored. This phenomenon, called *selective perception*, is not surprising considering all the stimuli individuals are bombarded with daily, including numerous advertising messages. Communicators are obviously interested in learning why consumers attend to some messages and ignore others. The remarks which follow on learning and psychographics should reveal some clues.

Learning

As Runyon[20] points out, knowledge of brands and their attributes are learned. One of the principal purposes of marketing communications, then, is to aid learning. Several learning theory concepts can be used in marketing communications to facilitate the process. They include:

Repetition
The repeated exposure of an advertising message in a given period of time. Media plans are formulated with this principle in mind.

Association
The idea is to associate a product or its use with a pleasing or enjoyable experience, e.g. the sound of a sizzling steak in a television commercial for a steak sauce or the sight of cool mountain stream waters as a setting for a soft drink. (The sight of a cool, bubbling mountain stream has been the backdrop

for a carbonated beverage on more than one occasion.) The concept bears consideration in practically any communication.

Reinforcement or reward

This principle has to do with a promise...the promise of an economic (save money), social (be more acceptable), or personal (look more attractive) reward. This is another learning principle which merits serious consideration when planning a marketing communication programme.

Meaning

The theory behind this principle is that individuals are viewed as problem solvers. With respect to marketing communications, it means that consumers should be given information which will enable them to relate the product or service to themselves in a meaningful way. For example, when Purina Dog Chow (food), a dry formulation as opposed to a canned product, was introduced, advertising for it claimed that it 'makes dogs eager eaters'. The idea was to dispel consumer fears that their pets would refuse to eat dry dog food.[21]

Psychographics

According to Wells,[22] 'advertisers use the term psychographics to refer to all the psychological variables that combine to shape our inner selves.' Psychographic studies are made to explain why some women serve frozen vegetables while others will only serve fresh vegetables; why some men drive a Porsche while others drive a Chevrolet. An understanding of attitude formation and life styles can help explain the different motivations for behaviour.

Attitudes

Wells points out that attitudes are a reflection of consumer values, indicating what a person stands for and feels is important. With respect to product advertising, the communicator wants to know in advance of preparing a campaign what product and brand perceptions and associations exist. This is true whether the product is Birds Eye Frozen Peas or Porsche cars. That is why advertisers engage in pre-campaign research on consumer attitudes and opinions. A case in point is the study undertaken by J.D. Powers which divided car buyers into six categories, each identified by their attitudes and buying habits. The groups varied from 'auto-philes', the people who like to be under the bonnet as well as behind the wheel, to 'auto-phobes', grandmothers who would rather have someone else drive them to the shops.[23]

Life styles

To many, life style research is the most significant means of understanding consumer behaviour. As Plummer[24] states, 'life style as a construct permits one to think about the consumer as a total person and how products and services fit into his or her daily living pattern.' Life style research has helped formulate advertising appeals for cat food, and isolate characteristics of heavy users of beer, the findings of which were used in developing a new advertising campaign for Schlitz Beer.[25]

According to Plummer,[26] life style has four components:

1 *Activities* — how people spend work and leisure time.
2 *Interests* — what's important to them in their immediate surroundings.
3 *Opinions* — how they feel about themselves and the world around them.
4 *Basic characteristics* — demographic and socioeconomic profiles.

Without going into the research technique at this point, findings from Plummer's cross-national life style research are shown in Tables 6.1 and 6.2. One is concerned with house-cleaning, the other with personal hygiene.[27] Table 6.1 shows the percentage of women in each country who are in 100 per cent agreement with the statement in quotes. Findings indicate wide differences in women's opinions held on dusting and polishing. Implications are present for the marketing of and communication about household cleaning products. Table 6.2 is read the same way as Table 6.1. Again, findings are very different with respect to opinions about use of a deodorant as are the implications for marketing and communication. Findings, however, are dated. Research results today could be very different than those reported above.

In planning marketing communication programmes practitioners like to have as much information as possible about the characteristics of their target

Table 6.1 *House-cleaning*

'A house should be dusted and polished three times a week'

Country	100% agreement (%)
Italy	86
UK	59
France	55
Spain	53
Germany	45
Australia	33
USA	25

Table 6.2 *Personal hygiene*

'Everyone should use a deodorant'

Country	100% agreement (%)
USA	89
French Canada	81
English Canada	77
UK	71
Italy	69
France	59
Australia	53

audience. For this purpose a consumer profile questionnaire might look like the one reproduced in Exhibit 6.1 at the end of this chapter. It contains questions about personal and household demographics, social class information, personality indicators, life style preferences and attitudes, media use and interest, use of a particular product or service, and trade with a particular store.

Summary

What this chapter underscores is that buyer behaviour and decision making is a complex process, possibly somewhat more so in the case of citizens than members of organizations. The reason is that organizational buying tends to be more rational, less emotional, and in this sense, then, less complicated. Complexities in organizational buying, however, arise in attempting to identify the key influencers and the strength of influence they exert.

Regardless of the circumstance, effective marketing communications are based on a thorough understanding of buyer behaviour principles outlined in this chapter. This includes the proper sequencing of cognitive, affective, and conative states to fit the particular type of product being marketed, and the psychological makeup of the consumer.

Exhibit 6.1 *Consumer profile questionnaire*

Consumer profile questionnaire

PERSONAL DEMOGRAPHIC INFORMATION

Mark the boxes that describe you.

1. Sex:
- ☐ Male
- ☐ Female

2. Age:
- ☐ Under 6
- ☐ 6 to 11
- ☐ 12 to 17
- ☐ 18 to 24
- ☐ 25 to 34
- ☐ 35 to 44
- ☐ 45 to 54
- ☐ 55 to 64
- ☐ 65 & over

3. Marital Status:
- ☐ Married
- ☐ Single (never married)
- ☐ Widowed
- ☐ Divorced or separated

4. Education:
- ☐ Grade school or less (grades 1–8)
- ☐ Some high school
- ☐ Graduated from high school (grades 9–12)
- ☐ Some college
- ☐ Graduated from college
- ☐ Some postgraduate college work

5. Principal Language Spoken at Home:
- ☐ English
- ☐ Spanish
- ☐ Other

6. Colour:
- ☐ White
- ☐ Nonwhite

7. Employment:
- ☐ Not employed outside the home
- ☐ Employed outside the home
- ☐ Employed full time (30 hours per week or more)
- ☐ Employed part time (less than 30 hours per week)
- ☐ Not employed – looking for work

8. Occupation:
- ☐ Professional and technical
- ☐ Managers, officials, and proprietors, except farm
- ☐ Clerical
- ☐ Sales
- ☐ Craftsman
- ☐ Foreman
- ☐ Nonfarm labourers
- ☐ Service workers
- ☐ Private household workers
- ☐ Farm managers
- ☐ Farm labourers
- ☐ Farm foreman
- ☐ Armed services
- ☐ Retired
- ☐ Student
- ☐ Other

9. Geographic Region:
- ☐ Northeast
- ☐ Metropolitan New York
- ☐ Mid-Atlantic
- ☐ East Central
- ☐ Metropolitan Chicago
- ☐ West Central
- ☐ Southeast
- ☐ Southwest
- ☐ Metropolitan Los Angeles
- ☐ Remaining Pacific

10. Geographic Area:
   □ Central City
   □ Urban Fringe (suburbs)
   □ Town
   □ Rural
   Population of city or town:
   □ 4 million or over
   □ Between 4 and 1 million
   □ Between 1 million and
     500 thousand
   □ Between 500 thousand and
     250 thousand
   □ Between 250 thousand and
     50 thousand
   □ Between 50 thousand and
     35 thousand
   □ Under 35 thousand

11. County Size:
   □ A county – one of the largest
     markets
   □ B county – not included in A but
     area over 150,000 population
   □ C county – not included in A or B
     but area over 35,00
   □ D county – all remaining counties
     under 35,000

HOUSEHOLD DEMOGRAPHIC INFORMATION

Answer these statements about your family:

12. Household Size:
   □ 1 or 2 members
   □ 2 or 3 members
   □ 3 or 4 members
   □ 5 or more members

13. Number of Children:
   □ None
   □ Two
   □ Three or more

14. Ages of Youngest Child:
   □ No child under 18
   □ Youngest child 12 to 17
   □ Youngest child 6 to 11
   □ Youngest child 2 to 5
   □ Youngest child under 2

15. Household Income:
   □ Under $5,000
   □ $5,000 to $7,999
   □ $8,000 to $9,999
   □ $10,000 to $14,999
   □ $15,000 to $24,999
   □ $25,000 and over

16. Wage Earners in the Family:
   □ Male head of household
   □ Female head of household
   □ Wife (non-head of household)
   □ One child
   □ Two children
   □ Over three children

17. Home Ownership:
   □ Own home
   □ Rent home
   Five years prior to survey date:
   □ Lived in same home
   □ Lived in different house
   □ In same county
   □ In different county

18. Dwelling Characteristics:
   □ House (unattached)
   □ Attached home
   □ Apartment
   □ Mobile home or trailer
   □ Single family dwelling unit
   □ Multiple family dwelling unit

SOCIAL CLASS INFORMATION

Mark the group your family belongs to.

19. □ The local elite with inherited
     wealth and family tradition.

20. ☐ Top executive or professional manager or owner.

21. ☐ Business, industrial, or professional manager or owner.

22. ☐ White-collar worker in industry or government and small business owner.

23. ☐ Semi-skilled worker in construction or industry. Probably blue-collar union member.

24. ☐ Unskilled worker, perhaps unemployed.

PSYCHOGRAPHIC INFORMATION

Personality Indicators

Mark the accurate statements about yourself.

It is my nature to:

25. ☐ Want to rival and surpass others.

26. ☐ Accept leadership and follow willingly.

27. ☐ Want things arranged, organized, secure, and predictable.

28. ☐ Want to be the centre of attention.

29. ☐ Seek freedom, resist influence, and do things my own way.

30. ☐ Form friendships and participate in groups.

31. ☐ Want to understand others, examine their motives and my own.

32. ☐ Seek aid, help, and advice from others.

33. ☐ Want to control others and be the leader of groups.

34. ☐ Feel inferior, guilty, and accept blame easily.

35. ☐ Want to help others, be sympathetic and protective.

36. ☐ Look for new and different things to do.

37. ☐ Stick to a task and work hard to complete a job.

38. ☐ Am attracted by the opposite sex, go out and enjoy company.

39. ☐ Belittle, blame, attack, and want to punish people.

40. ☐ Have frequent daydreams and fantasies.

41. ☐ Experience times of tenseness, self-pity, and am restless or excitable.

42. ☐ Am self-confident in social, professional, and personal dealings.

LIFE-STYLE PREFERENCES AND ATTITUDES

Mark the answers that fit you best.

Leisure

43. ☐ Enjoy entertaining formally and going to movies, concerts, plays, dances, or dinner.

44. ☐ Habitually read newspapers, magazines, and books.

45. ☐ Spend a lot of time listening to music (not just as a background).

46. ☐ Think I have the right to do absolutely nothing some of the time.

47. ☐ Anxious to be busy, go out and see people, participate in sports and other activities.

48. ☐ Would rather study or work than 'waste time' playing.

Cooking

49. ☐ Want to prepare good, healthy meals and think I am good at it.

50. ☐ Like convenience foods that are frozen, in cans, or packaged as mixes.

51. ☐ Judge my achievement on the basis of compliments I receive for enjoyable meals.

52. ☐ Try to stay out of the kitchen as much as possible and hate the drudgery of cooking.
53. ☐ Enjoy preparing fancy, exotic, or unusual dishes 'from scratch' and serving them in an unusual way.

Family

54. ☐ Think the man should be the boss and run the family.
55. ☐ Think the woman should be the boss and run the family.
56. ☐ Believe marriage should be a partnership with no bosses.
57. ☐ Think children should be considered in most family decisions.
58. ☐ Believe parents should make an effort to teach children and spend time with them.

Dress

59. ☐ Like to wear casual, comfortable clothes.
60. ☐ Want to look fashionable and stylish.

Physical Condition

61. ☐ Am in very good health.
62. ☐ Have an overweight problem.

63. ☐ Always on some kind of a diet.
64. ☐ Watch the scale, eat intelligently, and exercise.
65. ☐ Feel sickly much of the time.
66. ☐ Use over-the-counter drugs for minor ailments.
67. ☐ Seldom take anything for a headache or an upset stomach.

Finances

68. ☐ Have money in the bank and feel secure.
69. ☐ Just about break even every month.
70. ☐ Am in debt but believe the bills can be paid.
71. ☐ Am not optimistic about the financial future.

Risk

72. ☐ Am conservative and do not take chances.
73. ☐ Will take a calculated risk.
74. ☐ Take chances just to see what will happen.

Buying Style

75. ☐ Pick the same brand of products habitually.

76. ☐ Think about the products I buy and select them because they satisfy.
77. ☐ Look for bargains, deals, premiums, and usually compare prices.
78. ☐ Want quality in a product and will pay extra to get it.
79. ☐ Choose advertised brands and do not take chances on unknown products or manufacturers.
80. ☐ Keep trying new products to see what they are like.
81. ☐ Buy what I need when I need it and when a store is handy.
82. ☐ Plan shopping carefully with a list of needs and make an excursion out of the trip.
83. ☐ Judge brands on the basis of ingredients, weight, and package size.
84. ☐ Never read the information on a package to find out what it contains.
85. ☐ Am attracted to a brand by its name, colour of the package, and its design.
86. ☐ Usually buy what friends say is good.

87. ☐ Pay attention to advertisements and study them to make up my mind about what to buy.

88. ☐ Do not check into low-cost items much, but do shop intelligently and compare prices for high-priced products.

89. ☐ Respond to advertisements in:
   ☐ Newspaper
   ☐ Radio
   ☐ Magazine
   ☐ Television

MEDIA USE AND INTEREST

I use media at these times:

	Newspaper		Magazines		Radio		Television	
	Day	Wkend	Day	Wkend	Day	Wkend	Day	Wkend
90. 6:00 A.M. to 10:00 A.M.	☐	☐	☐	☐	☐	☐	☐	☐
91. 10:00 A.M. to 3:00 P.M.	☐	☐	☐	☐	☐	☐	☐	☐
92. 3:00 P.M. to 7:00 P.M.	☐	☐	☐	☐	☐	☐	☐	☐
93. 7:00 P.M. to midnight	☐	☐	☐	☐	☐	☐	☐	☐
94. Midnight to 6:00 A.M.	☐	☐	☐	☐	☐	☐	☐	☐

I pay attention to these types of stories or programmes:

	Newspaper	Magazine	Radio	Television
95. Local news	☐		☐	☐
96. National news	☐		☐	☐
97. Weather	☐		☐	☐
98. Sports	☐	☐	☐	☐
99. Business and finance	☐		☐	☐
100. Editorials and interviews	☐		☐	☐
101. Classified	☐			
102. Daytime serials				
103. Comics or comedy shows	☐	☐	☐	☐
104. Crime news or programmes	☐		☐	☐
105. Adventure				☐
106. Quizzes or game shows	☐			☐
107. Movies	☐			☐
108. Self-help stories	☐	☐	☐	☐
109. How-to-do-it	☐		☐	☐
110. Theatre arts, and entertainment	☐		☐	☐
111. Editorials	☐			
112. Interviews	☐			
113. Travel	☐			
114. Police shows				☐
115. Romantic programmes	☐	☐	☐	☐
116. Sexy stories and pictures				
117. Cooking programmes and stories				☐

USE OF A PARTICULAR PRODUCT OR SERVICE

(Statements must be adapted)

118. I am a

light _____
medium _____
heavy _____
or nonuser _____

119. I use your product/service

daily _____
once a week _____
once a month _____
once a year _____

120. I have used your product for a

short time _____
many years _____

121. I have tried similar products. The names are

_____
_____

122. I use your product in combination with _____

123. I buy your product at a

supermarket _____
drugstore _____
department store _____
discount store _____
hardware store _____
or other store _____

124. The quantity I buy at one time is a

single package _____
several packages _____
many packages _____

TRADE WITH A PARTICULAR STORE

125. I shop in your store

more than once a week _____
at least once a week _____
every two weeks _____
once a month _____
once a year _____

126. The distance from my home to your store is

less than five blocks _____
one mile away _____
two or three miles _____
five miles _____
over ten miles _____

127. I usually buy these types of products at your store:

_____
_____
_____

128. The part of my shopping I do with your store is:

All _____
Most _____

129. My favourite stores that are similar to yours (and including it) are:

First choice _____
Second choice _____
Third choice _____

130. Each year I spend this amount in your store $ _____

Source: Johnson, J. Douglas (1978) *Advertising Today*, Paradigm Publishing International, Eden Prairie, MN, pp. 32–35.

Questions

1 What types of people are involved in consumer buying decision process? Explain their roles in the buying decision.
2 Discuss the role played by different people in choosing your first major purchase.
3 How does organizational buying differ from consumer buying?
4 What kinds of risks are involved in purchase decision making? What steps should one take to reduce such risk?
5 Describe various stages in the decision process. Explain the decision process that would be involved in the purchase of a new car.
6 Briefly explain what is 'hierarchy of effects' including the principal steps. Do you think that the steps always follow the same order? Why or why not?
7 Why is it important for marketing communicators to know the hierarchy of effects sequencing?
8 What are the factors that influence individuals' response to marketing communications?

Notes

1 Berkman, Harold W., and Gilson, Christopher (1987) *Advertising*, 2nd edn, Random House, New York, p. 121.
2 Wells, William, Burnett, John and Moriarity, Sandra (1989) *Advertising Principles and Practice*, Prentice Hall, Englewood Cliffs, NJ, p. 120.
3 Strazewski, Len (1989) Tools — or toys? — of the trade. *Marketing News*, **23**, (11), 1.
4 Gething, Tom (1985) Boeing sells big planes overseas by stressing special features. *International Advertiser*, October, 18.
5 Rossiter, John R. and Percy, Larry (1987) *Advertising and Promotion Management*, McGraw-Hill Book Company, New York, pp. 166–7.
6 *Ibid.*, p. 167.
7 Wells, *op. cit.*, pp. 139–40.
8 Delozier, Wayne M. (1976) *The Marketing Communication Process*, McGraw-Hill Book Company, New York, pp. 7–3.
9 Ray, Michael L. (1982) *Advertising and Communication Management*, Prentice-Hall, Inc., Englewood Cliffs, NJ. © Prentice-Hall Inc. 1982.
10 *Ibid.*, pp. 184–5.
11 *Ibid.*, p. 185.
12 *Ibid.*, p. 186.

13 *Ibid.*, p. 187.
14 *Ibid.*, p. 187.
15 *Ibid.*, p. 188.
16 *Ibid.*, p. 189.
17 Wells, *op. cit.*, p. 124.
18 *Ibid.*, p. 125.
19 Runyon, Kenneth E. (1984) *Advertising*, 2nd edn, Charles E. Merrill Company, Columbus, Ohio, p. 156.
20 *Ibid.*, p. 165.
21 *Ibid.*, pp. 165–68.
22 Wells, *op. cit.*, p. 137.
23 *Ibid.*, p. 138.
24 Plummer, Joseph T. (1979) Consumer focus in cross national research. In *International Advertising and Marketing* (eds. S. Watson Dunn and E.S. Lorimor) Grid Publishing, Inc., Columbus, Ohio, p. 175.
25 Berkman, *op. cit.*, pp. 134, 138.
26 Plummer, *op. cit.*, pp. 175–6.
27 *Ibid.*, pp. 181–2.

Part Three *Planning, Preparing and Evaluating International Marketing Communication Messages*

As a prelude to Parts Three and Four, the planning process and organizational systems as developed in Chapters 2 and 3 will be combined in a single framework to show how the basic elements fit together. Exhibit A shows the interrelationship of plans for the main promotion variables and other marketing variables which, when combined, constitute a marketing plan.

As indicated in Exhibit A, the marketing plan is comprised of four parts: product, pricing, promotion and distribution. The promotion variable is further divided into personal (selling), non-personal communications, and deals and incentives. Since non-personal communications is the subject of this text, the emphasis in the remaining chapters will be on this topic.

Before going ahead, however, three more preliminary matters deserve attention: the planning cycle, communication targets and media alternatives, and direct versus indirect message response.

The planning cycle

The short-term marketing plan normal covers a twelve-month period which can coincide with the January–December calendar or an alternative twelve-month period to coincide with a company's fiscal year. The planning cycle, comprised of planning, implementation and evaluation, covers seventeen to nineteen months as depicted in Exhibit B. Planning begins four to six months prior to the new year and extends throughout two-thirds to three-quarters of the year. Evaluation often begins before the new year starts to determine the effectiveness of various promotion elements before being produced in final form, and extends past year end as the results of all aspects of the plan are being evaluated.

The objectives and strategies of a marketing plan will require approval before the new (business) year begins as will tactical plans for the first four to six months. Tactics for the remainder of the year are customarily developed as the year progresses. Evaluation can begin prior to the start of the year to test such things as new headlines and advertising executions, and continues throughout and after the end of the year to measure the effectiveness of all elements of the marketing plan. This brief visual and verbal explanation should give the marketing communicator a conceptual understanding of the planning cycle to which he/she will need to conform.

Exhibit A *Planning framework*

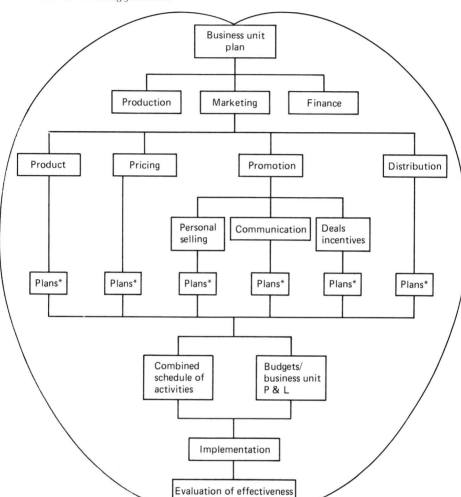

*Plans include objectives, strategies, tactics, a budget, a means of evaluation and timetable

Communication targets and media alternatives

Instead of referring to Chapter 1, communication targets and media alternatives will be reviewed in preparation for further treatment in the chapters to come.

Exhibit B *Time line for planning information and evaluation*

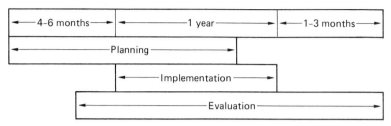

Targets

In designing information to be communicated within and across borders there are four basic target classifications:

1 company sales representatives
2 intermediaries: agents, brokers, manufacturers' representatives, distributors, wholesalers, and retailers
3 editors (print and broadcast)
4 prospects, users (consumers), and influencers

Classification of media alternatives

The manner in which communication activities are classified are by no means uniform from country to country. In the UK and other European countries a distinction is made between 'above-the-line' and 'below-the-line' media. Above-the-line media include advertising alternatives such as press (magazines and newspapers), television, radio, cinema, and posters for which a commission or a fee is paid to a recognized advertising agency. Below-the-line media usually include various types of non face-to-face communications designed to promote sales.[1] In Japan, the *Dentsu Marketing/Advertising Yearbook* classifies television, newspapers, magazines, and radio as 'major media'. Outdoor, transit, and movies along with direct mail, flyers, POP, telephone directories, and exhibitions/screen displays are classified under 'sales promotion'.[2]

For the purpose of classification in this text, the alternatives excluding face-to-face or voice communications and personal selling, are listed below.

Mass media
- newspapers
- magazines
- out-of-home
- *yellow pages*
- television
- radio
- cinema

Sales promotion media
- sales literature
- point-of-sale material
- audiovisual and films
- meetings and seminars
- exhibitions and trade shows
- sponsorships
- special events
- presentation aids

Mail

Publicity

Packaging

As for the communication alternatives, many marketers will use a combination of several, even many different techniques in carrying out a marketing plan. A consumer plan may include television, magazines, and yellow pages; trade shows, sales literature, point-of-sale material, and in-person presentation aids; direct mail, publicity, and packaging. A business-to-business marketer's plan is likely to include (trade) magazines, direct mail, publicity, trade shows, sales literature, and in-person and on-phone presentation aids. For example, a campaign for Wang Laboratories, Inc., Information Systems included media advertising involving television, radio, newspapers, business and general interest magazines; a companion direct response mail effort; a media kit (examples of the media advertising and the schedule); and an informational brochure for the Wang sales force to use in contacts with members of the distribution channel.[3] Other marketers, particularly ones that rely on direct response communications, will limit their activities to a few or possibly a single technique such as mail.

Direct versus indirect response

In designing a message the intended response should be determined in advance. This response can be either direct or indirect. The former is associated with 'doing' behaviour while the latter is associated with 'learning' or 'feeling' as discussed in Chapter 6. The 'doing' or direct response may involve behaviour other than a sale that results in, but is not limited to, the receipt of a price-reducing coupon, information (a descriptive booklet about the product or service), entry into a contest or sweepstakes or a purchase. The indirect response (learning or feeling) can involve behaviour that leads to a greater understanding of a particular product or results in a reassuring belief that a product being consumed is the most appropriate alternative to enhance or project one's self-image.

It is important to recognize that direct response as well as indirect response can be evoked in nearly, if not all media forms. This includes all types of mass media, sales literature, displays, point-of-sale material, exhibits, mail, publicity, on the inside of match-book covers, in aerial banner towing, etc. With the basic planning considerations involving targets, media alternatives, and message response options clearly in mind, attention can now be directed to topics of message development, execution and evaluation; subjects treated in Chapters 7 and 8.

Notes

1 Wilmshurst, John (1985) *The Fundamentals of Advertising*, Heinemann, London, pp. 95—97.
2 Publications Department (1989) *Dentsu Japan Marketing/Advertising Yearbook 1990*, Dentsu Inc., Tokyo.
3 Wells, William, Burnett, John and Moriarty, Sandra (1989) *Advertising*, Prentice-Hall, Englewood Cliffs, NJ, pp. 496—508.

7 Message strategy formulation

Introduction

The subject of this chapter is message strategy formulation. This subject is equated with 'what to say' in advertisements and other forms of communications. It is not sufficient to just tell a copywriter and art director to produce an advertisement for a given product or service. They might come up with a brilliant idea to attract much attention but be completely off target with respect to whom they attracted and what they had to say about the product or service. Instead, certain specific guideposts or instructions must be set forth in writing in advance so it is perfectly clear to the creative team who the target is and what should be said in the advertisement. Without such a discipline much time and (client's) money can be wasted.

This is true within a country market and also when crossing borders. For example, communication effectiveness can be negated by attempting to use the home country message and/or frame of reference. When a US concept for a laundry detergent was used in a Scandinavian country the message turned out to have a negative connotation. The concept involved the removal of 'body dirt'. What Scandinavian woman who showers two or three times a day would conceivably use a laundry detergent that removes body dirt?

As reported in an earlier chapter, to the surprise and chagrin of a New York copywriter who relocated in a Southeast Asian country, her great idea for a new miniature camera — 'Maxi's (skirts in USA) are out...Mini's are in' — simply didn't translate.[1]

As emphasized before, the ability to produce an effective message is based on a thorough understanding of buyers, influencers, and users as well as their characteristics, and the constraints imposed on them by every facet of their environment: economic, cultural, etc., and the principal characteristics of the product or service to be advertised. When the information gathered for this purpose is organized and thoroughly analysed, those responsible for formulating the message strategy should be able to produce a written strategy statement.

Global/local operating procedures

The means by which firms doing business in a number of countries develop advertising messages is by no means uniform. Some firms will advertise a product with a single message everywhere it is distributed. Others will localize their advertising. Take, for example, Hennessy Cognac, a brand with a wealth of tradition and a 227-year history.

Hennessy Cognac advertising aims for consistency without attempting to adopt a single style in all its markets. This is due to differences in consumers, their drinking habits, and their cultural heritage. While acknowledging that boundaries are receding and consumer differences are becoming more indistinct, a Hennessy advertising directive states:

> to be effective in a given country, we must express ourselves in a way which blends harmoniously with the existing advertising rhetoric of this country: for example, we cannot ignore that in the Far East it is usual to treat the product as something sacred, while the English, quite the contrary, respond to suggestion and humor.

In Japan a long-standing consumer campaign has been based on the praises of VSOP by wine waiters in prestigious European restaurants announcing that they have been serving Cognac for fifteen to twenty-five years or more (see Exhibit 7.1).

In the US Hennessy VS has been presented as the 'greatest accomplice to the intimacy of a couple', resulting in an evolving campaign that included advertising as depicted in Exhibits 7.2–7.4.[2]

In Germany, the campaign with (seventh generation) Gilles Hennessy as an authority has successfully established the brand as a credible and competitive one. He appeared in print advertisements with some 'surprising guests'. One is shown in Exhibit 7.5. To establish a 'presence of mind' among a broader population, a new campaign was subsequently launched on television.[3]

A study among twenty-four US and British multinational companies showed that some advertising planning and decision making was done at the local, subsidiary level and some was done jointly with headquarters' personnel.[4] As explained by one executive, 'product management with advertising agency develop plan/platform in each country for each market'. Where decisions are made interactively, it can be a matter of joint strategy development at country and regional group level with approval by international headquarters. Headquarters' personnel often are found in a coordinating rather than an authoritarian role. Reason and persuasion determine what ideas and concepts will be adopted.

With respect to industrial advertising, it is likely, if not a certainty, that advertisers of this type have a better opportunity to formulate one central creative strategy than consumer product advertisers. This is due to the similarity in customer needs and product technology and the importance of reason versus emotion in the message to be communicated.

One major consumer products company uses a 'lead country' decision process with respect to advertising executions. (This implies central strategy planning.) An execution which is considered to have outstanding communication

Exhibit 7.1 *Hennessy advertisement, Japan. Reproduced by permission of JAˢ Hennessy and Co.*

Exhibit 7.2 *Hennessy advertisement, USA. Reproduced by permission of JA' Hennessy and Co.*

Exhibit 7.3 *Hennessy advertisement, USA. Reproduced by permission of JA⁵ Hennessy and Co.*

Exhibit 7.4   *Hennessy advertisement, USA. Reproduced by permission of JA^s Hennessy and Co.*

Exhibit 1.5 *Hennessy advertisement, Germany*

Seit es sich herumgesprochen hat, daß Sie nach jedem Sieg Ihren herrlichen Cognac servieren, Monsieur Hennessy, gewinnt der Gaul jedes Rennen.

Merkwürdig, nicht wahr?

Dabei dachte ich auch immer, Araber trinken keinen Alkohol.

Unser Foto zeigt Gilles Hennessy als Gastgeber im Schloß der Hennessys.

NICHTS HAT SO VIEL ESPRIT WIE ALTER COGNAC UND NEUE GEDANKEN.

Hennessy

Das Vergnügen, Cognac Hennessy zu trinken,
ist durchaus steigerungsfähig: mit V.S.O.P., X.O. und Paradis.

values in one country is tested for use in other countries. If test results are favourable, the advertisement runs. If not favourable, the execution is modified or local advertising is developed.

Coca-Cola: a special case

Coca-Cola is one of the few brands that stands out for its global advertising approach. In 1962 it was decided that Coca-Cola should be presented to the world with 'one sight, one sound, one sell.'[5] Its first global advertising campaign was launched in 1964 under the theme, 'Things go better with Coke.' This theme subsequently was translated into twenty languages, including Spanish, 'Todo va mejor con Coca-Cola' and German, 'Besser gehts mit Coca-Cola.' This campaign ran for five years. It was followed by a campaign called 'It's the real thing' represented by the 1971 Italian hilltop television commercial, 'Buy the World a Coke.' As pointed out, there was 'no place it didn't work'...'no place where it was not effective.' This commercial was recreated as a 'Hilltop Reunion' and was launched during the 1990 Superbowl.[6]

Another US-made commercial, 'Mean Joe Greene', which employed US sport, US hero, US symbols, and US imagery, was successfully adapted for use in Thailand, Spain, and elsewhere. The sport changed to football. Country heroes, symbols, and imagery were used, but the basic strategy remained in tact. As Paul Harper said, 'These commercials were a great example of how to address one world and one customer with one message.'[7]

The Coca-Cola Company and its agency, McCann-Erickson, Inc. have evolved a system of management and testing which, along with the peculiarities of the brand, permit global advertising. The Company has a worldwide advertising council comprised of a balance of corporate and geographic divisional presidents and marketing directors which meet twice a year to review agency recommendations and select a limited number of advertising commercials based on strategy input from its divisional offices around the world.[8] On the agency side, McCann-Erickson has a special system of fifteen coordinators who are senior account managers located at sites where Coca-Cola Company has divisional offices. These coordinators report to the person in charge of the McCann-Erickson account group in Atlanta which serves the client's corporate marketing division.

In addition to the global account group there is an eleven-person senior creative team located in New York which is multi-national and multi-lingual in composition. The work of the New York group is supplemented when needed by international creative teams in London and Tokyo.

To aid in the global creative formulation and execution process, a standardized research system has been placed into operation. This permits pertinent cross-country comparisons which assesses the impact and appropriateness of

an advertising concept from one country to the next as in the case of the 'Mean Joe Greene' commercials.[9]

The luxury of such a system can only be afforded by a brand like Coca-Cola. Scaled-down versions of this system, however, can be used by brands with less resources.

Reasons for strategy variations

Coca-Cola is not typical of most consumer brands. In one study,[10] the following reasons were given why the same elements were not featured in all international advertisements:

- language and cultural nuances
- different products, users, and media alternatives
- specific product categories being developed in different countries
- different levels of local market sophistication in communication terms
- local needs vary
- localized strategy
- business priorities are different
- depends on brand, strategy, and local marketing status
- products sold, applications, and customers vary
- crops and products vary
- business priorities differ by geography and target audience and
- differing development of various countries/regions and levels of awareness

Another study among 120 senior executives concluded that the global approach is not universally accepted. Those products found to be most appropriate for global brand strategies were high technology products like computer hardware, airlines, photography equipment, heavy machinery, and machine tools. Considered less appropriate were products like confectionery, clothing, food, toiletries, and household cleaners.[11]

Walters[12] concluded that (global) standardization strategies are 'very situation specific'. Factors to be taken into account include the product itself, consumer behaviour, legal, and product use conditions as well as the firm's resources, objectives, and ambitions.

Message strategy formulation participants

In establishing what should be said in advertising messages, the traditional approach has the advertising agency account executive leading the way. Other

participants are customarily client representative (product manager), and a creative team (copywriter and art director) assigned to the account by agency management. The participants hammer out a creative statement to establish what the message should be. Before creative work begins, agreement is reached on both client and agency sides that the statement accurately reflects what the advertising should convey. Depending on the particular circumstance, the decision may not always be that democratic; the client may be more arbitrary in some situations than others.

Account planning

In Britain a somewhat different planning system has been created and widely used in advertising agencies over the past two decades. This could account for the high regard practitioners the world over hold for UK creative work.

The system is known as account planning. John Wood, veteran planner at Dorland Advertising (London) said the process (account planning) simply means 'having ideas about what leads people to respond to advertising'.[13] Planners attempt to determine '. . .the way in which advertising is received and interpreted in its effort to discover what binds a customer to a particular brand'.[14]

Account planning[15] was started about the same time at two London-based agencies (J. Walter Thompson and Boase, Massimi, Pollitt) during the 1967–68 period. This approach was conceived as a response to a business situation stemming from several converging factors, namely:

- The growth and concentration of power in a few supermarket chains, reducing the manufacturers' ability to control price.
- A more competitive market place.
- An increasing number of new product introductions.
- The growing importance of TV as an advertising medium.

This meant that advertisers had to do a better job of understanding what, in fact, they were selling. . .what people found valuable in brands. It led to an explosion of consumer research and the importation of brand management from the USA.

Research problems

Within the agency there existed a frustration over fractionated research from media, marketing (forecasting), and creative. The account executive was not able to tie all the information together. This person was using only what

seemed appropriate at the moment. Research was only called in to help solve a problem that already emerged.

At the same time there was a rejection of 'off the shelf' type of research such as day-after-recall, Schwerin, and Starch. (These techniques are discussed in Chapter 12.)

Qualitative research was poor; there was a lack of understanding of what the brand actually stood for and how to go about testing copy written about the brand. If humour was a part of the advertising message, the emphasis was on trying to measure degree of hilarity rather than tell a joke and then gauge the response.

Most advertising messages were found to be communicating attributes; some were communicating benefits; but the emotional possibilities of a message were being passed by because it was easier not to deal with this aspect. Messages like seven out of ten prefer', or 'drinking brand X beer will lead to a better life style' are examples of the typical approach.

Other factors causing problems for British advertising included the limited time available for TV advertising on the two existing channels and the belief that advertising was intrusive. Shouting to be heard didn't work. People are selective. They listen to what they want. There was a need, then, to understand that communication is an active, not passive process where people have to develop a relationship with a product which, if positive, will produce brand loyalty.

Account planning redefined

This leads to another way of expressing what account planning is all about. It can be expressed as an eternal quest for a relevant consumer message based on an understanding of why consumers behave the way they do and what motivates them, topics treated in Chapter 6. It places a demand on those involved in planning advertising to become more inventive.

As explained in an *Advertising Age* article,[16] account planning frees creative people from discovering what should be said in advertising by taking away part of the conjecture about how the market works, what the world is like, and how people think. It gives them specific input on what to say so that their attention and effort can be concentrated on execution (how to say it) of the advertising message.

How account planning works

For an idea of how the process of account planning works, the following example involving Chiat Day Mojo and their client, Arrow Shirt Company is given.[17] Arrow, maker of dress shirts for many years wanted to go into the sport shirt business. To develop the strategy, the account planner talked to men who wear, and women who buy and launder the shirts (i.e. users, buyers, and influencers).

The account planner went into focus groups (see Chapter 4) with material designed to get people talking about the category. You can't just ask, 'Why do you buy?' It isn't easy to articulate. You have to ask about things which will get at their feelings about fashion and the role of fashion in their lives. . .at the right price point. It isn't easy in this category.

The account planner also had to act as translator because what consumers say is not always what they mean.

In this particular instance, the advertising agency creative group and the client had the preconception that a classic male model was needed in the advertising. Merry Cutler explained:[18]

> Planning had to bring these guys back from the brink and tell them Arrow is not about high fashion, it's not about hip, it's not about natural fibers. It's about regular guys and $19 shirts that you can buy on sale for $14. Guys who wear a uniform all week. That's where the loosen-the-collar concept came from — people talking about how good it felt to get home after work, kick off their shoes and wind down. The key dynamic we tapped into is that it wasn't fashion forward; it was just waking up to the fashion conscious. We explained to the creatives and the client that they were kidding themselves (thinking this brand could be portrayed as fashion's cutting edge). The brand can't go there and the consumer doesn't want it to go there. Arrow had to ground itself. Its strength was the white dress shirt, and the strategy should not be to walk away from that equity.

The resulting TV commercial, 'Higher and Higher', depicted a solemn chorus of men in white shirts gradually being transformed into a gospel celebration of colourful sportswear with the Arrow tagline, 'We've loosened our collar.'

Organizational implications

In advertising agencies which have adopted account planning, multiple layers of account management are eliminated. A team is formed which is comprised of the account planner, the management supervisor (account management), and creative team (copywriter and art director). Media, production, traffic, etc., are considered support groups.[19]

Qualifications needed[20]

It's not easy to find account planning talent. The account planner must be a thinker, analyser, and hypothesizer, blessed with common sense as well as a person who can talk with customers, and work with both client and creative team. The ideal qualifications include:

- An understanding of psychology.
- Two years marketing research, acquiring good technical skills.
- Brand or account management experience.
- Curiosity and interest in people.
- A passion for advertising.
- A creative mind.

Analytical techniques

Different analytical techniques are used to aid in the formulation of message strategies. One advertising agency, FCB, reports the use of a two-dimensional scale called a 'Planning Grid' to aid in the formulation of message strategy. On this grid the degree (high/low) and nature (rational/emotional) of consumer involvement (Chapter 6) in a purchase can be plotted to help guide the development of the message to be communicated. Under other circumstances an advertiser may be interested in determining if a message concept in one country might have application in others. In this instance the nature and degree of involvement would be plotted for a single product in several different countries. In Figure 7.1, both of these approaches are illustrated. The grid on the left is for a shampoo product. It indicates a similar approach might be used in four different countries. The grid on the right indicates the degree and

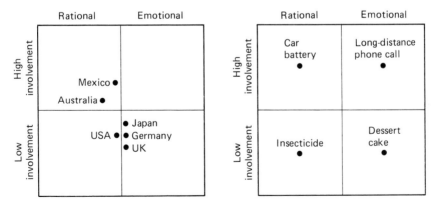

Figure 7.1 *FCB planning grids. Reproduced by permission of Foote, Cone & Belding Communications*

nature of involvement for a car battery, long-distance 'phone call, insecticide, and dessert cake.

Attribute analysis

Another useful approach, according to Runyon,[21] is 'attribute analysis'. This can be done by locating competitive products in one, two, or three-dimensional space. These attributes might involve price for cars; degree of sweetness and chocolate flavour for a hot chocolate drink mix; and strength, absorbency, and softness for a paper towel. See Figure 7.2 for a visual depiction of each of these attribute analysis examples.

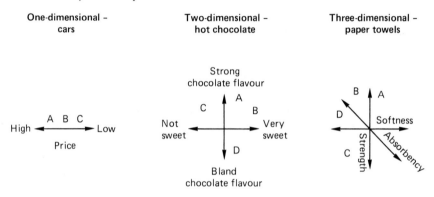

Products = A, B, C, D

Figure 7.2 *Attribute analysis in one-, two-, and three-dimensional product space*

An analysis of this nature presupposes that relevant attributes and the target market's direction and degree of interest in each attribute have been predetermined. Locating a company's brand and its principal competitors in product space will help define the brand's optimum position.

Positioning

What the aforementioned techniques are attempting to establish, as just mentioned, is the position for the brand. 'Proper positioning' was rated as the most important of nine key components of a successful marketing mix by 102 marketing executives.[22]

Positioning has been described by Ennis[23] as the basic selling concept for a product that provides its frame of reference, point of difference, and reason for it. He identifies and describes three major positioning classifications: product, category, and consumer.

Product positioning

Product positioning can take one of several forms. One form is the attribute or benefit that sets the product apart from other offerings of the same type. Crest, for example, was the first toothpaste with fluoride to prevent tooth decay. Maxim was the first freeze dried instant coffee that delivered a 'truer' coffee flavour.

Another form is the competitive orientation. Diet Coke, the number three cola brand behind Classic Coke and Pepsi has been positioned as the underdog to the latter product and attacks it by asserting that consumers are switching from sugared Pepsi to Diet Coke because of better taste.[24]

Sometimes product application, if the market potential is sufficient, can be an effective way to position a product. This proved to be the case for Lipton Onion Soup, promoted as the basic ingredient for a cocktail dip, and for Arm & Hammer Baking Soda, repositioned as a refrigerator deodorizer.

Finally, a packaging advantage can be used in positioning. Take, for example, the pump dispenser used by Henkel for their Thera Med Gel Toothpaste, or the drum-like container used for Janitor-in-a Drum Heavy Duty Household Cleaner.

Category positioning

Category positioning is the second major classification. It refers to a product category or segment in which a brand will compete. For example, Medi-Quik, the first aerosol first-aid spray, elected to announce its use as an all purpose antiseptic for the treatment of minor cuts, scrapes, insect bits, and sunburn. Solarcaine, another aerosol with essentially the same formulation, when introduced was positioned primarily for sunburn relief. The latter brand quickly surpassed Medi-Quik to become the leading seller in that category.

As Ennis[25] pointed out, it's best when you can create your own category, providing the category has sufficient potential users. This turned out to be the case for a highly successful product called Stove Top (bread) Stuffing Mix, an alternative for potatoes, rice or pasta.

Consumer positioning

Consumer positioning is the third major classification. According to Ennis,[26] it refers to the unique way in which the product is perceived based on some

distinguishing impression, regardless of physical properties, e.g. Schaefer —
'The one beer to have when you are having more than one;' Dial Soap —
'round-the-clock odour protection'; Johnson & Johnson Shampoo — 'for adults
who shampoo frequently and want a mild formulation'. In this classification,
the approach sometimes taken is to endow the product with a quality or
character that will set it apart from all brands in its category. This approach
can be visual or verbal. Examples of this approach include: 'The Man in the
Hathaway Shirt,' featuring a distinguished gentleman with an eye patch, and
the advertising line for a well-known investment house, 'When E.F. Hutton
talks, People Listen,' where the seemingly private conversation between two
individuals causes many heads to turn.

If a combination concept is used employing two positioning classifications,
e.g. product and consumer, a stronger message should result.[27]

Attribute ladders

As marketers compete to win share of market, the advertising they produce is
designed to win 'share of mind'[28] .... not an easy task, particularly in light
of all the information a given target audience is asked to process on a daily,
weekly, or monthly basis. For decision making with respect to any given
product the outcome can hinge on a single performance criterion.[29] This leads
to an evaluation of a product vis-à-vis its performance in relation to other
products in the same category. This is, in effect, another form of attribute
analysis. What is the product's relative standing or on what rung of a particular
'attribute ladder'[30] does the product offering rest? (Needless to say, the attribute
under consideration must be of major significance.) For a car, this might be
riding comfort, performance (acceleration, or cornering) or economy. With
respect to 'attribute ladders', when formulating a message for a given product
or service, the objective is to be foremost in the minds of the target market,
i.e., be on the top rung of that attribute ladder.

The job, then, of the international marketing communicator is to first
determine the rung of the ladder on which his/her product rests in the minds
of the consumer. If not at the top, or close to it, it is usually better to find a
new attribute ladder for which the product/service in question can attain top-
rung status. Crosier gave two examples of this approach:

The Bic/Biro case

'Biro' was synonymous with 'ball-point pen' for a whole generation of British
users. Today, it is still occasionally heard of as a generic term, but the product
itself has been entirely supplanted at the volume end of the market by the

throwaway Bic. It is one of those fine ironies of life that both names are, improbably, proper names. Laszlo Biro invented the ball-point mechanism, and promoted his new product as an alternative to the fountain pen, with some success. Baron Marcel Bich dared to gamble on the far more challenging notion of the disposable ball-point pen; instead of pitting it in a head-on competition with the Biro, he carried a new ladder into the prospect's mind by promoting it as the alternative to the pencil — which is, after all, the original throwaway writing instrument.

The Avis Rent-A-Car case

The second case example demonstrates how an established competitor can dramatically improve its market share by a change from the traditional locked-horns advertising strategy. After thirteen consecutive loss-making years of head-on competition with Hertz in America, Avis finally recognized the need to establish a ladder in the prospects' minds on which they could better their unequal rival from the outset. An advertising campaign was devised with the central proposition that 'Avis is only number two in rent-a-cars, so why go with us? Because we try harder.' One of the key tactical aims of this apparently self-deprecating headline was to position Avis in the same league as Hertz, rather than in a different one along with half-a-dozen other competitors as was actually the case. This could only be a short-term aim, however, for the 'number two' tactic was bound to lead to head-on clash with the market leader and the predictable consequence: number two would stay a long way behind number one. The longer term strategy is concealed in the second part of the headline, 'we try harder.' This slogan was repeated in all Avis promotional material: leaflets, order forms, swing labels inside the cars, complimentary road maps, lapel buttons, window stickers, and dozens of other items. By making the claim, Avis skilfully pre-empted any claim by Hertz to try hard themselves, unless it were to try second hardest. They succeeded, in short, in carrying a new ladder labelled 'conscientiousness' into the prospect's mind and establish themselves at the top of it. The tactics were an immediate success, as Avis turned their string of annual deficits into a million dollar profit within a year, increased their annual growth rate from ten to thirty-five per cent, and became an equal competitor with Hertz for market dominance.[31]

It has been said that perception is reality. If a brand can be perceived as occupying the top rung of an attribute ladder, this positioning can lead to and account for a significant share of mind and a major share of market.

Planning grids, attribute analysis, and positioning are useful techniques in message strategy formulation. The process, however, is more complex.

Advertising agency approaches to strategy formulation will vary

As one advertising executive indicated, there is no single formula which will guarantee success. Instead, his organization has developed a five-step, practical

approach which guides the 'efficiency oriented' creative product. These steps
describe:

1 *The market*
   To explain the competitive surroundings and an interpretation of the
   market in the eyes of the consumer.
2 *Target group*
   To identify the group that's economically and strategically the most interesting. It's defined demographically, psychologically, and behaviourally.
3 *Problems of the target group*
   To determine not what this group wants, but what it misses, what is
   bothering, not gained in terms of product functions and personality or
   brand character.
4 *The position*
   Based on the information developed in the first three steps, to define a
   clear, selective, unmistakable position for the brand (refer to prior section
   on this subject).
5 *The personality*
   To establish the functional and psychological qualities to be expressed in
   the advertising.[32]

Another agency executive explained the process in similar terms but with
special emphasis on certain elements.[33] In the past, the positioning of a
product was often based on its unique properties. However, in today's competitive environment many products and services are similar in terms of market
target, basic promise, and reasons for its existence. Because of this, a different
approach is needed; one that calls for a third dimension: *personality* – an
emotional link. For success in communications with the target market, a
brand character (or image) must be conceived. To accomplish this, three
elements are needed: product (efficacy), a position, and a personality. In
today's competitive marketplace all three elements are essential, not just the
first two. An example of this type of approach is drawn from Grey's advertising
for a major food chain in Belgium. Rather than attempt to compete with its
principal rival on price alone, a decision was made between the company and
Grey to differentiate itself from its rival by creating a unique image based on
the presentation of wines, an upmarket product category, to its customers.
The programme included the following.

● Special attention to the selection of wines from different producing countries
   which offered good value at reasonable, not cut, prices.
● Attractively displayed merchandise in a special wine department in each
   store.

- Hiring and training wine department managers who could offer personal assistance to customers in selecting wines for any occasion.
- A wine selection of the month which was advertised and promoted in a non-traditional way. For example, the advertising (print) would identify (on a map) the region from which the special offering came, describe the merits of the particular wine in some detail, offer serving suggestions, and announce the price but not shout about it.

Each element of strategy was there....the product(s), the position, and the personality. Who would think of a chain of supermarkets offering good value, a broad selection, *and* expert advice on a beverage category such as wine!

Creative strategy – the written statement

The end product of all the effort which goes into determining 'what to say' is a written statement called the creative strategy. Depending on location and advertising agency style, the name of these guidelines can vary. Two alternate names frequently used are 'copy platform' (USA) and 'creative brief' (Europe). Similarly, the elements to be treated can vary. However, the following points are normally covered and should be considered essential parts of the creative strategy though not necessarily in this order.

1 Product description (what it is, how it works, what its unique features are).
2 The target audience, demographically, geographically, psychographically, and behaviourally defined.
3 The audience's problem: what they miss or lack.
4 The advertising (communication) objective (see discussion below).
5 The product's position.
6 The principal selling idea (also called the promise or benefit).
7 The reason why the selling idea exists.
8 The personality; expressed in terms of mood, tone, and character.

As a written statement, covering the eight points listed above, the strategy is customarily no more than the length of a single page. If two or more target audiences exist for a single product or service, there should be a separate strategy statement for each.

As for the advertising objective (point 4), this is often misunderstood. As A.C. Nielsen, Jr has pointed out,[34] it is said that advertising's job is to increase sales and/or profits. But that's the job of all departments and functions working together in a coordinated fashion. Instead, it is necessary to define the tasks which 'advertising is assigned by itself'. They are the communication tasks involving changes in prospects' and/or buyers'. . .

1 state of mind
2 knowledge of product or service
3 attitude toward product/service versus competitive offerings
4 propensity to buy

These four changes can be expressed in terms of learning (2), feeling (1 and 3), and doing (4) as explained in Chapter 6.

As one senior marketing executive stated,[35] it is not what we want to convey, but what we want consumers to remember. For example, if the product were a dishwashing detergent, the benefit to be conveyed might be expressed as follows: 'The advertising will convince housewives 25−39 that Brand X will remove grease from pots and pans better than any other product of its kind.' Note that this benefit would be the response to the problem experienced by housewives in undertaking everyday dishwashing chores (creative strategy point 3).

The reason for the benefit's existence (point 6) would lie in the proof to support the claim. This might be:

- a special ingredient
- a special manufacturing process
- a torture test
- the linkage of the product's efficacy to a common grease cleaning problem; e.g., 'no presoaking needed'

This executive also emphasized what he called the brand character (the personality) to be created (point 8). It must conform to the desired image to be created. (A serious product, for example, should not be treated lightly.) Character can be expressed with words like *confident, reliable, user friendly, forward looking,* and *powerful*. For other types of products, descriptions might be: *intimate, sporty, romantic, adventuresome, concerned, sympathetic, caring, frivolous*.

While it was mentioned earlier that a creative strategy may, in its final form, be condensed into a one-page exposition, the subject of personality is complex and may take considerably more supporting explanation. For example, in the case of Hennessy Cognac, management has stated that 'the personality of a brand is not a simple formula and cannot easily be put into words' particularly with a brand with a 227-year history. The 'personality' of the Hennessy brand is treated in a four-page document which covers such topics as gender, status in society, authenticity, appeal to senses and the relationship it enjoys with its public.[36]

There is evidence to suggest, however, that the foregoing exposition on creative strategy formulation does not have universal acceptance despite the seemingly strong adherence on both sides of the Atlantic. While it has been said that few Japanese advertisers work without strategy, the content would be less specific on the one hand but more detailed and cumbersome on the other. This is due to the need to express the views of all participants. Because of the number of people involved in the decision process, emphasis is placed on the general direction and 'feeling' of strategies,[37] and not necessarily coverage of the seven specific points listed earlier.

What the experts say

To reveal the thinking of a number of well-known advertising agency executives on formulating creative strategy, Table 7.1 was prepared. Experts' comments were extracted from the *Wall Street Journal's* Creative Leaders Campaign which began in 1977.

These comments on creative strategy are tender morsels to chew on for anyone with a genuine interest in learning how compelling advertising is created.

Ideation

In this chapter the discussion has centred on developing creative strategy; determining what the message should be for a particular product or service.

This approach requires analytical skills, logic and reasoning as well as ideas. Information for the strategist comes from both internal and external sources. Internally, information can come from laboratory technicians, scientists, engineers, sales and service representatives, test kitchen personnel, quality control, and others who have worked with and studied the product or service. Externally, information is sought by means of informal meetings with users and non-users, from qualitative (focus group) and quantitative research studies, and from secondary sources.

In developing the best means to communicate the message once the creative strategy has been established, a different approach and orientation is required. This lies in the domain of the copywriter and art director, the creative specialists. (This does not mean that a person can do only one job or the other; some people possess both 'what to' and 'how to' communication skills.) Both 'what to' and 'how to' ideas are needed. The creative strategy must be on target. The resulting message requires freshness, originality, and memorability.

Table 7.1 *Experts' views on creative strategy*

Name and affiliation	Comments on creative strategy
Bill Backer, Backer/Spielvogel	Advertising needs an idea...requires sharp thinking about product and problem.
Norman Berry, Ogilvy & Mather (UK)	Strategies should be precise, tight, e.g., saying ad should be warm and friendly is not enough.
Jay Chiat, Chiat Day	The best work begins with a marketing solution...flows from strategy.
Gene Frederico, Lord, Geller, Frederico, Einstein	You must grasp both the marketing problem and the marketing environment.
Peter Geer, Geer DuBois, Inc.	'Writing that really communicates requires piercing insights into the heads and minds of your audience. Getting those insights is even harder than writing.'
Jim Johnston, Jim Johnston Advertising	Tone and style can create a personality that will reach, touch, and move readers.
Reva Korda, Oglivy & Mather	'....go right to the merchandise: feel it, wear it, eat it, know it.'
Burt Manning, J. Walter Thompson	Advertising must build a clear bridge between seller and buyer by showing how the product fills a genuine physical or psychological need.
Hal Riney, Hal Riney & Partners	'Advertising based on insignificant product differences won't provide significant leverage. Today, some important differences are simply *taste* and *style*.'
Robert Stone, Stone & Adler	'People won't switch brands, try a new product or service, unless they have a reason...there are only two reasons why people buy anything: to gain something or to protect what they already have.'

Source: Dow Jones & Co. Inc., June 1992.

Sometimes a group approach can be highly productive in aiding the development of creative strategy or in coming up with ideas for a compelling advertising message. One such approach is called brainstorming.

Brainstorming

Alex F. Osborn, a principal of the well-known advertising agency Batten, Barton, Durstine & Osborn, is credited with devising this technique. Silvano Arietti explains it in the following way:

> A group holds session together and advances new ideas (to solve a particular problem). Four basic rules are to be respected:
>
> 1 Criticism is ruled out.
> 2 Free-wheeling is welcomed — 'the wilder the idea, the better.'
> 3 Quantity is desired — the greater the number of ideas, the greater the likelihood of good results.
> 4 Combination and improvement are sought.
>
> Participants should suggest how ideas from other members of the group could be improved. The brainstorming session should be animated by a spirit of self-encouragement and a rejection of perfectionism. Osborn suggests that the ideal number of participants is between five and ten. The group has a leader who explains the rules, sees to it that they are not violated, and makes sure that ideas are not criticized and that the group does not break down into subgroups.

As Arietti pointed out, 'One (brainstorming) meeting turned up forty-five suggestions for a home appliance, another resulted in fifty-six ideas for a money-raising campaign, and another one offered 124 ideas on how to sell more blankets.'*

With respect to the topic or problem to be discussed, the group leader should exercise care in stating it at the beginning of the session. If too broad, interactively developed ideas may not result. If too narrow, ideas about the basic problem may not result, only some special way of handling it. For example, if the problem had to do with traffic control, 'better traffic control' would be too broad; 'to improve traffic lights would be too narrow'; 'method of improving traffic flow given the present arrangement of roads' would be appropriate. It is the responsibility of the chairman to formulate the problem statement as well as repeat it during the course of the session.[38]

Other functions of the chairman include:

* Excerpt adapted from Arietti, Silvano (1976) *Creativity: The Magic Synthesis*, Basic Books Inc., New York, pp. 367–368. Reproduced by permission of Basic Books, a division of HarperCollins Publishers Inc.

- Seeing that evaluation or criticism of ideas is avoided.
- Permitting only one person to speak at a time.
- Offering suggestions to fill in gaps.
- Suggesting different approaches, e.g., 'let's turn this thing upside down'.
- Ending the session at a set time or when ideas cease to be suggested due to fatigue and before boredom sets in.
- Scheduling a meeting to evaluate the ideas generated in the brainstorming session.

At each session a notetaker needs to be appointed for the purpose of recording all unduplicated ideas in an understandable and legible form. (It's also desirable to tape record the session.)

If the group assembled is unfamiliar with the brainstorming technique, it's a good idea to have a ten minute warm-up session dealing with a simple problem such as the design for a hand-held hammer. The purpose of the warm-up is to demonstrate the type of ideas welcomed, and to make sure participants understand that evaluation or criticism of ideas is strictly prohibited.

The length of a brainstorming session may vary from twenty to forty-five minutes. Often an informal luncheon with sandwiches in the conference room is an appropriate setting.

Because participants may continue to have ideas following the session, it's a good idea to circulate the list of ideas generated at the brainstorming session and request additional ideas to be added by each member of the group.

Evaluation is the final step in the process. It is carried out at a later date by the same or a different group. The result of this final assignment is to establish three separate lists:

1 Ideas of immediate usefulness.
2 Ideas for further exploration.
3 New approaches to the problem.[39]*

The individual as a source of ideas

Individuals, as well as groups, are called on to find solutions...come up with ideas to solve problems involving communications. In this regard, the process of individual ideation can be considered as a series of conscious acts. An understanding of the process should improve one's ability and efficiency in generating ideas to solve communication and other types of problems. It is

* The excerpts indicated by notes 39 and 41−48 are reproduced from de Bono, Edward (1970) *Lateral Thinking: Creativity Step by Step*, HarperCollins, New York by permission of HarperCollins Publishers. © Edward de Bono 1970.

with this thought that Frank Armstrong's five-step Idea Tracking approached is introduced.[40]

Step 1   Assess the situation

- Don't mistake assumptions for facts or rely on past experience which may not apply.
- Assume important facts are not yet known....more can be learned.
- Hold back opinions; avoid opinionated people.
- Examine the most taken-for-granted aspect of the entire situation...find out if it's really true.
- Ask endless questions...each flowing from the previous answer.
- Try to systematize the information-gathering process.
- Be on the lookout for a key factor, critical piece of information...try to isolate it.
- Use the time check: true yesterday...also today?
- Use the numbers check: what date, time? How many...few? How long ago...recently? How big...small?
- Check authoritative opinions and facts for source, conditions.
- Make personal observations: see, hear, feel.
- Record on cards so you can shuffle, order information.

Step 2   Define the problem

- Start with a tentative definition. This gives direction to your work in assessing the situation.
- Understand it will have to be expanded, refined.
- Key facts from the situation assessment will help establish the most accurate definition.
- Write the definition down and inspect each word for accuracy, completeness, appropriateness, clarity....use nouns, not adjectives.
- Apply numbers checks: times, dates, quantities.
- See if the problem statement means to others (try on colleagues) what it means to you.

Step 3   Use your subconscious

- After assessing situation and defining problem the subconscious will go to work automatically.
- Sleeping on the problem helps...tuck the problem into the corner of your mind as you begin the weekend...it won't intrude...it will simmer.
- If a complex problem, check your written statement often as a refresher, stimulant.

Step 4   The idea-producing stage

- After the subconscious has been given opportunity to reshape facts and produce new patterns of thought, the *conscious* mind must go back to work to produce ideas.
- Ideas will now come, partly by inspiration, partly through perspiration... but if adequately prepared, they will come.
- Mechanical stimulants help:
  - Clear your desk/mind.
  - Avoid intrusions, business or personal.
  - Set enough time aside...several hours without interruption.
  - Use pencil and pad...ideas not written down will flee.
  - After working a while, bounce ideas off people; don't worry about criticism; articulate, listen.
  - After pursuing one tack where you develop a number of ideas, drop it and start along a completely new path.
- When you finish, check each idea against the problem statement.

Step 5   Judgment to select the best idea

- Seek judicial criticism − expose to others for objectivity.
- Set up a balance sheet; points for....points against.
- Compare with visually stated expression of problem and apply the last double check: DOES THIS IDEA SOLVE THIS PROBLEM?

A manner of thinking

Whether attacking a problem in a group or by oneself, certain mind sets should be avoided. Edward de Bono in his book on *Lateral Thinking* provides a number of useful approaches for conditioning the mind to produce more and better ideas for problem definition and solution. Among them are:

1   *Searching for alternatives*[41]
   The purpose of searching for alternatives '...is to loosen up rigid patterns and to provoke new patterns'. This doesn't mean the most obvious approach is not used; however, instead of its choice as being the only one, '...it is chosen because it is obviously the best from among other possibilities'. De Bono advises that in the search for alternatives, a quota of three to five should be established. Of course, more are welcome, but a minimum are insured so that the search is not prematurely halted because an early alternative appears particularly promising. Here's an example:

A one pint milk bottle with half a pint of water in it.
How would you describe that bottle?

Alternatives
1   A half empty bottle of water.
2   A milk bottle half filled with water.
3   Half a pint of water in an empty one pint milk bottle.

2   *Challenging assumptions*
Assumptions imply certain boundaries and structures. Creative thinking requires restructuring. For this reason, assumptions must be challenged. Take for example the nine dot square problem. It was used to illustrate creativity in an exhibit on the showcase eighteenth floor of 485 Lexington Avenue in New York where McCann-Erickson, Inc. had its headquarters. The problem is to link all nine dots as shown below with only four straight lines, each connected and following the other without raising pen or pencil from the paper.

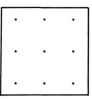

Can you solve the problem without reading on? While most of us would work until becoming frustrated trying to solve it by attempting to make the connections within the nine dot framework, the only solution, as McCann-Erickson put it, is to 'break out of the nine dot square'. This is done by extending two of the straight lines outside the nine dots. 'Breaking out of the nine dot square' is the means by which any problem should be approached.

3   *The 'why' technique*[42]
This technique is used to challenge assumptions. It is another means of trying to look at things in a different way. The initial question might be, 'Why are stop lights red?' When this question is answered, another 'why' question is directed at some particular aspect of the response. As de Bono explains[43] 'the idea is to show that any assumption whatsoever can be challenged'. 'One is much freer to use assumptions and cliches if one knows that one is not going to be imprisoned by them.'

4   *Suspended judgment*
Osborn, Armstrong, and de Bono all adhere to the suspension of judgment principle. As de Bono points out[44] judgment should be suspended at the

generation stage of thinking because a wrong idea at the preliminary stage can lead to a right one later on.

5 *Dominate ideas and crucial factors*

The thought with respect to dominant ideas and crucial factors is that they exert a strong influence without being consciously recognized. Even though a person may be confident in knowing what he/she is talking, reading, or writing about, when asked to pick out the dominant idea that person may have a problem. A dominant idea is 'the organizing theme in a way of looking at a situation'.[45] A crucial factor is a 'tethering point'. Both may influence without being consciously recognized. To surmount this hurdle... restructure a pattern...these questions must be asked:[46]

1 Why are we always looking at this thing in the same way?
2 What is holding us up, what is keeping us to this old approach?

6 *Fractionation*

Patterns tend to grow larger and as a result become harder to look at in a new way.[47] For example, a child cannot much more than use and admire a complete doll's house. However, if given a box of building blocks, they can be assembled in different ways to yield a variety of houses. The idea, then, is to break down a large pattern into fractions for the purpose of restructuring by putting the fractions together in a different way.

7 *The reversal method*

This method involves turning things around, looking at things from the other end, inside-out, upside-down.[48] To illustrate, de Bono used this example:

> A flock of sheep were moving slowly down a country lane which was bounded by high banks. A motorist in a hurry came up behind the flock and urged the shepherd to move his sheep to one side so that the car could drive through. The shepherd refused since he could not be sure of keeping all the sheep out of the way of the car in such a narrow lane. Instead he reversed the situation. He told the car to stop and then he quietly turned the flock around and drove it back past the car.

The idea is to free information so that it can come together in a different way.

Summary

The purpose of this chapter was to acquaint the reader with the preparation — what to say — phase of message development which involved the formulation of a creative strategy. In the process, organizational methods, analytical techniques, and approaches used by organizations and individual experts were introduced. In concluding this chapter both group and individual methods for idea generation were explained in some detail. The reader should now be prepared to explore the next topic: how compelling marketing communication messages are created.

Questions

1　Is it better to create the advertising message at the local country level or at headquarters in the home country?
2　What kind of advertising strategy is usually used in industrial advertising and why?
3　Explain what a 'lead country' decision process for advertising is.
4　Describe Coca-Cola's system of global advertising.
5　Give five reasons why the same elements may not be featured in all international advertisements.
6　Who are some possible participants in a message formulation process and what do they do?
7　Explain why account planning has become important in many advertising agencies around the world.
8　Who are normally the participants in account planning and how does it work?
9　Discuss the benefits of using planning grids and attribute analysis in formulating message strategies.
10　Define 'positioning'. Then explain product, category and consumer positioning.
11　How can the attribute ladder concept aid in developing message strategies.
12　Identify the principal topics that should be included in a creative strategy.
13　Explain why 'personality' is an important part of the creative strategy for consumer goods and services.
14　How should advertising objective be stated? Give reasons.
15　Describe the process of a brainstorming session and its objectives.
16　What other techniques can be used to produce useful ideas for marketing communications? Explain each briefly.

Notes

1　Roddy, John (1982) A speech, advertising & marketing in Southeast Asia: a lesson in give and take, New York, June 8.

2   Hennessy, Gilles (1990) Personal Presentation, Paris, 1 June.
3   Delmotte, Oliver (1991) Hennessy Cognac, Cognac, France, 15 November.
4   Griffin, Tom (1990) Advertising practice: a global or local affair? In *Advanced Marketing Research*, proceedings of the 19th Annual Conference of the European Marketing Academy, Innsbruck, May, p. 393.
5   Sugarman, Ron (1984) How one agency handles a global brand?, A presentation, the 14th Asian Advertising Congress, 18−21 June.
6   *Advertising Age*, 22 January 1990, 1.
7   Harper, Paul C., Jr. (1981) One world, one customer, one message: advertising's international opportunity. A speech at IAA Luncheon Meeting, New York, 10 March.
8   Cooper, Ralph (1989) Personal presentation, London, 7 June.
9   Sugarman, *op. cit.*
10   Griffin, *op. cit.*, pp. 393−4.
11   Peterson Blyth Cato and Cheskin and Masten (1985) *Survey of Global Brands and Global Marketing*, New York.
12   Walters, Peter G.P. (1986) International marketing policy, a discussion of the standardization construct and its relevance for corporate policy. *Journal of International Business*, **17**, (2), 55−69.
13   Wood, John, as quoted by Andrew Olds (1990) Planned and delivered. Creative insert in *Advertising Age*, 1 January, 8.
14   Olds, Andrew, *op. cit.*
15   This information is based on personal interviews with two account planners from the UK: Jane Newman, Chiat Day and a second executive (who cannot be located) working at Ogilvy & Mather, New York, July, 1985.
16   Olds, *op. cit.*, p. 10.
17   Kattleman, Terry (1990) Planning in action. Creative insert article in *Advertising Age*, 1 January, 38.
18   Kattleman, *op. cit.*
19   Newman, Jane (1985) Personal interview, New York, 22 July.
20   *Ibid.*
21   Runyon, Kenneth E. (1984) *Advertising*, 2nd edn, Charles E. Merrill Publishing Company, Columbus, Ohio, pp. 13−16.
22   Role of management in Marketing Mix (1983) *The Gallagher Report*, **XXXI**, Number (41).
23   Ennis, F. Beaven (1985) *Marketing Norms for Product Managers*, Association of National Advertisers, New York, p. 37.
24   Winters, Patricia (1990) Diet Coke's formula: stress taste, not calories. *Advertising Age*, 1 January, 16.
25   Ennis, *op. cit.*, p. 38.
26   *Ibid.*, p. 40.
27   *Ibid.*, p. 41.

28 Crosier, Keith (1982) A new strategy for advertising to overcommunicated target audiences. *The Quarterly Review of Marketing*, Summer, 13.

29 *Ibid.*, 15.

30 *Ibid.*, 15.

31 *Ibid.*, 15.

32 Schau, Jergen (1984) Personal interview, Team BBDO, Dusseldorf, May.

33 Godefroid, Alain (1987) Grey Advertising, Brussels, May.

34 Nielsen, A.C., Jr. (1985) Buenos Aires Speech, 18 August, 28.

35 Papas, Claude (1990) Personal interview, Procter & Gamble, Paris, 8 June.

36 Hennessy, *op. cit.*

37 Wagenaar, Jan Dirk (1980) Advertising in Japan. *Marketing Trends*, A.C. Nielsen Co., (2), 5.

38 De Bono, Edward (1970) *Lateral Thinking: Creativity Step by Step*, Harper-Collins, New York, pp. 152–157.

39 *Ibid.*, pp. 154–6.

40 Armstrong, Frank (1960) *Idea Tracking*, Criterion Books, New York, pp. 139–144.

41 De Bono, *op. cit.*, p. 64.

42 *Ibid.*, pp. 72–103.

43 *Ibid.*, p. 103.

44 *Ibid.*, p. 108.

45 *Ibid.*, p. 126.

46 *Ibid.*, p. 127.

47 *Ibid.*, p. 131.

48 *Ibid.*, pp. 142–7.

8 *Message making and evaluating effectiveness*

Introduction

This chapter is about message making and evaluating its effectiveness. The approaches used by a number of well known practitioners who could be called master chefs of modern day advertising in the USA are examined. This is followed by a discussion of recent creative efforts from a European and Oriental point of view, including criticism of US advertising and specific instructions from other practitioners. Then the interactive process by which creative strategy is transformed into advertising executions is discussed. Suggestions for developing different types of advertising are advanced. Finally, measuring effectiveness is treated.

The US school

The great names in advertising in the USA which became known in post Second World War days, particularly during the 1950s and 1960s, included Ogilvy, Bernbach, and Reeves. They join Burnett who started the agency in the 1930s which stills bears his name. Runyon described their approaches in some detail.[1]

Leo Burnett

Much of Burnett's most distinctive advertising 'involved romanticizing and personalizing the product'. Examples of his work included the creation of the symbol, Betty Crocker, for General Mills. Her name is found today on many of its branded products, and has been used in naming its test kitchens and cookbooks. Others are the 'Jolly Green Giant' for Green Giant Canned Peas, the symbol found on package labels and in advertising; the world-renowned 'Marlboro Man' and his 'Marlboro Country', as shown in Exhibit 8.1. This is one of the greatest advertising success stories of all times, a campaign which has run for thirty-six years.

David Ogilvy

David Ogilvy, is the founder of Ogilvy, Benson & Mather which began operations in the late 1940s. Like Burnett's organization, Ogilvy's has become

Exhibit 8.1 *Marlboro advertisement. Reproduced by permission of Philip Morris Incorporated*

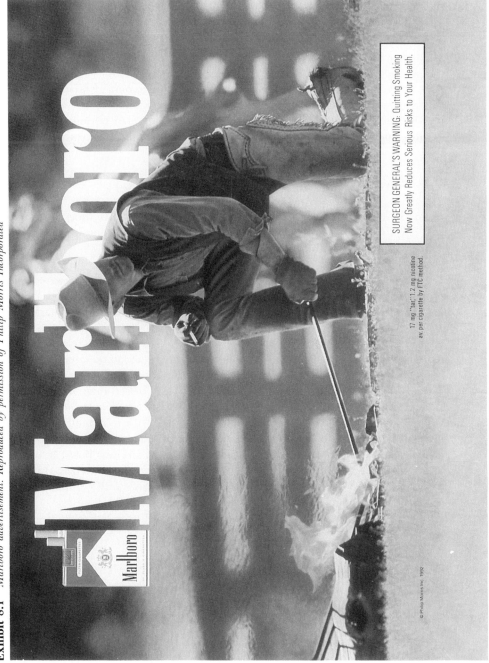

one of the world's top advertising agencies, Ogilvy himself is associated with the term *image* advertising. His image campaigns have included:

- 'The man in the Hathway Shirt', a tall, trim, distinguished looking gentleman with a black eye patch who became the symbol for that company's products for decades.
- Commander Whitehead, 'the man from Schweppes is here', who introduced Schweppes Tonic Water to the US market (see Exhibit 8.2).
- Advertising for Rolls-Royce cars with the headline, 'At 60 miles an hour the loudest noise in this new Rolls-Royce comes from the electric clock.'

Rosser Reeves

Rosser Reeves, author of the widely read book, *Realities in Advertising*, believed that effective advertising should contain a 'unique selling proposition' (USP) comprised of:

1 A benefit that is important to consumers and unique...not possessed by competitive products.
2 A promise − if a consumer buys that product she will get that benefit.

As Runyon pointed out,[2] the USP 'Cleans your breath while it cleans your teeth' helped Colgate achieve a 50 per cent share of market; only to be outdone by an even stronger USP for Crest Toothpaste, 'Look mom...no cavities.' Sometimes pictures can convey the USP better than words. For example, in the case of Uncle Ben's Rice, the USP read: 'Uncle Ben's is the rice without the surface starch that makes rice stick' − a mouthful! A simple demonstration for a television commercial communicated this benefit: two ice cream scoops of rice were placed on separate plates. A fork was thrust into the 'other' rice which could not separate the stuck-together rice kernels. In the case of Uncle Ben's the reverse was true, readily visualizing and communicating the USP − 'without the surface starch that makes rice stick'.

   In each example there was a reason why the benefit existed:

- Colgate contained GARDOL
- Crest contained fluoride...and the seal of the American Dental Association (as a result of extensive clinical testing).
- Uncle Ben's Rice was made by means of a patented process which produced the benefit.

Exhibit 8.2 *Reproduced by permission of Cadbury Beverages Inc., Stamford, Connecticut, USA*

The man from Schweppes is here!

MEET COMMANDER EDWARD WHITEHEAD, Schweppesman Extraordinary from London, England.

The Commander has come to these United States to make sure that every drop of Schweppes Quinine Water bottled here has the original flavor which has made it the essential mixer for an authentic Gin-and-Tonic all over the world.

He imports the original Schweppes elixir, and the secret of Schweppes unique carbonation is securely locked in his brief case. "Schweppervescence," says the Commander, "*lasts the whole drink through.*"

Now that Schweppes have given up transporting heavy bottles across 3,000 miles of Atlantic Ocean, you can buy their incomparable Quinine Water in handy six-bottle cartons, popularly priced, at grocers throughout Greater New York.

It took Schweppes almost a hundred years to bring the bitter-sweet flavor of their Quinine Water to its present perfection. But it will take you or the barman only thirty seconds to mix it with ice and gin in a highball glass. And *then*, gentle reader, you will bless the day you read this advertisement.

Schweppes now available in handy 6-bottle cartons of 10-oz. bottles.

William Bernbach

William Bernbach, co-founder of Doyle, Dane, Bernbach in 1949, created many memorable campaigns for clients over thirty years. As Runyon[3] pointed out, Bernbach believed that every advertisement should have a big idea which must be said in a way that's memorable. Taken from a videotaped interview with John Crichton, then president of the American Association of Advertising Agencies, these ideas amplified Bernbach's approach in creating advertising messages:[4]

- You must appeal to the instincts rather than the intellect . . . 'you've got to feel it in the gut'.
- Freshness is needed — by saying something in a way it has not been said before.
- Believability is important.
- It's better to under — than overplay.
- Respect for your audience is a must.

Some examples of Bernbach's work included the print campaign for American Airlines. To break away from the conventional approach of showing a plane photographically and announcing the schedule to this or that city, Bernbach selected a cartoonist, Chuck Saxon, to illustrate an airline service benefit with the headline, 'people are stealing our stewardesses'.

In a television advertisement the analogy of a (disastrous) day in the life of a paperboy — losing a paper out of the bike's basket, being chased by a dog, and falling off his bike and skinning his knee — was used to convey a message about insurance needs for small business. In another commercial, a gorilla was shown handling a US Tourister suitcase to demonstrate its durability.

To gain recognition for Volkswagen's rigorous quality control programme, Bernbach sold the idea of using the one-word headline 'Lemon' (in American terminology the classic put-down for a bad car) to induce people to read the body copy in the ad about the meticulous nature of this programme (see Exhibit 8.3).

Criticism of US advertising: a European perspective

As advertising messages proliferated and the industry matured in the USA, the quality of message output was seen as declining by observers elsewhere. 'Creatively, has America (the US) lost its way?' — that was a statement turned into a question which was directed to the US advertising industry by Jean-Michel Goudard in the early 1980s.[5] He believed that there had been a

Exhibit 8.3 *Use of the one-word headline. Reproduced by permission of DDB Needham Worldwide, New York*

Lemon.

This Volkswagen missed the boat.

The chrome strip on the glove compartment is blemished and must be replaced. Chances are you wouldn't have noticed it; Inspector Kurt Kroner did.

There are 3,389 men at our Wolfsburg factory with only one job: to inspect Volkswagens at each stage of production. (3000 Volkswagens are produced daily; there are more inspectors than cars.)

Every shock absorber is tested (spot checking won't do), every windshield is scanned. VWs have been rejected for surface scratches barely visible to the eye.

Final inspection is really something! VW inspectors run each car off the line onto the Funktionsprüfstand (car test stand), tote up 189 check points, gun ahead to the automatic brake stand, and say "no" to one VW out of fifty.

This preoccupation with detail means the VW lasts longer and requires less maintenance, by and large, than other cars. (It also means a used VW depreciates less than any other car.)

We pluck the lemons; you get the plums.

'rapid deterioration in the creative reputation of US agencies', and gave three reasons for it:

1 Ignorance based on poor intelligence work.
2 An excessive use of mindless research.
3 Growth of creativity abroad.

Frank Lowe, British ad man, became quite specific in identifying the problems with US advertising, one of which related to point 2 above.[6] After identifying advertising as 'essentially an American art form' and paying tribute to the creativity of advertising in the 1960s by referring specifically to DDB's Avis and Volkswagen campaigns, Lowe made reference to the increasing usage of high recall scores (see Chapter 12) as the criteria for selecting TV advertisements.

The strongest condemnation was the criticism as directed at the 'hard sell approach' of US advertising. These are his words:

> They suddenly look at the camera and say, 'Oh, hi! We were just chatting about hemorrhoids.' I believe in oblique communication. You can't come barging into someone's living room and expect them to be interested in diaper rash. They could be worried about their sick mother, or perhaps they can't pay the rent that month. I mean, people have a lot of real problems on their mind.

Barry Day has also questioned the US 'slice of life' television technique, used by many years by the largest companies such as Procter & Gamble.[7] 'Has the intelligent story type commercial outserved its usefulness?' To shed light on this question, Day introduced a number of TV commercials which involved a different approach including commercials for. . . .

● Kronenbourg and Tuborg Beers filled with scenes and situations to create a certain mood and feeling; product and brand appearing at the end only.
● Suntory Whisky with actions of real and mythical persons; also animals, symbols, and different scenes; only to close on a glass of whisky and a labelled bottle.

These commercials don't complete the circle, finish the story. . .that's up to the viewer.

The criticisms that Goudard, Lowe, and Day advance with respect to the quality of the US creative product may or may not have validity. Reasons given for the possible difference include the fact that the sheer volume of advertising output in the USA is so much greater as compared with most other countries; and there has been increasing pressure on the part of businesses for greater accountability. With the high cost of producing a commercial (which can be $200,000 or more for thirty second announcement) and airing it

($100,000 plus for prime time), the pressure for accountability to determine the return on the advertising investment mounts. It also must be acknowledged that the USA still possesses extraordinary creative talent and is turning out some highly imaginative work; subjects that will be discussed subsequently.

Advertising: a global art form

The truth of the matter is that advertising is no longer an 'American art form'. As with business in general, it has become a global art form. There is, as Goudard stated, a growth in creativity. . . . not just in Europe or Japan but in every country in the world, large and small, where advertising has become established as a legitimate means of economic growth.[8] As Phil Dusenberry said, 'As Americans, it's important to remember we don't have the world's advertising franchise. When I rejoined BBDO, I would look at the work from our agencies in England and France and simply drool. Well, they've continued to get better. So now, more than ever, it's not enough to be good: you have to be worldclass.'[9]

Differences in creative output can be attributed, at least in part, to particular environmental conditions such as the ones Wim Slootweg has identified.[10] For example, he referred to (disappearing) US constants − captive audiences, predictable mass markets, and saturation buying − which never existed in Europe. This meant that European advertising 'has always been more subtle, more prone to humour and more concerned with communication than hard sell'. In Europe, 'there is the feeling that maybe the product being sold is not the most important thing in the consumer's life'. . .hence there are not as many 'hit them hard' ads but more in which the advertiser 'jokes about the product, or sings about it, or talks about it in a way that underplays its importance'. Slootweg also found more emotional appeal in US ads whereas the emotional aspect is played down in European advertising. You don't get emotional about a toothpaste or an airline. This might be considered an invasion of privacy, just like you do not insult the consumer's intelligence. However, he believed that US advertising was moving away from the 'slice-of-life' and 'stand-up' pitch approaches which had characterized US advertising to the less direct methods of the European advertising community.

These and other comments about the US advertising industry may someday soon be levelled against Europe as more commercial TV stations are permitted in the various countries and as Europe as a whole moves closer to the realization of single market in the 1990s.

On the other hand, the so-called captive, mass markets are disappearing in the USA as traditional television viewing declines, as cable TV and VCR videotape viewing increases, and as magazines provide readers with more special interest alternatives. In combination these factors are likely to move US audiences closer to the characteristics of a European audience.

With respect to advertising message executions in various countries, any external evaluation must be made in context of the indigenous culture, otherwise the evaluation is meaningless. Take, for example, advertising in Japan and other parts of Asia.

The art of advertising in Asia

A French advertising agency executive recently remarked that he lacked understanding of advertising in Asia. This same comment is heard in the Americas as well. Jan Dirk Wagenaar explained that advertising in Japan, for example, 'reflects a concern for harmony'. For this reason, 'a Westerner is often totally lost in trying to understand what a particular ad or spot is supposed to communicate'.[11] Advertising and communications in general reflect a concern for harmony and a desire to please; not hard sell. Three main types of advertising were identified and discussed by Wagenaar:

1 *Follow the leader.* The Japanese advertiser is not concerned about differentiation and positioning in relation to competitive offerings. Instead, there is the feeling that if a certain approach worked for someone else, it should work for me too.
2 *Use of celebrities.* Both Japanese and Western celebrities are frequently used, often without a genuine relationship to the product as in the case of Sophia Loren for Honda motorbikes. Another product category where celebrities have been used, but with seemingly better reasons, is coffee. . . .

    - The US film actor, Kirk Douglas for Maxim Coffee (Americans are considered great coffee drinkers).
    - The Japanese actress Ayako Wakao for Yuban Coffee (the actress lends dignity and elegance to this premium coffee).

3 *Mood and nuance.* Symbols from nature such as skies, sunrises and sunsets set the mood, only to be followed by the product which comes as 'very much of a surprise to both Japanese and Western viewers'. Groups, rather than an individual in a group, receive the attention in the advertising. 'We' and 'us', are used instead of 'I' and 'me', e.g. 'Let us, simple men, use. . .' (Aggressiveness in marketing programmes are found at point-of-sale, in pricing and promotion, but not in advertising.)

In discussing advertising in Southeast Asia, John Roddy also indicated that aggressiveness in the form of asking for the order whether in written, voice, or person-to-person advertising is bad manners.[12] In contrast, 'symbolism and overt trappings of wealth and success' are perfectly acceptable. Roddy used these examples to illustrate the point. All made reference to the acceptance of the product/service in other parts of the world.

- *Toyota Tercel*. 'The number one range of imported cars in America is also number one in Hong Kong.'
- *Hong Kong and Shanghai Bank Visa Card*. 'The world's biggest card from Hong Kong's biggest bank.'
- *Marlboro cigarettes*. 'Marlboro is now no. 1 in the US according to the independent Maxwell Report.' (Unlike other parts of the world, 'Marlboro Country' was not a significant factor in the advertising.)

Proven how-to-say-it ideas from other US experts

Despite the earlier criticism of US advertising mentioned by some European authorities, there have been a number of very talented and successful creative leaders in the USA other than the four greats previously mentioned. Key ideas of some of these experts are recorded below as reported in the *Wall Street Journal's* advertising series, 'Creative Leaders Campaign' with respect to 'how-to-say-it':[13]

- *John Caples*. Start with your best idea; don't end with it. . .headlines make ads.
- *Jim Johnston*. Headlines can be visual. . . .words can stop readers.
- *Helmut Krone*. Begin by thinking, not drawing layouts. . .scribbles box you in. The page should look and smell like the product. If it's technical like a Porsche, that's how the page should look and feel.
- *Reva Korda*. Write like you are talking to one person – an intelligent friend. . .telling her what you want her to know.
- *Jerry Siano*. There are four success elements (in creating advertising):
  It's interesting or people won't read it.
  It's informative or they won't carry a message away.
  It's honest or it won't hold up when tested against reality.
  It's human or people won't relate to you or your message.

Image in advertising

Allen Rosenshine tells us that people don't really remember facts and figures. From advertising they receive a net impression: that's *image*. Through advertising, a brand image is created. That's the consumer's perception of the brand. To illustrate his point, he cited a two-page spread for Mercedes. There was copy, copy, and more copy accompanied by draughtsman's diagrams and 'automotive jargon'. The advertisement, in effect, was an 'engineering document'. Rosenshine asked, 'So where's the image?', then added, 'That is the image. It didn't matter whether you read a single word of copy. You got a net impression just from seeing the ad, for even a few seconds, that Mercedes Benz was state-of-the-art, a marvel of automotive design, a car so replete with quality, it took all those words and drawings to get it said. If you did actually read the ad, the image was reinforced. If you didn't, the image was still successfully communicated.' Net impression equals brand image.[14]

From creative strategy to production approval

Thus far in this chapter a number of advertising experts' ideas about making messages have been introduced. These ideas were introduced for the value they may possess as thought starters in transforming the creative strategy into a compelling advertising message. This transformation involves creative people and their work. The copywriter and art director assigned to the account and job at hand form the nucleus of the creative team. It is their responsibility to produce the copy (written matter) and layout (the illustrative material) for a print advertisement, a script for a radio commercial, or a storyboard for a television commercial, each of which should embody all elements of the creative strategy. Before any 'rough' (preliminary) creative work is shown to the client (the advertiser), it is customary to have it reviewed and approved within the advertising agency. In some agencies there is a formal review process often involving a committee of senior executives. In others, creative supervisors, account, and planning personnel will perform this function.

Client presentation

With respect to client presentation, the process will vary depending on the importance of the work to be approved, e.g. a revision of a trade advertisement versus a major new end user campaign, and the rapport of the agency's principal account representative with the client. Thus, a single representative may make the presentation or it may become a joint effort. In the latter instance, the account executive (or planner) will restate the prior-approved creative strategy, and then a representative(s) of the creative team will actually introduce and discuss the creative elements. The presentation may consist of one or more possible executions. If the latter is the case, each would necessarily respond to the creative strategy but represent different approaches and message concepts.

The outcome of this initial meeting can range from total acceptance to total rejection. In most instances, the outcome will lie somewhere in between.

However, if the agency account team has done its homework, put the appropriate talent against the assignment, and found their solution to the creative problem to be worthy of their agency's review process stamp of approval, changes will be minor.

Preparation of messages for different media

Returning to the creative message itself, the structure and elements of different types of advertisements will now be examined.

Print advertisements

In print advertisements the principal elements are headline, illustration, body copy, and signature or theme line. These elements can be observed in Exhibit 8.4 which shows the development of a print advertisement for Dannon Sprinkl'Ins, starting with an art director's rough and ending with the finished advertisement. The 'rough layout' (Exhibit 8.4(a)) is the form which the advertisement is presented to the client for the first time. Only the headline, caption and brand name are lettered in this layout. The remaining copy elements are indicated by lines or 'squiggles'. For this reason the layout would be accompanied by a separate copy sheet containing all the written content.

The 'comprehensive layout' (Exhibit 8.4(b)), though still an artist's rendition of what the finished ad would look like, is more precise in colour and detail. This layout is customarily presented to the client for final approval along with any possible copy revisions and an estimate of the cost to produce the advertisement in a form which is acceptable to the publication(s) in which it will run (Exhibit 8.4(c)). For this advertisement, it would involve photography, typesetting, artwork and mechanical assembly. (A technical discussion on preparing and producing advertisements whether for print or broadcast is beyond the scope of this text. If the reader wishes to explore this subject, several works cited in the notes, such as Wells et al.,[20] Mandell,[24] Dunn and Barban,[25] and Nylen,[39] are useful.)

Comments and suggestions are made about the principal print advertising elements in the paragraphs which follow.

Headlines. According to John Caples, the most important element in most advertisements is the headline.[15] David Ogilvy, who agrees with Caples, said, 'If you haven't done some selling in your headline, you have wasted 80 per cent of your client's money.' He supports this statement with the assertion, 'On the average five times as many people read the headline as the body copy.'[16] As Runyon points out, the headline 'should state a benefit, create interest, identify the brand, give information, or select the audience'.[17]

(a) Rough layout

Exhibit 8.4 *(continued)*

When your kids start asking for yogurt, there must be some sort of a mix-up.

Introducing New Dannon Sprinkl'Ins.

You're used to your kids asking for junk food, so imagine what a relief it will be when they ask for new Dannon Sprinkl'Ins. It's a unique real yogurt snack made with all the goodness and quality you expect from Dannon.

There are six custom kid flavors like strawberry, banana, cherry-vanilla and grape. And to make this yogurt even more irresistible, each comes with a pack of rainbow sprinkles that they can mix in any way they want.

It's no easy getting your kids to eat right, but at least now you can leave it to Dannon to find a way to get your kids to eat yogurt.

(b) Comprehensive layout

Exhibit 8.4   *(continued)*

(c) *Finished advertisement*

Illustrations. Illustrations are used to amplify the headline and in certain cases are the key element in the ad. The illustration should be designed to achieve any one or all four of these effects:

1 Attract attention of the target audience.
2 Communicate relevant product ideas or benefits.
3 Stimulate interest in the headline and body copy.
4 Express ideas or feelings that are difficult to express in words.[18]

A good way of determining the effectiveness of a photograph in an advertisement is to find out if it aroused the reader's curiosity.[19]

Body copy. Body copy is the text of the ad...the persuasive part of the message. It supports the headline, states the proof, provides the explanation.[20]

David Ogilvy offered these provisos:

- 'Don't beat around the bush − go straight to the point.'
- 'Avoid superlatives, generalizations, and platitudes.'
- 'Be specific and factual. Be enthusiastic, friendly, and memorable.'[21]

Length of copy. As for short or long copy, Ogilvy noted that the length depends on the product being advertised. With products like chewing gum there isn't much to tell; therefore, short copy is appropriate. However, if you are advertising a product with many qualities, such as a car, long copy is appropriate. Ogilvy's first Rolls-Royce and contained 719 words; his second, 1,400.[22] Jim Johnston added, 'People will read long copy. They won't read dull, confusing copy no matter how short.'[23]

Slogans. Slogans or theme lines can be found in print advertisements often at the bottom right side corner along with the advertiser's 'logo' (the signature or standard design for identifying the name or brand of the advertiser[24]). In television commercials the slogan normally appears as a 'super' (simultaneous overlapping of images from two cameras on one frame[25]) at the end along with the brand name and logo. In radio commercials, again placed at the end, the slogan is sometimes called a 'tag line'.[26]

The purpose of a slogan is to provide continuity in an advertising campaign, and through repetition it is supposed to achieve memorability among readers, viewers, and/or listeners. More important than memorability, the question for advertisers is: What meaning does it convey to customers and prospects? As Crosier points out...'claiming to be the favourite is no guarantee of success'. Of what possible communication value could these 'signature line superlatives' (slogans) have for an advertiser − 'Simply the best'...'The ultimate driving machine'?[27]

Keeping pace with Crosier's views (in Britain), Bob Garfield, writing in terms of the US experience, believes 'lightweight sloganeering (in the automotive field) is potentially dangerous'.[28] He does not believe the Chevrolet, 'a declining entry-level brand', is the *heartbeat of America*. He describes the Mercury slogan, 'nothing moves you like Mercury' as a 'boring and obvious play on words', and questions whether Nissan was really 'built for the human race'. Rather than going for what Crosier calls 'shallow and potentially self defeating', it is better to have a phrase at the end of the ad which realistically and believably communicates a benefit.

Client advice

Stavros Cosmopolus's advice is to beware of advertising agencies' presentations where 'the beauty of the layouts and storyboards exceeds the beauty of the ideas being presented...', where 'even the freckles on the redheaded boy are indicated'. Instead, as he points out, 'the idea should be king' where the message in the advertisement is focused on 'one single, salient point'. He relates, 'I've seen stick figures scribbled on wet lunchroom napkins so blurred you could barely discern what was represented. But an idea was there, and it had a life of its own. The words and pictures spring to life in your mind, stimulated and inspired by the basic strength and dynamism of the idea.... make the layouts rough and the ideas fancy.'[29]

Television storyboards

In the USA and other parts of the Western World, the television storyboard (see Exhibit 8.5) is used by the agency to show the client the manner in which the advertising strategy would be executed in television. A sequence of pictures or scenes, words, music, and sound effects are visualized and described in writing in the storyboard. Artists and writers join together to produce this work, sometimes in conjunction with people who are involved in casting (selecting) the individuals who will appear in the commercial and someone who is expert in creating music and/or sound effects. When a storyboard passes the screening process at the advertising agency it is then shown to the client. The presenter, usually a copywriter or art director, can add a flavour that is often not readily apparent by describing the action and information being imparted in each picture sequence (frame) of the storyboard. Note that the script for the storyboard shown in Exhibit 8.5 prepared by Grey Daiko Advertising Inc. for its client Procter & Gamble Far East Inc. is presented in both Japanese and English.

Television has an advantage over radio and print because the effects of sight, sound, and motion can all be employed to deliver an advertising message.

Exhibit 8.5 *Television storyboard. Reproduced by permission of Procter & Gamble Far East Inc. and Grey Daiko Advertising Inc.*

Client: Procter & Gamble Far East Inc.

Product: Bounce

Title: Twins

Timing: 30"

GREY DAIKO
ADVERTISING, INC.

Date: November 9, 1990

	VIDEO	ENGLISH AUDIO	JAPANESE
1.	Twins jumping into towel held by mother.	Singing: Wrap them up	Singing: つつんであげよう Tsutsunde ageyo
2.	Runner running into towel held by woman.	with more softness. Come on in Wrap them up	もっと柔らかく カモンイン つつんであげよう Motto yawarakaku Come on in. Tsutsunde ageyo
3.	CU of Bounce bottle revolving and label appearing.	with Bounce Softness.	バウンスの柔らかさ Bounce no yawarakasa
4.	CU of Twins enjoying soft towel and mother wrapping them up.	Come on in.	カモンイン Come on in.
5.	Bubble Demo. Super: Bounce (right) Other fabric softner (left)	NA: Bounce micro particles give more softness. Even a bubble doesn't burst.	NA: バウンスは ミクロ粒子だから もっと柔らか シャボン玉だって こわれない Bounce wa micro ryushi dakara motto yawaraka shabondama datte kowarenai

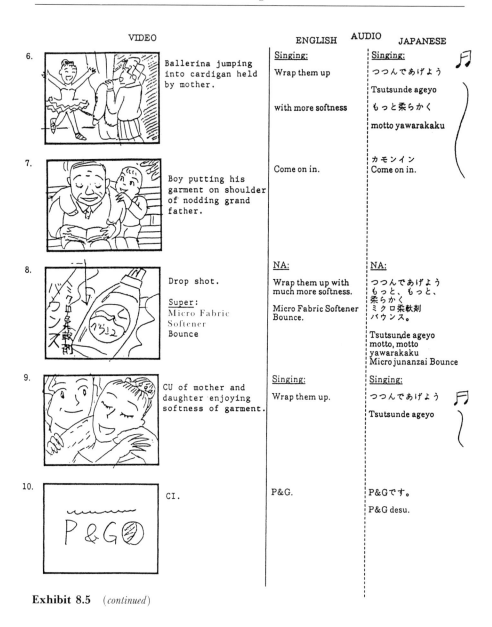

Exhibit 8.5 (*continued*)

The relatively high cost to produce and air a television commercial and/or the characteristics of the audience sought may preclude the use of television in many advertisers' media plans. In the USA the cost of a television commercial can run from $25,000 to a half a million dollars or more, depending on the situation and production values desired. (Media costs will be discussed in Chapter 10.)

Key factors to be considered in reviewing a storyboard include:

* the attention-getting device
* the drama, suspense, or humour
* the claim and its proof
* the story line, introduction to close
* the words, characters, setting
* the choice of voices, sounds, music
* the way the product appears

Other considerations prior to actual production are choice of the person or people to be cast in the commercial and their dress. If a testimonial type commercial, will a celebrity or ordinary person be chosen. The appropriate setting (room, porch, outdoor location) and objects (chairs, tables, drapes, place settings, for example, if indoors) must be selected.

In many countries legal approval of the storyboard will be required from company, agency, and television network(s) prior to production. In the USA it is customary to obtain legal clearance from both advertising agency and advertiser attorneys with respect to the claims being made in the commercial; the evidence offered to support the claim(s), such as a clinical test for a health claim, as well as the appropriateness of the message and the manner in which it is to be presented. In the USA the television networks have their own legal clearance procedures for approving messages before they are aired. Under these circumstances it would be unwise to produce a commercial before obtaining the necessary clearance(s).

Producing the commercial

In the USA and in other countries there are normally three parties involved in the development and production of the television commercial: the advertiser, the agency, and the production house. In the USA it is customary for the agency to obtain bids from several production houses after the storyboard has been agreed on. The low bidder usually gets the job unless another house has a particular talent which is needed in producing the commercial, e.g. special expertise in working with food products. During the production, the agency executive (producer) retains final authority over the production house and is responsible to the client for the finished product. In contrast, in Japan, a director of the production company is normally in charge of the project and has authority over the agency director.[30]

Radio commercials

Unlike television or print, radio commercials rely on sound to convey the message. Mental pictures, however, can be induced by the creative use of sound, either by the use of a particular voice to convey mystery, intrigue, or suspense...or by music and special sound effects. In the latter case, for example, the echo of footsteps was used to conjure up the illusion of walking through Victoria Station for Victorian Station Restaurants.

Radio commercial length normally varies from ten seconds to one minute. One of the critical factors is the number of words which can be communicated effectively in the given time span. For example, in a thirty-second commercial the average number of words which can be spoken in English is sixty-five.[31] The number of words spoken will vary depending on the language used. Whatever language, it is a good idea to read the commercial aloud in the manner in which it would be recorded for broadcast purposes while timing its length. Formats for commercials include any one or a combination of the following: jingle; narrative, which tells a story in monologue or dialogue form; personality using a well-known presenter; or straight delivery made by a radio announcer.[32] See Exhibit 8.6 as an example of how a radio commercial is written for presentation to the client and for reading (live) on air or for recording in a studio.

Whether writing or evaluating the work of someone else, these points and questions should be of value:

1 *Adherence to the strategy* Does the script contain the essential elements of the preagreed creative strategy?
2 *Simplicity* Will the listener be able to grasp the principal idea?
3 *Attention* Is a dramatic device or provocative statement used to get the attention of the listener at the start of the commercial?
4 *Communication language* Are familiar words, action verbs, short sentences, and easily understood references embodied in the message?
5 *Mood and tone* Is music and/or are sounds and voices introduced to enhance the message, stimulate emotions, induce mental pictures?
6 *Memorability* What techniques are used to aid memorability? (A catchy jingle, toe-tapping music, and repetition of brand name and principal benefit are proven techniques.)[33]

Out-of-home advertising

There are many forms of advertising which can be grouped under the heading of 'out-of-home'. The most common forms are posters which are pre-printed

Exhibit 8.6   *Radio commercial script. Reproduced by permission of AT&T. © AT&T 1992*

<u>**AT&T**</u>
<u>**'Partners in Business'**</u>
<u>**'Heard Around The World'**</u>
<u>**AXCIR 263**</u>
<u>**As of June 17, 1992**</u>

<u>**SFX:**</u>	Phone rings. 'Moshi, Moshi'
<u>**SFX:**</u>	Phone rings, 'Allo, ahhh bonjour'
<u>**SFX:**</u>	Phone rings, 'Bueno'
<u>**ANNCR:**</u>	At AT&T, we know some small businesses need to be heard around the world.
	But, we also know one calling plan simply can't fit all their needs internationally.
	That's why we've created the 'AT&T Partners in Business' International Programme. A range of AT&T savings plans specially designed for small businesses.
	Like an option that saves you money even if you only make a few short calls and faxes a month.
	Another option that gives you volume discounts to over 200 countries and extra savings to the country of your choice.
	And even a flexible savings option for companies whose needs change every month.
	So if your business needs to be heard around the world...
<u>**SFX:**</u>	Phone rings, Australian person answers - 'Allo'
<u>**ANNCR:**</u>	Here's something you should hear: 1 800 222−0900.
	Call us and find out how much 'AT&T Partners in Business' International can save you.
<u>**TAG:**</u>	**A World of Help from AT&T.**

sheets assembled in different sizes found in various high traffic locations. Sometimes a special sign with lights and/or motion devices is prepared for particular locations such as Piccadilly Circus, London, or Times Square, New York. In addition to being found at busy intersections, these signs are spotted along major arteries and highways, local laws permitting, see Exhibit 8.7. Other locations include bus and train stations, bus exteriors and interiors, and interiors of trains. Aerial banner-towing, sky-writing, blimps and balloons are other forms of outdoor advertising.[34]

Creatively, several overriding considerations should be taken into account including:

Exhibit 8.7 Out-of-home advertising for Calistoga Country Orchards. Reproduced by permission of Great Waters of France, Greenwich, CT, USA and its advertising agency, Atlas, Citron, Haligmant and Bedecarre

- start with a single idea
- proceed with a single expression of that idea
- concludes with a simple, dramatic, easily visible expression
- words, pictures, and layout should each contribute without overlapping
- lettering should be clear, simple, and bold[35]

Visibility is the key, particularly when the audience may pass a poster at a distance anywhere from 100 to 400 feet (30 to 122 metres). Test the poster design and message by drawing a four by nine inch (ten by twenty-three centimetres) sketch and view it from two to four feet (0.6 to 1.2 metres).[36]

Evaluating message effectiveness

David Ogilvy advises that research monies should be spent before the advertising is written (as well as after).[37] Research of this nature involves the techniques discussed in Chapter 4 to define the target market(s) and audience(s) to be reached in terms of their socioeconomic and psychological characteristics (Chapters 5 and 6), and to confirm the appropriateness of the creative strategy including the key promise or benefit to be conveyed (Chapter 7).

Preliminary message testing

In the process of finalizing the advertising message, headlines, illustrations, and complete messages can be tested by using focus groups or personal interviews. Communication tests of this type are considered to be small scale and qualitative in nature. People selected for these tests should be representative of the target audience for the message in question. Subjects for focus groups are normally recruited and pre-screened by telephone. Those with the right qualifications are invited to participate and given a gift or stipend for their cooperation. Personal interviews are commonly undertaken in a central location such as a shopping centre.

When various elements of an advertisement such as a headline, illustration, or slogan are tested, as many as five or six different alternatives can be evaluated at the same time. Opinions of the different alternatives are sought and ranked in terms of strength of appeal and importance.

Testing for television

In the case of television commercials, tests can be conducted on a commercial before it goes into final production by taping or filming the individual frames of a storyboard as they are passed beneath a camera in a fixed position to simulate motion. After completion of the visual sequencing of the message, voice-over can be recorded to match the visual action. Simulation of the commercial in this manner will cost only a fraction of a finished product. This preliminary result can be shown to individuals or a group in a central location. Afterwards, the viewers can be asked questions such as:

- What went on?
- What was said?
- What was the main point of the commercial?
- What, if anything, was hard to understand?
- What was liked and disliked?
- What was the name of the product being advertised?

Results of this type of testing will either strengthen the advertiser's conviction that the commercial has the communication values sought, or lead to changes and improvements.

Some drawbacks have been cited for preliminary message testing. Showing advertisements that have not been produced in final form may not include important details and thereby reduce communication effectiveness. Subjects being interviewed may not represent the real target market. Because of the artificial environment, the results may be inaccurate.[38]

Testing for print

When two different approaches are believed to have equal merit by those responsible for creating the advertising, a 'split-run' print testing technique can be used to determine their relative strength. This technique can be used to test alternate headlines, illustrations, and slogans. This is possible only where a newspaper or magazine to be used in the advertiser's media schedule can provide an 'A-B' split. Advertisements, using, for example, two different headlines, are produced. In all other respects, the advertisements are identical. The printing presses are then set to produce version 'A' in every other paper (magazine) coming off the press; the alternate paper carries version 'B'. All advertisements carry the same offer to induce reader response but are coded differently so that it can be determined how many responses each version produced. In that way, the relative strengths of the two headlines, or illustrations, or slogans can be measured. This technique can be used equally as well in testing alternate elements in a mail campaign.

Testing the finished product

A number of techniques exist for testing advertising messages once they have been produced. Among the most commonly used techniques are awareness, recognition, recall, attitude, and behavioural testing.

Awareness testing
This form of testing is designed to measure the effectiveness of an advertising campaign after it has begun and is in progress. Brand awareness is of crucial importance during the early stages of a new product launch. Tracking studies are undertaken to measure the level of brand awareness and month-to-month changes after the introduction. In other instances, advertisers are interested in determining levels of brand awareness versus competition on an annual basis. Yearly studies of this type are of particular interest to marketers of seasonal products like suntan lotion. Each year's marketing programme is like a new product launch.

Telephone surveys (if telephones are available) are common during test market programmes and new product launches because of the need to obtain feedback as quickly as possible in order to find out if the advertising is producing the intended levels of awareness. Personal interviews are used when not only awareness but other types of information is sought. In conducting these surveys, it is necessary to qualify the respondent at the outset to make sure that he/she is in the target market. For awareness, the first question may be of an unaided nature. For example, what brands of beer can you name? This may then be followed by a probe: Can you think of any others? On completion of this first portion, the questions become aided. That is, subjects are shown a list of brands and asked which ones they recognize. With some product categories the unaided recall may be so low that only aided questions are asked.[39]

For short-term tracking purposes, awareness studies are frequently conducted by phone. Under these circumstances little additional information may be collected other than classification data (age, education, occupation, family status, etc.). At other times, to keep in touch with the market for a particular type of product, advertisers may conduct in-depth studies periodically of which awareness studies are just one part. Product attributes and respondents' attitudes, opinions, and preferences may also be questioned. Typical awareness and advertising recall questions are shown in Exhibit 8.8.

Recognition testing*
A technique for evaluating magazine and newspaper advertisements which

---

* This section was written with the help of Laura Pezzi, Starch INRA Hooper Inc., Mamaroneck, New York, January 1992.

Exhibit 8.8 *Brand and advertising awareness: unaided and aided questions*

1 When you think of toothpaste, what is the first brand that comes to mind?
2 Please tell me all the other brands of toothpaste you have heard of. Any others?
3 Within the past six months, have you seen or heard any advertising for toothpaste?
4 Here is a list of different brands of toothpaste. (Hand list to the respondent.) Please read this list and tell me which brands you have heard of including those you may have already mentioned.
5 Do you recall seeing or hearing any advertising for each brand not mentioned in Question 3?
6 Where did you see or hear the advertising for each brand mentioned?
7 For each brand you saw or heard advertising for (ask separately) please tell me everything that you remember. What else did you remember seeing or hearing?

has been used for many years is the Starch Readership Service. Face-to-face interviews are conducted among a minimum of 100 respondents who have previously glanced through or read the specific study issue of a particular publication. After verifying this fact, interviewers go through the publication page-by-page with the respondent to find out which advertisements they remembered having seen in the issue being studied (noted score), the percentage who remembered seeing some part of the ad which clearly indicated the brand or advertiser (associated score) and the percentage who read half or more of the material in the ad (read most score). Exhibit 8.9 shows an advertisement with Starch scores.

The Starch Readership Service has been designed to be both inexpensive and reliable for use on a continuing basis. Therefore, it is possible to accumulate, study and analyse a large mass of readership data. The value of Starch data expands considerably when used over a period of time to track advertising performance.

Comparison is the key to using Starch Readership data effectively. More specifically, Readership Reports allow you to:

1 Compare current advertisements against those of competitors.
2 Compare the current campaign against previous campaigns.
3 Compare the current campaign against a competitor's previous campaign.
4 Compare current advertisements and campaigns against Starch Adnorms.

It is especially important to compare advertisements with identical or at least similar product interest levels. Starch strongly suggests that users average the figures for several insertions rather than use the scores for single advertisements.

Exhibit 8.9 *Magazine advertisement with Starch noted, associated and read most scores. Reproduced by permission of Fisher-Price and Starch INRA Hooper Inc.*

Recall testing

Recall tests have been devised for both television and print (press). The Burke Day-After Recall Test for television commercials is an unaided measurement technique which has been in use for many years. After a commercial has been produced, air time is purchased and the commercial is run in or adjacent to the type of programming that is consistent with the media plan for the product or service being advertised. The next day interviewers call a sample of consumers to first establish that they have been watching television on the channel and in the time segment in which the commercial was aired. Then these viewers are asked various questions about the commercials they recall seeing. The key determination is whether or not the respondents can identify the test commercial and relate it to the brand being advertised. This finding, expressed as a percentage, is compared with any and all prior commercials of the same brand and the same product category which have been tested in the same fashion. This comparison gives an indication of the relative strength of the commercial under investigation.

To reduce the cost of finding people who viewed the fifteen minute segment in which the test commercial ran, a theatre viewing technique can be used. Respondents are invited to view some form of entertainment in which the commercial is shown. Subsequently, respondents are telephoned to determine recall.

About one in five can remember something about a commercial the day after it is aired.[40]

Recall measurement for print, as devised by Gallup and Robinson, involves a process that conceptually is much the same as the television testing of Burke. A sample of 150 subjects located in different parts of the USA who regularly read the magazine in which the test advertisement will appear are identified. After giving these subjects a day to read the publication, they are contacted by phone for recall, brand name registration, and comprehension of the message being communicated. A specific, identifiable feature of the advertisement must be recalled and related to the brand in question in order for the response to count.[41]

Recognition and recall measurements have not been correlated with sales; however, as Ogilvy and Raphaelson pointed out, '. . . it is reasonable to assume that an ad that people notice is more effective than one they pass by, that it is better if an ad is read thoroughly than if it is only glanced at, and that it is better still if readers can remember some of what they read.'[42]

The first three types of tests — awareness, recognition, and recall — are associated with learning. If consumers indicate they are aware of a product (brand) or service, demonstrate interest by associating the offering with advertising for it, acquire information about it by reading, and can remember the principal benefit, they are more apt to become tryers and buyers.

Attitude and preference testing

Attitude and preference tests are associated with feelings. The former type of test is usually conducted by personal interview. 'Attitude measurement', according to Nylen, 'relies heavily on the use of rating scales', which he explains, 'is a device by which respondents can select one of several alternative answers and indicate how strongly they feel about the answer'.[43] Scales frequently used are of an agreement—disagreement or important—unimportant nature. For example, an attribute of crunchiness may be significant for a breakfast cereal. The rating scale to measure the importance of crunchiness might appear as follows:

	Very important	Fairly important	Not very important	Not important at all
The cereal you like to eat the most has a crunchy texture	[ ]	[ ]	[ ]	[ ]

Attitude profiles can be developed to measure consumers' feelings towards products and companies.[44] Take for example the brand image profiles of two beers. In this hypothetical example there are six bipolar attitude or semantic differential rating scales. Respondents were asked to choose one of seven points on the rating scales between one of the descriptors. As shown in Exhibit 8.10, the mean rating for each of the descriptors is then plotted to established an image profile of the two brands of beer.

Exhibit 8.10   *Brand image profiles for three brands of beer*

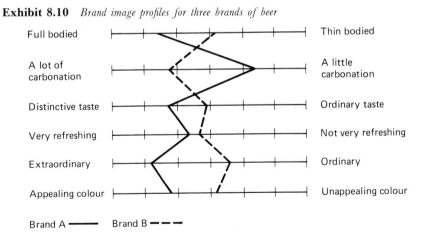

Brand A ———   Brand B — — —

In preference tests, a form of attitude change testing, purchase intentions are compared before and after exposure to the advertisement. This form of testing, pioneered by Horace Schwerin, involves subjects who are invited to a theatre, ostensibly to view a new television show. Before the show begins, subjects are asked about their preferences for various products. (They are also asked questions about their socioeconomic status for classification purposes.) In the case of the Schwerin test, they receive a shopping list of products and are asked how they would allocate a given amount of money for purchase of the products on the list. Then the show is presented. In it, one or more test commercials are screened. When the show is over, the subjects are again asked to allocate the same amount of money among the same list of products. Other questions are asked also about what they remember seeing or hearing in the commercials. However, the key measure is the pre-post gain (or loss) in the monies allocated to the test commercial product. This gain or loss is compared with prior commercials tested for the same product and also for all other brands in the same category. The pre-post gain in expenditures, expressed as a percentage of the total expenditures, is considered to be an indicator of the strength of the commercial in influencing brand preference.

Behaviour testing

This technique is a measure of 'doing', and involves the inclusion of some offer in the advertisement. The offer can be an informative booklet, a price-off coupon, some other incentive, or the product itself. The technique is essentially the same as the split-run technique. It is the basic manner in which direct response advertising is tested in mail or print campaigns. The test can be either monadic or comparative. If the former, the results can be compared against previously established norms for offers of the type being evaluated. If the latter, when testing two different mail messages, the samples can be drawn from the same mailing list. For print, when testing alternate executions at the same time, care must be taken in trying to match up the vehicles as closely as possible.

Research as an aid in message making

None of the testing techniques discussed in this section are foolproof. It is a virtual impossibility to hold all other variables constant than the two being tested. There may be biased responses, exaggerated readership claims, difficulty in interpretation, influences of uncontrollable factors, unnatural or forced conditions, and inappropriate selection of respondents for questioning.[45] However, all reasonable attempts to learn more about the impact of advertising messages on target audiences is a worthy endeavour for all parties involved in the marketing communication process.

The major research findings accumulated over time on the positive and negative executional factors has changed little according to Ogilvy and Raphaelson.[46] As they explained, brand preference change has been established as an indicator of purchase behaviour, and the following techniques have scored above average in their ability to change preference:

- problem solution
- humour (when pertinent to the selling situation)
- relevant characters (personalities, developed by the advertising, who become associated with the brand)
- slice-of-life (enactments in which a doubter is converted)
- news (new products, new uses, new ideas, new information)
- candid-camera testimonials and
- demonstrations

While use of celebrities scored above average (plus twenty-two) on twenty-four-hour recall tests, they were ranked below average (minus twenty-one) on changing brand preference. It could be that the message focused on the celebrity rather than the product!

Among television techniques that scored below average were these:

- cartoons and animation for adult commercials
- 'very short scenes and many changes of situations'
- 'commercials that don't show the package or end without the brand name'.

Even though print advertising measurement techniques, as explained earlier, haven't been correlated with sales results, it has been found that:

- print ads with news score above average
- 'story appeal' in illustrations attract above average attention
- 'before-and-after illustrations score above average'
- illustrations showing product in use and the result of having used the product are effective
- headlines with thirteen or more words work better than short ones
- high scores are achieved with headlines that quote somebody

The techniques discussed that have been identified as having had better than average effectiveness apply primarily to advertising based on a rational appeal. In setting forth these guidelines, it was not the intention of Ogilvy and Raphaelson to attempt to reduce the creative process to a set of rules; instead to attempt to aid creative people in avoiding pitfalls and enhancing message effectiveness by sharing their insights based on research findings over time.

Summary

There is much to be learned by studying the techniques successful creative people have used in the past. Even though advertising in the USA has drawn considerable criticism from experts in other parts of the world, a lot of good work continues to be produced. It is no secret, however, that creative products being developed in other countries rival if not surpass work produced in the USA. Advertising is a global art form, though the techniques will vary to fill the needs of different environments. For aspiring managers of advertising and marketing communications it is important to know the basic elements of the various forms of advertising − press, television, etc. − and the means by which they are created. It is also important to become familiar with the process by which advertisers and their agencies interact to progress from advertising concept to finished product, and with the methods by which messages can be tested both in preliminary and finished form.

Questions

1   What is a USP? Give an example not already given in the text.
2   What was Bernbach's approach? How did it differ from Ogilvy's and Burnett's?
3   Discuss the criticisms of US advertising. What are the explanations.
4   What is attributed for differences in creative output?
5   What are the similarities and differences in the advertising message in Asia, Europe, USA?
6   Give four suggestions on how to create compelling advertising.
7   What is image? Give an example.
8   Describe the people and organizations involved and the process by which advertising goes from an idea through to a finished product.
9   Describe the principal elements of a print advertisement and the purpose of each.
10 What are the key factors, before and after, to be considered in a television storyboard?
11 What factors should be taken into account in evaluating a radio advertising script?
12 Give pointers on how to create an outdoor advertisement.
13 Describe a process for preliminary testing of print and television advertisements.
14 Briefly explain awareness, recognition, recall, attitude and preference and behaviour testing.

Notes

1 Runyon, Kenneth E. (1984) *Advertising*, 2nd edn, Charles E. Merrill Publishing Company, Columbus, Ohio, pp. 276–285.
2 *Ibid.*, p. 277.
3 *Ibid.*, p. 283.
4 Bernbach, William (1977) Videotaped interview with John Crichton, American Association of Advertising Agencies.
5 Goudard, Jean Michel. President of Roux Sequela Cayzac & Goudard (1985) Presentation to the New York Chapter of the International Advertising Association, New York, 13 September, as reported by *Advertising World*, Oct/Nov, 28.
6 Walt, Vivienne (1983) British adman, Frank Lowe, crafting a creative take over. *The New York Times*, 27 November, F6.
7 Day, Barry (1988) A presentation to the New York Chapter of the International Advertising Association, New York, 18 February.
8 *Goudard, op. cit.*
9 *Wall Street Journal* (1989) Phenomenal Phil. An Advertisement, Dow Jones Company, Inc., New York.
10 Slootweg, Wim (1985) The demise of hard sell − learning from Europe's mistakes. *International Advertising & Media*, 15–28 February, (67), 1, 14.
11 Wagenaar, Jan Dirk (1980) Advertising in Japan. Reprint of an article appearing in *Advertising Age/Europe*, in *Marketing Trends, An International Review*, A.C. Nielsen Company, N. 2, 4–5.
12 Roddy, John (1982) Address on advertising and marketing to Southeast Asia delivered to the New York chapter of the International Advertising Association, 8 June.
13 *Wall Street Journal* (1989) Creative leaders 1977–1987, a composite of the campaign.
14 Rosenshine, Allen (1985) The image of images. Presentation made at a Seminar, Mexico City, 15 November.
15 Caples, John (1975) Fifty things I have learned in fifty years in advertising. *Advertising Age*, 22 September, 48.
16 Ogilvy, David (1964) *Confessions of an Advertising Man*, Atheneum, New York, p. 104.
17 Runyon, *op. cit.*, 329.
18 Runyon, *op. cit.*, 337–341.
19 Ogilvy, *op. cit.*, 116.
20 Wells, William, Burnett, John and Moriarty, Sandra (1989) *Advertising*, Prentice-Hall, Englewood Cliffs, NJ, p. 354.
21 Ogilvy, *op. cit.*, 108.
22 *Ibid.*, 108–109.

23   Johnston, Jim (1986) Creative leaders. *Wall Street Journal*, March.
24   Mandell, Maurice I. (1984) *Advertising*, 4th edn, Prentice-Hall Inc., Englewood Cliffs, NJ, p. 675.
25   Dunn, S. Watson and Barban, Arnold M. (1986) *Advertising*, 6th edn, The Dryden Press, Chicago, p. 793.
26   Mandell, *op. cit.*, 450.
27   Crosier, Keith (1982) A new strategy for advertising to over communicated target audiences. *The Quarterly Review of Marketing*, Summer, 13.
28   Garfield, Bob (1990) Engaging in safe slogans. *Advertising Age*, 22, January 5–14.
29   Cosmopolus, Stavros (1985) *Make the Layouts Rough and the Ideas Fancy*, 3rd edn, Cosmopolus, Crowley, and Daly, Inc., Boston.
30   Wagenaar, *op. cit.*, 5.
31   Runyon, *op. cit.*, 405.
32   *Ibid.*, *op. cit.*, 401–3.
33   *Ibid.*, *op. cit.*, 405–6.
34   Wilmshurst, John (1985) *The Fundamentals of Advertising*, Heinemann, London, p. 169.
35   Malickson, David L. and Mason, John W. (1977) *Advertising – How to Write the Kind that Works*, Charles Scribner's Sons, New York, p. 137.
36   Berkman, Harold and Gilson, Christopher (1987) *Advertising*, 2nd edn, Random House, New York, pp. 310–11.
37   Ogilvy, *op. cit*, 105.
38   Wells, *op. cit.*, 157–158.
39   Nylen, David (1986) *Advertising*, 3rd edn, Southwestern Publishing Co., Cincinnati, pp. 601, 602.
40   Wells, *op. cit.*, 514.
41   Nylen, *op. cit.*, 600.
42   Ogilvy, David, and Raphaelson, Joel (1982) Research on Ad Techniques that Work – and Don't Work. *Marketing News*, 17 September, 1982 Section 2, 2.
43   Nylen, *op. cit.*, 605.
44   *Ibid.*, *op. cit.*
45   Nylen, *op. cit.*, 593–612.
46   Ogilvy and Raphaelson, *op. cit.*, 2.

Part Four *Conventional Mass and Mail Media for International Marketing Communications*

The existence, use, and effectiveness of non-personal media options, of which there are many forms, will vary from country to country. To treat this subject material, Part Four is organized and presented in four chapters. The first three (Chapters 9, 10 and 11) cover print, out-of-home, yellow pages, broadcast and mail media. The final chapter (Chapter 12) treats the means by which these media are planned, purchased and evaluated.

By way of introduction, the distribution of advertising expenditures among the principal mass media in selected countries will be shown. First, it should be understood that it is not a simple matter to make precise media expenditure comparisons among countries because of differences in classification. The Starch INRA Hooper Inc. Worldwide Advertising Expenditure Surveys[1] do not distinguish between newspapers and magazines. In some in-country surveys the same situation exists: newspaper and magazine expenditures are combined under 'press'. As mentioned in the introduction to Part Three, television, newspapers, magazines, and radio are classified in Japan as 'major media'. Outdoor, transit, and movies along with direct mail, flyers, POP, telephone directories, and exhibitions/screen displays are classified under 'sales promotion'.[2] In the USA and Europe, outdoor, transit, and cinema are treated as mass media. Flyers, POP, and exhibitions/screen displays would be classified under sales promotion.

Media expenditures vary

Since media availability and relative importance will not be the same in all countries, plans may require adjustment in cross-border campaigns. By examining media expenditures in a number of countries in various regions of the world the differences will become apparent. Table 1 shows total media expenditures and the relative importance of mass media alternatives in twenty countries in the Americas, Europe, and the Asia/Pacific region.

In the twenty countries listed in Table 1:

- The number one media ranking goes to newspapers in fourteen countries and to television in six.
- The number two ranking goes to television and magazines in seven countries, to newspapers in five countries each, and to radio in one country.
- The number three ranking goes to magazines in seven, television in six, radio in four and outdoor in three countries.

Table 1 *Distribution of advertising expenditures — twenty country analysis (numbers in parentheses indicate rank within country*

	1990 Total ($ Millions)	Newspapers %	Magazines %	TV %	Radio %	Cinema %	Outdoor %
Europe							
France	9,322	(1) 29	(2) 27	(3) 25	(5) 7	(6) 0.1	(4) 12
Germany	13,321	(1) 49	(2) 30	(3) 13	(4) 4	(6) 1.0	(5) 3
Italy	7,252	(2) 22	(3) 22	(1) 46	(5) 3	(6) 0.2	(4) 6
Netherlands	2,555	(1) 53	(2) 24	(3) 13	(5) 2	(6) 0.3	(4) 7
Spain	7,630	(1) 38	(3) 16	(2) 32	(4) 10	(6) 0.7	(5) 3
United Kingdom	14,069	(1) 40	(3) 24	(2) 30	(5) 2	(6) 0.5	(4) 4
Denmark	1,076	(1) 62	(2) 21	(3) 13	(5) 1	(6) 0.8	(4) 2
Finland	1,253	(1) 68	(3) 11	(2) 14	(4) 6	(6) 0.1	(5) 3
Norway	776	(1) 78	(2) 16	(3) 2	(5) 1	(6) 1.2	(4) 2
Sweden	1,998	(1) 78	(2) 15	(4) 2	0	(5) 0.6	(3) 4
Asia/Pacific							
South Korea	2,897	(1) 42	(3) 6	(2) 29	(4) 5	*	*
Japan	29,014	(2) 32	(4) 9	(1) 38	(5) 6	NA	(3) 15
Australia	3,848	(1) 41	(4) 8	(2) 35	(3) 9	(6) 1.6	(5) 6
Taiwan	1,871	(1) 40	(4) 7	(2) 32	(3) 5	NA	NA
The Americas							
Canada	6,516	(1) 38	(2) 21	(3) 21	(4) 11	NA	(5) 10
United States	82,935	(1) 40	(3) 12	(2) 36	(4) 11	NA	(5) 2
Colombia	518	(3) 15	(4) 5	(1) 55	(2) 17	(6) 3.0	(5) 5
Chile	240	(2) 35	(4) 7	(1) 44	(3) 11	(6) 0.2	(5) 3
Mexico	1,031	(4) 9	(5) 4	(1) 67	(2) 15	(6) 1.0	(3) 4
Venezuela	441	(2) 28	(3) 3	(1) 62	(4) 2	(6) 1.8	(5) 3

NA = figures not available
* 19 per cent of total media expenditure is classified as 'other'. Amount spent on cinema is reported as 0.0 per cent; outdoor expenditures are not available.
Note: percentages may not equal 100 per cent due to rounding.
Source: Saatchi & Saatchi Advertising, Expenditure Forecasts December, 1991.

Overall, newspapers tend to dominate the media scene in terms of advertising expenditures in all regions except Latin America. Magazines earn the highest rankings in Europe, notably France and Germany. Television outranks all other media in Italy, Japan, and Latin American countries listed. Radio has special importance in the USA, Spain, Australia, New Zealand, and most Latin American countries. This is true for outdoor in France, Japan and Canada.

From the distribution of advertising expenditure analysis it is clear that wide variations exist among countries. The exception might be Latin America where the greatest similarity exists in advertising expenditures among the nations listed. A note of caution is also in order. Because the sources of information vary from country to country the degree of precision can also vary.

National versus local advertising expenditures

What Table 1 does not show is the relative importance of local versus national advertising...and what effect this might have on the proportions spent on different types of media. Take, for example, the situation in the USA as revealed in Table 2.

Newspapers dominate the local scene, 60 per cent of which is display advertising and 40 per cent is classified.[3] Local newspaper display advertising comes from various types of retailers. Though not to the same degree as newspapers, radio is considerably more important as a local medium. Nationally, television dominates. This is divided approximately 55 per cent for network purchases and 45 per cent for local (spot) purchases by national (or regional) advertisers.[4] Magazines are not broken out separately; however, it is believed that the major portion of these expenditures would be classified as 'national'.

Table 2 *National versus local advertising expenditures in the USA*

| | | | *1989 — $ billions* | | | |
Medium	Local	% of Total	National	% of Total	Combined	Total
Newspapers	$28.6	66.1	$ 3.7	14.6	$32.4	41.3
Magazines	(Not reported)				9.7	12.4
Television	7.9	18.2	19.0	75.1	26.9	34.3
Radio	6.3	14.5	2.0	7.9	8.3	10.6
Outdoor	.5	1.2	.6	2.4	1.1	1.4
Total	$43.3	100.0	$25.3	100.0	$78.4	100.0

Source: Coen, Robert J. (1990) Estimated annual US advertising expenditures 1980–1989. Prepared for *Advertising Age*, McCann-Erickson, Inc., New York.

The impact of television

Another factor to consider when studying the relationship among the principal media alternatives is the change in relative importance after television advertising first began. Again, using US figures, Table 3 shows the changes in ten-year intervals since television advertising expenditures were first recorded in 1949.

Table 3   *Per cent of advertising expenditures by medium in the USA*

Medium	1949	1959	1969	1979	1989
Newspapers	55.7%	47.9%	44.2%	42.7%	41.3%
Magazines	22.2	19.9	16.7	14.2	12.4
Television	1.7	20.7	27.8	31.2	34.3
Radio	16.6	8.9	9.7	10.2	10.6
Outdoor	3.8	2.6	1.6	1.7	1.4
	100.0%	100.0%	100.0%	100.0%	100.0%

Source: Percentages in this table were derived from Coen, Robert J. (1990) Estimated annual US advertising expenditures 1949−1989. Prepared for *Advertising Age*.

Television's share of advertising expenditures took a big leap between its initial use as an advertising medium in 1949 and 1959 when it captured more than 20 per cent of total advertising dollars. Since then television has steadily risen in importance, accounting for more than one-third of total expenditures in 1989. Newspapers suffered a major loss in advertising revenues over the first ten years of television advertising. Newspapers' loss in revenues have been more gradual since then. Magazines have lost share of advertising revenues steadily over the past forty years. Radio, however, presents an atypical picture. After suffering a major share loss between 1949 and 1959, it has actually gained share over each decade since then. Outdoor and transit advertising losses over the forty-year period may be more attributed to environmental constraints (such as scenic pollution) placed on the medium than to the inroads of television advertising.

Unlike the US experience, the growth of television and advertising in the medium has been constrained in many countries of the world. This can be observed by referring back to Table 1 and examining the relative importance of television in different European countries where culture and government regulations have inhibited the growth of television and its use as an advertising medium. In other countries of the world, such as in Eastern Europe and China, the constraint can be attributed to economic as well as other factors.

The media situation, however, in the regions and country just mentioned and elsewhere is by no means stable. Cable and satellite TV transmission and changes in regulatory policies have resulted, and are resulting, in the increased availability of television advertising time.

Attention will now be focused on a closer inspection of the major media alternatives in Chapters 9, 10 and 11. This is followed by an examination of media planning and evaluating systems in Chapter 12.

Notes

1 Starch Inra Hooper, Inc. (1990) Worldwide Advertising Expenditure Surveys.
2 Publications Department (1989) *Dentsu Japan Marketing/Advertising Yearbook 1990*, Dentsu Inc., Tokyo, 133.
3 Coen, Robert J. (1990) *Insider's Report*, McCann-Erickson, New York, June, (21), 2.
4 Coen, Robert J. (1990) Estimated annual US advertising expenditures, 1980–1989. Derived from the 1989 figures in this report prepared for *Advertising Age*.

9 *Newspapers, magazines, out-of-home, and yellow pages*

Introduction

This chapter is designed to equip the reader with a general knowledge of what to expect when considering the use of newspapers, magazines, out-of-home, and yellow pages in an advertising campaign in various countries of the world. The first two alternatives are the more widely used vehicles as revealed in the advertising expenditure summary found in Part Four introduction. Together these vehicles will be referred to as 'print'. However, in some English speaking countries, notably the UK, the more frequently used term is 'press'. When considering out-of-home and yellow pages, each has its special characteristics for application in an advertising campaign.

Newspapers

While newspapers are the most important medium in terms of monies spent on advertising in many countries of the world, their characteristics are by no means uniform. The differences can be demonstrated in several ways.

To begin with, considerable differences exist in the number of copies of daily newspapers sold for every 1,000 inhabitants in countries in Europe, the Middle East, North America, and the Far East. These differences are shown in Table 9.1.

Also shown are the percentages of the populations fifteen years and older who are considered literate. These figures, if accurate, demonstrate that reasons other than the ability to read and write must be sought to explain the variance. One could be level of education. Another could be the need of a particular society to be up-to-date on issues and events of the day, local, national, and international.

Readership

Differences in reading habits is also a factor. The figures in Table 9.2 show what a wide discrepancy exists in readership in six different European countries.

Weekly readership ranges from a high of 92 per cent in West Germany to a low of 22 per cent in Portugal.

Table 9.1 *Sales of newspapers and literacy rate*

Country	Copies sold per[a] 1,000 inhabitants	Per cent literacy[b] 15 years and up
Japan	526	99
Britain	443	99
Switzerland	391	99
Federal Republic of Germany	339	99
Austria	308	98
Netherlands	306	99
USA	284	99
Belgium	218	99
Canada	216	99
France	121	99
Israel	153	95
Italy	118	97

a   Axel Springer Verlag AG (1982) *Europaische Werbemarket Deutschland*, Berlin, August, Table 56.

b   Sivard, Ruth L. (1987) *World Military and Social Expenditures 1987–88*, 12th edn, World Priorities, Washington, DC, pp. 46, 48.

Table 9.2 *Who reads a newspaper?*

Country	All Adults Weekly (%)
West Germany	92
UK	90
Italy	67
France	58
Spain	38
Portugal	22

Source: TBWA World Media (1989) *A Review of the European Media Scene*, London, 15 February.

Uniform readership among men and women should not be taken for granted. For example, in Mexico, 48 per cent of males eighteen years and older read a newspaper yesterday. The same statistic for women was 35 per cent.[1] As for reading of individual publications, the leading newspaper in the Netherlands claims that its paper is read in one in five households.[2] In Portugal, it would be unusual for a newspaper to claim readership among more than 3 per cent of the population.[3]

Scope of distribution

With respect to the distribution of newspaper copies, in some countries national distribution predominates. For example, in the UK, there are twelve national dailies. The two largest, *The Sun* and *Daily Mirror*, have circulations respectively of 3.9 and 3.1 million.[4] In Japan there are three national dailies which are listed in order of circulation size: *The Yomiuri Shimbun* (9.8 million), *The Asahi Shimbun* (8.2 million) and *The Mainichi Shimbun* (4.2 million).[5] These large circulation figures are unheard of in a country like the USA where the newspaper business traditionally has been of a local nature. In New York City, for example, the greater metropolitan circulation of the largest paper, *The Daily News* is about 1.2 million. In Los Angeles, the number two US market, *The Times* has a circulation of about 1.0 million. Currently there is only one general newspaper, *USA Today*, with national circulation of 1.7 million. The national business paper *The Wall Street Journal* circulates about 1.9 million papers daily.[6] For a national advertiser to attain broad US coverage, it is necessary to advertise in many local papers. For example, if an advertiser wanted coverage of three-quarters of the US market, advertising space in papers in seventy different metropolitan areas would have to be purchased.

In Mexico, there are approximately 300 newspapers, most with local distribution. In the Mexico City metropolitan area, where more than 18 million people live, the circulation of papers is very fragmented. There are twenty-three dailies and the maximum circulation of one paper is about 300,000.[7]

Elsewhere in the world, regional papers have importance. In Hungary there are fourteen regional dailies along with another eleven that have national circulation.[8] In France some regional papers have larger readerships than 'national' papers.[9]

Language

Language is another variable. A number of countries have one dominant language which is used by all major papers other than those printed for ethnic minorities. In the USA and the UK newspapers are published in English; in France, French; in Germany, German. Other countries have a bi-lingual press: English and French in Canada; Flemish and French in Belgium. In other countries more variation exists. A case in point is India. The daily metro 'mainline', economic, and financial papers are printed in English. The regional daily papers are printed in several different languages, the principal one being Hindi. Other languages used by the regional daily press are Bengali, Gujarati, Malayalam, Marathi, Kannada, Tamil, and Telugu.[10]

Physical characteristics

Other differentiating factors among papers in various countries of the world include page size and number. In 1984 the newspaper industry in the USA adopted a six column format instead of the traditional nine columns for a standard size paper. (Tabloids are the other basic form.) With this change in columns, the depth became twenty-one or more inches. According to the Newspaper Advertising Bureau, Inc., the change was instituted to make the standard newspaper more visually attractive and easier to read. Also covered in this new standard were the tabloids which were specified as being fourteen inches deep and $9\frac{3}{8}$ to $10\frac{3}{4}$ inches in width and containing five columns.[11] In Table 9.3 a comparison is made between US papers and those in selected countries in Europe, Central America, and Japan. Judging from the figures shown, a uniform standard does not exist in either full size (broadsheet) or tabloid size papers. A variance in number of columns is also present.

Advertising material has to be adjusted to fit the formats of the various papers shown in Table 9.3.

Note that the Japanese paper has fifteen columns. This gives rise to a major difference between Japanese and Western papers. For example, in the *Asahi*

Table 9.3 *Newspaper sizes in selected countries*

Country	Size	Measurement inches	(Approximate) centimetres	Cols
USA	Broadsheet	21h × 13w	53h × 33w	6
	Tabloid	14h × 9–10w	35h × 24–26w	5
	(varies)	13h × 10w	33h × 26w	5
Netherlands	De Telegraaf	23h × 16w	58h × 41w	8
UK	London Daily			
	Telegraph	24h × 15w	60h × 39w	8
Germany	Three standards:			
	Rheinisch	19h × 13w	49h × 33w	
	Nordisch	21h × 15w	53h × 37w	
	Berlin	17h × 11w	43h × 28w	
Costa Rica	La Prensa Libre			
	(Tabloid)	15h × 12w	37h × 29w	4
				15
Japan	Asahi Shimbun	21h × 15w	53h × 39w	

h = height, w = width, cols = columns

Sources: US – Newspaper Advertising Bureau; Germany – Axel Springer Verlag AG, *Europaische Werbemarkete* (1982) Berlin, August, 44; Japan – *Asahi Shimbun* (1986) Advertising Department, Tokyo.

Shimbun, the columns run horizontally, while in the US broadsheet, as well as other papers listed in Table 9.3, the columns run vertically. Exhibit 9.1 shows the space a two column advertisement would occupy in the Japanese and US papers. (When actually buying space, an advertiser may buy all or part of a column and as many columns as needed up to a full page.)

The number of pages of advertising and editorial vary considerably from paper to paper. Most Japanese papers, for example, are relatively short in length. In the case of the *Asahi Shimbun* the maximum number of pages has been limited to thirty-two because of various historical, editorial and logistical reasons.[12] In contrast, the 30 October 1991 issue of *The New York Times* contained ninety-five pages divided in four sections.

Differences can also be found in the use of colour for either editorial or advertising purposes. These differences are noted in both flat or solid colours such as blue, red, and yellow and what is called full colour or four-colour process. Despite the relatively poor paper quality used in newspapers, the four-colour illustrative material in advertisements has improved significantly in some papers. The process used in the London *Daily Telegraph* is one example.

Exhibit 9.1   *Two-column advertising space in Japanese and US papers.* Note: *The striped area indicates the two column space*

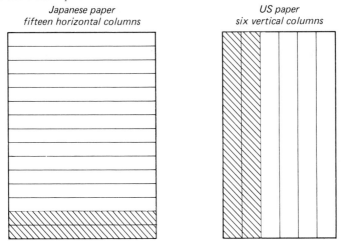

Japanese paper
fifteen horizontal columns

US paper
six vertical columns

Types of advertisements

There are three general types of advertisements found in newspapers: classified, display and supplement.

Classified

Classified advertisements are small in size, usually lack the visual elements of display advertising, and are grouped under specific headings such as 'rental', 'homes', 'furniture', etc.

Display

Display advertising will vary in size, shape, and location in the newspaper. Photographs, artwork, colour, and package illustration may be used to convey the message along with the copy (written) elements. Advertisements for men are often placed in the sports section while advertisements appealing to women will be found in the society section. Advertisements directed to business persons will be found on the financial and business pages.

Much of the display advertising in local newspapers will be placed by local businesses — bankers, merchants, and retailers. In both Germany and the USA national advertising, which is believed to be predominantly display, accounts for no more than one-eighth of total newspaper advertising revenues.[13]

Supplements

Supplements which are inserted in newspapers take different forms and possess different content. A magazine format with many or all pages printed in full-colour is commonplace. Three types of newspaper supplements are found in Germany:[14]

1 *Programme supplements* which contain information on radio and television programming appear once a week in dailies.
2 *'Quality' supplements* which are described as 'full colour extensions of certain papers'.
3 *Special topic supplements* which treat specific topics such as motoring and come out monthly or irregularly in certain dailies.

The magazine supplement may be a syndicated property of an independent publisher distributed to a number of newspapers across a country so as to form a national network as in the case of *Parade* in the USA. Local supplements printed by a single newspaper or a group of newspapers in the same geographic area are also found in the USA. An alternate type of supplement is called the 'free standing insert' (FSI) which contains no editorial, only coupons and other kinds of offers from participating manufacturers. In effect, the FSI is a compilation of preprinted (coupon) advertisements organized and distributed to newspapers for insertion on a particular day of the week, normally Sundays, by independent companies. The costs of preparation and distribution are borne by the participants. The FSI has been proven to be an effective means of delivering an attractive, full colour advertising message and coupon incentive in a cost effective manner.[15]

Of special advertiser interest

Characteristics of the newspaper medium which should be of particular interest to advertisers include these considerations:

- Mass coverage of markets where literacy is high. For example, *De Telegraaf*, a Dutch paper, reports readership in 20 per cent of all households in that country.[16]
- A means of reaching specific geographic markets with an advertising message by using local or regional papers.
- The ability to place an advertisement at short notice. For example, in Germany the booking date for a black and white (mono) advertisement is one to four days prior to publication; for colour, five to eight days.[17]
- Because of the basic news nature of this medium, newspapers are good vehicles for announcing new and/or improved products and services.

A major problem which international advertisers face is the variance in accuracy of circulation and readership figures, if available. In some countries of the world, such as the UK, the USA, Japan, and continental European countries, independent organizations such as the Audit Bureau of Circulation and the Joint Industry Committee for National Readership Surveys (UK) exist for the purpose of authenticating circulation and readership figures.[18] In other countries without such impartial and reliable organizations, the accuracy of the newspapers' own circulation and readership figures is sometimes questionable; the figures can be and often are misleading.

Advantages and disadvantages

As for advantages and disadvantages of using newspapers as an advertising medium, these considerations should be taken into account.

Advantages

- Can cope with detailed information.
- Flexibility in terms of coverage (with local and regional papers).
- News value; immediacy and currency of advertising.
- Cooperative advertising opportunities with retailers because newspapers are primarily a retail medium.
- Advertisement size and shape flexibility.

- High reader interest for both advertising and editorial content.
- An effective medium for delivering incentive such as a coupon or other promotion on a localized basis.
- Extensive national or local coverage is possible.

Disadvantages

- For market coverage, local or national, more than one paper maybe needed.
- Waste circulation — lack of audience selectivity.
- Colour limitations, though colour reproduction has improved greatly where new printing equipment is being used.
- Shortness of message life, normally a single day.
- Black and white as well as colour reproduction is often poor quality.
- Not suitable for products requiring demonstration or requiring emotional treatment.

Note
The advantages and disadvantages above were compiled from information in Wilmshurst, John (1985) *The Fundamentals of Advertising*, William Heinemann Ltd., London, p. 86; Ennis, F. Beaven (1985) *Marketing Norms for Product Managers*, Association of National Advertisers, New York, p. 67; Runyon, Kenneth E. (1984) *Advertising*, 2nd edn, Charles E. Merrill Publishing Company, Columbus, Ohio, pp. 457−8; Wells, William, Burnett, John and Moriarty, Sandra (1989) *Advertising Principles and Practices*, Prentice-Hall, Inc., Englewood Cliffs, NJ, pp. 279−81.

International marketing communicators must take into account both advantages and disadvantages of newspaper *per se* and the differences which exist among newspapers when this medium is scheduled to carry an organization's advertising message in various countries of the world.

Magazines

Magazines, also referred to as periodicals and journals, are the other major form of print advertising. However, in most countries they are significantly less important in terms of advertising monies spent than their counterpart, newspapers.

General characteristics
Magazines may be issued weekly, fortnightly, monthly, bi-monthly, and less frequently. The number and type of different magazine classifications can vary

from country to country. In the USA the major classifications are farm, business, and consumer. Within these general divisions, *Standard Rate and Data* has a total of sixty-eight subject headings ranging from Airline/Inflight to Youth.[19] In the UK, farm magazines would be classified under 'industrial' or 'business-to-business' journals along with publications that serve one industry such as *Caterer and Hotelkeeper* and others that may serve many industries such as *Industrial Equipment News*. Listings in this category also include trade magazines aimed at different classes of wholesale/retail trade like grocers and chemists, and technical and professional journals targeted to engineers, accountants, and doctors.[20] In France, where magazine advertising revenue comes close to that of newspapers, the principal consumer classifications include leisure, sport, news, television and radio programme guides, children's, women's, men's, home, and general.[21]

Post Second World War Developments

The introduction and growth of television in the post Second World War period impinged on and permanently altered the nature of magazines as a medium. In the USA, for example, television displaced the general interest magazine as the number one national display advertising medium. In fact, it was a major cause of the demise of such magazines as *Life*, *Look*, *Collier's*, and *The Saturday Evening Post*. These magazines and network radio programming were the principal alternatives for conducting a national advertising campaign prior to the advent of network television. Out of the ashes of these general interest magazines emerged special interest journals treating subjects like sports, cars, foods, and topics of particular relevance to males and females in different age groups, as well as television viewers. During the same period those publications whose success had been based on a special editorial format such as *Reader's Digest* and *National Geographic* along with others which had traditionally catered to women, the home, and the handyman held onto and continued to build their circulation bases.

Elsewhere in the world, where magazines held a prominent position, and the growth of television broadcasting and advertising was government controlled, magazines continued to enjoy a relatively larger share of the total advertising expenditures. Take a country like West Germany where magazine advertising entered the 1980s with a 35 per cent share of media monies and actually increased that share by 1985.[22] With deregulation now taking place in television, future figures, no doubt, will show a shift away from magazines to television as experienced in other industrialized countries such as the USA, Japan, and the UK.

In other countries where economic development and literacy are in marked contrast to the industrialized nations, and a number of languages and/or dialects exist, magazine advertising's importance will be minimal. Take Guatemala as an example. Illiteracy is 60, possibly 70 per cent. Many languages/dialects exist other than the offical one, Spanish. Among the total population, 80 to 90 per cent would be considered as lower class.[23] As for magazine advertising expenditures, McCann-Erickson indicated that it is about 2 per cent of the total. In their *MediaFact Book* they list only seven magazines with a total circulation of 71,000 in a country with over nine million population.[24]

With respect to magazine advertising in other parts of the world several regions and countries are examined.

Black Africa

In Black Africa, print media of a pan-regional nature has been published for the most part in London or Paris. These two points of origin reflect the partitioning of much of Africa into Anglophone and Francophone countries. London is said to be an ideal listening post for anyone interested in Africa. The same can be said for Paris depending on the African country of interest. Travel between African countries is often routed through these centres. 'Phone communications are more easily placed to and from London or Paris than many intra-African calls. It is not surprising, then, to hypothesize that information flows more rapidly between individual African countries and these two colonial 'capitals' than between two African countries. Added to this is the thought that writers and editors living off the continent give 'African' publications more credibility.[25]

Costs of and delays in distribution preclude weekly publications for the most part in Black Africa. Publishers are not inclined to invest in streamlining the distribution system because of the difficulty in recovering monies from publication sales in many African countries. Instead, Pan-African publications count on advertising to generate as much as 90 per cent of the total revenue. A major concern for advertisers is the reliability of figures supplied by publications regarding audiences' buying power and 'decision markers' reached.[26]

As for editorial content, it was reported that the original but now defunct Pan-African magazine, *Drum*, built its popularity, which included circulation in its home base, Nigeria, of 150,000, on articles about crime, sex, and sports. Readers since then apparently have become more inclined to read serious material.[27]

In regard to existing publications, *International Media Guide* included two news magazines published monthly, *Africa Now* and *New African*. The latter magazine has its concentration of readers in Nigeria. About one-half of all English speaking Black Africans reside in that country.[28] One French publication, *Afrique/Asie* (110,000 circulation), also has a very large English edition, *Africa/Asia* (55,000 circulation). The former is published fortnightly and the latter monthly. The other leading French magazine is *Jeune Afrique* a weekly with a total circulation of about 120,000; 50 per cent in Black Africa; 20–25 per cent in North Africa and the Middle East; the balance in Europe, inflight, and in the rest of the world. The magazines mentioned claim to have their readers concentrated among top executives and managers in business, bankers, educators, officials in government posts, and diplomats.[29]

Latin America

In Latin America, one characteristic of the consumer magazine business is that a number of publications have multi-country editions, all under the control of one organization. For example, in the general interest category, *Geomundo* (Editorial America, S.A., Virgin Gardens, Florida) has Central American, Chilean, Colombian, Ecuadorian, Mexican, Peruvian, Puerto Rican, and Venezuelan editions. *Selecciones Del Reader's Digest* (Coral Gables, Florida) has editions in the above regions and countries plus editions in Argentina, Brazil, and Uruguay. The science and technology magazine, *Mecanica Popular* (Editorial America, S.A.) has country editions in Argentina, Chile, Columbia, Mexico, Peru, Puerto Rico, Venezuela, and a Central American edition. As for women and fashion, a similar situation arises for *Buenhogar*, *Coqueta*, *Cosmopolitan* and *Harper's Bazaar en Espanol*, *Ideas Para Su Hogar*, and *Vanidades* all published by Editorial America, S.A. However, in Mexico, the women's magazine segment is dominated by the giant American Publishing Group.[30]

Japan

In Japan, despite the dominance of television and newspapers, the consumer magazine industry is well developed. Advertisers are offered a wide range of segmented, special interest audiences ranging from businessmen to housewives and sports enthusiasts.[31]

The number of monthly magazines in Japan outnumber the weekly magazines by thirty to one; however, the difference in total circulation is only three to two. With respect to audience, roughly one-third of total monthly magazine circulation is directed to the 'masses' or a 'general' audience, whereas over one-half of the weekly circulation is directed to these audiences. Despite the large number of titles – 2,253 – only sixty-five were audited in 1988.[32]

China

In mainland China, magazines (journals) occupy third place behind newspapers and a rapidly growing television industry with respect to advertising expenditures. There are many magazine titles which appear at intervals of one week to one year. Editorial content, according to the China Advertising Association, falls into two categories: natural science and social science. Many of these periodicals are of a theoretical, academic, technical and scientific nature. This indicates small, highly technical audiences. Also reported were comprehensive recreational and social titles.[33] *International Media Guides* list two general interest magazines, one called *After Work Hours* with a national circulation of one million copies (a fraction of 1 per cent of the total population). The other was a regional magazine, *Tianjin Broadcasting and TV Weekly*, with a weekly circulation of 400,000. The one scientific and technological publication listed was a Chinese language edition of *Scientific America* with a circulation of 20,000.[34]

Germany

In Germany, where more advertising monies are spent in magazines than in any country other than in the USA, the main classifications are supplements, 'ad mags', consumer magazines, customer magazines, and trade and technical journals. Supplements are loose inserts in newspapers or periodicals with a magazine format and with many pages printed in four-colour. The principal types are programme, quality, special topic, and trade and technical. Programme supplements, the most widely read, are published once a week and carried in daily newspapers. Editorial content is largely concentrated on previews of radio and television programmes. Quality supplements are found in some of the major newspapers and are largely read by males in managerial and professional positions. Special topic supplements come out at irregular intervals with various carriers. Trade and technical supplements focus on topics of interest to readers of the specialized journals in which the supplements are placed.[35]

Ad mags, also called 'free sheets', have the appearance of newspapers and contain little or no editorial. They are financed by advertisements, distributed free, and compete with regional dailies for advertising space. Unlike dailies, they can offer, theoretically, 100 per cent coverage of households in a given area. A disadvantage is their lack of data on coverage and readership. The bulk of advertising comes from small and medium retailers, department stores, and supermarkets.[36]

Among consumer magazines, the main classifications are topical illustrated weeklies, programme magazines (TV/radio guides), and women's magazines. Also widely read are news, business, sports, and motoring magazines.

The topical interest weeklies, such as *Stern* and *Bunte*, cover major news topics of a social, political, and society nature with emphasis on the sensational stories of the week. Pictures predominate over text with the principal emphasis on entertainment and advice versus education.

Programme magazines have increased their popularity due to the editorial shift from a narrow. in-depth focus on radio and TV to coverage of a broad range of topics of interest to the family, thus, putting themselves in competition with both women's magazines and topical illustrated weeklies. *Horzu* is the most popular magazine in this category with a readership of over 10 million.

Women's magazines treat fashions, cosmetics, the home, nutrition, raising children, and the social status of readers...stories and advice which can be found in similar publications in other countries of the world. The major titles include *Bild der Frau, Brigitte,* and *Freundin.*[37]

The UK

In the UK, which ranks number three in the world behind the USA and Germany on advertising monies spent in magazines, a category of major importance is the Sunday supplement.[38] By the end of 1991 every national Sunday newspaper except two had the added value of a magazine. The two exceptions published a Saturday magazine instead. In addition, one other daily paper had a Saturday magazine.[39] These widely distributed weekend magazines in newspapers as a group constitute the general interest magazine category. Also of note is the large number of women's weekly, fortnightly, monthly, and bimonthly magazines which vary in circulation from 40,000 to one million.[40] A total of sixty-eight women's magazines were reported by the Advertising Association in 1988, all with audited circulation. Of this, thirty-eight were monthlies and twenty were weeklies. The three largest weeklies' percentage of total women's readership ranged from 13 to 19 per cent as compared with a median of 1.5 per cent for the group as a whole. The top three monthlies women's readership ranged from 9 to 11 per cent with a median of 2.6 per cent for the group.[41]

International media

International media are comprised of both magazines and newspapers and can be classified in terms of editorial content and target audience.

Inflight

Inflight magazines are one of these categories. They cater to the individual traveller and business person. All major airlines have such a magazine published anywhere from two to twelve times per year. Some airlines, British Airways for example, have more than one publication. *Business Life* has three-quarters of its print run (six times per year) mailed to British Airways frequent flyers. *High Life*, a monthly, is apparently circulated among its airline passengers on certain routes. *Sinbad* is distributed solely on Middle Eastern routes.

Advertisers also have the opportunity to buy space in a publication distributed on more than one airline such as *In London*. It is available for in-bound first and executive class passengers on nine different airlines from the Americas, other countries in Europe and the Middle East.

Combination rate plans where advertising can be purchased in two or more magazines concurrently at a discount from the single magazine price are available for a number of different airline publications in both North and South America. The foregoing information can be found in greater detail from *IMG Consumers Magazines Worldwide*.[42]

Advertising which is frequently seen in inflight magazines range from perfumes and various duty free products to car rental, computers, cars, hotels, financial and communication services.

As an advertising medium, the editorial content and production values in most instances are found to be of a uniform high standard. However, what is lacking are meaningful comparative statistics on circulation and readership for decision-making purposes. Advertisers have only print runs, passenger flows and destinations on which to make judgments concerning media selection.[43] Nonetheless, inflight magazines provide a means by which advertisers can reach certain targets, namely the international business traveller and holiday makers.

Other international publications
Unlike inflight magazines, other international publications are not as easy to classify. When examining the analyses of a leading trade journal, a major advertising agency, and competitive media which publish/distribute across borders, different comparisons are found. For example, *Advertising Age* classifies global media by these basic categories: dailies, weeklies, monthlies, and other.[44] Saatchi & Saatchi's European compilation *Focus* classifies print media on the basis of general (interest), business, French language international editions, financial and daily newspapers.[45] *Time* magazine compares itself with its US counterpart *Newsweek*, *The International Herald Tribune*, *Fortune* and international business magazines and newspapers when addressing a European media audience.[46] *Reader's Digest* (not on *Time's* list) compares itself with *Time* and *Newsweek*, as well as business and non-business publications in all parts of the world.[47] These publications will make comparisons on a global, regional, or country-by-country basis depending on the client or prospect's request.

With respect to circulation and readership on a global (and regional) basis, the *Reader's Digest* outdistances all other publications by a wide margin. It has 100 million readers, 43 million of which are outside the USA who are reached by thirty-eight different editions in fifteen languages.[48]

Most of the 'global' or regional publications with significant circulations are printed in English, which, by itself, is a major constraint. The findings of a European language comprehension study conducted by Gallup are shown in Table 9.4.

Table 9.4 *Per cent of population who speak English*

Country	%	Country	%
Austria	25	Norway	80
Belgium	26	Spain	13
Denmark	51	Sweden	68
France	26	Switzerland	26
Ireland	99	UK	100
Netherlands	68	West Germany	43

Source: TBWA/World Media Limited (1989) *A Review of the European Media Scene*, London.

While these figures are based on the percentage who 'speak' English, they should be indicative of the relative fluency, speaking or reading.

Among the 'global' publications with the most circulation in three regions outside of North America are those shown in Table 9.5.

In Latin America there is one strong regional contender for readers' attention: *Vision/Visao* (Spanish/Portuguese) with a circulation of over 300,000. In S.E. Asia the leading regional contender is *Asia Magazine* with a circulation of over 700,000.

In addition to the magazines already mentioned, there are a number of well-established periodicals, most of which are business or financial in editorial content with regional or multi-regional circulation. These titles include *L'Express* (International), *Paris Match* (International), and *International Management* in Europe; *Asiaweek*, and the *Far Eastern Economic Review* in Asia.[49]

Advertising Age's global media lineup (19 November, 1990 issue) shows a

Table 9.5 *Regional circulation of selected magazines*

	Circulation (000)			
Publication	Europe	S.E. Asia	Latin America	Total
Reader's Digest (monthly)	6,623	542	1,220	8,385
National Geographic (monthly)	804	130	100	1,034
Time (weekly)	560	135	95	790
Newsweek (weekly)	281	115	65	461

Source: Personeni, Jane (1992) Pleasantville, New York, 13 January. (Figures are based on 1992, rate cards.)

much broader mix of publications with different editorial formats. Included are daily newspapers, and weekly and monthly magazines catering to business, general, and special interest readers. Of the eighteen publications listed, eleven originate from the USA where their circulation is also concentrated. The exception is *World Paper* with its largest circulation in Latin America followed by the Soviet Union and Asia/Pacific. The number two publication behind *Reader's Digest* for circulation outside the USA is *Cosmopolitan*. Only in China does another publication — *The People's Daily* — dominate.

Regional advertising

Regarding regular readership of selected international publications, one thirteen-country European study among economically active adults meeting certain minimum educational and income requirements indicates it is difficult to achieve much uniformity.[50] (Thirteen publications in this study were also in *Advertising Age's* global media lineup.) The implication of this finding is that advertiser's would have to supplement a pan-European selection of print media with local publications to achieve uniform weight of advertising against such a regional audience.

Opportunities for pan-regional advertising appear to be better in Latin America and the Arab world where single languages dominate. The Latin American situation was discussed earlier in this chapter. In the Arab countries of North Africa and the Middle East, pan-Arab weekly and monthly magazines receive the majority of advertisers' monies as opposed to local and national weeklies and monthlies. In a ten-country survey where weekly and monthly magazines accounted for 31 per cent of total 1987 press and TV advertising expenditures, the pan-Arab publications accounted for over three-fifths of the total.[51]

Business to business publications

For those organizations engaged in international business-to-business advertising, there are four basic media alternatives: international publication; national publication; general management audience; and industry specific audience.

The aviation industry is used to demonstrate these alternatives. For a US manufacturer of small business aircraft to use periodical advertising as a means of delivering a message in Sweden to various participants in the buying process, alternatives include:

1   International/general management
    - *Business Week* International   (US)
    - *Newsweek* International   (US)
    - *International Management*   (UK)
    - *Financial Times*   (UK)

2 National/general management
   - *Veckans Affaerer*   (Sweden)
   - *Ledarskap Ekonomen*   (Sweden)
   - *Affaersvaerlden*   (Sweden)
   - *Svensk Handelstidning Justita*   (Sweden)
3 International/industry specific
   - *Aviation Week & Space Technology*   (US)
   - *Commuter Air*   (US)
   - *Interavia*   (Switzerland) .
4 National/industry specific
   - *Flyghorisont*   (Sweden)
   - *Flygrevyn*   (Sweden)

The purchase of magazines in group 1 or 3 would mean that the manufacturer is using international general management and aircraft industry magazines to reach prospects in Sweden (as well as in other countries). To use group 2 or 4 magazines would mean that Sweden is being targeted for special coverage. The choice of general management or industry specific is dependent on whether the target should be passengers as opposed to operators and maintenance personnel. Decision makers and influencers should be found in both audiences.

References to specific media in this section were drawn from *International Media Guides* (IMG) business/professional Europe edition.[52] IMG publishes similar editions for Asia/Pacific, Middle East/Africa, and Latin America. In addition to the general business and industry category there are fifty-three specific industry classifications where professional, business, technical, and trade publications are listed on a multi-continent and country basis. Other information reported includes rates, page size, closing dates, circulation and readership (where available). Country overviews giving information on exchange rates, populations, media alternatives, research services, and advertising taxes are also included. A sample listing on 'boating' is shown in Exhibit 9.2.

Magazines: advantages and disadvantages

In considering magazines in the advertising media mix, these advantages and disadvantages should be taken into account:

Advantages

- The most selective (non-direct) medium for reaching a target audience where geographic confinement is not a factor.

Exhibit 9.2 *A page from* IMG Business/Professional Europe. *Reproduced by permission of* International Media Enterprises Inc., *South Norwalk, USA (December 1991)*

8.5 – Boating

CLASSIFICATION 8.5

BOATS – BOATING EQUIPMENT – BOATING – MARINE SUPPLIES –
BOAT MOTORS – MARINAS

DEFINITION OF MARKET SERVED:

Publications listed in this classification are directed to boat and boat equipment dealers, distributors, manufacturers and suppliers; marina and boat yard managers; boat users and other persons involved in the boating industry.

SAMPLE OF SUBJECTS COVERED BY THESE PUBLICATIONS:

Boat Construction Materials – Boat Maintenance – Boat Merchandising – Boat Shows – Boatyard Management – Cruising Areas – Marina News – Marine Legislation – Marine Problems – Marine Products – Marine Safety – Power Boat Models – Regattas – Sail Boating – Seamanship

Related Classifications:

Marine, Fishing & Shipping (Classification 54)

MULTI–CONTINENTAL

Major distribution in two or more continents or worldwide; circulation breakdown for Europe.

INTERNATIONAL BOAT INDUSTRY
Boating Communications Ltd., 1 St. John's Court, St. John's Street Farncombe, Surrey GU7 3BA, UNITED KINGDOM (Tel: 44–4868/25817; Telex: 859130 265871 MONREF G)
Bi–Monthly (3rd week of prec. month) in English. Est.1968⁶
Ed: N.D. Hopkinson; Ad Mgr: Carolyn Gooch
Reps: US: Reed Business Publishing, Inc. Ge: Knevels Marketing Services Jpn: Trade Media Japan, Inc. Swe: Martin Eden Reklam AB Swi: intermar Tai: Alpha Trading Company
Rates effective 1988, in British Pounds Sterling. Agency Comm: 15%
1 L = $1,696
  1 pg (b/w): L 820 or $1,392
  1 pg (2 color): 10% extra
  1 pg (4 color): $1,620 or $2,750
Type pg: 179x260 mm or 7" x 10-1/4"
Trim sz: A4. Offset
Ad Closing: 6 weeks prec. publication
Circ (ABC): 9,300 (Europe: 7,000; UK: 1,985)
Readership: wholesalers, marine dealers, retailers, manufacturers, boat builders, import/export agents & manufacturers representatives, naval architects, designers & consultants.

YACHTING WORLD
Reed Business Publishing, Quadrant House, The Quadrant, Sutton, Surrey SM2 5AS, UNITED KINGDOM (Tel: (01) 661–3314; Telex: 892084 BIS PRS G; Fax: (01) 661–3263)
Monthly. Est. 1894
Ed: Dick Johnson; Ad Mgr: David Wilson
US Sales Office:
New York, NY 10017: Reed Business Publishing, 205 East 42nd Street (Tel: 212–867–2080; Telex: 238327; Fax: 212-687-6604). Contact: Gail Taverman
Newport Beach, CA 92660: Reed Business Publishing, 3700 Campus Drive, Suite 203 (Tel: 714-756-1057/8/9; Telex: 238327; Fax: 714-756-2514). Contact: Larry Arthur
Rate Card: 9/89, in US$. Agency Comm: 15%
  1 pg (b/w): $1,792
  1 pg (2 color): $2,607
  1 pg (4 color): $3,304
Type pg: 178x254 mm or 7" x 10". Screen: 100–120
Trim sz: 216x295 mm or 8-1/2" x 11-5/8". Offset
Ad Closing: 4 weeks prec. publication
Circ (ABC): 45,317 (Western Europe: 11,546; Eastern Europe: 53)
Readership: top yachting people, boat owners, potential buyers.

Pan Europe

Media distributed throughout Europe; each publication listed has more than 50% of its circulation distributed outside the country of its publication

MOTOR BOAT & YACHTING
Reed Business Publishing, Quadrant House, The Quadrant, Sutton, Surrey SM2 5AS, UNITED KINGDOM (Tel: (01) 661 3312; Telex: 892084 REEDBP G)
Monthly. Est. 1904
Ed: Tom Wills; Ad Mgr: Chris Rogers
US Sales Office:
New York, NY 10017: Reed Business Publishing, 205 East 42nd Street (Tel: 212–867–2080; Telex: 238327; Fax: 212-687-6604). Contact: Gail Taverman
Newport Beach, CA 92660: Reed Business Publishing, 3700 Campus Drive, Suite 203 (Tel: 714-756-1057/8/9; Telex: 238327; Fax: 714-756-2514). Contact: Larry Arthur
Rates received for 1988, in US$. Agency Comm: 15%
  1 pg (b/w): $1,740
  1 pg (2 color): $2,390
  1 pg (4 color): $3,770
Type pg: 187x267 mm or 7–3/8" x 10-1/2"
Trim sz: 216x296 mm or 8-1/2" x 11-5/8". Offset
Ad Closing: 6 weeks prec. publication
Circ (ABC, 1-88-12-88): 37,150
Readership: yachtsmen, boat builders, engine manufacturers, yacht chandlers, dealers, marinas, brokers & architects.

AUSTRIA

1 Austrian Schilling (S) = $.0758
Language: German

YACHTREVUE (Yacht Review)
Verlag Orac, Schlossgasse 10–12, A–1050 Vienna (Tel: (0222) 551621313; Fax 222–551621–78)
Ed: Luis Gazzari; Ad Mgr: Peter Schimek
Rate Card: 1/89. Agency Comm: 15%
  1 pg (b/w): $ 37,560 or $2,847
  1 pg (2 color): 25% extra
  1 pg (4 color): $ 63,852 or $4,840
Type pg: 185x253mm or 7–5/16" x 9–15/16"
Trim sz 212x280mm or 8–3/8" x 11". Offset
Ad closing: 2 weeks prec. publication
Circ (VOZZ): 48,000
Readership: sailors; powerboat operators.

BELGIUM

1 Belgian Franc (BFr) = $.0255
Languages: French & Flemish

LE COURTIER NAUTIQUE (The Nautical Broker)
Infor–Nautic, Ruedu Sceptre Straat 8, B–1040 Brussels
Monthly (1st) in French. Est. 1970
There has not been a response to questionnaires since 1983. Please contact the publisher for advertising rates and data.

YACHTING SUD – SURE L EAU (Southern Yachting–On The Water)
Belgian Yachting Press, Rue Caroly 37, 1040 Brussels (Tel: 2/5131104)
10x yearly (Dec/Jan & July/Aug combo), in French & Flemish editions. Est. 1923. Ed & Ad Mgr: Charles Bertels
Official organ of the Lgue Regional du Yachting Belge
Rates received 2/89. Agency Comm: 15%
  1 pg (b/w): BFr 21,000 or $536
  1 pg (4 color): BFr 29,900 or $762
Type pg: 175x235 mm or 6–7/8" x 9-1/4".
Trim sz: 215x275 mm or 8–7/16" x 10–3/4". Offset
Ad Closing: 1 month prec. publication
Circ (PS): 8,000
Readership: yachtmen.

- High reader involvement due to editorial content.
- The ability to reach a large number of readers/households in certain countries, e.g. *Horzu* in Germany and the Sunday supplements in the UK.
- Long life, depending on frequency of issue. One study showed the average person picked up a monthly magazine on four different days.
- Pass along from one person to another increases readership and extends life.
- A high quality medium with excellent full colour reproduction.
- Ability to provide detailed information.
- Readers tend to rank above national averages in terms of income and education for many magazines.
- Certain magazines due to reader characteristics and quality of content lend prestige to goods/services advertised.
- Can provide special reader attention-getting devices, e.g., inserted samples, scent strips and micro-recordings.

Disadvantages

- Lack of local penetration other than for Sunday magazine supplements and publications like German 'Ad mags.'
- Lack of message immediacy; reading may be spread over life of issue.
- Usually difficult to vary advertising pressure geographically within a country.
- Long lead times for the placement (eight to nine weeks for a monthly) and cancellation of advertising.
- Circulation delivered outside of an advertiser's market area is wasted.
- Relatively high production costs, particularly for full colour advertising.

The above advantages and disadvantages include information from: Wilmshurst, John (1985) *Fundamentals of Advertising*, William Heinemann Ltd., London, pp. 150–152.
Runyon, Kenneth E. (1984) *Advertising*, 2nd edn, Charles E. Merrill Publishing Company, Columbus, Ohio, pp. 465–6.
Shimp, Terence A. (1990) *Promotion Management and Marketing Communications*, 2nd edn, The Dryden Press, Chicago, pp. 395–7.
Dunn, S. Watson and Barban, Arnold M. (1986) *Advertising*, 6th edn, CBS College Publishing, Hinsdale, IL, pp. 593–5.

Out-of-home advertising

Of the major media, out-of-home advertising, also called outdoor advertising, usually ranks behind newspapers, television, and magazines in advertising expenditures. In some countries, however, it is more important than radio and can even outrank magazines and newspapers. In the comparative advertising expenditure analysis at the beginning of Part Four, expenditures in this medium as a per cent of total ranged from zero to 12 per cent.

Out-of-home advertising is located outdoors and indoors away from the home. The advertisements themselves have many different names including signs, posters, billboards, bulletin boards, placards, spectaculars, signboards and hoardings. Out-of-home advertising may appear on or in frames built especially for this purpose. They are found along highways, city streets, at intersections, train, bus and underground stops; also in trains, in or outside buses and taxis, and on other vehicles. When identified with transportation, it is customary to use the term 'transit advertising'. Other locations include on buildings and storefronts, often in and around shopping malls.

Global usage

Use of out-of-home advertising in different parts of the world is characterized by these observations:

- *China* Many forms of outdoor advertising can be found in China. The more traditional types include billboards, neon signs, and posters. Electronic, power-driven, multi-sided displays lighted in different ways are being introduced throughout the country. 'The varied and colourful outdoor ads have added both atmosphere to the commercial areas and beauty to the City's life.'[53]
- *Japan* Outdoor advertising showed strong growth in 1988, particularly on the part of tobacco companies and banks.[54]
- *India* 'Hoardings have grown in large numbers in the bigger towns of India in the recent past.'[55]
- *Hungary* 'Posters, billboards and neon signs are popular vehicles in Hungary.'[56]
- *Saudi Arabia* Outdoor advertising has become well established in this country and should be carefully considered as a part of an advertiser's media mix.[57] One reason for this can be attributed to its largely visual nature which is a way of bypassing the language barrier to reach both Arabs and expatriates.[58]
- *UK* In 1987 and 1988 investment in outdoor advertising came 'from a wider product base than the traditional drink and tobacco market'.[59]
- *Continental Europe* There is a high demand for outdoor advertising in Belgium, France, Italy, The Netherlands, Norway, Sweden, and Switzerland. In Austria and West Germany the demand can exceed the supply. The demand varies in Finland and Greece. In Denmark, only city advertising

is permitted; not along highways. Portugal stands alone as a country where the medium is underdeveloped.[60]

As for specific types of out-of-home advertising, the basic alternatives will be discussed in the next several sections.

Storefront

Signs which name the business and/or products sold are unquestionably the most widely used and pervasive form of out-of-home advertising. Signs are found in a great variety of materials, sizes, and shapes, two- and three-dimensional with or without lighting and motion. Airspace can become crowded as advertisers compete for visibility as the photo of a busy Guatemala City shopping street as Exhibit 9.3 indicates. Elsewhere municipal ordinances, which control size, shape, colour, and location of the signs, may not permit this kind of crowding and appearance.

Uniformity is also controlled by manufacturers, retail chains, and franchisors that wish to project a uniform image where their retail operations are located. Take, for example, the Michelin Man in Exhibit 9.4. He looks and acts the same wherever he appears.

Exhibit 9.3 *Shopfront advertising on a busy street in Guatemala*

Exhibit 9.4 *Outdoor advertising for Michelin Tyres. Reproduced by permission of Michelin, Manufacture Français des Pneumatiques Michelin, Paris*

Outdoor

With respect to outdoor posters, they will normally be found in a limited number of standard sizes, large, medium, and small. Standards, however, will vary from one country to the next. A frequently used size in the UK is called a 'forty-eight sheet' poster. Its counterpart in the USA is a 'thirty sheet' poster. The former measures ten feet high by twenty feet wide;[61] the latter nine feet seven inches high by twenty-one feet seven inches long.[62] A 'standard' outdoor poster in Mexico measures ten feet high by twenty-four feet wide.[63] The term 'thirty (or forty-eight) sheet' signifies the number of individual printed sheets which have to be pasted together on a flat surface to complete a poster. With the larger printing presses available today, a fewer number of individual sheets are needed. Medium sized posters (eight to sixteen sheets) can run six to seven feet in height and from five to six feet in width. Small sizes (three or four sheet posters) can range from five to seven feet in height and run about three feet in width. Standardization of sizes within country markets is needed to keep printing and locational costs down. Posters are often lighted for night viewing. See Exhibit 9.5 which pictures a standard large size poster.

Other types of outdoor advertisements found in the USA (and elsewhere) include painted bulletins and spectaculars. Painted bulletins are painted on

Exhibit 9.5   *Outdoor advertising for Moosehead Dry. Reproduced by permission of Moosehead Dry and its advertising agency, Harrod and Mirlin, Toronto, Canada*

Exhibit 9.5 (*continued*)

moveable panels or directly on location. Their special features are extra large size, illumination, and embellishments (extensions) to give a three-dimensional effect.[64] Spectaculars, because of their size, special lighting and motion effects, and cost are found in very high traffic locations such as Picadilly Circus, London, and Times Square, New York. See the spectaculars at Picadilly in Exhibit 9.6.

Transit

Transit advertising also comes in many sizes and shapes to fit the surface to which it is affixed. This could be the front, back, sides, or top of buses, tram cars, and taxis; on station platforms; on the concave walls of an underground system at stations, at bus stops and inside trains, underground trains and buses. Exhibit 9.7 shows a typical bus stop poster.

The outdoor audience

Mass audience would be the media planner's answer to the question about out-of-home advertising audience delivery. When advertising is located at a busy intersection like Picadilly Circus or along a major shopping street such as the one pictured earlier in Guatemala City, a large, diversified audience will be reached — shoppers, travellers, business people — all with varying socio-economic characteristics. However, viewers can be targeted if the advertising locations are properly selected. Posters placed along certain arteries; on certain transit system vehicles, stops, or platforms; in specific neighbourhoods or adjacent to certain plant sites can reach a concentration of executives, grocery shoppers, affluent homemakers, or blue collar workers.

In some major markets a mass audience may be difficult to reach through the conventional broadcast and print media. In these circumstances, out-of-home advertising may be an important supplemental medium. Los Angeles, the number two metropolitan market in the USA, is a case in point. It is known as a 'drive' market because most people commute to work by car rather than public transportation. Advertising coverage on a broad scale is also hard to achieve by means of television or the press, or a combination of the two. Out-of-home, therefore, is often used by advertisers to augment other media choices when attempting to reach a mass market.

Audience measurement
In countries where media research services are readily available more audience information for planning and evaluating out-of-home advertising will be found.

Exhibit 9.6 *Outdoor spectaculars at Piccadilly Circus*

Exhibit 9.7 *Examples of transit advertising for Harp Lager, Dublin, Ireland. Reproduced by permission of Guinness Brewing GB, London*

For example, in the USA 'The Traffic Audit Bureau audits outdoor advertising plants to validate the number of panels available, the quality of their locations, and the number of potential viewers passing each location.'[65] (Outdoor advertising plants are independent business firms that own or lease sites, erect structures, sell advertising space, put up and take down the advertising; length dependent on terms of the advertising contract.) In the UK the Outdoor Advertising Association has devised a system for evaluating outdoor audiences by auditing all poster panels and measuring visibility of each as well as potential vehicle and pedestrian traffic.[66] Outdoor media research in Germany provides information on poster coverage and viewer information by region, sex, age, education, occupation, and household income.[67] In the USA, information on audience size and demography are available from several different sources along with reach and frequency information.[68]

Even though out-of-home advertising is available in many countries throughout the world, the information available and research techniques used for planning and evaluation purposes are apt to be less sophisticated and accurate . . . . and in many instances not nearly as readily available.

Advantages and disadvantages

While the creative and buying aspects of out-of-home advertising are treated more fully in other sections of this text, the principal advantages and disadvantages of the medium are summarized below.

Advantages

- A dominant form of advertising due to size . . . can achieve a striking effect.
- Can build audience coverage quickly.
- Can reach a very broad or selective audience depending on placement.
- Has geographic and seasonal flexibility.
- On a cost-per-1,000 basis, relatively inexpensive.
- Can provide high frequency (on worker routes for example).

Disadvantages

- Very brief viewing span when in a moving vehicle.
- Non-intrusive in nature; therefore may become part of the background.
- May deliver a high percentage of wasted viewers.
- Limited opportunity to deliver a written message.
- Audience figures can be ambiguous; duplication figures don't exist.
- Cost of design, artwork, and printing small quantities, particularly in larger sizes, may be prohibitive for small advertisers.

The above advantages and disadvantages were compiled from information from Wilmshurst, John (1985) *The Fundamentals of Advertising*, William Heinemann Ltd., London, pp. 170−1; TBWA World Media (1989) *A Review of the European Media Scene*, TBWA, London, 15 February; Nylen, David W. (1986) *Advertising*, Columbus, Ohio, South-Western Publishing Company, Cincinnati, 3rd edn, p. 395; Runyon, Kenneth E. (1984) *Advertising*, 2nd edn, Charles E. Merrill Publishing Company, Columbus, Ohio, pp. 499, 500, 503.

Yellow pages advertising

Introduction

A former associate who introduced bowling and other products, consumer and industrial, in about sixty countries around the world reported that whenever he went into a new market he invariably used the yellow pages to find local distributors as well as suppliers of goods and services needed in his business. That is probably a good explanation why professional and managerial employees rank as the number one users of yellow pages among all socioeconomic categories in the USA.[69]

The fact that sources which have been used elsewhere in this text to report on other media forms in various countries did not treat yellow page advertising gives an indication of its specialized nature. Considerable information is available in the USA on this medium due to the efforts of the Yellow Pages Publishers Association.

Recognizing that 'phone networks and yellow page advertising exist in most all markets of any consequence in the world, a discussion of this type of advertising is deemed to have significance. The wisdom with respect to its use, of necessity, is based on the US experience.

The medium's importance
In 1989, estimated annual expenditures on yellow page advertising amounted to $8.3 billion. This was greater than monies spent on consumer magazines and roughly equivalent to funds expended on radio. In comparison with all categories of advertising, yellow pages accounted for roughly 7 per cent of the total. Like radio, and unlike magazines, yellow pages is predominantly a local medium; only 12 per cent of the $8.3 billion was estimated to be national.[70]

The medium will be examined further to identify its principal characteristics.

Use of yellow pages

Use of yellow pages is broadbased in the USA. Over four-fifths of the adult population use this medium at work, at home, or elsewhere. Greater than average usage occurs among professionals and managers as previously noted. It also occurs among technical, clerical, and sales people; and among higher income, better educated males and females in the thirty-five to forty-nine age bracket.[71]

Unlike other forms of mass media, yellow pages is not considered as a medium for creating awareness or building desire (learning and feeling). Rather, it is considered as a medium which directs people to places where they can compare those brands that have previously been chosen as possible buying alternatives, or where the best place to purchase the preselected brand of their choice is located. Yellow pages, void of entertainment or editorial, is the place to go when the consumer is ready to spend his or her money but is not sure where the purchase should be made.

Availability of yellow pages

In many countries of the world only one entity, public or private, may have the right to publish a yellow pages directory for the country as a whole or for all areas where telephone service is available. This is not the situation in the USA. In many metro areas two or more directories are apt to be found. These could be directories published by a telephone utility in its own region or even in a region that another utility serves. Independent directory publishers also exist...some have been in business for many years and possess considerable expertise in this field. Independents in the USA can produce a directory in any area which they believe represents a good business proposition for profitable growth. The possibility of a multi-directory market and other considerations must be taken into account by the advertiser.

Planning yellow page advertising

Directory selection
As in the development of any advertising plan, decisions must be reached with respect to vehicle selection and message. If only a single directory exists in the area in which a firm operates, the problem is narrowed to the consideration of breadth of coverage. If directories exist in adjacent territories will the advertiser draw sufficient customers to justify the added expense? This is a question for the local, not national, advertiser. The answer will depend on the nature of the merchandise being sold. Customers in need of low-priced, convenience items, such as foodstuffs and health and beauty aids, normally want convenience of location and therefore will not travel far afield when making a purchase. The converse is true of high-priced, durable goods like refrigerators and furniture

where extensive search activities are normally conducted before the purchase is made.

The national advertiser will approach the problem from a different viewpoint, seeking broad geographic coverage with a minimum of duplication. This leads to the question of selection when two or more directories are available in the same area. Several factors should be studied in this respect. One involves competition. In which of the directories are the competitive products being advertised? Another concerns the method of distribution. Is it achieved by mail or door-to-door? Do businesses receive a copy for each 'phone in service? Ultimately the advertiser will want to compare costs of advertising in the directories which serve the same territory.[72]

Heading selection

While heading selection may not pose a problem for airlines, banks, or dentists in order to reach the greatest number of customers, an appliance retailer should consider listing under such headings as ranges and ovens, refrigerators, dishwashers, microwave ovens, and television and radios. Similarly, a dealer selling electrical equipment and lighting fixtures would want to be listed under both headings to maximize customer reach. Manufacturers that supply stores of the types just mentioned will also be interested in heading selection.

National and regional advertisers

Firms that compete on a regional or national basis may conduct their own yellow pages campaign or use yellow pages as an advertising medium in conjunction with their dealer network. Take, for example, the category of computers. AT&T and Honeywell Bull are listed on their own, indicate their basic services, and give their 800 telephone numbers to call for information. Apple Computer runs a yellow page advertisement listing their local dealers for customers to call. IBM in its advertisement gives numbers to call for sales, service, and supplies as well as listing its local authorized dealers.

In the yellow pages advertising where both names of manufacturer and dealer are listed, this could be an example of cooperative advertising where the dealer participates in the cost of the manufacturer's ad. In other cases, the manufacturer may include dealers in yellow page advertising as a matter of advertising policy.

Creating the advertisement

Format, size, copy, and layout are factors to be reckoned with in creating the advertisement. There are numerous possibilities. The advertisement can vary from a simple name, address, and 'phone number to a display advertisement of a one-half page size or greater.[73]

Here are several do's and don't's regarding copy and layout:

Do's

- Think of your customers in terms of their needs in addition to 'phone number and location, e.g. days and hours of operation, lines carried.
- Find a way to set yourself apart, e.g. 'years in business'.
- Make your location easy to be found, e.g. 'one block south of the fire station'.
- Keep the ad clean and simple.

Don't's

- Start with your company name unless it describes your business.
- Use more than two type faces...it makes the ad too busy.
- Include detailed illustrations or drawings in small space.
- Clutter up the ad with too many elements or too much copy.

Evaluating effectiveness

No advertising effort of any type should be conducted without first determining how its effectiveness should be evaluated. Several alternatives are suggested by Alan Fletcher including the installation of a special telephone number that only appears in the yellow page advertising in order to track incoming calls, or the inclusion of a special discount offer only run in the yellow page advertising to gauge its effectiveness. To judge the source of information whether it be yellow pages or some other medium, a simple tracking form can be used. This is shown in Exhibit 9.8.

The usefulness of this method is that it is designed to evaluate the effectiveness of all communication types for both telephone inquiries or walk-in customers if a retail establishment. To be effective, employees must be schooled as to its importance and trained to use the form at all times; otherwise the method will not produce reliable results.

Summary

An understanding of the basic similarities and differences of print, out-of-home, and yellow pages media is useful when working with media representatives and advertising agencies on cross border advertising campaigns. Many factors need to be taken into account. These include readership, coverages, languages variances, physical characteristics, opportunities for using publications with circulation in more than one country. Of vital importance is a knowledge of the advantages and disadvantages of each vehicle. All of these points were

Exhibit 9.8 *Yellow pages tracking form.* Source*: Fletcher, Alan D. (1991)* Target Marketing through the Yellow Pages, *Yellow Pages Publishers Association, Michigan, p. 29. Reproduced by permission*

Yellow Pages Tracking Form

Date _____

Store Name _____

Branch/Location _____

YPPA
Yellow Pages Publishers Association

Telephone Inquiry	OR	Walk-In Customer	Source of Information (check as many as appropriate) Yellow Pages	Newspaper	Magazine	Radio	TV	Direct Mail	Word-of-Mouth	Other
☐		☐	☐	☐	☐	☐	☐	☐	☐	☐
☐		☐	☐	☐	☐	☐	☐	☐	☐	☐
☐		☐	☐	☐	☐	☐	☐	☐	☐	☐
☐		☐	☐	☐	☐	☐	☐	☐	☐	☐
☐		☐	☐	☐	☐	☐	☐	☐	☐	☐
☐		☐	☐	☐	☐	☐	☐	☐	☐	☐
☐		☐	☐	☐	☐	☐	☐	☐	☐	☐
☐		☐	☐	☐	☐	☐	☐	☐	☐	☐
☐		☐	☐	☐	☐	☐	☐	☐	☐	☐
☐		☐	☐	☐	☐	☐	☐	☐	☐	☐
☐		☐	☐	☐	☐	☐	☐	☐	☐	☐
☐		☐	☐	☐	☐	☐	☐	☐	☐	☐
☐		☐	☐	☐	☐	☐	☐	☐	☐	☐
☐		☐	☐	☐	☐	☐	☐	☐	☐	☐
☐		☐	☐	☐	☐	☐	☐	☐	☐	☐
☐		☐	☐	☐	☐	☐	☐	☐	☐	☐

treated in this chapter. On completion of the following two chapters on electronic and mail media, the reader should be prepared to explore the ways by which media programmes are planned, purchased and evaluated, the content of Chapter 12.

Questions

1　Why do you think readership and circulation of newspapers vary from country to country?
2　Discuss the nature of display and classified advertising in newspapers.
3　Describe the principal advantages and disadvantages of newspaper advertising.
4　Indicate the general characteristics of magazines.
5　Give a synopsis of magazines as an advertising medium in different parts of the world.
6　What are the constraints and obstacles faced by international publications?
7　What opportunities exist for advertising in business publications in different parts of the world?
8　Describe the principal advantages and disadvantages of magazines.
9　Identify the various types of out-of-home advertising.
10　Discuss the variations that will be found in out-of-home advertising from country to country.
11　Describe the nature of the out-of-home advertising audience.
12　Explain the advantages and disadvantages of the out-of-home medium.
13　What are the principal steps in planning yellow pages advertising?
14　How can yellow page advertising be evaluated?

Notes

1　Leo, José, L. (1991) A media presentation at Colgate Palmolive, Mexico City, 16 January.
2　*De Telegraaf* (1985) Promotional brochure, September.
3　Saatchi & Saatchi Compton Worldwide (1987) *MediaFact Europe*. Compiled for *Focus*, Crain Communications, Inc., London, January, p. 95.
4　The Advertising Association (1990) *Marketing Pocket Book 1991*, The Advertising Association, London, p. 107.
5　Grey Daiko (1991) *US versus Japan, a Media Comparison*, a presentation, Tokyo.

6   A/S/M Communications, Inc. (1991) *Media Week's Guide to Media*, New .
    York, **14**, (2), 138, 139, 161.

7   Barroso, Lilia (1991) *Mexico's Media Scene*. A presentation at J. Walter
    Thompson, Mexico City, 15 January.

8   Serenyi, Janos (1991) A memorandum on marketing communications,
    McCann-Erickson, Budapest, 2 January.

9   Saatchi & Saatchi Compton Worldwide, *op. cit.*, p. 56.

10 Hindustan Thompson Associates Limited, *Thompson Pocket Reference To
    Media in India 1991*.

11 Newspaper Advertising Bureau, Inc. (1983) *The Six Wide Design*. A pro-
    motion piece, The Bureau, November.

12 Akari Kitagawa (1990) Phone interview, New York, 28 September.

13 Coen, Robert J. (1990) *Insider's Report*, McCann-Erickson, Inc., New
    York, (21), June; and Axel Springer Verlag (1982) *Europaische WerbeMarkte
    Deuschland*, Berlin, August, p. 44, Table 60.

14 Axel Springer Verlag, *ibid.*, p. 45.

15 Wells, William, Burnett, John and Moriarty, Sandra (1989) *Advertising
    Principals and Practice*, Prentice-Hall, Inc., Englewood Cliffs, NJ, pp. 503–7.

16 *De Telegraaf*, *op. cit.*

17 Axel Springer Verlag, *op. cit.*, pp. 31–34.

18 Wilmshurst, John (1985) *The Fundamentals of Advertising*, William
    Heinemann Ltd., London, p. 145.

19 Dunn, S. Watson and Barban, Arnold M. (1986) *Advertising*, 6th edn,
    Hinsdale, IL: CBS College Publishing, Hinsdale, IL, p. 591.

20 Wilmshurst, *op. cit.*, p. 145.

21 Saatchi & Saatchi Compton Worldwide, *op. cit.*, pp. 58, 59.

22 Team/BBDO (1987) *The German Media Scene*. A presentation, Dusseldorf:
    Team/BBO, 26 May, p. 7.

23 McCann-Erickson Guatemala (1991) *Media Fact Book*, McCann-Erickson,
    Guatemala City, p. 66.

24 *Ibid.*, p. 145.

25 Obe, Ad'Obe (1990) Print media in Black Africa struggle for recognition.
    Advertising World, April–May, 26, 27, 29.

26 *Ibid.*, 26.

27 *Ibid.*, 27.

28 *Ibid.*, 29.

29 Directories International, Inc. (1986) *International Media Guide* (IMG)
    Consumer Magazines Worldwide, Directories International, Inc., New York,
    pp. 142–44.

30 Barroso, *op. cit.*

31 Furniss, John D. (1983) Eye on Japan – the Asian misconception.
    Ad World, June/July, 18.

32 Publications Department (1989) *Dentsu Japan Marketing/Advertising Yearbook*,
    Dentsu Inc., Tokyo, pp. 184–5.

33 China Advertising Association (1990) Information presented at a reception, New York, 19 March.

34 Directories International, *op. cit.*, p. 152.

35 Axel Springer Verlag, *op. cit.*, pp. 45−6.

36 *Ibid.*, pp. 47−8.

37 TBWA World Media, *op. cit.*

38 Personeni, Jane (1990) *Magazines − A Worldwide View*. A presentation, Pleasantville, NY, 9 November.

39 *Ibid.*, (January 1992 update.)

40 TBWA World Media, *op. cit.*

41 Berlin, L.C. (1988) *Marketing Pocket Book 1988*, The Advertising Association, London, February, pp. 106−7.

42 Directories International, *op. cit.*, pp. 1−20.

43 Saatchi & Saatchi Compton Worldwide, *op. cit.*, p. 25.

44 Advertising Age's global media lineup. *Advertising Age*, 14 December 1987, p. 54.

45 Saatchi & Saatchi Compton Worldwide, *op. cit.*, p. 23.

46 Waterkeyn, Martin (1990) *Time For the 1990's*. A presentation, Paris, May.

47 Personeni, *op. cit.*

48 *Ibid.*

49 Waterkeyn, *op. cit.*

50 Research Services, Ltd. (1988) *Pan European Survey 4*, Research Services Ltd., Wembley, England.

51 Tawil, Fouad (1988) Bulk of advertising expenditures in Arab world spent on television. *Arab Ad*, **2**, (4), 17.

52 Directories International, Inc. (1990) *International Media Guide* (IMG) Business/Professional Europe Directories International, Inc., New York.

53 China Advertising Association, *op. cit.*

54 Publications Department, Dentsu, Inc., *op. cit.*, p. 227.

55 Hindustan Thompson Associates Limited, *op. cit.*, p. 20.

56 Serenyi, Janos, *op. cit.*

57 *Arab Ad*, Special Report, January, 1988, **2**, (1).

58 Ghazi, Jameel (1982) Outdoor advertising in Saudi Arabia. *International Advertiser*, March/April, 36, 39.

59 Lintas London, *op. cit.*, p. 25.

60 TBWA, *op. cit.*

61 Berlin, *op. cit.*, p. 115.

62 Nylen, David W. (1986) *Advertising*, 3rd edn, South-Western Publishing Co., Cincinnati, Ohio, p. 390.

63 Commite Medias Mexico (1990) *Medios De Publicidad en Mexico*, Asociacion Mexicana De Agencias De Publicidad, Mexico City.

64 Nylen, *op. cit.*, p. 392.

65 *Ibid.*, p. 398.

66 Berlin, *op. cit.*, p. 115.

67 Axel Springer Verlag, *op. cit.*, p. 64, Table 96.

68 Nylen, *op. cit.*, pp. 398, 400.

69 A/S/M Communications, Inc. (1989) *Adweek, The Marketer's Guide to Media*, First Quarter **12**, (1), 161.

70 Coen, Robert J. (1990) Estimated annual advertising expenditures 1980–1989. Prepared for *Advertising Age*, McCann-Erickson, Inc., New York.

71 *Adweek, op. cit.*, 161.

72 Fletcher, Alan D. (1991) *Yellow Pages Advertising*, Yellow Pages Publishers Association, Troy, Michigan, p. 15.

73 Information for this section has been drawn from Fletcher, Alan D. *Yellow Pages Advertising*, Yellow Pages Advertising Association, Troy, Michigan; and Yellow Pages Advertising Association, *Yellow Pages and the Media Mix*, Troy, Michigan.

10 *Television, radio and cinema*

Introduction

This chapter follows in the footsteps of Chapter 9 by examining the nature of television, radio and cinema media. The first two, television and radio, are often collectively described as broadcast. The third, cinema stands by itself. Each medium will be discussed in terms of its general characteristics in various countries. This will be followed by a more in-depth investigation in selected environments and conclude with a summary of the advantages and disadvantages of each medium.

Television

Television has already been identified as the most dynamic advertising medium in the USA, replacing and outdistancing both magazines and radio to become the premier national advertising medium. The growth of this medium in other countries of the world in many instances, however, has not paralleled the US experience. The reasons for this include economic conditions and development, communication's infrastructure, and governmental constraints.

China

At one end of the spectrum is a country like China. Business was reopened in the 1970s with the non-communist countries of the world. Advertising has been making a comeback since 1979. Twenty-one years prior to that time the first television station was established. A 1981 article on advertising in China indicated that five million television sets existed and were being viewed by 200 million people.[1] In 1986, the number of stations in operation amounted to 363, sets in use jumped to sixty-five million, and the average daily audience climbed to 350 million.[2] By 1988 the figures were up sharply again, this time to 140 million sets and nearly 600 million viewers each day, roughly one-half of the total Chinese population.

The beginning of television advertising coincided with the rebirth of the advertising industry. In 1979 the Shanghai TV Broadcasting Station aired the first commercial. By 1983 television accounted for 14 per cent of the total advertising expenditures in journals, newspapers, radio, and television. This figure climbed to 29 per cent of the total by 1988, becoming roughly one-half as important as newspapers as an advertising medium. The cost of television time — about $6,000 for a thirty second commercial (less for local — was remarkably cheap by Western standards. (The advertising industry as a whole in 1987 was comprised of 11,000 firms, 122,000 people, and total expenditures of $500 million US dollars.[3])

Japan

Television advertising dominates the media scene in Japan where average household viewing amounted to seven hours fifty-six minutes per day[4] compared to US household viewing of seven hours two minutes per day.[5] Despite television's dominance, Cable TV (CATV) has only recently begun to grow with vigour. The pattern of development appears to be following the US model. CATV systems have been small and used to overcome poor reception by retransmitting regular TV broadcasts. It wasn't until March 1989 when a Japanese satellite was successfully launched from French Guiana that satellite communication operations were started in Japan. Three more satellites were put into orbit the same year. These four private satellites cover all of Japan and provide ample capacity for that country's telecommunication needs. This includes cable television which is expected to experience rapid growth. As in the USA, up until satellite transmission became available the cable systems, as previously mentioned, were confined to terrestrial transmission. Now programme suppliers, including general trading companies and television stations, are entering the business with news, entertainment, and sports pro- gramming along with large-scale, multi-channel CATV systems. Households subscribing to multi-channel CATV are expected to reach about eight million (20 per cent of total households) by 1995. In the early twenty-first century the industry overall is expected to be relatively comparable to its counterpart in the USA.[6]

India

In India the medium is controlled by a department of the Information and Broadcasting Ministry. There are approximately 22.5 million TV sets in this country which has a population of about 837 million people. This means that the TV set penetration is roughly 17 per cent. In urban areas the penetration amounts to about 61 per cent. Set penetration is greatest in Delhi in the North (97 per cent) and Maharashtra in the West (87 per cent). It is lowest in the 'NE' Region in the East (37 per cent) and in the Tamil Nadu region in the South (40 per cent). The ratio of colour to black and white sets is roughly one to three. Viewing is greatest during prime time evening shows featuring films, soap operas, and serials. Viewing follows a normal pattern with the low point during breakfast hours, then building throughout the day up to prime hours in the evening.[7] Hindustan Thompson reports that a code, as shown in Exhibit 10.1, exists for commercial advertising on television and radio in India.

Exhibit 10.1 *Code for commercial advertising on television and radio*

'A code of ethics comprising the general rules of conduct for both Advertisers and Advertising Agencies is applicable in India, for advertising on either of the above government-owned media. Broadly these ensure that:

1 Advertising is designed to conform to the laws of the country and does not offend morality, decency or religious susceptibilities
2 does not divide any race, caste, creed
3 protects the consumer against false or exaggerated claims
4 disallows the promotion of cigarettes and other tobacco or tobacco related products, wines and other intoxicants
5 disallows advertisements concerning

   – money lenders
   – chit funds
   – saving schemes and lotteries other than those conducted by Central and State Government bodies, etc.
   – matrimonial agencies
   – unlicensed employment services
   – fortune tellers or soothsayers, etc.
   – foreign goods and foreign banks
   – betting tips or guide books on horses or other games of chance

Guidelines for advertisers
All advertisements due for telecast/broadcast in India, are required to be examined by the respective Commercial Directorate of Doordarshan/All India Radio, so as to enable them to verify that the advertisement does not contravene any of the rules laid down in the code of ethics.

   No advertisement can be telecast/broadcast without obtaining this mandatory approval/clearance.'

Source: Quotation is from Hindustan Thompson Associates Limited, *Thompson Pocket Reference to Media in India 1991*, Bombay, 29.

Hungary

Currently there are about five million television sets in Hungary with about four-fifths of households equipped with colour TV. Until recently television existed as a two-channel state monopoly.

Channel I operates from breakfast until late night seven days a week. Channel II operates weekdays from 5pm until late night and on Sundays and holidays starting at 3pm. Advertising rates peak during prime time hours. Two new private channels began operations in 1990. One operates three times a week from 5 to 8am. The other operated during the summer from 5pm to 1am daily in the Balaton area where 60 per cent of the visitors are foreign, mostly German. Both German and Hungarian languages were used during broadcasts.[8]

Latin America

In Latin America where television has had a longer history than in China, i.e. more than one-third of a century, there is generally greater television viewing among the various populations. Consumer product advertisers concentrate their media expenditures in television. For example, in Costa Rica 92 per cent of the people in the Central Valley, where approximately three-quarters of the population is concentrated, view television regularly.[9] A distinction, however, must be made in Latin American countries like Mexico between the major economic centre(s) and elsewhere in the country inhabited largely by an indigenous population which may or may not be counted in the official economic statistics of a country. This distinction concerns the ability and desirability of delivering an advertising message on television and is based on both economic conditions and the ability to reach the hinterland with a television signal. For example, a leading advertising agency in Guatemala reported that television coverage in the capital, Guatemala City, and the area around the capital was 96 per cent of all households, whereas the television coverage nationally was 34 per cent.[10] (This made radio the preferred medium outside the metropolitan area of Guatemala City.)

Western Europe

In Europe there is considerable disparity with respect to television character-istics among countries in that region of the world. Table 10.1 presents several of these characteristics to highlight the differences.

Examination of the information in Table 10.1 reveals the variance in number of national stations or channels which accept advertising from one in Sweden

Table 10.1   *European television advertising: selected characteristics*

Country	(A) Number of channels	(B) Per cent of total media expenditures	(A) Average commercial Air time minutes/day
Austria	2 national	24	40
Belgium	4 channels/2 language areas	34	220
Denmark	1 national + 1 satellite	14	20
Finland	2 national + 1 regional	19	110
France	6 national/semi-national	30	250
Greece	5 national/semi-national	43	100
Ireland	2 national	27	110
Italy	6 national + 1 semi-national	48	780
Netherlands	4 national	18*	51
Norway	3 satellite/semi-national	4	120
Portugal	2 national	44	300
Spain	4 national + 5 regional	39	200
Sweden	1 national + 1 satellite	0	0
Switzerland	3 language regions	10	20
UK	2 national + 1 breakfast	40	300+
W. Germany	2 national + 4 semi-national	22*	300+

Note
* No Sunday advertising on state channels
Source: Finnegan, Tony (1992) *MJP*, Carat International Ltd, London.

to six national channels in Italy and six national/semi-national channels in France. As for per cent of total media expenditures allocated to television, the figures again show major dissimilarities. In Italy, Portugal, and Greece the percentages run from 43 to 48 per cent whereas in Switzerland, Norway and Sweden, television accounts for 10 per cent or less of the total media expenditures. The average commercial air time minutes per day is a third factor where wide variations occur; from 780 minutes per day in Italy to zero minutes in Sweden. Comparisons made between television as a per cent of total media expenditures and the television air time minutes per day on a country-by-country basis indicate that a correlation does not exist.

Another significant difference for advertisers are the dissimilarities in lead time required in various countries for the placement of television advertising. For example, in Austria and Switzerland and for West German and Italian state-owned channels application for television advertising time must be submitted in September or October of the previous year. In Portugal and Spain, the lead time is two weeks or less.[11]

A closer look at commercial television in selected European countries

UK

The UK currently has three commercial television networks. A new network is expected to go into operation in 1993. The existing networks include one that is national (ITV) but which is operated by fourteen programme companies (two in London) which sell advertising in their own regions and through their own sales departments.

The second network, Channel 4, is national with a 'minority-based appeal'. Advertising time on this network is sold by ITV sales contractors. The third network, TV-am, is an early morning national programme for which air time is sold by its own sales force.[12]

As for television advertising time, it is limited to six minutes an hour, averaged over the day's programmes, with normally a maximum of seven minutes in any 'clock-hour' (e.g. 6−7pm, 7−8pm).[13]

It must be pointed out, however, that the British Broadcasting Company (BBC) operates two non-commercial channels funded by licence fees which are paid by households with a television.[14] Table 10.2 indicates the viewing hours attributed to each channel.

The figures in Table 10.2 show that the hours of television viewing are quite equally divided between non-commercial and commercial television.

Commercial broadcasting in the UK is controlled by the Independent Broadcasting Authority (IBA), a central body appointed by the Home Secretary. The IBA, in accordance with the provisions of the Broadcasting Act is involved in all matters pertaining to the 'planning and formulation of policy, and is ultimately responsible for the content and quality of everything transmitted'. The IBA appoints the programme companies, mentioned earlier, that derive their revenue from the sale of advertising time and pay rent to the IBA to cover the costs of operating the national network of transmitters. While the individual companies are responsible for programme content, the appropriate

Table 10.2 *Average daily viewing hours − homes*

Network	Av hours	% of total	Av hours	% of total
BBC 1	1.8	36.7	1.9	36.5
BBC 2	0.5	10.2	0.6	11.5
ITV	2.4	49.0	2.2	42.3
Channel 4	0.2	4.1	0.5	9.6
Total	4.9	100.0	5.2	99.9

Source: BARB/AGB Hours Viewed In Lintas (1989) *Media Fact Book 1989*, Media Research Department, London, March, 16.

quality and balance in programming is overseen by the IBA. This includes the allocation of sufficient time for different types of programmes including education, religion, news documentaries, local interests, and programmes made in the UK.[15]

With respect to satellite and cable television advertising in the UK, in 1989 it was estimated that 260,000 UK homes were connected to cable and receiving satellite transmissions though more than that number of homes were connected to (ground) cable relay systems called MATV. In addition to this wired cable system of transmission, two companies were engaged in developing direct-to-home from satellite transmission requiring subscribers to own a 'dish' for reception. One system using the ASTRA Satellite was expected to transmit eleven English channels including Rupert Murdoch's six 'sky' and sport channels, and Robert Maxwell's Premiere and MTV channels. The other, British Satellite Broadcasting (BSB), via its own satellite was preparing to transmit three channels including sports and films, and possibly two additional channels if given the award by the IBA. By mid-1990 it was anticipated that 1.5 million UK homes would be receiving satellite television which would account for 7 per cent of UK homes and 3 per cent of adult hours viewed. In mid-1992 these figures were projected to grow to 4.8 million homes, 23 per cent of the total and 6 per cent share of adult hours viewed. Not all of the satellite channels will carry advertising. As for the impact of this new medium, it is believed that satellite television will be a peripheral medium for advertisers for some time to come.[16]

West Germany
In West Germany the opportunity for television advertising has its own special limiting characteristics. There are three state-owned television networks, two of which are run by (nine) regional independent public corporations which operate under the laws of the '*Lander*' (land). Jointly these organizations form the Association of German Broadcasting (ARD) but each is self-governed and financed by licence fees of viewers and advertisers in the regions in which they operate. However, only one of the two networks (Channel 1) accepts advertising; the other, Channel 3, does not. ZDF is the second channel to accept advertising. It is owned jointly by the *Lander*.[17]

The ARD advertising Channel 1 broadcasts nationwide with the same programming each day except for two hours between 6 and 8pm when nine regional stations which form the network broadcast their own individual programmes.

Advertising messages, limited to twenty minutes per day, are only allowed between 6 and 8pm over regional stations. These messages are transmitted in blocks (pods) lasting five to ten minutes and are interspersed with non-commercial reports. Advertising announcements normally vary in length from seven to sixty seconds, occasionally longer.

The ZDF Channel 2 only operates on a national basis and accepts television advertising on a similar basis as ARD Channel 1, but from 5.35 to 7.30pm.[18]

Television advertising is not accepted on Sundays and holidays. If television is to be included in an advertiser's media schedule, application for time on the state-owned channels must be made by 30 September for scheduling the following year. An average television advertising schedule could consist of four thirty-second announcements per month on both state channels.[19] Even given these circumstances, demand for television time generally exceeds supply.

With respect to private television, there are two stations of significance — RTL Plus and SAT 1 both with growing national reach currently about 70 per cent of total households.[20]

At this moment a new chapter is being written on television as the East and West are merged into one united Germany.

Pan-European satellite television*

In 1991 there were nine satellite communications systems offering television programming in various countries in Europe. These systems included Super Channel, Eurosport, Screensport, CNN, MTV and Scandinavia/Scansat TV3. Super Channel, Eurosport, Screensport and MTV have had the same degree of success in acquiring subscribers. On the Continent, The Netherlands, Belgium/Luxembourg, and Switzerland had the highest degrees of household penetration; 47 to 72 per cent of the total households in these countries were connected to one or both systems. In the Scandinavian countries, West Germany, and Austria household connections ranged from 30 to 42 per cent. In France, Greece, Italy, Spain, and Portugal 8 per cent or less of the households were connected.

These are problems which television Pan-European satellite transmission is facing:

- Heavy dependence on cable connection; possibilities of which vary by country.
- Low advertising demand and too few real Pan-European advertisers.
- Inflexible...inability to adjust market weight with audience viewing.
- Language — English is not a widely understood language other than in The Netherlands and Scandinavia. It is questionable if expensive, multi-language soundtracks can attract sufficient additional viewers to be cost effective. On the positive side more advertisers are using the medium and the thematic channels are progressing.[21]

---

* Information in this section was originally supplied in 1989 by Tony Finnegan (MJP/Carat International Ltd. London). It was updated in February 1992.

Television in the USA

The growth in household usage of television since the beginning of commercial broadcasting is one measure of its power as a communication medium. Table 10.3 indicates the relationship between households and television ownership from 1950 to 1990.

Television's penetration of US households rose rapidly between 1950 and 1960. Since then it has continued to climb at a decelerating pace as the saturation point is approached.

Keeping pace with these penetration figures are the growth in multi-set and colour ownership. Multi-set households have risen gradually from 40,000 or 1 per cent of total television households in 1950 to 60 million or 65 per cent in 1990. In 1955 the first incidence of colour television was recorded. By 1975, twenty years later, over two-thirds of the television households owned at least one colour television set. By 1990 the per cent penetration increased to 98 per cent.[22]

A second measure of the medium's power is the trend in advertising dollars spent on television. Table 10.4 shows this trend in ten-year intervals since 1950.

The growth in dollars and in share of total advertising expenditures was extraordinary in the 1950 to 1960 interval. In subsequent intervals the dollar growth has been very large but the share of total advertising expenditures has grown at a decreasing rate.

A third measure of television's power is its reach according to a 1990 survey. Around 89 per cent of the adults watched television yesterday for 245 minutes.[23]

As for television household usage, the average daily viewing of approximately seven hours did not change appreciably during the 1980s.[24] As might be expected, usage starts the day (6–7am) at a low level, builds throughout the

Table 10.3 *Growth in television households 1950 to 1990*

Year	Total US households (000)	TV households (000)	Per cent with TV
1950	43,000	3,880	9.0
1960	52,500	45,750	87.1
1970	61,410	58,500	95.3
1980	77,900	76,300	97.9
1990	93,760	92,100	98.2

Source: TVB Research Department (1990) *Trends in Television*, Television Advertising Bureau, New York, 3.

Table 10.4   *Estimated annual television advertising expenditures*

Year	Dollars (millions)	Per cent change	Per cent of total advertising expenditures
1950	$ 171	—	3
1960	1,627	851%	14
1970	3,596	121	18
1980	11,469*	219	21
1989	26,891*	134	22

* includes cable television

Source: Coen, Robert J. (1990) *Estimated Annual Advertising Expenditures 1950–1989*, McCann-Erickson, Inc., NY.

day, peaks between 8 and 10pm, and thereafter falls rather rapidly into the early morning hours. This pattern of usage can be seen in Exhibit 10.2.

Viewing by selected age and sex characteristics are ranked below:

	Viewing hours:minutes/week
Women 55+	41:19
Men 55+	38:22
Women 18–34	29:16
Children 2–5	27:49
Male teens (12–17)	22:18
Female teens (12–17)	21:16

Women and men, fifty-five and over, view the most television; male and female teens, the least.[25]

Similar findings of more viewing by both men and women fifty-five years

Exhibit 10.2   *Daily television usage*

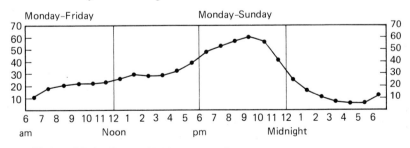

Source: Nielsen Media Research, *Nielsen 1990 Report on Television*. Northbrook, Illinois.

old and over were indicated in the (Brushkin) survey mentioned earlier which also reported greater reach among the fifty-five plus age category. Other demographic findings included a skew to greater reach as well as more time spent among these with lower income and less education.[26]

US television industry structure
The USA has its own distinctive features when it comes to television industry structure.

Regulation and ownership
To begin with, the industry is characterized by private ownership under licence from the Federal Communication Commission (FCC).

Under this licensing authority the FCC has the power to control both programme and advertising content, but as Runyon has pointed out, '. . is reluctant to do so'.[27] Instead, the FCC refers complaints to another governmental agency, customarily the Federal Trade Commission (FTC). The FTC, with its power to exact remedies such as cancellation of contracts, refund money, payment of damages and public notification in cases involving false and deceptive advertising, has an influence over advertisers. Since all legitimate advertisers wish to keep customers satisfied with their product offerings, every precaution would be taken to make sure advertising communications are not deceptive.[28] (The FTC's powers extend to all forms of advertising, not just television.)

Regulation is not only an interest of governmental agencies. The advertising industry, itself, is concerned with matters such as deception, operating with the philosophy that it is better to be self-policing and pro-active rather than to have to respond to the dictates of governmental authority. Professional associations of the advertising industry joined forces with the Council of Better Business Bureaus in 1971 to establish a system for dealing with deceptive advertising.[29]

Other participants in the regulatory process include television networks, advertising agencies, and advertisers. The networks and all legitimate advertisers and agencies will have internal systems, including legal counsel, to ensure that advertising messages can be properly documented as to accuracy of factual content, are neither false or deceptive. . .nor in bad taste.

The availability of television advertising time
When it comes to the placement of advertising on television, it is possible to buy time on a national or local (spot) basis. National advertising is normally accomplished by purchasing television advertising time from a network on either a sponsorship or participation basis. Sponsorship means that the advertiser takes financial responsibility for producing the programme and the advertising within it. This, in turn, means control of both the programming and

advertising content. At today's costs, it also means a sizable investment and sole responsibility for the gain or loss resulting from viewer acceptance of the programme and size and nature of the audience. That's why 90 per cent of the commercial advertising time on television is purchased on a participation basis where the advertiser becomes one of several advertisers that buy announcements in a particular programme. The advertiser in this instance loses control of the programming and any benefits that may accrue from sponsorship identification. On the other hand, the advertiser stands to gain a lower cost in delivery of the advertising message and is able to advertise during more than one programme rather than be confined to announcements on just one, single show.[30]

Local or spot advertising refers to announcements which are placed on individual stations by either local or national advertisers. These announcements may be placed between national programmes or within (or between) local programmes.[31]

Guidelines for the number of non-programme minutes per hour have been set by the National Association of Broadcasters as follows:[32]

				Minutes
1	For network affiliates:	prime time		9.5
		non prime time		16.0
		Children's:	Sat/Sun	9.5
			Mon/Fri	12.0
2	For independent stations:	prime time		12.0
		non prime time		16.0

Non-programme minutes not only include commercial announcements but also promotional announcements for other programmes, presentation of the sponsor(s) at the beginning and end of a programme (called billboards), and programme credits exceeding thirty seconds.[33] As for commercial length, the thirty-second commercial is the most frequently used length although fifteen-second commercials have been increasingly used to offset the rising costs of television advertising time.

The network situation

Nationally, the three major networks, Columbia Broadcasting System (CBS), National Broadcasting System (NBC), and American Broadcasting System (ABC) have been in existence since the early days of television. These networks have been joined recently by the Fox Broadcasting System (FBS). FBS, under the control of Rupert Murdoch, is comprised of a network of independent stations which cover approximately 80 per cent of US television households.[34] The traditional networks each own fifteen stations. The remainder and major portion of their network is comprised of approximately 200 privately owned affiliates each.[35] These affiliated stations are contractually obligated to carry network-originated programming during their daily schedules, normally comprised of certain daytime programmes such as 'soap operas', news, and prime time programmes of various types. In this manner, the networks are able to provide advertisers with national coverage.

With reference to network coverage, it is defined as 'the number and percentage of all US television households that are able to receive a given programme.[36] Table 10.5 provides an example of the coverage of several different network programmes, including the number of affiliated stations in each network's lineup for that particular programme.

Over the years the three major networks have held a dominant position with respect to share of the national viewing audience. However, their combined share has been declining in recent years. For example, the three network share has declined from 89 per cent in 1978–79 to 73 per cent in 1985–86,[37] and to 58 per cent in 1990.[38] Developments since the early 1970s involving FCC rulings lessened the control accorded to the big three networks over programme production, scheduling and re-run syndication. This stimulated growth of independent programme producers, syndicators, and local stations. Another phenomenon in the 1970s was the emergence of satellite delivery systems for basic and pay cable television. More recently there has been rapid acceptance of VCR technology. All of the foregoing factors have contributed to the erosion of the major networks' share of the nationwide television audience.[39]

Syndication
Syndication involves the sale of re-run of original programmes (television or radio) to local stations (affiliates or independents) to fill gaps in programming which are likely to occur during the morning, late afternoon, early evening, and late night. The rapid growth in syndication throughout the 1970s and 1980s is related to the general need for programming, and particularly because of the increase in number of independent stations.[40] Table 10.6 provides information on the status of syndicated programming in 1988. While Table

Table 10.5 *Network programme coverage*

Network programme	Household coverage (%)	No of stations in lineup
CBS 60 Minutes	99	209
ABC Monday Night Movie	93	178
NBC News Digest	77	148
CBS Dallas	99	208

Source: Sissors, Jack Z. and Lincoln Bumba (1987) *Advertising Media Planning*, 3rd edn, NTC Business Books, Lincolnwood, Illinois, p. 46.

Table 10.6 *Selected syndicated programme information (1989)*

Daypart	Time Period	No of programmes	% US TV household coverage	Normal frequency	Normal length
Daytime	6am−4.30pm	16	70−95	1or5xWk	1/2−1 hr
Early Fringe	5pm−7.30pm	13	75−99	1or5xWk	1/2 hr
Prime Access	7.30pm−8pm	43	70−99	1xWk	1/2 hr
Prime Time	8pm−11pm	33	80−99	1xWk/1xMo	2 hrs
Late Fringe	11.30pm−1am	13	70−90	1or5xWk	1/2−1 hr
Children	− am −	37	70−95	5xWk	1/2 hr
Specials	As occurring	50	70−95	1xonly	2 hrs
Sports	As occurring	8	80−97	1xonly	1 hr
		213			

Source: *Adweek, Marketer's Guide To Media*, First Quarter, 1989, 15,22.

10.6 does not show all the syndicated programme offerings, the 213 programmes it does list cover all day parts as well as special types of programmes, all of which have the potential of being viewed in 70 per cent or more of total US television households. (In 1989 The Nielsen Syndication Service provided audience information on over 450 programmes.[41])

The organization which syndicates a programme may sell advertising time to an advertiser and/or make arrangements with local stations to run the programme on a one-time or regular basis depending on the programme format, e.g. special or serial. When a station agrees to run a show, a predetermined time period is also established.[42] Advertising time may be sold on either a national or local (spot) basis. All of the top 100 advertisers use syndication to air their advertising messages. This can account for 10 per cent or more of their television network budget.[43]

The syndication industry is not without its problems. Some experts believe that the top-rated programmes are priced too high and that the 'marginal' shows are not good buys because of poor quality. In contrast, other experts believe that syndication offers lower costs than network programming. The greater risks are with the new rather than the established programmes. This is because advertisers don't know in advance what kind of rating a particular show will get, and sometimes don't know which daypart the show will be placed in as the syndicator attempts to put together a nationwide station lineup. Despite these problems, one observer felt that the outlook for syndicated television in the 1990s would be 'mostly sunny.'[44]

Independents
In keeping with an increasing number of non-network programme producers, syndicators, and syndicated shows, independent television stations increased

from sixty-one in 1969 in thirty-four markets providing 53 per cent coverage of US households to 339 stations in 1989 in 137 markets providing 92 per cent coverage.[45]

The new network

Fox Broadcasting System (FBS), the fourth television network, has emerged as a real challenge to the big three networks in recent years by syndicating live programming beginning with a late night talk show (1986) and then moving into prime time programming (1987). The number of independent stations under contract in the late 1980s provided coverage of 80 per cent of US television households.[46] As a result of independent stations availing themselves of the syndicated programme opportunities of FBS and as a result of becoming part of its network, they have been able to double the number of their viewers[47] to the detriment of competing independents and network affiliates.

Cable

Cable television is another major factor to consider in the assessment of the trends in the overall television industry in the USA. When cable television was initiated in the late 1940s it was known as 'community antenna television' or CATV. Its purpose was to deliver an original or improved signal to households where 'over-the-air' transmission was a problem. Growth was modest until 1975 when satellite transmission . . of first-run films . . . began. Cable operators discovered that speedier and more efficient transmission was possible via satellite and dish reception than over land. This sparked the rapid expansion of cable systems and cable subscribers.[48] The penetration of total US homes has risen from 14.2 per cent in February 1967 to 57.8 per cent in February 1990. In this latest period, cable is found in over 53,000,000 homes. The average annual increase in cable television homes over the past five years has been over 3,000,000.[49] The penetration of cable television, however, is by no means uniform. Table 10.7 shows the cable penetration in selected US markets, numbered and ranked in order of importance in terms of total television households.

The variation ranges from less than 50 per cent penetration to 75 per cent. Among those markets listed, there appears to be no correlation between rank and per cent cable penetration.

Cable television is transmitted to homes in a given area by operators who have been awarded contracts by local governments. Cable programming can originate locally or be received via satellite[50] from various networks that provide news, entertainment, sports, children, special audience, and religious programmes.[51]

Cable programming is classified as either basic programming or pay programming. Both are charged to the subscriber on a monthly basis, but the latter involves an added fee to receive current or recent movies, special programmes, and certain sports events not otherwise available. The Cable

Table 10.7 *Cable Television Penetration of Selected US Markets*

Market	Ranking	% Penetration
New York	1	56.8
Los Angeles	2	54.0
Chicago	3	49.0
Philadelphia	4	67.1
San Francisco-Oakland-San Jose	5	62.8
Houston	10	51.0
Phoenix	20	48.5
Kansas City	30	56.1
Salt Lake City	40	46.6
West Palm Beach-Ft. Pierce	50	74.5

Source: Nielsen Station Index News (1990) *Cable Penetration Estimates July 1990*, Northbrook, ILL, Nielsen Media Research.

Advertising Bureau (CAB) listed twenty-eight satellite-fed national networks, thirteen regional networks, and three shopping service networks, all advertiser-supported.[52] As for pay programming one source reported ten networks.[53]

Advertising revenues in 1990 from various cable programming amounted to nearly twenty-four billion dollars. See the pie chart in Exhibit 10.3 which shows the relative importance of national network, regional sports and local/spot cable.

Relative importance: network, independent, cable and public television
One way to look at the relative importance of different forms of television transmission is by weekly usage. Total weekly television usage amounted to

Exhibit 10.3 *Division of advertising revenues by type of programming*

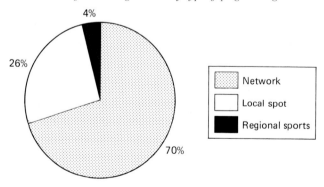

Source: Paul Kagan Associates, Inc. *Cable TV Facts 90*.

over forty-seven hours in April 1990. Shares of weekly household usage were reported to be as follows:

		%
Network affiliates:	ABC 19	
	CBS 18	
	NBC 18	55%
Independent stations:		23
Cable:	Basic 18	
	Pay 7	25
Public television:		3
Total		106*

* Figures exceed 100 per cent due to simultaneous viewing
Source: TVB Research Department (1990) *Trends in Cable TV*. Based on A.C. Nielsen Monthly Cable Status Report April.

The big three networks with their affiliates, despite declining shares, still dominate the television media as observed in the figures on weekly household usage.

The one remaining factor that has also contributed to the decline in network dominance is the rapid expansion in household acquisition of VCRs. This growth has been fuelled by the introduction of (relatively) low-priced equipment and proliferation of video software available in various types of retail outlets.[54] Since 1980 when 400,000 homes or 0.5 per cent of total television households were reported to be owners of VCRs, household ownership increased to 63,917,000 or 69.4 per cent of the total by May 1990.[55]

Over the past four years (1987–1990) there has been a moderately declining trend in total weekly minutes of VCR recording and playing. For the first six months of 1990, the total minutes of play in an average week came to 230...approximately thirty-three minutes per day. (This is slightly greater than the time spent per week on pay cable.) During prime time evening hours, the number of minutes of play per week amounted to sixty-one...peaking over the weekend.[56]

To summarize the recent developments in the US television situation, there have been many new opportunities for viewing in television households. This is evidenced by the growth of independent stations, in basic and pay cable, and in VCR ownership. Programme viewing alternatives are much greater than they were ten years ago and are forecast to continue to grow throughout the 1990s. This means that the audiences for shows in general will continue to shrink. A premium will be placed on effective programming in order for stations and operators of all types to survive. The bottom line, as one expert has said, is that all television is (and will be) driven by programming.[57] This will hold true whether it involves the television industry in the USA, Europe, or the Far East.

Advantages and disadvantages

The advantages and disadvantages of television as an advertising medium include these considerations:

Advantages

- Offers the combined impact of sight, sound, and motion.
- The best medium for product demonstration.
- Can deliver a large national or local audience, i.e. broad reach.
- Possible to reach males, females, teens, and children through programme selection.
- Can have flexibility in terms of geographic coverage; national, regional, and local.
- Due to its established reputation in some countries as a source of news, entertainment and education, TV can lend credibility to an advertiser's message.
- Delivers a captive audience; viewers must make a special effort to miss seeing a commercial.

Disadvantages

- The cost of a unit of advertising time may be beyond the means of many advertisers.
- The preparation of good quality television commercials can be very costly.
- Tends to deliver a non-selective audience other than sex and broad age classification resulting in wasted coverage.
- Availability of advertising time in or adjacent to quality programmes which deliver large audiences is limited and costly.
- The life of a television message is short-lived, not giving the viewer much opportunity to reconsider the details.
- Due to the transitory nature of the advertising message it cannot be used by consumers as a means for searching out product alternatives and making choices.
- In some countries due to the number and (short) length of commercials their visibility and persuasiveness are diminished. (This is called commercial clutter.)
- Where advertising time has to be bought six to twelve months in advance, the advertiser has limited, if any, flexibility in scheduling advertising or making scheduling adjustments.[58]

Radio

The role of radio in the advertising budgets of most advertisers around the world is distinctively supportive. This is evidenced by radio's position among other media alternatives as shown in Table 1, Part Four Introduction. Radio ranks as number five out of six among media alternatives in Europe and Asia, fourth in the USA, and third in Latin American countries. This does not mean radio as an advertising medium should be ignored. For some small advertisers with low advertising budgets, it has been proven to be effective as the principal medium. However, generally it is used as a supportive medium to extend reach or increase pressure in a particular market. Radio usage will be examined in different countries of the world and will be considered in terms of its advantages and disadvantages as a medium. To set the stage for a discussion of radio in today's market place, a brief historical sketch of radio advertising in the USA will be given.

Radio in the USA

In the 1930s and 1940s radio emerged as a major national medium to rival magazines for the national advertiser's dollar.[59] It provided general family entertainment for adults and youth as well as coverage of athletic events such as baseball for sports enthusiasts, soap operas for homemakers, and mystery and adventure serials for teenagers and children. Much of the advertising in those days was purchased on networks providing national coverage.

Shortly after network television became available it quickly moved past radio as the dominant broadcast advertising medium. This resulted in the transformation of radio into an entirely different advertising category. Instead of being a family medium delivering a broad national audience, it became a specialized medium delivering different programme formats to different, more specialized audiences on a local rather than national level. Formats included news, talk shows, and music to appeal to different tastes and preferences and behavioural patterns. Listening takes place when shaving and showering, preparing breakfast, driving to and from work or just for pleasure, when relaxing, and/or after turning out the bedside lamp when going to sleep at night. As a result, radio is found today predominantly as a local medium with local programming specializing in various musical and talk show formats and news. The variety of music to be enjoyed will vary from hard rock to country and western to classical. . .attracting different socioeconomic audiences.

Talk show formats include sports commentary, medicine, gardening, managing your money, local politics and government, religion, and contemporary and controversial issues. While personal visits to the microphones are still popular, increasingly guests are being interviewed by phone. In many instances the listening audience has a chance to participate by calling the station to have questions answered by the talk show host or his/her guests.

Technological advances in radio sets continue to expand opportunities for listening. One example is the increasing popularity of the small, portable headset which people use when walking or jogging.

Current situation

Estimates indicate that radio accounts for 10 per cent of the total measurable advertising expenditures in the USA. As a communications medium, radio usage is pervasive. Here are a few statistics to support this contention. . .[60]

- 99 per cent of all households have a radio(s)
- the average number of radios per household is 5.6
- car commuters spend 97 per cent of their driving time listening to radio
- the average US person listens to radio two hours fifty-nine minutes per day
- radio's listening levels are consistent throughout the year
- radio listening peaks between 7 and 8am and declines from that period throughout the day and evening
- the highest reach levels for radio are among teens and males eighteen to thirty-four.

Due to specialized programming and segmented listeners, the average ratings for thirty-second announcements are 1.3−1.4 for adults and 0.7 for teenagers. This means that any one advertisement reaches a very small portion of a group of listeners. To build reach against a given target the addition of a number of stations is required.[61] (Refer to Chapter 12 for an explanation of ratings and reach.)

China

In this great country the radio transmission network, run by provinces, municipalities, autonomous regions, cities and counties under provincial jurisdiction, provides 80 per cent coverage. There are approximately 300 million radios owned by its citizens and eighty million loudspeakers in the countryside. Regular listeners comprise 53.7 per cent of the total population.

Advertising on radio includes various types of presentations such as 'peetry (poetry), opera, guyi, music, crosstalk, and story-telling'.

According to the China Advertising Association radio is the most effective medium in China for fast and large-scale coverage of the country.[62]

India

Radio in India ranks number four in media expenditures behind print, television, and outdoor, accounting for 3 per cent of the total. There are approximately ninety-four million radio sets in India or one set for every nine people. Radio penetration is 78 per cent in urban areas as compared with 61 per cent in rural areas. Radio is owned and controlled by the government through its agency, All India Radio. Advertising time can be purchased by metropolitan area groupings, by type of market covered, and by breadth of station coverage. Programme sponsorships are possible for certain geographic groupings of stations for a period of time from five to thirty minutes. Commercial length can be purchased in increments from seven to thirty seconds. Programme types include rural/farm, women's, light music (Indian and Western), and 'film' music.[63]

Hungary

In Hungary there are presently somewhere between five and six million radio sets. Listeners have the opportunity to tune into three state radio channels and three commercial channels. Radio Danubius, which covers all of Hungary and East Austria and broadcasts in both Hungarian and German, is the only channel which has conducted survey research to provide listeners' information. Advertising rates vary by length of commercial (ten to sixty seconds) and time of day with highest prices paid in peak morning hours.[64]

Japan

Up until the late 1980s radio advertising, which accounts for about 5 per cent of total advertising expenditures in Japan, had been in a slump for several years. The year 1988 was characterized as a year of recovery for commercial radio. Factors which accounted for this recovery included the start up of five new FM stations (three in the Tokyo area), reprogramming on the part of established AM and FM stations, more advertising time availabilities for the very popular night time baseball games in and out of season, and increased promotional pressure. Instead of depressing the business of the existing stations, the advent of the new FM stations brought about the opposite effect. Growth in radio advertising expenditures occurred among both traditional (food/beverage/tobacoo) and less traditional (office equipment/industrial-machinery/precision-equipment) spenders. Car advertising, normally number one, declined, however.

Listening among female salaried workers increased in response to more programming with social and economic content of interest to this group.

Targeting programming to narrower listener groups by means of new news and information programmes, special musical formats, and special topics of interest to young people and adults attracted more listeners and advertisers.

Considerable promotional pressure was exerted by means of issuing comic magazines showing the value of radio, encouraging student station visits, preparation of special earthquake disaster drill programming, and using a mobile remote studio to attract listener interest.

The popularity of night baseball during which advertisers could air commercial messages on either a spot or network basis produced listening averages among men and women twelve to fifty-nine of between 7 and 8 per cent.

The foregoing information paints a healthy picture for advertising on the forty-seven AM and short wave and twenty-nine FM private radio stations in Japan.[65]

Latin America

As indicated at the outset, radio is significantly more important as an advertising medium in selected Latin American countries than in Europe, South East Asia, and Japan. In Guatemala, for example, it was reported that 20 per cent of the total advertising expenditures were invested in radio, twice the level experienced in the USA. The penetration of radio in urban homes reaches a high of 98 per cent in the capital city and ranges from 83 per cent in the Northeast to 90 per cent in the Northwest. In the capital there is an average of 2.4 radios per home. As for number of radio stations, 132 are commercial, ten are religious, and seven governmental, making a total of 149 stations in operation in 1991. With respect to station ratings between 8am and 6pm, they range from a high of 14.9 per cent in the twenty to twenty-nine age category to a fraction of 1 per cent in various demographic categories such as housewives and adults aged thirty to thirty-nine. Average station ratings across all demographic classifications range from 0.7 to 2.3 per cent. Station ratings are relatively uniform for both high and low economic groups. A varied musical format is the most popular programme type. No regulations govern the use of radio.[66]

In Costa Rica, 90.4 per cent of the people in the Central Valley listen to radio regularly, somewhat more for those aged fifteen to twenty years old and somewhat less for people in the thirty plus category. As in most other countries radio listening peaks during the morning hours and is significantly lower at other times of the day as shown by these figures (figures show per cent listening at different hours):

5am−12 Noon	12pm−1pm	1pm−7pm	7pm−Midnight	Midnight−5am
73.2%	31.5%	45.1%	34.1%	14.5%

Most of the radio listening is done at home. Music and the news are the most popular programme formats. Radio listening is equally popular between sexes and across all educational categories. The most popular commercial form is the jingle followed by testimonials. Only 9 per cent of the regular listeners don't like the radio commercials.[67]

In Mexico 80 per cent of homes and 78 per cent of cars have radios — similar to listening habits in Costa Rica and elsewhere. The peak occurs during morning hours by 10am and declines throughout the remainder of the day. There are close to 900 stations in Mexico, three-quarters of which are AM stations and the balance FM. A varied musical format is the most popular programme type followed by rock in Spanish and then ballads in Spanish. Individual station ratings are characteristically low in the three largest cities, ranging from 0.4 to 1.4 per cent.[68]

Based on a media study by Nielsen in February 1989, it was found that 61 per cent of the people surveyed listened to radio 'yesterday'. There was relatively little difference between economic classes (60—65 per cent) and men and women over eighteen (59—62 per cent). The biggest variation in listening was found between males under eighteen (55 per cent) and females under eighteen (68 per cent).

As for coverage, there are no national stations. Among all stations 85 per cent are found in other parts of the country than in the three principal cities (Mexico City, Guadalajara, and Monterey). This produces a coverage of 95 per cent of the country by radio. Commercial length varies between ten and sixty seconds, and commercial time can be as much as twenty minutes per hour as compared with nine minutes per hour in a country such as the UK. Sales are controlled by twenty-seven companies. Price negotiations and discounts are a matter to be resolved between advertiser or its agency and the stations. Like Guatemala there are no advertising restrictions.[69]

Europe

Looking at the relative importance of radio as a vehicle for conveying advertising messages in thirteen European countries in terms of per cent of total advertising expenditures, the range varied from a high of nearly 13 per cent in Austria to zero per cent in Sweden where the medium is unavailable for advertising. As to rank in relative importance among six major media alternatives, in seven of thirteen countries it was ranked number five. In eight of those countries the budget was 2.5 per cent or less of the total advertising expenditures.[70] Conditions for radio advertising will be discussed for selected European countries.

Germany
The story on radio and other forms of media advertising is being rewritten now as East and West Germany are reunited. In West Germany there are

fifteen state-owned local/regional stations and a growing number of private German stations which currently number about 200.[71] Estimated adult coverage is 80 per cent.[72] This means that four-fifths of West Germany and West Berlin can be covered by radio advertising. As observed in other countries, reach is greatest in the morning — over 27 per cent of the total population can be reached in the 7 to 8am hour. Thereafter the listening declines irregularly throughout the day to a low of less than 1 per cent in the 8 to 9pm hour.

One problem area with respect to coverage is the Nordhein-Westfalen region where five of the top markets are located. The state-owned station there does not accept advertising. This means that the only way to obtain coverage for this area is by means of Radio Luxembourg.[73]

Other characteristics of interest to advertisers include:

1 *State channels*

- advertisements are delivered in five-minute blocks between programmes
- commercials, normally ranging between fifteen and sixty seconds in length, are aired from 6am until 9pm
- time must be bought by 30 September for the entire year ahead; selection can be made by day and hour of transmission
- supply and demand will vary from station to station
- no radio advertising is permitted on Sundays and public holidays

2 *Private radio*

- commercials can be aired during late evening hours, on Sundays and public holidays
- opportunities exist for creating live spots and sponsored programmes
- if not sold out earlier, closing dates are fourteen days prior to transmission

Restrictions with respect to commercial announcements on radio cover cigarettes, prescription drugs, and use of children in or as targets of radio advertising.[74]

British radio
British radio presents an interesting combination of government operated and government controlled stations, and some coverage from stations outside the UK.[75] The British Broadcasting Corporation (BBC) under direct government control operates four stations, each of which provide national coverage, and one station which provides local coverage; none of which permit advertising.

The government-regulated Independent Broadcasting Authority (IBA) appoints independent companies to serve separate areas within the UK. These companies which provide their own programmes derive revenue from advertising time sales and pay rent to the IBA to cover administration costs and also to pay for the operation of its network transmitters. The Independent Local Radio (ILR) companies must meet IBA programme standards with respect to content and variety.

The ILR stations came to forty-six in 1989 with eight additional ones planned to serve various areas in the near future and three national channels in the 1990s.

Advertising time is limited to nine minutes per hour and can be bought on a spot-by-spot basis or in packages designed to reach specific audiences. Network packages are also available on certain programmes. Radio audiences skew to the lower socioeconomic group, especially heavy listeners. The listener profile is also younger than television with greatest reach among males fifteen to thirty-four and females fifteen to twenty-four.

Share of listening is divided 65−35 per cent between BBC listeners and ILR and other stations (RTL Ireland and Radio Luxembourg). While 90 per cent of the population can receive radio, weekly ILR radio reach is only 42 per cent, Radio Luxembourg 2 per cent (a youth-oriented audience), and other radio 9 per cent.

Other European countries[76]

In Sweden there is no commercial domestic radio. Instead, reception is now permitted by government from foreign radio stations via cable. This situation could change in the future.

In France, radio accounts for 11 per cent of total advertising expenditures. Traditionally it has been a regional medium served by three foreign stations with a young, male, urban-based audience. More recently domestic commercial radio has been developed.

In Austria where radio accounts for 12 to 13 per cent of total advertising expenditures, there are two state-owned commercial stations which deliver a female-biased audience. It is described as an over-demanded medium along with its counterpart television. The latter provides only forty minutes of total advertising time per day on two national state-owned channels.

Italian commercial radio accounts for less than 2 per cent of total advertising expenditures. This is the case even though there are two state-owned, three foreign stations with regional listenership, and over 2,000 local private stations.

Spain, a country where radio accounts for 11 per cent of total advertising expenditures, has six national networks with over 300 stations. Large female audiences exist during daytime hours.

Advantages and disadvantages of radio

To conclude this section on radio as an advertising medium, its advantages and disadvantages are summarized below.

Advantages

- relatively low cost
- ability to deliver a message preceding consumption and buying, e.g. before a meal or the most important shopping day
- geographic flexibility
- ability to deliver a message at or away from home, especially driving to and from work
- can deliver a highly selective audience
- particularly effective in delivering a teen/young adult audience
- short lead time for placing advertising on air, i.e. in the USA copy can be submitted up to air time
- can create mental images through creative combination of words, music, and special sound effects

Disadvantages

- limited effectiveness in delivering a nationwide audience
- audience reach for any given programme is very low
- must add stations (many) to build reach
- appeals to only one of the senses; this can hamper message effectiveness
- a background medium during musical programming resulting in the likelihood of a less attentive audience than TV
- when message is repeated often there is an early 'wear-out' of message effectiveness causing a need for message variation
- 'clutter' may result if a number of competing stations exist and many commercials are permitted each hour thereby reducing message effectiveness.[77]

Cinema advertising

Cinema advertising in terms of monies spent is of little consequence in most countries from which figures have been obtained. However, its existence in many parts of the world is acknowledged. A 1985 European survey covering sixteen countries reported cinema advertising in eleven with share of expenditures ranging from 2.2 per cent in France to 0.1 per cent in Finland and Switzerland.[78] In Table 1 in the Introduction to Part Four cinema advertising was reported in three of five Latin American Countries accounting for 1 to 4 per cent of total advertising expenditure. (The 9.41 per cent share of advertising for cinema in Japan cannot be confirmed and, therefore, is believed to be in error.)

In two very different countries in terms of location and environmental characteristics, Germany and India, the growth of television (and video) has brought about a gradual decline in cinemagoers. In Germany the trend began in 1960 and ended in 1978 when interest in cinema was rekindled and cinema visits began to increase again.[79] The downward trend in cinema advertising in India as reflected in the distribution of expenditures by medium is a much more recent phenomenon with cinema's share declining from 4 per cent in 1985 to 1 per cent in 1989.[80] Throughout Europe generally, the declining trend that was previously noted for Germany has stopped.[81]

As for type of audience, in most countries in Europe the cinemagoers are younger and slightly skewed to men over women.[82] In Hungary, for example, two-thirds of the audience is under thirty with a core target of fifteen to twenty-four years.[83] In the UK, the average audience profile shows a split of 52 per cent male and 48 per cent female with 79 per cent being between the ages of fifteen and thirty-four. This profile also shows a skew towards the top socioeconomic categories.[84]

The composition of the Mexican cinema audience indicates a similar profile with respect to age, but a reverse profile in terms of sex and socioeconomic level. Around 53 per cent of the average Mexican audience is women, 47 per cent male, and two-thirds of the audience are in the low socioeconomic category.[85]

In India it is reported that the audience is predominantly male because of

TBWA gave the roundup below on cinema advertising in Europe:

Country	No. of Screens	Remarks
Austria	520	Considered a minor medium
Belgium	355	Demand in North high (TV in South)
Denmark	300	Strong demand
Finland	360	Good availability
France	3,000	Demand = supply
Greece	550	Low demand
Ireland	145	Low demand
Italy	3,500	Heavy demand for young categories
Netherlands	450	Good availability − declining medium
Norway	310	High demand
Portugal	340	Low attendances/low priority
Spain	2,300	Good availability − steady audience size
Sweden	510	Demand exceeds supply − steady audience levels
UK	1,230	Very high demand
West Germany	3,200	Low demand

Source: TBWA World Media Limited (1989) *A Review of the European Media Scene*, TBWA.

the 'cinema's inherent outdoor characteristic'. Additionally, its reach lies among the lower income classes in large urban centres and the lower population strata towns.[86]

In the USA, the use of cinema advertising is of little consequence dollar-wise. It is largely found in drive-in movie theatres and other theatres scattered in different parts of the country. The idea of seeing commercials by an audience which has paid money to see a film is not acceptable to some cinemagoers.[87] No doubt this is a major reason why cinema advertising does not have more widespread acceptance and use in the USA.

As for cinema commercials, they are usually viewed in one group when the house lights go down prior to the showing of the feature film. These commercials tend to be longer in length and can be very dramatic due to the larger than life images that can be projected onto the cinema screen and the accompanying high quality sound systems. This type of advertisement, however, is costly, and likely to be affordable only by the large national or international firm. The medium can be affordable to the local business person by using slides or pre-made films to which their name, phone, and address can be added.[88]

Summary

Television has become the premier mass medium in many countries of the world, while print and radio have had to make radical adjustments to survive and grow. Cinema has been and will continue to be a specialized medium reaching small numbers of people but providing unique possibilities for message transmission. Like all other media forms, television, radio, and cinema exhibit different characteristics in different countries. Television broadcasting networks and stations are experiencing growth in coverage and viewers in many countries, frequently due to government deregulation and permission for use as an advertising vehicle. Elsewhere, traditional television audiences are switching to cable channels and VCRs. Pan-regional systems are not experiencing the growth anticipated due to language barriers and programming limitations. Radio has found a niche by disseminating specialized programming and delivering segmented audiences in a country like the USA. In less developed countries like Guatemala, where literacy is low and electricity is scarce, it is the principal medium for news in rural areas. When making preparations for conducting advertising campaigns in countries and across borders, the advantages and disadvantages of all media alternatives should be known.

Questions

1 Describe the differences in television as a communication and advertising medium in China, Japan, and India.

2 Which three countries in Europe account for the greatest percentage of total media expenditures on television? Which three are the lowest?

3 What are the major problems that Pan-European satellite television is currently facing?

4 Explain the functions of the Independent Broadcasting System in the UK.

5 How does television advertising differ in the UK and West Germany?

6 Describe how television viewing varies during the course of a typical day in the USA and how television viewing varies among ages and sexes.

7 Contrast the system of ownership and regulation of television in the UK and the USA.

8 Define television syndication. What problems does syndication face in the USA?

9 What effect, if any, does cable television and VCR ownership have on network and independent station television?

10 Identify four advantages and four disadvantages of television as an advertising medium.

11 Contrast the role of radio to television as an advertising medium and explain how the medium has changed since the advent of television in the USA.

12 Point out the major differences of radio in Hungary, Japan, and Latin America; in Germany and the UK.

13 List five advantages and five disadvantages of radio as an advertising medium.

14 Explain the current status of cinema advertising in different countries of the world. Do you think its status will remain the same in the future? Give reasons for your answer.

Notes

1 Pei, Wang (1981) The big sell came to China. *Advertising World*, Feb/March, 46.

2 Hook, Michael (1987) World advertising congress: growth in advertising assured. *ARAB AD*, **I**, (6), 123.

3 China Advertising Association Presentation (1990) New York, 19 March.

4 Dentsu Inc. (1989) *Dentsu Japan Marketing/Advertising Yearbook 1990*, Dentsu, Tokyo, 193.

5 Nielson Media Research (1990) *Nielson 1990 Report on Television*, Nielson, New York, 6.

6 Dentsu Inc., *op. cit.*, 199–200.

7 Hindustan Thompson Associates Limited (1991) *Thompson Pocket Reference To Media in India 1991*, Hindustan Thompson, Bombay, pp. 10–13.

8 Serenyi, Janos (1991) A memorandum on marketing communications, McCann Erickson, Budapest, 2 January.

9 Garnier, Alberto H., S.A. (1988) Estudio sobre los habitos de exposicion a la television en Costa Rica. *Dirrecion De Medios*, (3), 1.1.

10 Munoz, Maria Mercedes (1990) A presentation on Guatemala in Media given at Guatemala City, McCann-Erickson, January.

11 Finnegan, Tony (1992) MJP/Carat International Ltd, London, February.

12 Crain Communications, Inc. (1987) *Focus, Media Fact Europe*, London, January, 119.

13 Wilmshurst, John (1985) *The Fundamentals of Advertising*, William Heinemann Ltd, London, pp. 158−9.

14 *Ibid.*, p. 155.

15 *Ibid.*, p. 157. (Extracted from Independent Broadcasting Authority.)

16 Lintas London (1989) *The Lintas Media Yearbook 1988*, The Media Department, London, February, p. 14.

17 Axel Springer Verlag A.G. (1982) *Europaische Werbe Markte Deutschland*, Berlin, p. 57.

18 *Ibid.*, p. 58.

19 *Focus, op. cit.*, p. 129.

20 Finnegan, *op. cit.*

21 Finnegan, *op. cit.*

22 TVB Research Dept. (1990) *Trends in Television*, Bureau of Advertising Inc., New York, p. 4.

23 TVB Research Department (1990) *Media Comparisons*, Bruskin Associates, p. 3.

24 Nielsen Media Research (1990) *Nielsen 1990 Report on Television*, A.C. Nielsen Company, NorthBrook, New York, p. 6.

25 *Ibid.*, p. 8.

26 TVB Research Department, *op. cit.*, Media comparisons, p. 4.

27 Ruyon, Kenneth E. (1984) *Advertising*, 2nd edn, Charles E. Merrill Publishing Company, Columbus, Ohio, pp. 619−20.

28 Wells, William, Burnett, John and Moriarty, Sandra (1989) *Advertising Principles and Practices*, Prentice-Hall, Englewood Cliffs, NJ, pp. 54−60.

29 *Ibid.*, pp. 61−62.

30 Runyon, *op. cit.*, pp. 482−3.

31 Sissors, Jack Z. and Bumba, Lincoln (1989) *Advertising Media Planning*, 3rd edn, NTC Business Books, Lincolnwood, Illinois, p. 439.

32 A/S/M Communications, Inc. (1988) *Adweek's Marketers' Guide to Media*, First Quarter 89, New York, **12**, (1), 12.

33 Ruyon, *op. cit.*, pp. 479, 480.

34 Sissors, *op. cit.*, pp. 396−7.

35 Wells, *op. cit.*, pp. 247−8.

36 *Ibid.*, p. 395.

37 *Ibid.*, p. 395.
38 Cable Advertising Bureau (1990) *Cable TV Facts 90*, New York, CAB, 6.
39 Sissors, *op. cit.*, p. 375.
40 Wells, *op. cit.*, pp. 250, 594.
41 Nielsen Media Research, *op. cit.*, p. 14.
42 Sissors, *op. cit.*, p. 395.
43 *Ibid.*
44 *Adweek Media Outlook 1991* (1990) Supplement to *Adweek's Marketing Week*, 1 October, 26, 28.
45 Independent TV Supplement (1990) Independent television, an advertiser's Guide for 1990. Advertising Age, p. 7.
46 Sissors, *op. cit.*, p. 397.
47 Television bad year for networks with little improvement likely. *New York Times*, 24 December 1990, 32.
48 Sissors, *op. cit.*, p. 397.
49 Derived from Cable Television Fact Sheet (1990) Increases in home presentation, February, 1986 through February, 1990.
50 Wells, *op. cit.*, p. 248.
51 Sissors, *op. cit.*, p. 378.
52 Cable Television Advertising Bureau, Inc. (1990) *CAB TV Facts 90*, The Bureau, New York, pp. 38−45.
53 Sissors, *op. cit.*, p. 400.
54 *Ibid.*
55 TVB Research Department (1990) *Trends in VCR Usage*, Television Bureau of Advertising Inc. New York, 3.
56 *Ibid.*, pp. 3, 7, 9.
57 Alter, Robert in *Adweek's Media Outlook 1991*, *op. cit.*, p. 23.
58 Sissors, *op. cit.*, pp. 194−5; Runyon, *op. cit.*, p. 486; and Wells, *op. cit.*, pp. 259−261.
59 Nylen, David W. (1986) *Advertising*, 3rd edn, South-Western Publishing Co., Cincinnati, Ohio, pp. 366−367.
60 Radio advertising Bureau, Inc. (1990) *Radio Facts For Advertising*, The Bureau, New York.
61 Sissors, *op. cit.*, p. 305.
62 China Advertising Association (1990) The broadcasting commercials in China. Information presented at an HDM sponsored meeting, New York, 19 March.
63 Hindustan Thompson, *op. cit.*, pp. 14−19.
64 Serenyi, *op. cit.*
65 Dentsu, Inc., *op. cit.*, pp. 187−190.
66 McCann Erickson (1991) *Media Fact Book-Information General De Medios 1991*, Guatemala City.
67 Garnier, Alberto H, S.A. (1987) *Estudio Sobre Los Habitos De Exposicion Ala*

Radio En Costa Rica, Garnier, San Jose.

68 Asociacion Mexicana De Agencias De Publicidad (AMAP) (1990) *Comite Medios Mexican*, AMAP, Mexico City, pp. 33—47.

69 Barroso, Lili (1991) *Mexico's Media Scene*. A presentation, J Walter Thompson, Mexico City, January.

70 The Advertising Association (1990) *Marketing Pocket Book 1991* NTC Publication Ltd, Henley-on-Thames, England, pp. 130—131.

71 *Team/BBDO* (1987) *The German Media Scene*. A presentation, Dusseldorf, pp. 15—18.

72 *TBWA* (1989) *A Review of the European Media Scene*, World Media Ltd, London.

73 Axel Springer Verlag, *op. cit.*, p. 59.

74 TEAM/BBDO, *op. cit.*, pp. 16—17.

75 British Radio Information drawn from Wilmhurst, *op. cit.*, pp. 154—5, 157, 163; The Advertising Association, *op. cit.*, pp. 120—121; TBWA, *op. cit.*; Lintas London, *op. cit.*, pp. 29, 30, 65, and *Focus*, *op. cit.*, p. 119.

76 Other European radio drawn from Focus, *op. cit.*, p. 51; and TBWA, *op. cit.*

77 Runyon, *op. cit.*, p. 489; Wells, *op. cit.*, pp. 266—269; and Wilmshurst, *op. cit.*, pp. 156—7.

78 *Focus*, *op. cit.*, p. 17.

79 Axel Springer, Verlag, *op. cit.*, p. 61.

80 Hindustan Thompson, *op. cit.*, p. 19.

81 TBWA, *op. cit.*

82 *Ibid.*

83 Serenyi, *op. cit.*

84 The Advertising Association, *op. cit.*, p. 122.

85 AMAP, *op. cit.*

86 Hindustan Thompson, *op. cit.*, p. 19.

87 Wells, *op. cit.*, p. 445.

88 Wilmshurst, *op. cit.*, p. 172.

11 *The medium of mail in marketing communications*

Introduction

Mail as a medium provides a communication channel of extraordinary dimensions bounded primarily by the development and operation of the postal systems of the world. There are two other factors which can influence its importance. One is the extent of newspaper and magazine penetration and readership when they are used as the transmitting medium and mail is used as the response mechanism. The other is the penetration of telephone when this vehicle is the preferred response mechanism.

The outstanding features of mail as a medium for marketing communication are two-fold:

1   the precision by which the medium can deliver a message
2   the ability to measure the effectiveness of any given mail media effort

Providing the postal service in a country is reliable and the address is accurate, the mail can deliver a marketer's message directly to the front door of a consumer or the office of a business person.

When the mailed message calls for a response, as is often the case, because the number of pieces mailed is known, the number of the responses can be counted to evaluate the effectiveness with an exactness which is hard, if not impossible to replicate with other forms of non-personal communications. Small samples of any given mailing target can be used to test any aspect of the mailing − the offer, and words and pictures of the message − before the complete programme is implemented.

The medium's importance

For an idea of the importance of mail as a medium, information contained in several studies will be examined.

A 1990 report on international mail order statistics in thirteen European countries, Japan, Australia, Canada, and the USA showed per capita mail order sales ranging from $8 in Spain to $550 in the USA. The average per capita sales in Europe was an even $100 compared with $94 in Japan, $124 in Australia, and $255 in Canada. Mail order was growing at the highest rates in these five countries:

- Spain 34.0 per cent
- Australia 25.0 per cent
- Japan 16.2 per cent
- Finland 10.0 per cent
- USA 8.0 per cent[1]

In Europe, one study among 200 companies showed that 'addressed direct mail' ranked as the number one medium in terms of usage in business-to-business advertising, and ranked as the number three medium after newspapers and magazines in consumer advertising.[2] In Switzerland, direct mail is reported to account for over 35 per cent of all advertising media expenditures. In the Netherlands, nearly 25 per cent is spent on direct mail.[3]

In the USA, according to one authority, direct mail also ranked as the number one medium among business-to-business advertisers, accounting for one-third of total advertising expenditures.[4] Again similar to European findings, direct mail ranked as the number three medium in overall US annual advertising expenditures with a whopping $21.9 billion reported in 1989.[5]

Usage around the world

Mail as a medium for marketing purposes is at various stages of development and is subject to various constraints in different countries around the world.

Japan

In Japan, a criticism levelled against direct mail was based on the issue of privacy. This factor, coupled with the lack of a discounted bulk postage rate up until recently impeded the growth of the medium. Since its inception as a viable media alternative about a decade ago, the medium has been used primarily for catalogue distribution purposes and for marketing books, records, and video clubs. Mailing lists have been scarce. Marketers have had to build their own. To obtain a preferential mailing rate, a vendor's catalogue had to have a certain percentage of editorial so that the appearance was somewhere between a magazine and catalogue, hence the name 'magalogue'.[6] In the latter part of the 1980s the medium began to grow at a rapid pace. This growth was fuelled by several factors including increased usage by specialty stores and large department stores, the entrance of new companies into the field, the realization of a new discounted bulk mail system, the spread of free phone dialing, credit cards, and new, improved home delivery systems. General merchandise catalogues are giving way to specialized catalogues that offer merchandise catering to different life styles.[7]

China

In China, there is some use of mail for marketing communication purposes. However, its use as a means of reaching and gaining responses from prospects is not recommended. The reason for this is China's decentralized purchasing system which permits 'hundreds of thousands of "work units" with foreign exchange credits' to purchase necessary goods. Advertising in specialized journals in such fields as chemicals, computers, electronics, and medicine is a better way to prospect. This can stimulate inquiries for catalogues and price quotations. In responding to inquiries, a firm's catalogue or brochure may be the only contact with the buyer; therefore, this printed material may be more important than the quality of the product itself. This means that the mail response package must be an effective communication tool in terms of language, style, and presentation, including precise product specifications, in order to get the business.[8]

Italy

Italy is a country that has lagged behind the rest of Europe with respect to mail order business. The per capita sales figure is only $22. This is the second lowest among thirteen European nations and less than 1 per cent of Italian retail sales according to the Fishman report.[9] The rate of growth in recent years, however, is accelerating. An in-country survey indicated that 70 per cent of the respondents were favourably disposed towards the receipt of direct mail. Even so, a relatively few companies as compared with the number of companies in other European countries use the medium. Among those that do, clothing is the number one selling item in contrast to other countries in the region where books head the list of products sold by direct mail.[10] While not mentioned, it is quite likely that the development of marketing by mail has been hampered by the speed and reliability of the postal service.

Mail order: Europe versus the USA and elsewhere

A number of factors have been cited to differentiate mail order in Europe from the USA.[11] In Europe there are these factors to consider:

- limited availability of mailing lists
- higher costs of and wide variance in country postal rates
- stricter advertising and promotion claim regulations
- lower penetration of credit cards for payment purposes
- agents, not mail, are used to distribute catalogues, take orders, collect payments in at least one major market
- variances exist among countries not found in the USA such as:
  - tastes in fashions
  - clothing sizes
  - taxes
  - postal regulations

   — legalities of credit sales
   — exchange rate fluctuations
   — differences in merchandise returns across borders

With respect to mail order offerings, general merchandise was mentioned most frequently by the leading mail order companies in nine of twelve countries in the Fishman report. Included in the report were eight countries in Europe plus Canada, Japan, Hong Kong, and Australia. Among the specialized types of merchandise offered were books, magazines, and periodicals in six countries; clothing/apparel in four countries; records in three countries; and collectables and coins in two countries. Mentions by type of merchandise and number of different countries are shown in Table 11.1.

When it came to the means by which mail order offers were conveyed, catalogue and non-catalogue direct mail was reported in the majority of countries. These were followed by print, then TV advertising, inserts, and agent-distributed catalogues as shown in Table 11.2.

Agent distributed catalogues were only reported in the UK; inserts only in Australia; and TV only in West Germany and Japan.

Principal characteristics

The purpose in using mail as a medium can be to inform or keep in touch with customers and prospects. For example, companies mail quarterly and annual reports to stockholders. Libraries inform library card holders of the arrival of

Table 11.1 *Merchandise offered by mail order*

	General	Books Mags etc	Total number of mentions = 99			
			Clothing Apparel	Records	Coins/ colectables	Other
% of mentions	53	12	11	5	5	14
# of different countries	9	6	4	3	2	7

Table 11.2 *Means of conveying mail order offers*

	Mailed catalogue	Non-catalogue mailing	Space	TV	Inserts	Agents
# Countries where used	10	8	4	2	1	1

new books and special events. Politicians report on issues affecting their constituents. Commercially, however, some form of response is commonly sought. The response varies and may involve an initial or repeat purchase, the generation of a prospective customer, or the solicitation of membership which provides preferred customer status.

Various goods and services are offered

A great variety of goods and services, consumer and industrial, are marketed by mail. In many instances, particularly with respect to consumer offerings, mail is the only form of solicitation. Merchandise sold by mail include:

- books and records
- magazine subscriptions
- food
- computer software
- clothing
- household goods
- personal care products
- office supplies

Services frequently offered by mail:

- investment instruments
- credit cards
- banking services
- home improvements
- insurance
- lawn and garden care.

The means by which these goods and services are marketed include catalogues (mail order), cooperative mailings and individual mailings.

Examples of mail order usage

Among the users of mail is possibly the most famous department store in the world, Harrods of London. This organization publishes about 250,000 catalogues twice a year, 85,000 of which are sent free to customers. The balance is sold in the store itself, and at bookstores in the UK, Europe, Southeast Asia and in America including the USA where about 40,000 are purchased.[12]

Another well-known London institution, Fortnum & Mason of Picadilly, is undoubtedly one of the oldest catalogue mail order purveyors in the world. International delivery began by sending hams, tongues, cheese, and assorted food delicacies to Wellington's hungry officers in Spain, and to those serving during the time of the Colonial Wars in Africa, Afghanistan, and China.[13] See Exhibit 11.1 for a picture and description of Fortnum & Mason's export hampers.

Cooperative mailings

Cooperative mailings could be a US invention. These mailings represent an assemblage of items organized by a single manufacturer to offer two or more products of the house, or by an independent organization that solicits participation on the part of different manufacturers. A manufacturer of household cleaning products might decide to run a spring cleaning promotion. An element in the promotion could be a mailing to a certain type and number of households in a country featuring coupons offering a price reduction on selected products in the manufacturer's line.

The term 'cooperative mailing' is more commonly associated with an independent organization like Donnelly Marketing in the USA. Periodically this company organizes a mailing under the name of 'Carol Wright' which will reach anywhere from thirty to fourty-five million households. Offers in this mailing may include car insurance, leather wallets, stationery, clothing, upholstery cleaning, books for pre-school children, and money-off coupons on food, health and beauty aids, and household products. (This was the primary medium for delivering coupons of the type just described. However, the bulk of the couponing business has passed to the 'free standing' inserts carried in newspapers which was discussed in Chapter 9.)

Individual mailings

Individual mailings can be aimed at the consumer, professional, or business-to-business market. *Advertising Age* ran an article in their 24 July 1989 issue with the title, 'Direct mail becoming the hottest incentive conduit.' The reference was to car makers where automotive direct mail has been growing at an annual rate of about 20 per cent since the early 1980s. Included among those placing greater emphasis on direct mail were names like Porsche, BMW, Cadillac, and Buick. Porsche, for example, with a model line that starts at over $30,000, has a limited target audience. A mailed invitation to test drive a Porsche which included a poster showing the 944 and a licence on the front of it with the recipient's name drew an unexpectedly high 6 per cent response.[14]

Exhibit 11.1 Fortnum & Mason export hampers. Reproduced by permission of Fortnum & Mason plc, Piccadilly, London

A well-known pharmaceutical manufacturer in the UK uses direct mail to improve awareness and understanding, and develop a doctors' prospect list for personal sales call follow-up. One campaign for birth control tablets included a three-part mailing quiz, a brochure about product efficacy, and the offer of high quality (Gladstone) doctors' bags and briefcases for the first forty-nine correct responses. This mailing to between 8,000 and 9,000 doctors drew a 36 per cent response rate.

Gillette used direct mail in a unique way to launch the Paper Mate NonStop Plastic Pencil all across Europe. The Pan-European launch was needed to generate sufficient sales volume to compete pricewise with the wooden pencil, cover the costs of construction and operation of a new automated plant in Italy, and over time, return a satisfactory profit. The market opportunity was seen as being located in the business, not consumer, market. The pencil consumption in this sector was estimated at about 1.5 billion pencils a year. The advantage in the Gillete plastic pencil besides its cost was convenience — no sharpening — and a life three times longer than an ordinary wooden pencil. The challenge was to get the job done on a budget of $250,000 without the benefit of a sales force. (The Gillette sales organization called on the stationery trade, not business organizations.)

As for the business market, it was learned that stationery buying as such was the responsibility of many different types of employees. . .from secretaries to managing directors of small firms. . .and occupied considerably less than 10 per cent of any buyer's time. The idea, then, became one of reaching both buyers and users. The first objective was to find a list of these people in the various countries of Europe. List suppliers were able to provide 'possible users' but could not positively identify 'buyers'.

With a prospective user list in hand, the first mailing was launched. The information contained in the mailing had to be translated into twelve languages because the type of recipient for the most part could not speak English. Three sample plastic pencils were enclosed with each mailing package: one for the secretary, one for the executive, and one for the buyer. Replies were abundant, the sales produced adequate volume for plant operations, and information was obtained about purchasing habits of those who bought pencils and other stationery items of the type which Gillette marketed. Two subsequent mailings, both containing samples, drew responses of between 10 and 20 per cent. The result was increased sales from new and repeat customers and more information on buying behaviour all across Europe. This information produced a comprehensive list of European stationery buyers and influencers for future mail media campaigns.[15]

International mailing considerations

Point of origin and the Postal Union Convention are two factors for consideration.

Point of origin

Production and mailing locations are matters for consideration when planning a cross-border mailing campaign. The alternatives are print and mail from the originating country, print in the originating country and mail in the receivers' country(ies), print and mail in the receivers' country(ies).

A case in point is a US marketer who is planning a multi-country European mail campaign. If it is planned that large audiences are to be reached in separate countries along with message translation to accommodate the national language(s), assistance from local direct mail companies is needed and local dispatch is preferred. Production might occur at home or in the individual countries. This would be dependent on production costs, air shipment to points of dispatch, handling charges, and differences in timing.

If it is determined that the message in English will be understood by recipients and their numbers are not too large (e.g. managing directors or managers of departments in business organizations), then it may be possible to print and mail from the USA. Before this decision is made a comparative cost and timing analysis would also be needed.[16]

Postal union convention

For international mail there is a Postal Union Convention to which most countries of the world subscribe. (Subscribing to this Convention, however, is no guarantee of the speed and/or reliability of the service in any given country.) Within the framework of this Convention three basic categories of international mail are found:

1 Postal Union mail which is further divided into:
   - *Letters and cards* (in French, lettres et cartes) or LC-letters, packages, post cards, and aerogrammes.
   - *Other articles* (in French, autres objects) or AO-printed matter, books and sheet music, publishers' periodicals, matter for the blind, and small packages up to four pounds in weight; also sacks containing printed matter being sent to one addressee.

2   *Parcel Post* (in French, Colis Postaux) or CP mail which contains merchandise but no current personal correspondence, written or recorded.

3   *Express Mail International* which is based on agreements and understandings between specific countries.

All categories of mail (surface and air delivered) are subject to regulations with respect to size, weight, and instructions for processing. Reply paid cards and double cards are not generally accepted in international mails. Letters and packages may or may not be permitted to contain dutiable merchandise. Senders are responsible for their determination and compliance with all rules and import regulations. Mail delivery charges will vary according to specifications that are set by the country of origin.[17]

System changes

The international mail system is by no means static. For example, in the latter part of the 1980s agreement was reached among many European countries 'to honour postage paid responses from any member country to any other'. This means that a mailing from London or Amsterdam to other member countries can be returned to the London or Amsterdam address.[18]

In-country system differences

Marketers using mail systems at home and abroad must either have in-house expertise or retain an organization which specializes in mail media services to understand the peculiarities of and keep abreast of changes in the systems in which they operate. For example, in South Africa there is no third-class mail service at reduced postage rates.[19]

In the UK there is a 'freepost' system whereby a marketer can advertise a product via mail or mass media with a direct response device. So long as a return address and freepost number is provided, a person may reply free of mail charge when taking advantage of the offer.[20]

The information file and the mailing list

If mail is going to be the medium for the solicitation of a response, a mailing list must be developed or selected. Depending on the target audience the list may be based on in-house information. The source of this information can include warranty cards, current and prior customers, stockholders, and others who have made inquiries about the product(s) to the company. The source may also be the response to a mass media campaign when individuals write or phone in, often to an 800 (free) number, to obtain information and give their address and phone number.

Mailing lists are also available in many countries from companies in the business of compiling lists of different groups of people that companies may wish to reach. In the USA the Standard Rate and Data Service has a comprehensive directory of mailing lists of all types which are available to advertisers. If that type of directory is not available in a particular country, then the availability of lists can be determined by contacting local advertising or direct response agencies, advertising or direct mail associations, or what are called 'list brokers'. One such company in the USA that sells lists is Edith Roman Associates, Inc. This organization publishes an encyclopedia which is offered as 'a comprehensive guide to the names and addresses of virtually every sought-after direct response prospect in the United States today'.

The encyclopedia organizes the lists alphabetically and by various industrial and educational classifications. See Exhibit 11.2 for a sample of an alphabetical page.

Pricing is based on the number of names per thousand purchased and can vary from $20 to $50 depending on the total number purchased. The minimum order is 5,000 names. Lists purchased come complete with mailing labels sorted into the postal mailing code sequence in order to meet third-class bulk mailing requirements. Additional information can be ordered along with the list and labels. This includes key coding (for response classification purposes), telephone numbers, title addressing, and title and function. Lists are guaranteed to be 93 per cent deliverable.[21]

External mailing lists are either compiled from various sources such as directories, trade magazines, newspapers, trade show registrations, or are lists already and regularly used for direct response purchases. In the latter case it may be possible to purchase a list from another company or from a magazine whose target market is similar to the audience required by the marketer.

These types of lists are readily available in the USA. In fact, one expert described the growth of mailing lists in the USA as reaching 'astonishing proportions'. In a country of 250 million people there are over 'four billion names for rent'.[22] This is not the case, however, in most countries around the world. In Europe, for example, many publishers are reluctant to permit others to use their exclusive list of readers.[23]

In the long run, for companies planning to use mail as a medium, it pays to develop a basic in-house customer and prospect information file ready to be drawn on when needed for use in a mail campaign. This requires that someone inside or outside the firm be assigned the responsibility to build and maintain the list(s) of names, addresses, and phone numbers; to make additions, changes, and deletions as needed; and to gather other pertinent information.

Exhibit 11.2 *A page from* Edith Roman Direct Mail Encyclopedia. *Reproduced by permission of Edith Roman Associates Inc., New York*

QUAN.	DESCRIPTION	SIC
	INSURANCE	
6,201	Adjusters	6411A
195,115	Agency Offices	6411
395,292	Agents & Brokers	
8,716	Bonding & Surety	
	Companies	6351
	Companies - Home Office	
8,494	Life & Health	6311,6321
386	Property & Casualty	6331
14,036	Consultants	6411B
20,161	Executives	
395,292	Fire & Casualty Agents	
52,900	High Volume Producers	
	(CLU's, MDRT's...)	
500	Investment Specialists	
11,800	Lawyers	
868,585	Life & Disability Agents	
	INTERIOR DESIGN/ SPACE PLANNING	
36,025	Corporate Design Magazine Subscribers	
28,869	Interior Decorating Services	7399E
27,497	Decorators & Designers	
835	Suppliers	5023E
37,500	Interior Design Magazine Subscribers	
27,190	Interiors Subscribers	
145,266	National Association of Home Builders	
35,000	Professional Remodeling Magazine Subscribers	
14,030	Internal Auditors	
21,300	International Trading Companies	
216,852	Executives	
14,139	Export Companies	
142,321	Executives	
1,290	Import Companies	
9,275	Executives	
8,499	Companies That Both Import & Export	
57,189	Executives	
	INVESTORS	
13,214	Financial Analysts	
152,634	Financial World Active Subscribers	
197,818	Futures Magazine Subscribers	
21,317	Investment Advisory Services	6281
2,164	Investment Advisory Specialists	
4,398	Investment Bankers	
261	Investment Newsletters	
4,495	Investment Portfolio Managers	
95,000	Investments & Tax Publications	
	Seminar Attendees, Book & Tape Buyers	
867,760	Investors (please inquire for selections by interest) (see Best Sellers Section)	
1,471,964	IRA Holders	
406,356	Kiplinger Washington Newsletter Subscribers	
156,296	Oil & Gas	

QUAN.	DESCRIPTION	SIC
166,268	Real Estate	
41,187	Security Dealers & Traders	
1,706,140	Ultra Affluent Investors	
1,471,964	IRA Holders	
	J	
22,679	Janitorial & Cleaning Services	7349A
4,743	Janitorial Supplies Wholesalers	5087E
	JEWELRY & WATCHMAKING	
16,779	Jewelry, Clock & Watch Repair Services	7631
17,295	Jewelry, Precious Stone & Watch Wholesalers	5094
47,233	Jewelry Stores	5944
2,678	Manufacturers	391X
8,513	Repair Services	7631E
8,058	Southern Jeweler Magazine Subscribers	
6,448	Job Training & Rehabilitation Services	8331
4,392	Judges	
4,015	Judo & Karate Studios	7995A
2,729	Junior Chambers of Commerce	
1,807	Junior Colleges	8222
13,491	Junk Dealers	5093
	K	
7,963	Kennels	0752A
36,736	Kindergarten & Nursery Schools	
21,323	Kitchen Cabinet Dealers	5712N
18,404	Manufacturers	2434
6,649	Kiwanis Clubs	
8,272	Knights of Columbus	
1,640	Knitting Mills	225X
22,163	Knitting Yarn & Embroidery Shops	5949
471	Knitwear Shops	5631B
	L	
1,371	Labor Attorneys	
40,639	Labor Unions with Top Official	
	LABORATORIES	
1,080	Chemical	
4,812	Commercial Testing	
11,362	Dental	8071C
3,176	Hospital Pathology	
10,074	Industrial Research	
26,557	Executives	
6,634	Medical	8071A
19,495	Photo Finishing	
5,838	Research & Development	7391
3,700	Research at Universities	
432	X-Ray Laboratories	8071B
111,445	Ladies' Apparel Shops (see Apparel)	562X,563X
46,796	Ladies' Club Presidents	
10,779	Ladies' Custom Tailors	5699C
946	Ladies' Dress Mfrs.	2335

QUAN.	DESCRIPTION	SIC
1,321	Lamp & Lampshade Stores	5719D
782	Wholesalers	5023F
22,691	Land Developers	6552
12,935	Surveyors	8911F
26,618	Landscape & Garden Contractors	0782A
6,263	Landscape Architects	0781
43,599	Landscape Services	0782
	Laundries	
412	Industrial	7218
11,431	Power	7211
13,661	Self-Service	7215A
	LAW ENFORCEMENT	
19,651	Agencies	
60,366	Agencies & Institutions	
5,375	Correctional Facilities	
20,564	County Level	
20,205	Courts	
1,211	Federal Level	
4,392	Judges	
1,686	Medical Examiners	
22,864	Municipal Level	
5,807	Police Chiefs	
3,798	Probation Agencies	
8,733	Prosecution Agencies	
837	Public Defenders	
3,040	Sheriffs	
12,226	State Level	
3,519	Township Level	
842	Law Libraries	
61,612	Lawn & Garden Supply Stores	5261
43,599	Lawn Maintenance Services	0782
26,452	Lawn Mower Dealers	5261C
8,453	Repair Shops	7699E
6,962	Lawn Sprinkler Installation Services	0782C
	Lawyers & Law Firms (see Attorneys)	
4,433	Leather Goods & Luggage Dealers	5948
2,849	Manufacturers	31XX
7,068	Manufacturing Executives	
2,412	Wholesalers	5199J
4,509	Leather Goods Cleaning & Repair Services	7699F
7,348	Legislators, State	
6,404	Letter Shops	7331A
	LIBRARIES	
	Libraries by Book Funds (please request data)	
30,093	Librarians by Name	
	Libraries by Type	
5,995	College & University	
48,000	Elementary School	
901	Government	
29,000	High School	
1,501	History	
1,186	Law	
2,766	Medical	
5,670	Public Branches	
8,683	Public Main	
782	Religious	
3,462	Scientific & Technical	
4,383	Special Subjects (please request data)	
1,167	Lighting Fixture Dealers	5719N
3,607	Manufacturers & Wholesalers	5063M
6,083	Limousine Services	4119D
1,905	Linen Shops	5719E

Respondent input

What opportunities exist for obtaining pertinent input for planning purposes from mailing list respondents? The answer appears to be excellent, at least in the USA, based on information supplied by George Wiedemann. Wiedemann based his conclusion on a study done by Grey Research which, when projected to the US population as a whole, indicated that at least one-half of all household heads would be very or somewhat likely to supply some information beyond name, address, and phone number when 'ordering, requesting, or participating in a frequent user programme'.

The profile of this 'interactive' type of consumer included these characteristics: slightly more females than males, more married than single and most importantly, more upscale in terms of income and occupation...white-collar, well-educated, with children.

These 'interactives' will tell what they think about present products and services and will volunteer certain personal data such as age, sex, family size and occupation. They decline to discuss income and are reluctant to provide information on their planning and purchasing processes. Overall, they are more ready to buy than non-interactives.

The implications and suggestions made by Wiedemann for those using direct response communications in the USA are these:

- 'Never make contact with a consumer without asking for input.'
- 'Never take input without acting on it.'
- The order form and/or coupon should be designed to provide for input.
- Customer files should be segmented by interactive and non-interactive groupings.
- In soliciting information, tell the respondent how the information will be used.

Before instituting such a programme, special note should be made of the finding that the interactive group 'does not believe that selling information about them is at all appropriate'. Caution, therefore, is needed to 'protect the trust implied in this relationship'.[24]

While prospects for obtaining respondent input in the USA are exceedingly favourable, the assumption that this same condition prevails in other countries would be a serious mistake. A reliable study is needed first.

Enhanced information files

Considerable work has been done in the US on attempting to make information files and mailings derived from these files more productive. This is being accomplished by combining purchase characteristics with demographic and lifestyle information. While this approach has considerable intellectual appeal, its application thus far has been limited. The costs and benefits have not yet been properly substantiated.

Optimizing use of the customer file

When a prospect makes a purchase the person's name can be added to the firm's customer base. The question will then arise as to when the customer should be recontacted. To answer this question the type and variety of product(s) or service(s) offered and purchased requires consideration. The answer will be different for catalogue sales as compared with limited lines, single product sales or services. Catalogues give rise to purchases that range from children's toys to clothing, swimwear, tyres, bedding, washing machines, furniture and television sets. (The Spring/Summer 1991 issue of the Sears Catalogue contained nearly 1,600 pages of merchandise.) Companies that offer underwear, Porsche cars, and life and health insurance are faced with very different patterns of buying behaviour. Because of these differences, well-managed mail order companies have long since learned to manipulate customer files in ways to reveal purchasing patterns that include the following factors which when weighted will indicate when and with what type of merchandise the customer should be contacted:

1 frequency of purchase
2 recency of purchase
3 amount of purchase
4 type of product/service purchased

Analysing what purchases were made in what amount with what frequency in a given time period such as one quarter or one year can lead to a customer contact strategy to answer the questions of when to contact and with what merchandise.

A 'cross-selling' strategy can also be adopted when you know what customers buy. As Bob Stone points out, commercial checking accounts are prime prospects for car loans; savings accounts are prime prospects for car loans; life insurance policy holders are prime prospects for medicare insurance when they reach sixty-five. (For a more complete treatment on manipulating customer files, on which the foregoing discussion was based, see Stone, Bob (1989) *Successful Direct Marketing Methods*, 4th edn, NTC Books, Lincolnwood, Illinois, pp. 29–33.)

Developing new business from customer files

Referrals from satisfied customers have always been a powerful means of generating new business. That's how a Porsche mail campaign in South Africa led to the sale of six new cars worth $360,000 and a 5 per cent dealer sales increase in a down year for cars and business in general. Porsche clients, incidentally, were professionals, not corporate, and wealthy. This made prospects difficult to target. The idea behind the campaign was to encourage satisfied Porsche owners to introduce the car to prospective clients.

The initial mailing of the campaign directed at 2,300 registered Porsche owners offered a limited-edition video called the 'Porsche experience'. Respondents − an extraordinary 96 per cent − were sent the video and an invitation to enter a Porsche twenty-four-week endurance classic contest with a $9,000 grand prize for the winning driver and co-driver. The hook in the invitation was the entry requirement: 'to nominate three 'co-drivers' who had the 'style and resources' to become Porsche owners'. Points were awarded for introducing prospects, getting prospects to test drive the cars and for making a purchase. Subsequent mailings were made to prospects with invitations to test drive (for those who had not already done so) and to request ratings of their test drive experience; also to send thanks for purchases and telegrams to announce the race's winners.

From this campaign, eighty-two leads (3.7 per cent) were generated and six sales were made. The 'member-get-member' campaign, led by a strong mail effort, was considered by the dealer to have produced a significant result in a very difficult sales year.[25]

Creating mail media messages

In this section, techniques in creating catalogues and other forms of personal communications to be sent through the mail will be discussed. The focus will be on general guidelines, not specific instructions. For a more complete explanation of these techniques books that concentrate in this field should be consulted.[26]

Prior to the conception of a catalogue or mailing packet a creative strategy in writing developed along the lines suggested in Chapter 7 is needed. This will provide the necessary guidelines for writers and artists assigned to the project. As with any form of communication thorough preparation is needed before the creative strategy is attempted. The type of product(s) offered, the prospective target audience, the competitive situation, including all elements of the marketing mix, must be clearly understood. Marketing research should be undertaken to identify the demographic and psychographic (activities, interests, opinions) characteristics of the intended audience. The strengths and weaknesses of a marketer's product should be evaluated in relation to competitive offerings. Communication content analyses should also be made comparing principal elements of prior catalogue or mailing packets against competitive offerings.

The offer: it can make the difference

Along with the development of the creative strategy, the offer to be made in the mail presentation needs to be established. It is a critical factor in determining the success or failure of a mail campaign. For example, in the Porsche case just cited, the $9,000 was not awarded as a free gift. It had to be 'spent on something exotic like hosting a black tie dinner in the middle of Botswana's Okavango Swamps' in order to 'accentuate the exotic nature of Porsches'.[27]

Several factors require consideration in establishing the offer. *Pricing* the offer is the most important consideration. This, as in the case of all other elements of the marketing mix calls for research and analysis. What are the features of the product or service? What comparisons can be made between the price and benefits of your product versus competition? Will *shipping* and *handling* be included in the price or will they be extra? If extra, how much can be charged realistically? How will *payment* be made: by cash, cheque, money order or credit card? Will a *special incentive* such as a free gift or a discount be a part of the offer? How about a *guarantee*? If a customer is not completely satisfied, will a *refund* be made?[28] All of these questions should be resolved before the actual job of creating the mail communication package begins. However, if legitimate alternatives exist, small-scale testing can be undertaken to determine the strongest offer before the overall campaign is launched.

Catalogues

The catalogue, as a marketing communication tool, is used by retailers, manufacturers, and intermediaries to present a large assortment of merchandise for sale. The catalogue may contain merchandise which caters to either the consumer or business-to-business sector. The products offered can be either general line merchandise or be of a limited nature such as fashion items for consumers or cleaning supplies for offices or factories. The target can be an individual, household, or business organization.

Prior to the initiation of creative work there should be a meeting of the minds among those working on the project. Participants may include a marketing director, writer, artist, and production manager. Their initial assignment is to hammer out the direction or creative strategy as mentioned earlier. Elements of this strategy include the target audience, type(s) of merchandise to be offered, and the image or personality to be created. This will involve guidelines for format, graphics, and quality of reproduction.

The catalogue cover is the most critical element in the entire catalogue. It's akin to a print ad without the body copy and must pique the reader's interest in a matter of seconds so that the page is turned and the inner content is perused.[29] Exhibit 11.3 shows the cover of a Sears catalogue. (Sears is a major US retailer that has been running a successful catalogue business for years.)

Exhibit 11.3   *Sears catalogue cover. Reproduced by permission of Sears National Catalog Home Office, Skokie, Illinois*

Bob Stone offers these ingredients for catalogue success:

1   Positioning − the catalogue should have a reason for being: why it can fill the needs of an identifiable and reachable target.

2   Merchandise selection — the items included must be appropriate for the target.
3   Grouping of merchandise — items should be grouped to maintain through-the-book reader interest with the most popular items up front.
4   Graphics — photography should be used in a way that will satisfy the target audience.
5   Colour — background colours should be selected to enhance the merchandise offered.
6   Size — 8—1/2″ × 11″ size is most appropriate for businesses and catalogues in the USA. If consumer catalogue is less than twenty-four pages, it is better to reduce size; a thicker look and feel lends authority, can induce inspection of content.
7   Copy — subordinate to photography but should give basic information and/or stimulate emotions (for consumers).
8   Incentives — their purpose is to encourage browsing, trigger orders. Examples are free gift if ordered by a specific date, free phone number, charge privileges, and free trial period.
9   Order form — it should be designed to facilitate ordering, e.g. a bound-in order form with return envelope has been proven to pull more orders than an on-page order form.
10 Sales analysis — a page-by-page sales analysis of every catalogue should be made to build on successes and avoid future failures.[30]

The individual mailing

Mail communications involving a product or service normally contains several elements, each of which must be considered carefully for its communication value. These elements are the envelope, a personalized letter, brochure, reply form, and return envelope. The packet is by no means limited to these elements. A number of specialized devices may be a part of the packet. Common devices include a stamp which must be removed and affixed in a specified location, a specially designed paper construction which pops up when the mailing piece is opened, a second letter in a sealed envelope with instructions to open only if the recipient has decided not to respond, a formal invitation, a telegram format. If a special device is used, it in no way should take the reader's attention away from the basic sales message.[31]

Preparations

Making preparations for a personalized mail packet is much the same as making preparations for a mass media message. Before any creative work is initiated, a thorough understanding of the product(s), target customers, and competitive offerings is needed. This understanding should preceed the preparation of a creative strategy which was explained earlier in this chapter.

Creation

The personalized mailing packet concept should be based on guidelines established in the creative strategy. Before getting into the specific elements of the packet, several general observations will be made. First, the approach to a customer should be different than an approach to a prospect. In the former instance give the idea that 'it's me again and I have something new and different to offer'. Second, an upscale product deserves upscale treatment in terms of look and feel. Conversely, sale or low-priced items should not give that appearance. Third, a well-known brand should play on its established reputation using its distinctive logo.[32] As for individual elements, the principal ones are listed below along with executional ideas that have worked for others:

Envelope
Envelopes with only logo and address work well for companies with established reputations when sent to regular customers. The weight and feel of the envelope itself should be in keeping with the type of company and offer. *Windows* which highlight an important feature of the offer such as 'free bonus' or show a piece of the product such as clothes material can stimulate opening action. A teaser statement such as an 'urgent' stamp is another way to stimulate action. . .but just be sure that your message is urgent.[33]

The letter
Stone describes the letter as the 'key ingredient' in the packet. . .it should look and feel like a personal, one-on-one communication. These are his guideposts in writing the letter or reviewing the work of someone else:

- Promise a benefit (the most important one) up front in a headline or first paragraph.
- Amplify your benefit immediately thereafter.
- Explain to the reader exactly what will be received, e.g. width, length, height, material, and colour.
- Offer proof of the benefit through testimonials, case histories, stress tests or other means.
- Explain why the reader should act. . .what will be missed if the order isn't placed by a specified date.
- Restate your principal benefit(s).
- Close with a logical call for immediate action.[34]

Wilkison offers several pointers as to how the letter ought to look including these suggestions:

- A letter should look like one, meaning it should be typed in a commonly used font, not typeset as in the case of printed matter.
- Consider placing the benefit headline in a box so it jumps right out at the reader.
- Reading aids help. This includes short handwritten notes in the margin, action words like 'urgent' and 'reply now', and the inclusion of a 'PS' – 'it's the most read part of the letter'.
- Use paper stock that makes the letter look special and loose sheets which, unfolded, give the appearance of being important.[35]

Brochure

The brochure or printed piece to accompany the letter should have a theme and visual concept that relates to and amplifies the offer made and the benefit to be derived as stated in the letter. The piece can vary in size and appearance from a one-sided, two-colour sheet to a full-colour brochure with photography of several pages in length. A fold out which increases the size of the piece (called a broadside) can also be effective. The design will be enhanced by carefully selecting a *readable* type face, weighting headlines in relation to their importance, boxing in key elements, keeping paragraphs short – four to five lines, using subheadings to draw the eye, and using photographs that show product in use and real people.[36] As in the case of print advertising, the words and illustrations, photography preferred, should be there to help create a personality for the product as well as show its key features and demonstrate its use.

Reply form

One expert suggests that reply forms should 'look too valuable to throw away'. Size, special seals, receipt stubs, specially designed borders, are some of the ways which can help project that appearance. Involve the reader by asking he or she to affix a stamp and/or tear off the written guarantee that goes with the order. But never call it an *order form*; instead, it could be called a 'reservation certificate' or 'trial merchandise application'. A final note of importance: the reply form 'should be able to stand alone and do a complete selling job'.[37]

The ideas just expressed are general guidelines for basic mailing packets. Often other elements are included such as free gifts, related objects, and additional illustrative matter.

A variety of approaches can be used effectively in creating any of the elements described. A study of approaches used previously and by others will benefit anyone attempting to create or direct the creating of this form of communication. One special advantage is the ability to test any element in the mail packet – envelope, letter, brochure, reply form, etc. – for effectiveness.

Physical questions

Taking for granted that envelope and paper sizes are the same in all countries could be a costly mistake. Standards do vary among countries and/or regions of the world. First, the US is out of step with most other countries in type of measurement. Inches and feet are used instead of millimetres (the international metric system). Standard of measurement, then, is a factor. Envelope and paper sizes also differ. Table 11.3 gives a comparison between the USA and other countries.

In planning mailings from or to the USA, if design and production of the physical elements takes place in different countries, coordination is needed to ensure that the proper dimensions are established.[38]

Will creative approaches travel?

An expert who has been asked to evaluate mail communication packages which have proven successful in the USA for use internationally reports that a US copy approach can and has worked in other English speaking countries. However, if translation is required, that is a different matter because copy cannot be translated effectively. An interpretation and then 'a rewrite by a skilled direct mail copywriter in the host country is essential'.[39]

Strategic concerns

Marketers that sell direct to consumers by seeking responses from their non-personal communication mail efforts limit the potential of their business to the names on their mailing lists. These marketers have tended to emphasize testable tactics such as headline and/or premium offer testing to determine which alternative produced the greatest response. Even if the tactics are brilliant, any such effort will suffer if the strategy is not appropriate.

Table 11.3 *Measurement standards*

	US system (inches)		Metric System (millimetres)	
	US	*Overseas*	*US*	*Overseas*
Envelopes				
No. 10	4½ × 9½	4 × 9	114 × 241	102 × 229
C 4	6 × 9	6⅜ × 9	140 × 229	162 × 229
C 5	9 × 12	9 × 12¾	229 × 464	229 × 324
Paper				
A 4	8½ × 11	8¼ × 11¾	221 × 279	216 × 298
A 3	17 × 22	16½ × 23½	442 × 559	432 × 596

Strategic concerns include such questions as: Is it better to concentrate on activities to expand the category in which a product competes? Or is it better to obtain a greater share of the existing business? These are valid questions. However, prior to these answers, it is necessary to know where both the marketer's product and the category stand on the life cycle curve as well as the product's position in relation to the principal competitive brands. Marketing research studies, original, syndicated, or informal, are needed to shed light on these questions when developing the marketing plan.

Another strategic concern, well-known to consumer packaged goods marketers, is positioning. What is needed in this instance is knowledge of your competition. This is easy to obtain when the competitive product is stocked on the same shelf and it is being advertised on television or in print. This task is more difficult when mail is being used as the only medium, making it more difficult to obtain competitive information.

A third concern involves media alternatives. Should marketing efforts be concentrated in a single medium or be spread among two or more alternatives? The answer to this question in part is a function of budget, but deserves periodic review and evaluation. One direct response marketer that had relied on direct mail for prospecting switched to space advertising for that purpose. In a span of four years the budget for space advertising was increased 200 per cent. This indicates that a multimedia approach may be more effective than a single mail approach for direct response marketers.

A fourth concern is the frequency with which costumers should be contacted. It is likely that present customers can be contacted more often with existing products and services. Needed is a contact strategy using a 'frequency, recency, amount, and type' formula to identify the best customer categories and weight accordingly to determine when each group should be recontacted. For example, one catalogue firm divided its customer list into four segments. The best customer segment received twelve catalogues per year; the others received eight, six, and three respectively. This strategy increased sales and also reduced mailing costs as a result of 20 per cent fewer catalogues being sent.[40]

Obstacles to and opportunities for growth

Two major factors stand out when attempting to assess the prospects for future growth of mail media on an international scale. One is delivery system. The other concerns the mailing list and the related issue of privacy.

With respect to delivery system, this will vary on a country-by-country basis and be influenced by the nature of the system, economics, regional cooperation, and culture. Generally speaking, the more advanced economies will have the more highly developed, efficient, and reliable systems. For several years now, overnight mail delivery and small parcel delivery service have been made possible through the US Postal Service. In many countries door-to-door mail service is provided; in others it is not. As recently as 1987, in parts of South Africa door-to-door mail delivery service did not exist...and parcel delivery was non-existent.[41] 'In parts of the Middle East', Ian MacKelder, President of the New York Office of the Marcoa DR Group, was quoted as saying, 'the streets have no names and the houses have no numbers. Women are not allowed to receive mail unless it's approved by their husbands first.'[42]

Real progress has been made in reply mail in Europe as previously cited. A number of European countries now will honour postage paid reply mail from other countries.

Facilitating the use of mail as a medium is growth of the 0800 freephone number in and among countries. For example, the freephone number (numeri verdi) became available in Italy in 1987.[43]

Harrod's of London has used an 800 toll free number for customers from the USA to order merchandise, and permitted the use of a credit card for payment purposes.

Mailable addresses present a problem in Asian and South American countries.[44] Mailing list creation and duplication are other problems. In Brazil, money for this purpose has to be spent on mass media to generate names, involving 'substantial inducements' for cooperation. Lists that are available in Brazil, Australia (and no doubt in many other countries) can result in multiple mailings to the same individual.[45]

Privacy could be the most serious threat to the growth of the mail communication medium. Privacy laws have been adopted for this purpose in Germany.[46] Consumers not wishing to receive mail advertising can have their names left off or removed from mailing lists in the USA. Recently, a mailing list joint venture involving information on 120 million US citizens was cancelled because of consumer complaints and the unanticipated costs required to accommodate consumer privacy issues.[47]

In contrast to what has been just said, Sweden has relatively lax privacy laws. As a result, marketers using the mail medium can access accurate mailing lists through a government computer centre for a fee. The information obtained can include name, address, ID number, marital status, birthplace, citizenship, income, and number of children. This information can be supplanted by other accurate lists that include information on home and car ownership. As a consequence, mail became Sweden's fastest growing medium.[48]

Summary

As target marketing gains in importance the world over and as information gathering systems retrieve more precise characteristics on the buying behaviour of citizens and industrial buyers and influencers, the medium of mail will continue to increase in importance as a marketing communication medium.

Chances are that there will always be a wide variance in one's ability to deliver a message among countries of the world. This will continue to be due to differences in political ideology, social and cultural beliefs, religion, economic development and the inner workings of countries' postal systems.

The international mail system has always been hampered by the lack of standardization in rules, regulations, and costs among nations of the world. This situation is improving among nations that are working towards economic unions and standardization of requirements for business and communications as exemplified by the European Community.

The growth of the medium is not without its threats. In the nations of the world with advanced postal systems, rising costs and consumer outcries over the swapping of their names and dossiers along with the proliferation of unwanted commercial mail may severely blunt the growth of mail as a domestic or international channel of communication in the years to come.

Questions

1 How does mail rank as a medium for advertising in different parts of the world?
2 Why isn't mail recommended as an advertising medium in China?
3 With respect to ordering goods through the mail,

   a What type of goods and services are commonly offered?
   b In what media are these offers made?
   c What factors differentiate mail order in Europe from the USA?

4 Explain the meaning of a cooperative mailing.
5 Give two examples of how mail has been used successfully as a marketing communication tool.
6 Of what importance is the Postal Union Convention to users of mail as a medium internationally?
7 How can mailing lists be compiled and used most effectively?
8 Explain the procedure for the following.

   a Developing mail media strategy.
   b Deciding on the offer.
   c Designing a catalogue.

9 Identify the principal elements of an individual mailing packet and offer two creative guide posts for each.
10 Explain the major strategic concerns which have been expressed with

respect to the use of established principles of mail as a marketing communication medium.

11 How important do you believe the use of mail as a direct response medium will be in the future?

Notes

1 Fishman, Arnold (1990) International mail order guide. *Direct Marketing*, October, 48.

2 Kesler, Lori (1987) Direct marketing special report. *Advertising Age*, 12 January, S−14.

3 Lowen, Irwin (1990) Eyes on Europe. *Direct Marketing*, October, 45.

4 Direct Marketing Association (1991) 1989 Business-to-business marketing communications budgets by per cent per type of advertising. *1990/91 Statistical Fact Book*, The Association, New York, p. 209.

5 Coen, Robert J. (1990) *Estimated Annual US Advertising Expenditures 1980−1989*. Prepared for *Advertising Age*, McCann-Erickson, Inc., New York.

6 An interview with Lester Wunderman *Direct Marketing* (1986) March, 76.

7 Dentsu, Inc. (1989) *Japan Marketing/Advertising Yearbook 1990*, Publications Department, Tokyo, pp. 218−219.

8 Hughes, Lyric (1985) Why and how to advertise in China. *Advertising World*, June, 14−15.

9 Fishman, *op. cit.*, 48.

10 Raphael, Murray (1985) Direct mail in Italy? Bene!, Bene! *Direct Marketing*, February, 102−3.

11 Fishman, *op. cit.*, 48, 49, 56−58.

12 Sanghavi, Nitin (1987) Harrods reaches out with its plush touch. *Direct Marketing*, April, 44.

13 Fortnum & Mason, *The Delectable History of Fortnum & Mason*, a brochure, London.

14 Steinberg, Janice (1989) Direct mail becoming the hottest incentive conduit. *Advertising Age*, 24 July, S−4.

15 diTalamo, Nicholas (1990) Selling in Europe without a sales force. *Direct Marketing*, May, 22−25.

16 Davies, R.R. (1982) International direct mail. *Advertising World*, November, 23.

17 Information on international mail service was obtained from the *Export Shipping Manual, International Trade Reporter* (1991) The Bureau of National Affairs, Inc., Washington, DC, pp. 12, 15, 17−21, 23, 25−35, 37−41.

18 Ralston, Richard (1988) Transnational direct mail. *Direct Marketing*, April, 32.

19 Kilalea, Des (1987) South Africa. In Kesler, Lori, Direct marketing special

report. *Advertising Age*, 12 January, S−20.

20 Lowen, Irwin (1990) Eyes on Europe. *Direct Marketing*, October, 48.

21 Edith Roman Associates, *Direct Mail Encyclopedia*, The Associates, New York.

22 Stevenson, John (1987) Database demystified. *Direct Marketing*, July, 78.

23 Davies, *op. cit.*, 21.

24 Wiedemann, George S. (1987) Interactive marketing: the consumer talks back. *Direct Marketing*, December, 62, 64, 66.

25 Kilalea, *op. cit.*, 8, 9.

26 Well-known books on this subject include Stone, Bob (1989) *Successful Direct Marketing Methods*, 4th edn, NTC Business Books, Lincolnwood, IL, Rapp, Stan, and Collins, Tom *MaxiMarketing* (1987) McGraw-Hill Book Co., New York; an Katzenstein, Herbert, and Sachs, Williams S. (1986) *Direct Marketing*, Merrill Publishing Co., Columbus, Ohio.

27 Kilalea, *op. cit.*, S−8.

28 Stone, *op. cit.*, 46−47.

29 Stone, Bob (1984) *Successful Direct Marketing Methods*, 3rd edn, National Textbook Company Lincolnwood, IL, pp. 308−309.

30 Stone, *op. cit.*, 3rd edn, p. 321.

31 Stone, *op. cit.*, 3rd edn, 253−4.

32 Wilkison, Dave (1987) Designing for your market and budget. *Direct Marketing*, February, 48.

33 Wilkison, Dave (1987) The envelope. *Direct Marketing*, March, 66.

34 Stone, *op. cit.*, 3rd edn, 272−273.

35 Wilkison, Dave (1987) The letter & the personalized letter. *Direct Marketing*, April, 74.

36 Wilkison, Dave (1987) The brochure. *Direct Marketing*, May, 62−63.

37 Stone, *op. cit.*, 3rd edn, 268.

38 Davies, R.R. (1982) International direct mail. *Advertising World*, October/November, 23.

39 *Ibid.*

40 Kobs, Jim (1987) Marketing strategies for maximum growth. *Direct Marketing*, May, 32−34, 36−39, 155.

41 Kesler, Lori (1987) Direct marketing special report. *Advertising Age*, 12 January, S−20.

42 *Ibid.*

43 *Ibid.*, S−19.

44 Roel, Raymond (1987) The global perspective. *Direct Marketing*, April, 4.

45 Kesler, *op. cit.*, S−16, 17.

46 Roel, *op. cit.*

47 Culnan, Mary J. (1991) An issue of consumer privacy. *New York Times*, *Forum*, 31 March, F 9.

48 Kesler, *op. cit.*, S−10.

12 *Media planning buying and evaluating effectiveness*

Introduction

The purpose of this chapter is to identify and treat the essential factors involved in planning, buying and evaluating the effectiveness of a media programme within an individual country or across borders. The international media planning process is the same as it is domestically, covering such topics as objectives, strategies, competition and budget.[1]

As a prelude to developing a media plan, the relative importance of three fundamental media variables should be established. These variables are reach, frequency and continuity. Ratings and gross rating points are two related concepts.

Reach, frequency, continuity and related concepts

Reach

This is the extent to which a given audience is exposed to an advertising message a single time. It is a net, unduplicated figure expressed as a percentage. For example, if the target audience is airline executives of which there are 250,000 and an advertisement is run in a publication that is received by 50,000, the reach is 20 per cent. If the target is households of which there are 10,000,000 and a television commercial is run (aired) in a programme viewed by 1,500,000, the reach is 15 per cent.

A rating is a directly related concept applicable to magazines, television, and radio, but is used more often for broadcast than print in planning and evaluating media programmes. It determines the size of an audience that reads, sees or hears a particular advertising vehicle. A rating is measured as a percentage of total households or some other demographic characteristic such as men, women or teenagers. If a television commercial is run in a programme which reaches 15 per cent of a given target as explained above, it would receive a fifteen rating.

Seldom will an advertiser wish to deliver an advertising message to one audience a single time. The exception may be to announce an end-of-range (close-out) sale of a particular item, the deliverance of a price-off coupon or some other special promotion offer. One pillar of learning theory involves repetition. Reception of a communication message, in this case advertising, is aided by repetition. This leads to the second fundamental media variable, frequency.

Frequency

This is the average number of times a message is received by a target audience in a given time period. If an advertisement is run in the same magazine in five issues, readership of each issue (as well as the ad) will vary. Some will read only one issue of the magazine while others will read two, three, four, or all five issues. The average frequency will fall somewhere between one and five. A similar result will occur when advertising is aired on radio or television.

When the same advertising message is run in several print vehicles at the same time or in the same broadcast vehicle, duplication will occur. This, of course, is a form of frequency which media planners often try to minimize. In print, for example, it is customary to select a list of magazines aimed at a particular target such as adult women with the least amount of duplication. With one insertion in each magazine selected, reach will be maximized. Frequency can be achieved by repeated insertions in the magazines selected.

Reach and frequency for television and radio are normally measured over a four-week period. In the case of print, reach and frequency may be determined monthly, quarterly or for a full year. The reach and frequency of different media vehicles can be aggregated to provide a combined total for both.

Reach and frequency have a mathematical relationship. Previously, the term rating was defined. When advertising for a product is run in the same or different vehicles at the same or different times, the ratings for the individual vehicles can be summed. The term for this summation is *gross rating points*, often referred to as GRPs. GRPs are equal to the product of reach times frequency. During a four-week period, if a television commercial is run weekly in two different night-time programmes, one of which has a rating of twelve and the other fifteen, the total gross rating points are equal to 108. From mathematical tables computed to indicate reach for different levels of gross rating points, the reach is found to be fifty-two. The average frequency, then, equals 2.1 as shown in this computation:

$$\text{GRPs: } (12 + 15) \times 4 = 108 \quad R \times F = \text{GRPs} \quad F = \frac{\text{GRPs}}{R} = \frac{108}{52} = 2.1$$

The remaining basic variable is *continuity*. Continuity refers to the scheduling of advertising throughout an entire planning period, normally one year. Will advertising be continuous, will it be intermittent, or will it be concentrated during one or a few periods of the year?

Each of these basic variables — reach, frequency, and continuity — should be addressed in a media plan. The relative importance of each should be established along with reasons why.

Balancing reach and frequency in the media plan[2]

Equipped with an understanding of the relationship between reach and frequency and the means by which one or the other can be built in television and print, the next consideration is their optimal relationship in any given media plan. By way of illustration, the medium of television will be used for the reason that most research and debate over the interrelationship between the two concepts has involved this medium. In 1979, from many different studies on the subject, Michael Naples[3] concluded that three exposures within a product purchase cycle were believed to be optimal. In other words, an advertising message should be repeated at least three times in order to be effective. Naples also postulated that advertising becomes more effective after three exposures but at a decreasing rate. In media planning, effective frequency is the key. Once defined mathematically, the number for reach is just a matter of computation since reach equals gross rating points divided by frequency.

Following the appearance of the Naples' conclusion, Sissors and Bumba have pointed out that much debate arose and continues to be centred on the question of what constitutes effective frequency. Factors needing consideration include the type of product, the 'threshold' at which an audience begins to respond to a message, the quality (creativeness) of the advertising message, and the exposure at which the message wears out, i.e. starts to produce a negative effect. This lead to their recommendation that beginning with an effective frequency benchmark of three plus, a media planner should do the following:

- weight pertinent marketing, copy, and media factors mathematically,
- sum the result, and
- add or subtract the sum from the benchmark to determine the effective frequency level.

Selected factors and the direction of weighting are shown in Exhibit 12.1. In countries where reach and frequency numbers are available to planners, mathematical treatment can be undertaken. (The four-point scale recommended by Sissors and Bumba ranged from −.2 to +.2.) In Exhibit 12.1 a number of key marketing, copy, and media factors are shown which suggest either lower or higher levels of effective frequency.

In countries like the USA and the UK, reach and frequency estimates can be made by a firm's advertising agency. However, in many countries of the

Exhibit 12.1 *Marketing, copy and media factors that affect effective frequency*

		Lower frequency	*Higher frequency*
Marketing:		• Established brands	• New brands
		• High market share	• Low market share
		• High brand loyalty	• Low brand loyalty
		• Long purchase cycle	• Short purchase cycle
Copy:		• Simple copy	• Complex copy
		• More unique copy	• Less unique copy
		• Continuing campaign	• New copy campaign
		• Product sell copy	• Image type copy
		• Larger ad units	• Small ad units
Media:		• Less ad clutter	• More ad clutter
		• Compatible editorial environment	• Non-compatible editorial environment
		• Attentiveness high	• Attentiveness low
		• Continuous advertising	• Pulsed or flighted advertising
		• Few media used	• Many media used

Source: Sissors, Jack Z., and Bumba, Lincoln (1990) *Advertising Media Planning*, 3rd edn, NTC Business Books, Lincolnwood, ILL., p. 180

world, due to lack of reliable information and trustworthy research techniques, such estimating is not possible. Nonetheless, the relative importance of reach and frequency should be considered in the media planning process. Here are guidelines for building either reach or frequency in a television plan:

	To build reach use	*To build frequency use*
• number of different types of programmes	many	few
• dayparts (morning, afternoon, evening)	several	one
• number of different shows	many	few
• day of week	different	same
• stations or networks	several	one

Source: 4A Media Letter (1977), New York, American Association of Advertising Agencies.

In a similar manner it is possible to emphasize one variable or the other in print:

	To build reach use	To build frequency use
● number of different vehicles	many	few
● editorial format	different	same
● audience target	broad	narrow
● scheduling of publications (daily, weekly, monthly)	varied	same

Equipped with an understanding of these concepts, attention can next be focused on three important questions which require answers at the beginning of the media planning process: who, where, and when.

Who

Who is the target audience? Is it a mass or specialized audience? Are they engineers, financial executives, housewives, factory workers, or teenagers? Are they in a certain income bracket? What occupation(s) are they in? Are they average consumers of your product or do they consume more or less than average? — i.e. are they heavy, medium, or light users? Are they consumers, buyers, influencers, or intermediaries? What kind of life style do they lead? What are their activities, interests, and opinions?

Understanding the marketplace

To answer these questions, an understanding of the dynamics of the marketplace are needed. Take the USA for example. BBDO New York profiles the changes taking place in the consumer marketplace. In introducing these factors no suggestion is being made that the USA is a model for all of the industrialized world; rather that here are the kinds of conditions that communicators may face in planning media programmes for consumer products. The BBDO profile included these factors:

● a better educated society
● more women in the work force (over 50 per cent)
● more active lives
● greater interest in health and fitness
● more convenience oriented, evidenced by:
  − 24-hour and in-home banking
  − convenience and fast foods
  − TV shopping channels and catalogue shopping
  − home delivery services

This has resulted, according to BBDO, in a dominant need for control on the part of consumers, including control of the information and entertainment they choose to receive. This covers media viewing, listening, and reading habits.

The media has responded by offering more choices, such as:

- a fourth television network
- an increasing number of pay and ad-supported cable channels
- more special interest magazines at the expense of the large, mass circulated publications
- 20 per cent more radio stations than ten years ago with listening formats that range from 'rock to news, classical, talk, sports, oldies, black, country and western'
- growth in weekly suburban newspapers at the expense of large, centre city papers

For the media planner reaching the target audience, the job has become more difficult and selection has become more critical. The importance of 'selectively targeted vehicles' has never been more important.[4]

Targeting made easier

Some years ago Michael Manton, a UK direct mail expert, discussed the same idea as that expressed by the BBDO planners of the 1990s. By the mid 1980s media developments in the UK were tending toward greater selectivity on the part of audiences and those who developed media alternatives for the UK market. Press circulations and cinema audiences were on the decline and poster sites were dwindling. The remaining 'truly mass medium' had become television. Even in the case of television, new alternatives had emerged with the advent of Channel 4 and TV-AM along with the introduction of free newspapers, free magazines, regional editions, and local radio. Much greater segmentation and improved targeting of audiences were becoming a reality. 'Single-medium scheduling' had become history.

Manton pointed to two factors which were making it possible to target audiences more precisely: more sensitive and reliable marketing information and a greater ability to manage (electronically) the mass of information being generated from sources like the Census, sales records, retail turnover, and market research.[5]

The ACORN system, for example, which stands for 'A Classification of Residential Neighbourhoods', organizes Census data into eleven groups of thirty-eight neighbourhood types and their respective shares of Great Britain's fifty-four million population. The eleven groups and their shares of total 1990 population are shown in Exhibit 12.2.

The eleven groups shown in Exhibit 12.2 are further broken down into anywhere from two to five additional sub-groups. For example, 'better-off

Exhibit 12.2   *The ACORN groups and their shares of total population*

Group name	% of 1990 population
Agricultural areas	3.4%
Modern family housing, higher incomes	17.5
Older housing of intermediate status	17.9
Older terraced housing	4.2
Council estates – category I	13.2
Council estates – category II	8.8
Council estates – category III	7.0
Mixed inner metropolitan areas	3.8
High status non-family areas	4.1
Affluent suburban housing	15.8
Better-off retirement areas	3.8
Unclassified	0.5
	100.0%

Source: CACI Market Analysis (1990) In *Marketing Pocket Book 1991*, The Advertising Association, Henley-on-Thames, 12.

retirement areas' are subdivided into 'private houses, well-off older residents', and 'private flats, older single people'.

By means of bar coding, retail responses can be matched with circulation of a print vehicle in one of the ACORN areas or groups. Through other research services, such as TGI, the purchasing behaviour of every ACORN classification can be identified and matched against the electoral register. This means that a mailing list with names and addresses can be generated for mail media purposes.

These types of developments resulted in media campaigns, like the one for Mazda, where television was used for image-building purposes along with a mail effort designed to stimulate selected potential customers to take a test drive. In another instance, British Airways combined television to promote its corporate image with local press and a local message aimed at special target groups such as Jersey Island London-bound Christmas shoppers...offering special seasonal low-cost round trip air fares.[6]

Where
Is your target audience located in many countries of the world, in a region of the world, or within a single country? Is the audience national, regional or local? Is it urban, suburban or rural? Is the audience located in a few or many parts of the country? Are there targets within a regional grouping of countries or within a territory of a country that needs special advertising effort?

Geographic media decisions can be aided by several relatively simple calculations. The difficulty encountered concerns the figures that may or may not be available with which to make the calculations. To begin with, it is necessary to focus on the amount of monies budgeted for advertising and the countries or regions in which these funds will be expended. Whether the monies will be allocated among countries, among regions, or (metropolitan) areas within regions, the same principles apply.

Allocating advertising expenditures by territory

The first set of calculations involves the past (if one exists) and projected sales along with the funds spent and budgeted for media advertising (or it could be for any form of promotion). The figures might look like those shown in Exhibit 12.3.

Exhibit 12.3   *Sales and advertising: brand X by territory*

| | Year ago | | | | Year ahead | | | |
| | Case sales | | Advertising | | Case sales | | Advertising | |
Territory	*(000)*	*% of Total*	*Monies (000)*	*% of Total*	*(000)*	*% of Total*	*Monies (000)*	*% of Total*
A	4,922	16.5	9,440	18.0	4,850	15.9	8,600	15.9
B	8,890	29.9	14,200	27.1	9,500	31.1	16,800	31.1
C	11,500	38.7	19,450	37.1	12,300	40.2	21,700	40.2
D	4,441	14.9	9,360	17.8	3,900	12.8	6,900	12.8
Totals	29,753	100.0	52,450	100.0	30,550	100.0	54,000	100.0

Examining the figures for a year ago in Exhibit 12.3, it can be observed that sales ran ahead of advertising expenditures in territories B and C, and sales lagged advertising expenditures in A and D. In plotting sales for the year ahead, territories B and C were considered to be growing markets and A and D declining markets. The advertising budget was adjusted to conform with sales projections. If the numbers are available only for the prior year and the sales estimates for the year ahead, using percentage of sales for the new year to allocate the advertising budget, as shown in Exhibit 12.3, has merit. However, prior to making the sales projection or setting the advertising budget, other factors such as sales trends, competition, customers, and environmental conditions should be taken into account.

Indexing: an aid in allocating expenditures
In product-market situations where competitive and category information is

available, another, even more useful geographical analysis can be made. By linking both brand A's sales and the total sales for the brand's category (e.g. instant coffee) to the same base statistic such as population, a comparison can be made of the brand's performance against the overall performance of the category by territory. This is called *indexing*. Brand and category development indexes are computed and compared to enhance the geographic decision-making process. See Exhibit 12.4 for an example of this computation.

Exhibit 12.4 *Category and brand X development indexes*

Territory	% of total population	% of total category sales	Category development index	% of total brand sales	Brand development index
A	19.2	18.0	94	16.5	86
B	27.5	28.3	103	29.9	109
C	30.0	25.6	85	38.7	129
D	23.3	28.1	121	14.9	64
	100.0	100.0		100.0	

To determine the index numbers, the per cent of population of a territory is divided into the per cents of category and brand sales, then multiplied by 100. For example, in territory A:

$$\frac{\% \text{ of category sales}}{\% \text{ of population}} \quad \frac{18.0}{19.2} \times 100 = 94$$

In looking at the indexes in Exhibit 12.4, it can be assumed that any number between approximately ninety and 110 is average. As the index numbers move away from the average range on the up or down side, the indexes become increasingly more important.

What actions do these figures suggest with respect to the allocation of advertising monies? First, potential exists in all territories so that some level of advertising should be considered for each. Second, in territory A, the brand development index is somewhat below average in an average category market. Third, in territory B, both brand and category indexes are average. Fourth, there is a marked contrast in territory C with a below average category development index and a well above average brand development index. Fifth, the reverse is true in territory D. While other factors, as mentioned earlier, must be taken into account before advertising budget allocation decisions are reached, the analysis gives clear signals as to courses of action. Territory D deserves special attention because of the category's importance. Territory C deserves some extra effort as well because of the brand's importance.

When

When will advertising be conducted: year-round, in conjunction with peak sales periods, to support a promotion, or to extend the seasonal demand for a product by attempting to entice consumers to buy during a slow period? Purchasing patterns of a brand and its competition are needed to answer the 'when' question.

It is also important to distinguish between consumer and industrial goods in order to answer the timing question. Purchasing cycles for the two categories can be very different. Some consumer products such as milk can be repurchased several times a week, in some cases, daily. Manufacturing plants can last for decades. Equipment can be used up or become obsolete in five, ten, or twenty years. When putting industrial or business-to-business product life cycles and demand into a global context, opportunities for sales may occur at different times in different countries.

Seasonality

In the consumer goods sector where purchases are often made by large numbers of people on a regular basis, the timing question is apt to centre on seasonality. All other things being equal, extra advertising and promotion effort will coincide with the up side of the seasonal sales curve. Two examples will be used to illustrate the seasonal nature of products in the USA (see Exhibit 12.5). The first is for Canned Peas which rises above the annual volume average of 100 in the Autumn months to a peak of 119 in November, dips to 105 in December, rises again to 114 in January then falls through 100 to a low of eighty in June.

The second seasonal curve for prepared mustard must be tied to the American consumer's penchant for hot dogs and hamburgers cooked on the backyard grill. Observe how sales of this product peak in the months of May, June and July.

In each instance, it would be customary to heavy up advertising and promotion expenditures on the up side of the sales curves.

Other planning considerations

There are other important preliminary considerations in planning the media programme within or across borders. They are dealer/distributor involvement, product feature and perceptions, price and quality, editorial adjacency, space size/length of commercial, separate but complementary markets, and media availability and budget.

Exhibit 12.5 *Monthly index of sales of canned peas and prepared mustard. Twelve months' basis, annual average = 100*

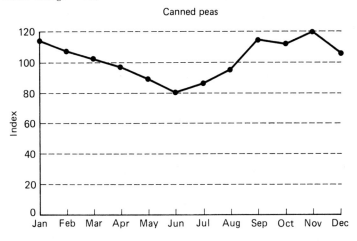

Canned peas

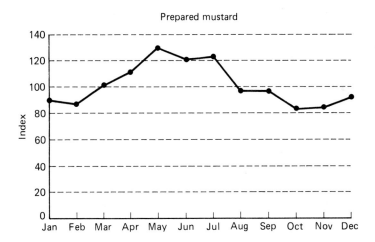

Prepared mustard

Dealer/distributor involvement

For a company that sells industrial equipment through distributors in various countries, the international advertising budget may be relatively small but nonetheless important in producing inquiries and sales leads. Host country distributors can be very helpful in planning a media programme by suggesting which local trade magazines are most widely recognized and read. Their input can supplement information obtained from publications like *International Media*

Guides or from individuals or organizations that represent publications in the countries where the advertising programme is being planned. The local distributors can also check on the advertisements which have been run for position, quality of reproduction, and the number of leads generated by the advertising. For the export marketer, then, the host country intermediary can aid in the media planning process which, under other circumstances, would be the job of a local advertising agency.

Product features and perceptions

Media planners and message creators need to work in concert so that the appropriate medium(ia) is selected. If the product requires demonstration, which of the media alternatives available is preferred? In the consumer product sector, where television exists and is affordable, there is no better alternative. Sight, sound, and motion are combined to produce the message effect. When three dimensions are needed, it is the media planner's job to try to come up with a means by which this effect can be produced, for example, by the use of a special construction that can be inserted into a magazine.

Price and quality

Where price and quality are important, it becomes the media planner's job to select the vehicle(s) to project this image. Some magazines reaching a general audience tend to be upscale, more sophisticated and worldly while others tend to be more earthy and sensational in their stories and news coverage. The editorial treatment should be in keeping with the price/quality perceptions of the message being communicated.

Editorial adjacency

Editorial adjacency can also be an important consideration. For medicaments, if the advertising can be placed in a position adjacent to an editorial column on health and medicine, it should, by nature of its position, achieve higher readership than if placed run-of-press (anywhere).

Space size/length of commercial

One of the media planner's jobs is to work closely with the creative group to learn of the nature of the message. Will it introduce a new product or service, or is it for an established product? Will the media be used as a vehicle to carry some form of promotion, e.g. a coupon, contest, or sweepstake? This will influence the choice of media and also the amount of space or length of time to be devoted to the advertising message. If there is to be a major promotion to create extra attention and awareness, two pages or a spread may be recommended in place of a single advertising page. If the purpose of the campaign is to introduce a new product into an existing market, or to introduce an existing product into a new market, this may call for greater space or a longer message on television or radio. Again, this is why media and creative planners must work closely together in developing advertising plans.

Separate but complementary targets

Valid reasons may exist for running separate advertising campaigns against two (or more) different target markets. In the consumer goods field, a breakfast cereal may have two targets — mothers and children — and two creative strategies — nutrition and taste — necessitating separate media strategies: women's magazines to reach mothers and Saturday morning television (cartoons) to reach children.

Similarly, the international marketer of industrial products may have to run two different campaigns: one to keep the name and reputation of the company in the buyers' and influencers' minds; the other to present a specific product offering in an environment where a potential sales opportunity exists. For example, one of the commercial aircraft manufacturers runs an ongoing 'umbrella' campaign in the major international publications that reach a broad cross section of industry leaders, government officials, and opinion leaders. However, the company's major advertising effort is one designed to support the sales mission in a specific country where it may take several years before a purchase decision is made. Objectives and strategies for the campaign are worked out with the person in charge of the sales effort in that country. The targets (which may include airline executives and technicians, bankers, government officials and travel agents); the message; and the media to reach the targets are decided jointly between corporate communications and the sales group. When launched, the campaign may last six months or several years.

Media availability and budget

Included among the important considerations are the availability of a medium in a given market and the budget to be put behind the product or service. Both are crucial in media planning. As already observed, across Europe there still persists a wide discrepancy in the availability of television as an advertising medium. For a Pan-European television campaign in Germany and some of the Scandinavian countries where television time is limited or not available, the media planner will have to compensate by using alternative media forms.

Finally, the size of the budget will have a direct bearing on the selection of media. If the budget is low, conventional wisdom dictates that the major portion if not all of the media funds should be concentrated in one medium rather than scattered among two or more. The idea here is to be important, important as possible in one medium before planning the use of a second. Competitive spending will be the indicator of importance. In fact, if other competitors are outspending a product in a given medium, it may be better to pick an alternative medium in which the product advertising will be more visible, possibly dominate...providing that the medium will deliver a satisfactory target audience.

The media mix

If adequate media funds are available, then more than one medium can be considered. Under these circumstances, the choice of media alternatives must be thought out and defended with logic and imagination. Several possible media mix strategies for consumer products are:

1 National magazine advertising for continuity with additional advertising weight provided by national television during or immediately prior to the peak selling period to boost levels of reach and frequency.
2 National television advertising scheduled in each of four quarters to attain satisfactory reach and frequency levels and for continuity. For increased frequency and/or extended reach local television will be added in selected high potential markets.
3 A variation of 2 above would be the replacement of television with magazines to achieve reach, frequency, and continuity goals on a national level along with the local (spot) television in high potential markets.
4 National television advertising to attain satisfactory levels of reach and frequency across the country in combination with local radio in selected markets to extend reach and build frequency.
5 A multi-media effort involving television, radio, newspapers and outdoor to maximize reach during the introduction or reintroduction of a product or service.
6 Magazines for continuity and frequency against a selected target year-round plus local newspapers during the peak selling period to implement a cooperative advertising programme with retailers to stimulate sales activity.

Other combinations incorporating outdoor, mail, and/or yellow pages along with print and/or broadcast are possible combinations. It depends on the product-market situation, media availabilities, the media objectives to be realized, and the budget.

In the case of business-to-business advertising, various media combinations can also be selected such as a blend of general business magazines, trade directories, and mail. A mix that an industrial promotion board in Ireland used in order to interest electronic manufacturers in Silicone Valley, California in locating production facilities in Ireland combined local radio with outdoor posters.

Scheduling patterns

With respect to the scheduling of advertising, there are three widely accepted patterns: continuous, flighting, and pulsing.

Continuous
A continuous pattern, which addresses the continuity variable mentioned at the beginning of this chapter, calls for advertising to be maintained throughout the entire planning period or year as indicated below:

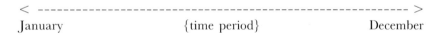

January   {time period}   December

An example of a continuous pattern is a media plan which calls for running a commercial announcement in a weekly television programme fifty-two times a year, or running an advertisement in a monthly magazine twelve times per year. This pattern keeps the advertiser's message before a given audience continuously while the reach is limited to the vehicle or vehicles selected. It is a pattern used for products or services that are purchased frequently and at regular intervals. However, depending on the size of the budget, the advertising weight (reach and frequency) in any one week may be relatively low.

Flighting
Flighting involves advertising that is run at different periods throughout the year. Here is an example:

Advertising	*Flight 1*		*Flight 2*		*Flight 3*	
Flights	Feb−Mar		June−July		Oct−Nov	
Hiatus Jan		April−May		Aug−Sept		Dec

In this instance, radio or television announcements are scheduled weekly during the three, two-month periods as shown. Advertising that is concentrated in bursts at set intervals through the year is interspersed with periods of no advertising at all (hiatuses). One possible drawback of this approach is that recipients forget the advertising message, particularly if the interval between flights is too great.[7] However, studies have shown that while awareness drops off after a flight is terminated, it does not disappear. In fact, it increases once the next and subsequent flights are underway.[8]

Though commonly concerned with broadcast media, flighting can also be used with print, particularly daily and weekly newspapers and magazines. Due to the interval between monthly publications, flighting does not lend itself to these vehicles.

Pulsing

Pulsing combines the strategies of continuity and flighting as shown in the following illustration.

Flighting	xxxxxxxx		x xxxxxxxx		xxxxxxxx	
Continuity	xxxxxxxxxxxxxxxxxxxxxxxxxxxxxxxxxxxxxxxxxxxxxxxxxxxxxxxxxx					
	Feb−Mar		June−July		Oct−Nov	
Jan		April−May		Aug−Sept		Dec

When compared to a continuity or flighting schedule, a pulsing strategy would appear to require a larger budget. This may or may not be the case. It depends on how funds are allocated among heavy up (high) and sustaining (low) periods, and also the selection of media. For example, magazines (normally a lower cost medium) may be used for continuity and be supplemented with television (a higher cost medium) for added advertising weight during peak periods of demand. The benefit of this strategy is that both continuity and increased reach and frequency during peak selling periods are achieved. A programme of this nature must be costed out to determine if sufficient impact is being delivered at any time throughout the planning period as well as during peak seasons.

At this point it should have become clear that in many circumstances, particularly when a media programme is being planned for a consumer product with a budget of a size that will allow for use of two or more media, the planning alternatives are numerous. That is why the variables discussed earlier should be clearly in focus before selection and scheduling of media is attempted. Clear, unambiguous answers to the who, where, and when questions are needed. Basic marketing considerations such as the competitive environment and need for dealer support should have been taken into account. The relative importance of reach, frequency, and continuity should have been established.

Then, and only then can media choices and their application throughout the entire planning period be made.

Media information for planning purposes

Beginning with a global perspective, *International Media Guides* (IMG) provide planners with facts and figures on business publications, newspapers, and consumer magazines in 140 or more countries. Information on publications that are regional and 'global' is also provided. Their newspaper edition contains the name and address of each publication, who to contact for editorial and advertising purposes, rates for weekday and Sunday advertising, technical specifications, closing dates (when advertising materials have to be received for printing purposes), circulation, and area of distribution. See Exhibit 12.6 to obtain an idea of the type of information reported in an IMG for newspapers.

The Standard Rate & Data Service (SRDS) of Wilmette, Illinois in the USA also publishes directories of international business and consumer publications. Exhibit 12.7 shows how the SRDS information is presented.

Regional media information is not as easy to find. European media scene information has been available from time to time from different sources. One source, now outdated, provided a comprehensive analysis of general economic and demographic statistics along with advertising expenditures by media in sixteen countries, selected statistics, and basic cost information on all forms of mass media.

On a country level, specialized publications, associations, and individual advertising agencies provide detailed information about media alternatives and costs. In the USA, *Adweek* publishes a quarterly *Marketer's Guide to Media*. This guide provides media rates and costs per thousand, circulation and readership data, and television and radio ratings along with selected demographic information. The media include newspapers, magazines, national and spot television and radio, cable, yellow pages, outdoor, and specialized media to reach Hispanic and teen markets. The *Standard Rate and Data Service*, also in the USA, publishes rates, circulation, and specifications for all forms of mass media as well as a special directory on mail media. Associations representing different types of media and the advertising industry as a whole are also sources of media planning information. For example, the Advertising Association, London, publishes an annual *Marketing Pocket Book* that not only contains detailed facts on media but also on various aspects of marketing. Subjects covered are economic and demographic statistics; consumer expenditures; distribution; advertising and other marketing expenditures. Also included are marketing and media maps in Great Britain. In addition, selected marketing and media topics are also included for other countries in Europe. In fact, this *Pocket Book*

Exhibit 12.6 *IMG: Newspapers in Malaysia. Reproduced by permission of International Media Enterprises, Norwalk, CT, USA*

MALAYSIA

1 Malaysian Ringgit (M$) = $.3755
Languages: Malay (official); English, Chinese & Indian
languages also spoken

Newspapers

Selangor

STAR and SUNDAY STAR
Star Publications (Malaysia) Berhad, 13 Jalan 13/6, 46200 Petaling Jaya, Selangor (Tel: (03) 757-8811; Telex: MA 37373; Fax: (03) 755-4039)
General morning newspaper in English. Est. 1971
Ed: V.K. Chin; Ad Mgr: Linda Ngiam
Rate Card: 1989
  Weekdays:
    1 col/cm: M$ 14.80 or 1 col/inch: $14.12
    Full pg: M$ 3,833 or $1,439
  Sundays:
    1 col/cm: M$ 15.90 or 1 col/inch: $15.16
    Full pg: M$ 4,118 or $1,546
  4 color & double-truck ads possible
Type pg: 267x370 mm or 10-1/2" x 14-9/16". Offset
7 cols, width: 35 mm or 1-3/8". Screen: 85
Ad Closing, b/w: 5 days before publication; color: 4 weeks before publication
Circ (ABC): 148,184 (daily); 173,497 (Sunday)
Distribution: national

Kuala Lumpur

THE BERITA HARIAN
The New Straits Times Press (Malaysia) Berhad, Balai Berita, 31 Jalan Riong, 59100 Kuala Lumpur (Tel: (03) 2745444; Telex MA 30259; Cables: NEWTIMES; Fax: (03) 274-9434)
Daily (Mon-Sat) morning newspaper in Bahasa. Est. 1957
Group Ed: BHSB; Ed: Ahmad Nazri Abdullah;
  Gen Adv Mgr: C.C. Lo
US Rep: Dow Jones International Marketing Services
Rate Card: 4/88
  National Edition (Malaysia only):
    1 col/cm: M$ 11.00 or 1 col/inch: $10.49
  International Edition (Malaysia & Singapore):
    1 col/cm: M$ 16.19 or 1 col/inch: $15.44
  4 color and double-truck ads possible
Type pg: 389x555 mm or 15-1/4" x 22"
10 cols, width: 35 mm or 1-3/8". Screen: 100
Ad Closing, b/w: 2 working days before publication; color: 4 working days before publication
Circ: 207,812
Distribution: Malaysia & Singapore, Brunei

THE BERITA MINGGU
The New Straits Times Press (Malaysia) Berhad, Balai Berita, 31 Jalan Riong, 59100 Kuala Lumpur (Tel: 03-2745444; Telex MA 30259; Cables: NEWTIMES; Fax: (03) 274-9434)
Weekly (Sun) morning newspaper in Bahasa. Est. 1960
Group Ed: BHSB; Ed: Ahmad Nazri Abdullah;
  Gen Adv Mgr: C.C. Lo
US Rep: Dow Jones International Marketing Services
Rate Card: 4/88
  National Edition (Malaysia only):
    1 col/cm: M$ 11.50 or 1 col/inch: $10.96
  International Edition (Malaysia & Singapore):
    1 col/cm: M$ 18.13 or 1 col/inch: $17.29
  4 color and double-truck ads possible
Type pg: 389x555 mm or 15-1/4" x 22"

10 cols, width: 35 mm or 1-3/8". Screen: 100
Ad Closing, b/w: 2 working days before publication; color: 4 working days before publication
Circ: 291,730
Distribution: Malaysia & Singapore, Brunei

THE CHINA PRESS
40 Jalan Lima, Off Jalan Cahn Sow Lin; P.O. Box 10346, 552200 Kuala Lumpur (Tel: (03) 2218855; Telex: 03-2214310; Fax: (03) 2214975)
General daily morning newspaper in Chinese. Est. 1946
Ed: Wong Ah Lek; Ad Mgr: Jeremy Goh
US Rep: S.S. Koppe & Co., Inc.
Rates received 5/89, in US$
  1 pg (b/w): M$ 2,385 or $896
  1 pg (4 color): M$ 5,830 or $2,189
Type pg: 355x530 mm or 14" x 20-7/8"
Trim sz: 370x570 mm or 14-9/16" x 22-1/2". Offset
10 cols, width: 35 mm or 1-3/8". Screen: 100
Ad Closing, b/w: 3 days before publication
Circ (ABC): 73,000
Distribution: national

THE MALAY MAIL
The New Straits Times Press (Malaysia) Berhad, Balai Berita, 31 Jalan Riong, 59100 Kuala Lumpur (Tel: (03) 2745444; Telex: MA 30259; Cables: NEWTIMES; Fax: (03) 274-9434)
Daily (Mon-Sat) afternoon newspaper in English. Est. 1896
Group Ed: NSTSB; Ed: A. Kadir Jasin;
  Gen Adv Mgr: C.C. Lo
Rate Card: 4/88
  1 col/cm: M$ 11.00 or 1 col/inch: $10.49
  4 color & double-truck ads possible
Type pg: 270x375 mm or 10-5/8" x 14-3/4". Offset
7 cols, width: 35 mm or 1-3/8". Screen: 100
Ad Closing, b/w: 2 working days before publication; color: 4 working days before publication
Circ: 60,211. Distribution: National

UTUSAN MELAYU/UTUSAN ZAMAN
Utusan Melayu (Malaysia) Berhard, No. 46M, Jalan Lima Off Jalan, Chan Sow Lin, 55200 Kuala Lumpur (Tel: 2217055; Telex: MA 30489)
Adv Address: Utusan Pear & Dean, P.O. Box 12590, Kuala Lumpur (Tel)/795488; Telex: MA 37776)
General daily newspaper in Mingguan Malaysia
Rates effective 1988
  1 col/cm: M$ 5.20 or 1 col/inch: $4.96
  Full pg: M$ 2,246 or $843
  1 pg (4 color): M$ 7,800 or $2,929
Trim sz: 410x578 mm or 16-1/8" x 22-3/4". Offset
8 cols, width: 45 mm or 1-3/4"
Ad Closing (copy): 3 days before publication
Circ (PS): 26,554 (weekdays); 30,611 (Sunday)

MINGGUAN MALAYSIA
Utusan Melayu (Malaysia) Berhad, No. 46M, Jalan Lima Off Jalan, Chan Sow Lin, 55200 Kuala Lumpur (Tel: (03) 2217055)
Adv Address: Utusan Pear & Dean, Sdn Bhd, No. 59 Jalan ss 22/19 Damansara Jaya, 47400 Petaling Jaya (Tel: (03) 7195488; Telex: MA 37776; Fax: (03) 7172284)
General weekly (Sun) newspaper in Mingguan Malaysia. Est. 1964
Ed-in-chief: Zainuddin Maidin; Ad Dir: Abd Latiff Nordin
Rates received 8/89. Agency Comm: 15%
  1 col/cm: M$ 14.50 or 1 col/inch: $13.83
  Full pg: M$ 7,830 or $2,940
  1 pg (4 color): M$ 16,326 or $6,130
  Double-truck & hi-fi ads possible
Type pg: 356x540 mm or 14" x 21-1/4"
Trim sz: 382x578 mm or 15" x 22-3/4". Offset
10 cols, width: 32 mm or 1-5/16". Screen: 120
Ad Closing: 2 days prec. publication
Circ (ABC, 6/88): 407,292
Distribution: national

Exhibit 12.7 *Business Publication Rates and Data. Reproduced by permission of Standard Rate and Data Service, Wilmette, Illinois*

INTERNATIONAL
20 Business

AMERICA ECONOMIA—cont

Seoul—Jo Young Seng, Biecom. Phone 739 7840-1. FAX: 732 3662.
Tokyo—Fumihiro Tanaka, Shinano International Inc. Phone 3584 6420. FAX: 3505 5628.
Bogota—Gertrudis de Saportas, Gersamedios. Phone 236 6568.
Buenos Aires—Gustavo Lichtmajer y, CarlosBablo, AmericaEconomia. Phone 311 3472. FAX: 313 9987.
Caracas—Cecilia Spitia, AmericaEconomia. Phone 910489. FAX: 929 229.
Mexico D.F.—Dolores Siguenza y, Sergio Lopez, AmericaEconomia. Phone 286-6400/286 7063. FAX: 211 5923.
Santiago—Ana Maria Casanueva, BernarditaMenchaca y Carmen Toro, AmericaEconomia. Phone 235 2496/494171. FAX: 223 1903.
Sao Paulo—Antonio Scavone, SIX. Phone 881 4068. FAX: 852 1893.

3. COMMISSION AND CASH DISCOUNT
15% to recognized advertising agencies.

ADVERTISING RATES
Effective January 1, 1992.
Rates received March 24, 1992.

5. BLACK/WHITE RATES

	1 ti	6 ti	12 ti
1 page	5510.	5410.	5190.
2 columns	4140.	4060.	3900.
1/2 page h	4000.	3930.	3770.
1 column	2270.	2230.	2130.

6. COLOR RATES

2-Color:	1 ti	6 ti	12 ti	18 ti	24 ti
1 page	6890.	6750.	6480.	6210.	5930.
2 columns	5160.	5060.	4850.	...	...
1/2 page h	4970.	4870.	4670.	...	...
1 column	2830.	2770.	2660.	...	...

4-Color:	1 ti	6 ti	12 ti	18 ti	24 ti
Sprd	16,690.	16,360.	15,690.	...	...
1 page	8,600.	8,430.	8,090.	7,750.	7,400.
2 columns	6,890.	6,750.	6,480.	...	...
1/2 page h	6,460.	6,330.	6,060.	...	...

7. COVERS

4-Color:	1 ti	6 ti	12 ti
2nd cover	10,320.	10,120.	9,700.
3rd cover	10,320.	10,120.	9,700.
4th cover	12,040.	11,810.	11,330.

9. BLEED
No charge.

10. SPECIAL POSITION

	1 ti	6 ti	12 ti
Centerspread	19,790.	19,400.	18,610.
Extra			15%

15. GENERAL REQUIREMENTS
Also see SRDS Print Media Production Data.
Printing Process: Offset Full Run
Trim Size: 10-7/8 x 8-1/16.
Binding Method: Saddle Stitched.
Colors Available: 4-color process.

AD PAGE DIMENSIONS

Sprd	9-5/8 x 14-13/16	1 col	9-5/8 x 2-3/16
1 pg	9-5/8 x 6-13/16	2 col	9-5/8 x 4-1/2
1/2 h	4-13/16 x 6-13/16		

16. ISSUE AND CLOSING DATES
Published 12 times a year.

Issue:	Issued	Closing (+)	Closing (*)
Jan-Feb	1/1	12/6	12/13
Mar	3/1	1/10	1/31
Apr	4/1	2/7	2/28
May	5/1	3/6	3/27
Jun	6/1	4/3	4/24
Jul	7/1	5/8	5/29
Aug	8/1	6/5	6/26
Sep	9/1	7/3	7/24
Oct	10/1	8/7	8/24
Oct "500"	10/26	9/4	9/25
Nov	11/1	9/4	9/25
Dec	12/1	10/2	10/23

(+) Space
(*) Material

17. SPECIAL SERVICES
A.B.C. Supplementary Data Report Dec/91.

18. CIRCULATION
Established 1966. Single copy 5.00; per year 60.00.
A.B.C. 12-31-91 (6 mos. aver. qualified)

Tot.Pd.	(Subs)	(Single)	(Assoc)
36,870	35,359	1,511	...

Average Non-Qualified (not included above):
Total 8,000
GEOGRAPHICAL DISTRBUTION 12/91—37,768

Argentina	1,871	Panama	662
Bolivia	704	Paraguay	121
Chile	5,218	Peru	675
Colombia	2,547	Uruguay	494
Ecuador	6,266	Venezuela	4,959
Guatemala	182	Others	229
Mexico	13,840		

Publisher states: Effective with April 1992 issue, guaranteed average net paid 46,114

ANDOVER BUSINESS

Location ID: 7 BINT 20 **Mid 062909-000**
Published quarterly by Andover Business Publications LTD., P.O. Box 664, Andover, Hampshire England SP11 0YE. Phone UK 0264 772828. FAX: UK 0264 772828.
For shipping info., see Print Media Production Data.

PUBLISHER'S EDITORIAL PROFILE
ANDOVER BUSINESS is a news and features magazine for chief executives, proprietors and senior management of professional, industrial and commercial business in the Andover area. Rec'd 6/26/91.

1. PERSONNEL
Pub—Alex White.
Adv Mgr—Linda White.

3. COMMISSION AND CASH DISCOUNT
10% to recognized agencies.

4. GENERAL RATE POLICY
All invoices are billed in Sterling. Advertising rates will, therefore, vary according to the exchange rates in effect at the time of billing.

ADVERTISING RATES
Effective January 1, 1991.
Rates received June 26, 1991.
NOTE: Rates quoted in pounds.

5. BLACK/WHITE RATES

	1 ti	2 ti	3 ti	4 ti
Sprd	830.	810.	790.	770.
1 page	425.	415.	405.	395.
1/2 page	220.	215.	210.	205.
1/4 page	115.	113.	110.	105.
1/8 page	65.	64.	62.	60.

6. COLOR RATES

4-Color:	1 ti	2 ti	3 ti	4 ti
Sprd	970.	950.	930.	910.
1 page	495.	485.	475.	465.
1/2 page	270.	265.	260.	255.
Spot color, black/white rates, extra				10%

7. COVERS
4th cover, extra 15%

10. SPECIAL POSITION
Extra 10%

14. CONTRACT AND COPY REGULATIONS
See Contents page for location—items 1, 2, 3, 8, 14, 15, 17, 20, 21, 28, 29, 30, 35, 36.

15. GENERAL REQUIREMENTS
Also see SRDS Print Media Production Data.
Printing Process: Offset Full Run
Trim Size: 8-1/4 x 11-3/4.
Binding Method: Saddle Stitched.
Colors Available: 4-color process.

AD PAGE DIMENSIONS

1 pg	7 x 10-1/2	1/4 v	3-1/4 x 5-1/4
1/2 h	7 x 5-1/4		

16. ISSUE AND CLOSING DATES
Published quarterly.

Issue:	Closing	Issue:	Closing
Mar 8	2/7	Sep 13	8/16
Jun 14	5/17	Dec 13	11/15

18. CIRCULATION
Established 1986. Single copy 1.25; per year 5.00.
SWORN 6-30-91 (6 mos. aver.)

Total	Non-Pd	Paid	(Subs)	(Single)	(Assoc)
1,731	1,719	12	8	4	...

Unpaid Distribution (not included above):
Total 140
TERRITORIAL DISTRIBUTION 5/91--1,731
England 1,731

BUSINESS ANALYSIS OF CIRCULATION

	Total
CEOs of All Business	1,731

Asian Business

A Far East Trade Press, Ltd. Publication
BPA

Location ID: 7 BINT 20 **Mid 041818-000**
Published monthly by Far East Trade Press, Ltd., Kai Tak Commercial, 317 Des Voeux Rd., 2nd Fl., Central Hong Kong. Phone 5-453028. FAX 5-446979. Telex 83434 FETPHX.
U.S. Ofc: Reed Business PublishingGroup, 205 E. 42nd St., New York, NY 10017. Phone 212-867-2080.

For shipping info., see Print Media Production Data.

PUBLISHER'S EDITORIAL PROFILE
ASIAN BUSINESS is designed for the business executive manufacturer, trader, bankers and investor interested in keeping up with major trends in the key growth economies of Southeast and East Asia and with commercial developments in major financial and industrial sectors. We report the news that interests Asia's business leaders. Rec'd 4/9/90.

1. PERSONNEL
Dir—Jack Maisano, Koh Hock Seng

2. REPRESENTATIVES and/or BRANCH OFFICES
New York, NY 10017—Reed Business Publishing Group, 205 E. 42nd St. Phone 212-867-2080. Phone 212-867-2080. FAX: 212-687-6604.
Des Plaines (Chicago), IL 60018—1350 E. Touhy Ave. Phone 708-635-9920. Telex: 984819 SOX WIN. FAX: 708-635-0602.
Newport Beach (Los Angeles), CA 92660—3700 Campus Dr., Suite 203. Phone 714-756-1059. FAX: 714-756-2514

3. COMMISSION AND CASH DISCOUNT
15% of gross billing to agencies.

4. GENERAL RATE POLICY
If and when new rates and circulation base are announced, such announcement will be made at least 13 weeks in advance of issue date of the 1st issue to which such an increase of rates shall apply. Contracts placed prior to such announcement will, however, be honored at the original rate for the duration of such contract, up to a maximum of 12 months from the 1st insertion. No cancellations after closing date.

ADVERTISING RATES
Effective December 1, 1991.
Rates received January 7, 1991.

5. BLACK/WHITE RATES

	1 ti	3 ti	6 ti	12 ti
1 page	6645.	6450.	6310.	5980.
2/3 page	5015.	4870.	4765.	4510.
1/2 page	3930.	3815.	3735.	3540.
1/3 page	2780.	2700.	2645.	2505.
1/4 page	2440.	2370.	2320.	2200.
1/6 page	1765.	1710.	1675.	1595.

6. COLOR RATES

2-Color:	1 ti	3 ti	6 ti	12 ti
1 page	7935.	7695.	7535.	7140.
2/3 page	5965.	5790.	5675.	5370.
1/2 page	4745.	4610.	4510.	4275.
1/3 page	3250.	3155.	3090.	2930.
1/4 page	2850.	2770.	2710.	2570.
1/6 page	2115.	2060.	2010.	1900.

4-Color:	1 ti	3 ti	6 ti	12 ti
1 page	9640.	9550.	9350.	8860.
2/3 page	7535.	7310.	7160.	6785.
1/2 page	5870.	5695.	5575.	5280.
1/3 page	3865.	3750.	3670.	3480.
1/4 page	3465.	3360.	3290.	3120.
1/6 page	2460.	2390.	2340.	2225.

7. COVERS

	1 ti	3 ti	6 ti	12 ti
2nd cover	10,760.	10,440.	10,225.	9,685.
3rd cover	10,485.	10,175.	9,960.	9,440.
4th cover	11,450.	11,105.	10,875.	10,300.

8. INSERTS
Available.

9. BLEED
Extra 10%

10. SPECIAL POSITION
Specified positions, extra 10%

14. CONTRACT AND COPY REGULATIONS
See Contents page for location—items 1, 2, 3, 4, 5, 7 thru 22, 24, 26, 28, 30, 31, 32, 33, 34, 35.

15. GENERAL REQUIREMENTS
Also see SRDS Print Media Production Data.
Printing Process: Offset Full Run
Trim Size: 8-1/16 x 10-3/4; No./Cols. 2 & 3.

AD PAGE DIMENSIONS

1 pg	7-1/16 x 10	1/2 h	7-1/16 x 4-7/8
2/3 v	4-5/8 x 10	1/3 v	2-1/6 x 10
1/2 v	3-3/8 x 10	1/4 v	3-3/8 x 4-7/8

Binding method: Saddle-stitched.
Colors available: AAAA/ABP; Matched.

16. ISSUE AND CLOSING DATES
Published monthly.

Issue:	Issued	Closing	Issue:	Issued	Closing
Jan	1/1	12/1	Jul	7/1	6/1
Feb	2/1	1/1	Aug	8/1	7/1
Mar	3/1	2/1	Sep	9/1	8/1
Apr	4/1	3/1	Oct	10/1	9/1
May	5/1	4/1	Nov	11/1	10/1
Jun	6/1	5/1	Dec	12/1	11/1

SPECIAL FEATURE ISSUES
Jan/92—Investment Handbook.
Feb/92—Regional TV: Cable and Satellite.
Mar/92—The new South Africa.
Apr/92—Health Care / Asian Development Bank 25th Meeting.
May/92—Fashion Industry.
Jun/92—Office Automation.
Jul/92—Mexico: Gateway to North America.
Aug/92—Banking.
Sep/92—Cargo.
Oct/92—Europe 1992.
Nov/92—Telecoms.
Dec/92—Auto Industry.
May/90—Japan; Duty Free Shopping.
Jun/90—Korea; Office Automation.

18. CIRCULATION
Established 1965.
Summary data—for detail see Publisher's Statement.
B.P.A. 12-31-91 (6 mos. aver. qualified)

Total	Non-Pd	Paid
85,916	82,620	3,296

Average Non-Qualified (not incl. above):
Total 7,233
TERRITORIAL DISTRIBUTION 11/91—86,444

W.S.Cen.	Mtn.St.	Pac.St.	Canada	Foreign	Other
...	...	...	...	86,444	...

BUSINESS ANALYSIS OF CIRCULATION

Manufacturer	17,897
Banking Insurance, Finance	8,603
Research, Development	2,311
Building, construction	5,706
Importers, Exporters	17,056
Prof. Services	10,503
Power Generation	888
Communications.	2,577
Transport, Tourism.	5,830
Agriculture, Forestry, Plantations.	1,239
Gov't Officials.	3,224
Others Allied to the Field.	1,129
Single Copy Sales.	2,019
Bulk Subscriptions to Hotels, Airlines, and Companies.	7,462
Total.	86,444

ASIAN FINANCE

ABC

Location ID: 7 BINT 20 **Mid 050967-000**
Published monthly by Asian Finance Publications, 233 Hollywood Rd. 3/F, Hong Kong. Phone 815-815-5221. FAX: 852-854-2794.

PUBLISHER'S EDITORIAL PROFILE
ASIAN FINANCE is edited for financial and investment professionals and senior executives in corporations and government. Its regular features include articles on Corporate Finance, Risk Management, Portfolio Strategy, Information Technology, Country Profiles, International Finance, Global Custody Services and Investment Banking. Rec'd 11/29/90.

1. PERSONNEL
Pub—Joan Howley.

2. REPRESENTATIVES and/or BRANCH OFFICES
Mt. Kisco, NY 10549—GW Associates, 125-131 E. Main Street. Phone 914-241-4558.

ADVERTISING RATES
Effective January 01, 1991.
Rates received November 29, 1990.

5. BLACK/WHITE RATES

	1 ti	3 ti	6 ti	12 ti
1 page	3310.	3250.	3100.	2830.
2 columns	2380.	2340.	2240.	2040.
Jr. page	2110.	2060.	1940.	1800.
1/2 page	1910.	1870.	1770.	1640.
1 column	1250.	1230.	1190.	1060.
1/4 page	1120.	1110.	1060.	920.

6. COLOR RATES

2-Color:	1 ti	3 ti	6 ti	12 ti
1 page	3500.	3450.	3290.	2970.
2 columns	2570.	2520.	2410.	2180.
Jr. page	2190.	2100.	1990.	1860.
1/2 page	1930.	1890.	1800.	1700.

is the model which all country advertising or marketing communication groups should adopt.

Elsewhere, the best in-country source of information on media availabilities and costs may be one of the leading advertising agencies. In India, for example, Hindustan Thompson Associates publish an annual *Thompson Pocket Reference to Media in India* which is filled with useful information for media planners. In similar fashion, McCann-Erickson Guatemala publishes an annual *Media Fact Book*.

The ultimate source of media costs, specifications, and comparative data on reading, listening, or viewing is the individual media vehicle. As to costs, a typical rate card, in this case for the *Reader's Digest*, is shown in Exhibit 12.8.

Conventional space and time units

In buying space or time, the conventional units for cost estimating purposes are:

Newspapers: by the column centimetre or inch; by the page in mono (black and white) or colour
Magazines: by the quarter-page, half-page or page in mono, two-colour, or four(full)-colour (Other space units are also available)
Radio: ten to sixty seconds with thirty seconds widely quoted
Television: : same as radio, though in countries like Japan and the USA the fifteen second length is also widely quoted (and used)

Cross border media planning

As Erika Engels Levine pointed out, the job of the international media planner is to 'translate the advertising objectives into media strategies appropriate to the various international markets'. What the planner has to avoid is thinking that the media planning information and alternatives elsewhere will be the same as in the home country. A prerequisite for answers to the who, where, and when questions is a basic understanding of the country-markets in which advertising will be scheduled. This understanding will be gained by considering the following factors.[9]

Climate and season
Summers and winters are the opposite in the northern and southern hemispheres. In between, there may be little or no distinction among seasons. In August, the Plaza Mayor in Madrid is empty; in July, all of Sweden is on vacation and businesses are closed. Climate and season will have an effect on

Exhibit 12.8 Reader's Digest *international advertising rates. Reprinted by permission of Reader's Digest Association Inc., Pleasantville, New York*

INTERNATIONAL RATES* LOCAL CURRENCY

Region	EDITIONS	1992 Circ. Rate Base (000)	Local Curr.	SINGLE PAGES			HALF-PAGES			SPREADS		
				B&W	2-Color	4-Color	B&W	2-Color	4-Color	B&W	2-Color	4-Color
EUROPE/SCANDINAVIA	BELGIUM											
	Flemish	80	B. Franc	55,500	63,500	79,500	33,500	38,000	47,500	111,000	127,000	158,500
	French	88	B. Franc	54,500	62,500	78,000	33,000	37,500	47,000	109,000	125,000	156,000
	FRANCE	1,077	F. Franc	96,000	115,000	132,000	67,000	78,000	87,000	192,000	230,000	264,000
	GERMANY	1,250	D. Mark	25,700	38,100	44,500	14,100	21,100	24,600	47,500	70,600	82,400
	ITALY	650	Lira (000)	13,100	17,900	21,500	9,000	12,200	14,700	26,200	35,800	43,000
	NETHERLANDS	390	Guilder	13,000	14,305	21,270	7,155	7,865	11,945	24,705	26,905	41,265
	PORTUGAL	256	Escudo (000)	600	640	690	310	330	360	1,100	1,200	1,350
	SPAIN	74	Peseta	335,000	385,000	450,000	180,000	205,000	245,000	630,000	720,000	835,000
	SWITZERLAND											
	French	85	Sw. Fr.	4,320	5,180	7,190	2,600	3,110	4,310	8,210	9,840	13,660
	German	256	Sw. Fr.	9,260	10,670	14,330	5,540	6,390	8,590	17,590	20,270	27,230
	UNITED KINGDOM	1,500	Pound	13,500	13,500	18,500	7,400	7,400	10,000	27,000	27,000	37,000
	DENMARK	110	Kroner	9,800	11,600	13,900	6,800	7,800	9,500	16,700	19,800	23,600
	FINLAND	345	Markka	23,900	28,200	34,500	16,700	19,200	21,300	43,600	49,500	62,000
	NORWAY	163	N. Kroner	13,100	15,400	20,000	8,100	9,400	12,800	23,600	27,700	36,000
	SWEDEN	149	Kroner	10,720	12,070	13,335	6,980	8,330	9,010	18,650	20,000	22,700
	MIDDLE EAST	58	U.S. $	2,625	3,100	4,410	1,470	1,785	2,520	4,885	5,670	8,245
	SOUTH AFRICA	370	Rand	10,360	11,955	15,500	5,705	6,565	8,520	20,255	23,910	31,000
	HUNGARY	50	U.S. $	850	975	1,200	520	600	730	1,580	1,815	2,230
	RUSSIA**	100	U.S. $	1,400	1,600	2,000	850	975	1,220	2,600	3,000	3,750
ASIA/PACIFIC	ASIA											
	Chinese	300	U.S. $	12,620	13,835	15,200	8,205	8,995	9,880	22,715	24,905	27,360
	English	242	U.S. $	14,695	16,080	17,700	9,550	10,450	11,505	26,450	28,945	31,860
	AUSTRALIA	476	Aus. $	6,500	7,300	8,600	3,740	4,200	4,950	12,220	13,720	16,170
	INDIA											
	English	350	Rupee	59,000	59,000	89,000	33,000	33,000	48,000	106,000	106,000	159,000
	Hindi	55	Rupee	2,835	2,835	5,670	1,575	1,575	3,150	4,770	4,770	9,540
	KOREA	120	Won (000)	780	860	1,500	470	510	900	1,400	1,550	2,700
	NEW ZEALAND	170	NZ $	4,300	4,300	5,990	2,600	2,600	3,600	7,750	7,750	10,750
LATIN AMERICA	ARGENTINA	137	U.S. $	2,800	3,250	4,430	1,825	2,105	2,865	5,040	5,850	7,970
	BRAZIL	75	U.S. $	740	900	1,055	440	530	630	1,330	1,610	1,900
	CENT. AMERICA	35	U.S. $	1,345	1,525	1,820	865	990	1,185	2,415	2,745	3,280
	CHILE	38	U.S. $	1,585	2,110	2,500	1,185	1,355	1,625	2,855	3,780	4,500
	COLOMBIA	55	U.S. $	1,865	2,100	2,470	1,370	1,510	1,810	3,360	3,780	4,450
	ECUADOR	11	U.S. $	780	895	1,055	505	520	690	1,405	1,615	1,900
	MEXICO	700	U.S. $	5,760	6,480	7,680	3,745	4,210	4,990	10,370	11,665	13,825
	PERU	33	U.S. $	1,050	1,200	1,420	675	785	925	1,890	2,160	2,555
	PUERTO RICO/D.R.	67	U.S. $	1,575	1,970	2,100	1,010	1,260	1,345	2,835	3,545	3,780
	URUG/PARA/BOL.	36	U.S. $	1,015	1,180	1,390	660	735	895	1,825	2,120	2,505
	VENEZUELA	33	U.S. $	1,990	2,275	2,695	1,280	1,485	1,760	3,580	4,095	4,850
N.A.	CANADA											
	English	1,264	Can. $	20,545	21,830	25,680	13,355	14,190	16,690	36,980	39,290	46,225
	French	319	Can. $	7,460	7,925	9,325	4,850	5,150	6,060	13,430	14,265	16,785
	UNITED STATES											
	Hispanic	131	U.S. $	2,925	3,655	3,900	1,830	2,285	2,440	5,265	6,580	7,020

**NOTE:* For discounts, taxes, bleed, etc., see general information.*

***A maximum of 50% of the rate may be paid in rubles.*

consumption of many products from electricity to carbonated beverages. . . as well as the timing and nature of advertising campaigns. (Recall the seasonal sales pattern for canned peas and prepared mustard in the USA.)

Population

An analysis of population is needed in the determination of a target audience. This analysis should include literacy rate, age, those counted in the commercial market, and geographic distribution. In a country like India where 43 per cent of household heads have no education[10] the ability to deliver a written advertising message would have its limitations. In Guatemala, 57 per cent of the population is below the age of twenty.[11] This is in contrast to the UK where 33 per cent of the population is below twenty-five. In Mexico possibly as many as 25 per cent of the inhabitants are not counted in the commercially active population. Of those that are, over 71 per cent were located in urban areas in 1990, principally Mexico City.[13] This latter statistic is more than reversed in India where 85 per cent of the population is rural.[14] When such variances as just pointed out are taken into account in media planning, markedly different strategies will emerge.

Language
It is foolhardy to be lulled into the belief that because English is considered by many to be the international language of business that English language publications where available will be the appropriate media choice. As Levine has pointed out, 'Using the local language for our message is not just a matter of making ourselves understood but also demonstrates respect for the local culture.'[15]

Religions and laws
It is important to get to know the local religious customs, taboos, and laws. Ramadan is a month-long holy season celebrated by most Moslem countries in the Middle East and Africa, where, under Moslem law, no advertising is allowed during that period.[16]

In most Latin American countries businesses shut down to celebrate the Christian holidays from Christmas to Three Kings Day (Tres Reyes), a period that lasts from 24 December to the first Sunday after New Year's Day.

In Saudi Arabia, females are not permitted in advertising, nor are alcoholic beverages and tobacco. Cosmetics are best sold by means of a private house party arranged and attended by women only.[17]

With respect to advertising restrictions in Europe, pharmaceutical and beer/wine advertising on television is not permitted in six countries. Greek television bans advertising aimed at children. New European Community directives are being formulated on tobacco, alcohol, pharmaceuticals, food, direct response and comparative advertising.[18]

Political orientation
Media in Italy, the Middle East, Latin America, and elsewhere may have a strong political bias. It is in the best interests of a media planner to know the political orientation of a particular media vehicle before recommending its inclusion in a client's media plan.

The foregoing five points were cited by Levine as important preliminary considerations prior to the establishment of the target audience and the selection of vehicles for an international media plan.

Developing international business-to-business media plans

To complement Levine's consumer oriented planning guidelines, Jo Lhoest has proposed a useful six-step system for international business-to-business media planning as explained by Robert Roth.[19] This system, with some modifications, is outlined below.

Screening the market
For each country or group of countries a grid which looks like the one shown in Exhibit 12.9 should be constructed...in this case for the information processing equipment market. Across the top the industry sectors are listed — financial institutions, general manufacturing, etc. Down the side the job titles of the buying influencers are listed — Managing Director, Financial Manager, etc.

Exhibit 12.9   *Business to business screening grid information processing equipment*

	Financial institutions	General mfg	Retailing	Local govt
Managing directors				
Financial managers				
Production managers				
Data processing managers				

*Weight each target according to its importance

Target group identification
This next step is taken to establish the target audiences. As previously discussed, industrial buying is normally participated in by representatives from different functional areas of business. Accordingly, the appropriate industrial sector and job function grid boxes must be checked.

Assignment of relative importance
A numerical weighting system should be devised such as a scale of one to five with five being most important. Each grid box checked should be assigned a value to indicate relative importance as sales prospects. (If the information processing industry structures are similar among countries, e.g. in Europe, it may be possible to use international [English language] media. If it turns out that wide variances occur in structure, then indigenous media would be the preferred alternative.)

Horizontal or vertical strategy
To what extent should horizontal versus vertical advertising pressure be exerted? This will be dependent on the number and weighting of the industry sector/job function grid boxes. If several industry sectors and few job functions are considered important, more emphasis should be placed on horizontal media. In case the reverse is true, then more vertical pressure would be appropriate.

Media screening and selection
Once the basic direction has been established in terms of targets and relative importance of horizontal and vertical media pressure, the planner can screen and select the media in the best alternate combination that can be purchased within the budget. This may include indigenous or international print media, mail, seminars, company-sponsored newsletters and the like.

Consolidation and write up
As a final step, the objectives, strategies, and plan details must be written up and supported with rationales, a budget and schedule of media activities.

International media planning checklist
A useful checklist when planning cross border advertising campaigns can be found in all editions of the *International Media Guide*. While this checklist shown in Exhibit 12.10 was developed for US advertisers, advertisers in any country who wish to reach audiences beyond their own borders will find it helpful.

The media planning, buying and selling relationship

Up until this point, attention has been focused on the information needed to develop media plans. Now it is necessary to attend to the manner in which planning is linked with selling and buying media. The key participants include:

1 *The media planner* The planner is normally found as an employee of an advertising agency or as a member of the advertiser's marketing communications department.

Exhibit 12.10 *Checklist for international media planning from a US base. Reproduced by permission of international Media Enterprises Inc., South Norwalk, CT, USA*

A. Basic Considerations
(Who Does What?)

What is the client's policy regarding supervision and placement of advertising? Make sure you know when, where, and to what degree client and/or client branch offices abroad want to get involved.

1. Which client office is in charge of campaign? U.S. headquarters or local office or both? Who else has to be consulted? In what areas (creative or media selection, etc.)?

2. Is there a predetermined media mix to be used? Are there any 'must' media? Can international as well as foreign media be used?

3. Who arranges for translation of copy if foreign media are to be used?
   a) Client headquarters in the U.S.
   b) Client office in foreign country
   c) Agency headquarters in the U.S.
   d) Foreign media rep in the U.S.
   e) Foreign media advertising department
   f) Other

4. Who approves translated copy?

5. Who checks on acceptability of ad copy in foreign country (prior to completion of ad production, please!)? Certain ads, especially those of financial character, sometimes need special approval by foreign government authorities.

6. What is the advertising placement procedure?
   a) From agency branch office in foreign country, after consultation with agency headquarters, directly to foreign media.
   b) From U.S. agency to U.S.-based foreign media rep to foreign media
   c) From U.S. agency to U.S.-based international media
   d) From U.S. agency to affiliated agency abroad to foreign media
   e) Other

7. What are the pros and cons of each of these approaches? Is commission-spirit with foreign agency branch or affiliate office necessary or can campaign be equally well-placed directly from U.S.? Does the client save money by placing from U.S. to save certain ad taxes (in Belgium and the Netherlands, for instance)? Some publications quote local rates and higher U.S. dollar rates. In those instances local ad placement results in a lower rate. Therefore, in what currency does client want to pay?

8. Who receives checking copies?

9. Will advance payment be made to avoid currency fluctuation possibilities? What will the finance folks in the back room have to say about your choice?

10. Who bills whom? In what currency? Who approves payment?

Exhibit 12.10 (*continued*)

B. Budget Considerations
1. Is budget predetermined by client?
2. Is budget based on local branch or distributor recommendation?
3. Is budget based on recommended media schedule of agency?
4. Is budget based on relationship to sales in the foreign markets?
5. What is the budget period?
6. What is the budget breakdown for media, including ad taxes, sale promotion, translation, production and research costs?
7. What are the tie-ins with local distribution, if any?

C. Market considerations
1. What is your geographical target area?
   a) Africa and Middle East
   b) Asia, including Australasia
   c) Europe, including U.S.S.R.
   d) Latin America
   e) North America
2. What are the major market factors in these areas?
   a) Local competition
   b) GNP growth over past four years and expected future growth
   c) Relationship of country's imports to total GNP in per cent
   d) Membership of country in a common market or free trade association
   e) Literacy rate
   f) Attitude toward U.S. products or services
   g) Social and religious customs

3. What is your basic target audience?
   a) Management executives across the board in business and industry
   b) Managers and buyers in certain businesses
   c) Military and government officials
   d) Consumers: potential buyers of foreign market goods

D. Media Considerations
1. Availability of media to cover market: Are the desired media available in the particular area (e.g., business magazines, news-magazines, trade and professional magazines, women's magazines, business and financial news-papers, TV, radio, etc). Also see Section E below.
2. Foreign media and/or international media: Should the campaign be in the press and language of a particular country, or should it be a combination of the two types?
3. What media does competition use?
4. Does medium fit?
   a) Optimum audience quality and quantity
   b) Desired image editorial content and design
   c) Suitable paper and colour availability
   d) Justifiable rates and CPM (do not forget taxes on advertising which can vary by medium)

Exhibit 12.10   (*continued*)

e) Discount availability

f) Closing dates at U.S. rep and at the publication head-quarters abroad

g) Type of circulation audit

h) Agency commission (when placed locally abroad at the agency commission is sometimes less than when placed in the U.S.)

i) Availability of special issues or editorial tie-ins

j) For how long are contracted rates protected?

5. Does foreign or international publication have U.S. representative to help with media evaluation and actual advertising placement?

2 *The media buyer* This specialist can work for an advertising agency, an independent media buying organization, or can be on the payroll of advertisers that decide to perform the buying function on their own.

3 *The media representative* This person may work for a particular media vehicle, or work for an independent sales organization or as an individual performing the selling function for one or more media vehicles.

The planner

The media planner needs to deal with all the variables mentioned earlier in this chapter in order to perform his/her job effectively. In so doing, it is customary for planners to work closely with and obtain information from media buyers and representatives on such matters as current costs, and cost trends, ratings, audience characteristics, editorial content and changes, and any important developments affecting the media being considered.

The essence of the media planner's job is to formulate media strategies and tactics to deliver the target audience in conformance with reach, frequency, and continuity specifications, and the budget. This requires a knowledge of current and projected media costs, the characteristics of all media alternatives, and the analytical techniques and planning tools described earlier in this chapter.

The planner's knowledge base must be updated regularly to keep pace with the dynamics of the media marketplace. To do this, the planner should maintain close contact with both media buyers and representatives.

The buyer

The media buyer is the individual who negotiates price and does the purchasing. This requires a different talent than that needed by planners. Analytical skills are of paramount importance for the former; bargaining skills for the latter. In the performance of the buying job the buyer must be in close contact with the media marketplace and the trends that will impact on media costs. For example, in print advertising, production and labour costs have been associated with media price advances; whereas, in the case of television, price changes are closely aligned with the forces of supply and demand.[20] By regular contact with media representatives, the buyer can keep abreast of events in the marketplace and be in a position to anticipate price changes. This gives rise to the need for interaction between buyers and planners so the planners can benefit from the media cost changes which buyers anticipate will occur and also so planners can match up audiences delivered, cost per 1,000 incurred and reach and frequency levels attained against those predicated.

In some agencies, particularly smaller ones, one person may be found performing both the planning and buying functions. In many large advertising agencies the functions will be performed separately but with close coordination.

With respect to buying, often it is done by medium and market rather than by brand. This results in the formation of a group of experts, one or a few concentrating on national (network) television, another or others concentrating on one or more spot (local) television markets. Further specialization may take place with radio and various print classifications.

Division and coordination of work

The division and coordination of work of a modern media department in a large, full-service advertising agency, such as BBDO New York, consists of five interactive functional groups as shown below:

Group	Functions
1 Media planning services	Develops media plans, supervises plan execution, controls budget and workflow, and executes (buys) print portion of plans.
2 Media buying	Comprised of national and local buying units which negotiate the purchase of all radio, television, and cable time, and syndication; monitor buys which have been made for performance according to specifications; perform post schedule analyses.
3 Programme development	To meet specialized needs of certain clients, develops and distributes programming to provide effective delivery of clients' messages.
4 Media research	Provides research data gathered from syndicated and audited research services to aid in the planning and buying processes.

5   Media systems   Develops systems and planning models to
                                      meet clients' needs; uses in-house computer
                                      hardware to assess, summarize, and tabulate
                                      information from various sources to aid in
                                      client media planning and evaluation.

For clients that have needs for a multi-media approach, BBDO forms a
media team headed by a senior media executive and comprised of planning
and network television buying experts with support as needed from various
media specialists. These specialists may have expertise in any one of the
following functions:

- media research
- international media
- media systems
- local TV/radio buying
- out-of-home media
- yellow pages
- business-to-business media
- special markets, e.g. medical
- TV programme development
- promotion
- new technologies

The media team coordinates its activities throughout the media planning,
buying, and evaluating process with account service, creative, and marketing
research to maximize the effectiveness of clients' marketing communications
programmes.[21]

Note is made once again of the fact that not all experts agree media
planning and buying should be performed separately. Mike Jarvis, managing
director of a UK media agency, believes that the buying function is best
performed by the planner. The planner, working closely with the client and
media owners, has the 'best understanding of the overall creative and media
objectives', and, therefore, should control and be responsible for the overall
media programme, including buying.[22]

International media representatives

International media representatives can be found in most if not all of the
major business centres and many countries of the world. A 1989 IMG Directory
contains a listing of media representatives in over sixty countries. Vehicles
represented are predominantly print. Television and radio are bought locally

on a country-by-country basis. As one media expert stated, 'you can't buy
TV from here (USA) any more. Even if you could, you can't import your
commercial'.[23] One European study on space representation in four countries
indicated that over 5,300 publications from other Western European countries
and the USA had representatives in those four countries, 62 per cent of which
were business or trade journals.[24]

In the USA, the majority of foreign publications have no representation,
direct or indirect. Listing in media reference books, such as IMG, and word of
mouth are the only means by which US advertising is attracted. The 2,000 or
so foreign publications with representation rely on either independent firms
(indirect) or establish their own sales offices (direct). Since the latter approach
is costly, only a few, large publications like *The Economist*, the *Financial Times*,
Handelsblatt, and *Vision* along with publishing houses such as Gruner + Jahr
and the Axel Springer Group provide direct representation.

The primary role of the media representative is to sell advertising space for
the media owners represented, and to provide the owner with information on
the host country market conditions and trends that have or will have an effect
on space sales. The number of publications represented may vary from one
(direct) to as many as twenty or thirty (indirect).

From a media buyer's point of view, representatives should be able to
explain who and where their readers are, what they do, and how they match
up with the target audience sought. They should be equipped with rate cards
that have been translated into the host country language and include technical
specifications for production purposes, also exchange rate information. A
representative who gives the buyer a feeling of confidence in terms of following
through with the publisher for quality of reproduction and good position is the
one who is more apt to get the buyer's business.[25]

From the media representatives' point of view, media buyers are often seen
as novices, unfamiliar with international markets, primarily interested in numbers, and not caring much about editorial concept and why people read a
particular publication. Another problem expressed by US representatives concerned the buyer's mindset on 'American' international media as opposed to
indigenous media which often provide better market penetration. A sensible
approach under these circumstances is first, to determine exactly what the
buyer is trying to accomplish; second, to gather information about how the
publication will deliver the audience the buyer is seeking; and third, to then
make a presentation to show how participation in the publication will help
attain the buyer's objectives.[26]

While it is true that most media owners will not continue to compensate a
representative if the buying is transferred to another point, often to the
owner's home country, Sandra Ourusoff observed that if the international
marketing director remains in the host country, some cultivation of that
person should continue. Under these circumstances the host country represen-

tative should receive compensation. Ourusoff concluded with this advice for media buyers:

> My advice is never buy space in a publication you haven't looked at. Even if you can't read it, physically get hold of it, understand the size, the coloration, the frequency. If you look at the table of contents, you can get an idea of the kinds of articles in most publications and from that the kind of people buying it.[27]

Survey of media buying practices

In surveying recent literature Stewart and McAuliffe found that '...much of the advertising that is referred to as international is in reality purchased locally by a local country representative for the firm that is headquartered elsewhere'. (To underscore this point, Andre Bernard, Chairman of Initiative Media International, in a presentation on European media in Chicago, October 1990, reported that 'About 95 per cent of all media is still negotiated and placed locally.')

They also found that '...the majority of the media available to advertisers remains local or regional. There are few genuinely international media'. Those that qualify, such as *The Economist*, *Time*, and *Newsweek*, are circulated in many countries and are read by well-educated business executives with fluency in English.[28] No other magazine, however, comes close to the global presence of the *Reader's Digest* which is published in fourteen languages in addition to English and circulates twenty-eight million copies among 100 million readers.[29]

Stewart and McAuliffe's survey on media buying practices revealed that nearly one-half of the advertising agency media directors contacted in the USA indicated that international media was placed locally; that over two-fifths of the twenty-eight respondents had less than three years media buying experience; and nearly three-fifths had booked less than $500,000 of international media in the course of a year and worked for a single client. Buying did occur in a number of countries in both international and local media. The most common type of media purchased were the trade magazines, followed by consumer magazines and newspapers. Among the most frequently mentioned types of clients were financial services, aircraft/aerospace, travel goods and services, and office equipment. Important sources of information for decision-making included syndicated research, ABC/BPA circulation audit figures, the rate card, and sales calls by media representatives. The single most important selection criteria was 'targetability', followed by 'strong editorial content and general prestige'. Cost related factors were perceived as being less important.[30]

Media buying trends

Centralization and negotiation have emerged as the two main themes in media buying and selling in recent years as the three principals — advertisers, agencies, and media owners — vie for survival and dominance. By means of acquisitions, mergers, and growth, certain entities of all three types have increased dramatically in size and in relative bargaining power. This brings to mind names like GM, Toyota, Phillip Morris, Unilever, Philips, and Sony among advertisers; Saatchi & Saatchi, Dentsu, and Y & R among agencies; and Murdoch, Maxwell, Bertelsmann, Berlusconi, and Time Warner among media owners. Despite the growth in size and importance of a number of advertising agencies, there has been a tendency toward the polarization of power between the multinational advertisers and media owners.

As for negotiability of media rates, this depends in part on the country. In Europe, press media is negotiable in the UK, France, and Portugal; inflexible in Switzerland, Germany, and Holland (owner strength). In Europe, TV is state-owned and non-negotiable in Austria, Portugal, and Switzerland; however, private TV is negotiable in France and Italy, and is becoming more flexible in Germany, Spain, and Greece.[31] In countries like the USA where government media ownership has never existed, broadcast media has always been negotiable, but up until recently print media was basically sold off the rate card. Now, all media is negotiable.

Despite the polarization of power, media intermediaries have not been standing idly by. In the 1960s, independent media buying services began to operate in the USA and Europe, notably France. These independents, such as Vitt International in the USA, established and built businesses on the premise that the advertising agency was not getting the best (lowest) price from the media, principally broadcast, for clients. Since advertising agencies were paid by commission from the media (15 per cent was the standard), they had no incentive to attempt to negotiate lower prices. If they did, they would be reducing their own revenues. However, as media buying services grew, advertising agency media services had to adopt more agressive buying practices in order to survive and prosper.

In Europe, the growth of independent media buying as practiced in France took on a somewhat different shape. As described by Mike Jarvis, it became a form of 'brokering' where media space and airtime were treated as 'commodities'. Chunks of space and time are committed as far ahead as a year in advance. The commitments are sold throughout the year 'a piece at a time to advertisers or their agencies at fixed rates agreed with the media, or at whatever rates the traffic will bear'. Jarvis contends 'Bulk buying can result in conflict between what the broker has to sell and what his clients need. Clients also lose out when the broker pushes certain titles where rates are low and commission high.' Jarvis further contends that the development of large buying-only agencies has led to the practice of sub-commisions paid by media owners to these agencies at the end of the year, the amount being dependent on the volume of business conducted. It is an off-the-record practice that has become widespread in Spain, Belgium, and Norway as well as in France. Under these circumstances, the media buying agency's ability 'to secure real client savings' is reduced.[32]

One effect of bulk media buying by independent agencies has been to put a squeeze on media owners' profit margins. The owners' retaliation has been or is likely to be to reduce the standard 15 per cent commission to compensate for lowered advertising space or time rates.

The advertising agency response has been to form special media buying networks to serve all affiliates of an agency conglomerate or to serve a group of independent agencies. One of these networks is Zenith, formed to serve a number of Saatchi & Saatchi companies in the UK. In 1989 this network was reported to have accounted for 18 per cent of total UK media buys. Among the reasons listed for creating this entity, according to John Perriss, were:

1 escalating media costs which were outpacing inflation rates became an issue with clients
2 the trend toward bigness among media owners put advertisers (and their agencies) at a disadvantage
3 increased competitiveness among media owners made everything negotiable
4 increased complexity of the media environment
5 greater demands by clients on media buying performance.[33]

Other European media buying networks which have been formed include:

Network	Agency members
PMI	Lintas/Initiative Media, McCann-Erickson, Lowe
Carat	Carat and affiliated agencies, EWBD, HDM
The Media Partnership	O&M, BBDO, DDB, JWT, RSCG.[34]

One UK client director of advertising services siding with the buying network approach, pointed to his own situation. Before going to centralized buying, he was using ten different agencies among some twenty different brands. Now he considers his organization as a 'multi-brand' advertiser instead of being a complex of small, individual advertisers. In Europe Unilever also buys centrally at a discount from the standard 15 per cent commission which is determined and agreed on locally. This organization does not believe that centralized buying results in significant media cost savings. Rather it looks for improved quality of buying and lower costs through savings in general management and administration.

Despite the advantages seen by some, others, including Jarvis, see negatives in the centralized system. These negatives include the possibility of violation of client confidentiality and product conflicts, lessened client/account management control, and duplication of effort between main agency and buying unit media management.[35]

The World Federation of Advertisers (WFA) has given this entire matter serious consideration and issued a memorandum on the state of the art and offered policy guidelines. The memo described the different types of prevailing buying media buying structures, identified the existence of possible conflicts of interest, affirmed the importance of advertiser autonomy, and made recommendations for advertisers in establishing their relationships with prospective media buying entities. See Exhibit 12.11 for selected portions of the WFA brochure.

Evaluating media effectiveness

For a company that spends money on communications, whether the funds allocated for this purpose are 1 or 10 per cent of sales, a means of evaluating pre- and post-campaign effectiveness should be an integral part of the international marketing communications plan. For low budget communications, inexpensive research techniques can be employed. For example, questions can be asked on purchase warranty forms to find out through what medium the customer learned about the product or service. Distributors and dealers can be surveyed by 'phone, fax, mail, or in person to obtain their ideas and opinions on media (and message) effectiveness. Media owners and their representatives can be asked to prepare facts and figures on the advertisers' intended audience which their vehicles deliver. Advertising agencies can be asked for and are expected to provide pre- and post-media buy analyses. As media budgets increase, more complex surveys can be conducted to evaluate effectiveness. The available industry, syndicated, and proprietary media studies can be purchased for this purpose.

The existence, quality, and variety of information for planning and measuring the effectiveness of media programmes varies considerably from country to country. These are subjects for further exploration.

The level of sophistication in media measurement information is apt to parallel industrial development. In most European countries, Japan, and the USA, syndicated, industry, and specialized research services are available to provide a variety of tracking information which is equally useful for planning purposes.

Media research services in the UK

In the UK, a number of different media research services can be found. For example, audited circulation figures for newspapers and general consumer

Exhibit 12.11 *World Federation of Advertisers: media buying trends and policy guidelines, September 1990. Reproduced by permission of Paul P. de Win, Director General, World Federation of Advertising and J.H. Cassin, Advertising Services Manager, Procter & Gamble, France*

Current trends

From discussion with members very active in this area, WFA has identified what we believe are the prevailing media buying structures:

Traditional agency
Currently encompassing planning and buying. In some agencies planning and buying are separate departments. Some print-buying units are being set up as self-standing departments.

Potentially, buying may be split-off as a separate buying unit subsidiary of the Agency. Another relatively new dimension is program production, which can serve the agency's advertisers or act as a separate base for the agency.

Agency consolidation
An agency conglomerate assigns the buying from various wholly owned subsidiaries to one central group.

Agency co-operative
A number of traditional agencies combine their resources in order to achieve claimed significant buying leverage.

Advertiser co-operative
A group of advertisers or advertiser/agency will form their own buying group.

Independent media shop
A structure whose primary function is the buying of media, and whose clients are either advertising agencies or advertisers directly. The group may have consulting and planning capability.

Potential new players could be companies who own, finance or sell programming. In exchange for the program rights, they obtain media time from the channels, which they subsequently re-sell to interested advertisers. This is common practice in the US and is being developed in a number of other countries.

WFA's policy guidance

Conflict of interest
These new media structures may result in the same group having an interest in a channel or owning media time and at the same time being charged with the planning and/or buying of an advertiser's schedule.

It is WFA's position that any potential conflict of interest resulting from the media buyer owning, selling or representing the medium should be clearly and explicitly identified as part of the media recommendation to the advertiser.

Exhibit 12.11   (*continued*)

Advertiser's autonomy
The relationship between each advertiser and its agency or media planning/
buying group is the sole and exclusive domain of these parties. This arrangement, be
it contractual or other, should be based on the total freedom of each party, without any outside influence, other than the applicable laws of the country or state.

Perspective

Because of the autonomy principle, and also because each advertiser's needs may
vary, WFA cannot advise its members as to the 'best' service.
   However, to assist advertisers in fully understanding what can be a complex
relationship, WFA recommends that advertisers seriously consider these factors:

Economy − demonstration of the financial advantage of the advertiser in the
proposed new set-up, and guarantee that the media group will secure the most
advantageous value for each advertiser according to each advertiser's volume
commitment in a specific medium.

Equality − assurance that the advertiser will receive a fair and at least pro-
portionate share of the media opportunities secured by the media unit.

Individuality − assurance that the advertiser benefits entirely from all volume/
frequency discounts earned by himself directly, and proportionately to its volume
commitment from the negotiations and rebates generated by the media unit.

Security − guarantee that the advertiser's marketing knowledge, policies, strategies, plans, and media expertise are safe from competitors.

Autonomy − right to maintain or exercise the right of approval or rejection.
Right to assign the business to more than one unit.

Flexibility − freedom, within industry practice, to change strategies, plans or
buys and not to be tied to any 'bulk' commitments made by the media unit.

Clarity − clear definition of the individual responsibilities of the partners involved
(advertisers/agencies/media shops) prior to appointment of the media group.

Liability − guarantee that the advertiser participating in a media contract will
be liable only to the degree of his subsequent commitment and will not be liable
for any changes by other participating advertisers.

Transparency − access to media contracts and invoices, files and records for
proof-of-performance and auditing purposes.
   The WFA strongly recommends that an advertiser seriously considers a formal
letter of agreement that details all terms and understanding between the two or
more parties.[36]

magazines are measured by the Audit Bureau of Circulation (ABC) annually. This is a non-profit company set up jointly by advertisers, agencies, and publishers. Circulation information, while not audited, is also obtainable on a geographic and type of subscriber basis for business, professional, and special interest consumer magazines. Readership information comes from the National Readership Survey conducted under the auspices of the Joint Industry Committee for National Readership Surveys. These surveys, which cover national daily and Sunday newspapers and certain large national magazines, are published quarterly and contain information on readers by age, sex, social grade, region, certain consumer durable possessions and by amount of TV viewing and radio listening.[37] These studies are augmented by the British Market Research Bureau's Target Group Index (TGI). TGI information is based on mailed questionnaires to 24,000 respondents in 200 areas. The periodic reports treat the demographic characteristics and readership, viewing, and listening habits of heavy, medium and light users of over 2,500 branded products.[38]

Along with TGI, radio and television audience research is provided under the direction of the Broadcasters' Audience Research Board. Television research is based on electronic meters which record sets-in-use by channel on a minute-by-minute basis and which is supplemented by a quarter-hour household diary maintained by survey panel members whose socioeconomic characteristics are known. A separate panel of viewers aged four to fourteen has also been created to measure children's viewing habits and reactions to various programming.[39] According to the Advertising Association, monitoring of video cassettes' use in live viewing and recording of television programmes has been in effect since 1985.[40] Television research gives information on population profiles that include households, social class, age of housewife, size of household, existence of children under fifteen, average number of people per household as well as TV ratings by adults, men, and women.[41] Audience measurement of independent local radio stations provided by the Joint Industry Committee for Audience Research is also available to advertisers. Radio research provides information on weekly reach and weekly hours of listening by adults.[42]

Media research services in other industrialized countries

Similar types of media research information is found in and among other industrialized countries. In German-speaking Europe, seven major studies of two basic types are available for media planning and evaluation purposes. One is a mass or general audience type. The other covers readership habits of business people or 'decision-makers'. In addition, there are other studies which focus on special interest groups of both a consumer and industrial nature. The two largest general audience studies, which are jointly sponsored by the advertising and media industries, have similar methodology, employing personal interviews of adults fourteen years and older, but differ in the kind of data collected and sample size. While both report on the coverage and structure of the basic advertising media, one provides more detail on the purchase and usage of consumer package goods. The choice of survey should be based on a clear definition of the target audience and the media vehicle of primary interest.[43]

It would appear that in European countries, as in the UK, the research services provided are sponsored by industry groups and/or government agencies to a large degree. This is not the experience in the USA where, other than the Audit Bureau of Circulation sponsored by advertisers, agencies, and publishers, research services are under private ownership...for example, the Nielsen National Television Index and Arbitron spot radio and television reports which are available to agencies and their clients on a fee basis. Syndicated studies from Simmons Market Research Bureau and MediaMark Research supply information on usage of media along with demographic and psychographic characteristics of users of a great variety of products. Exhibit 12.12 shows how demographic information and magazine readership are reported.

Pan-regional studies

In Europe, the Middle East, and Asia, media planners and evaluators will find pan-regional readership studies among certain target audiences such as business people. One of these is the thirteen-country Pan European Survey (PES) conducted by Research Services Ltd. of Wembley, England in conjunction with twelve other national research companies. The fourth such survey of this type was conducted between September 1987 and June 1988 among a sample of 8,604 'high status' professional men and women representing an estimated total universe of nearly 5.4 million people. Average issue readership for the twenty-three daily, weekly, fortnightly, monthly and bimonthly publications in the survey was one area of investigation.

Profiles of the average issue readers were also given covering demographic characteristics, types and reasons for travel, and involvement in business purchase decisions and other business activities. Readership of the major publications other than the twenty-three internationals in each of the thirteen countries was also treated.[44]

A study like PES, however, is the exception, not the rule in Europe according to one authority. Media planning and evaluation remains a predominantly local affair. Lack of data harmonization persists with respect to reader and viewer definitions and diary user systems. After advertising campaigns are conducted, the post campaign evaluation is dependent on the local availability of data. For TV, this varies between countries such as the UK and Germany. In the

Exhibit 12.12 Demographic information and magazine readership for users of canned soup and broth – usage in last seven days (female homemakers). Reproduced by permission of Simmons Market Research Bureau Inc.

	Total US '000	All users				Heavy users (four or more)				Medium users (two–three)				Light users (one or less)			
		A '000	B % Down	C % Across	D Index	A '000	B % Down	C % Across	D Index	A '000	B % Down	C % Across	D Index	A '000	B % Down	C % Across	D Index
Total female homemakers	86,361	67,837	100.0	78.6	100	16,391	100.0	19.0	100	30,763	100.0	35.6	100	20,683	100.0	23.9	100
18–24	7,911	5,822	8.6	73.6	94	1,481	9.0	18.7	99	2,342	7.6	29.6	83	1,999	9.7	25.3	106
25–34	20,745	16,386	24.2	79.0	101	3,969	24.2	19.1	101	6,787	22.1	32.7	92	5,630	27.2	27.1	113
35–44	17,764	14,403	21.2	81.1	103	3,692	22.5	20.8	110	6,386	20.8	35.9	101	4,325	20.9	24.3	102
45–54	12,328	10,073	14.8	81.7	104	2,541	15.5	20.6	109	5,028	16.3	40.8	114	2,504	12.1	20.3	85
55–64	10,847	8,692	12.8	80.1	102	1,970	12.0	18.2	96	3,922	12.7	36.2	102	2,800	13.5	25.8	108
65 or older	16,765	12,461	18.4	74.3	95	2,738	16.7	16.3	86	6,297	20.5	37.6	105	3,425	16.6	20.4	85
18–34	28,656	22,208	32.7	77.5	99	5,450	33.2	19.0	100	9,129	29.7	31.9	89	7,629	36.9	26.6	111
18–49	53,038	41,999	61.9	79.2	101	10,543	64.3	19.9	105	18,154	59.0	34.2	96	13,302	64.3	25.1	105
25–54	50,837	40,862	60.2	80.4	102	10,202	62.2	20.1	106	18,201	59.2	35.8	101	12,459	60.2	24.5	102
35–49	24,383	19,791	29.2	81.2	103	5,093	31.1	20.9	110	9,025	29.3	37.0	104	5,673	27.4	23.3	97
50 or older	33,322	25,838	38.1	77.5	99	5,848	35.7	17.5	92	12,609	41.0	37.8	106	7,381	35.7	22.2	92
Graduated college	14,461	12,027	17.7	83.2	106	2,138	13.0	14.8	78	5,288	17.2	36.6	103	4,601	22.2	31.8	133
Attended college	15,754	12,726	18.8	80.8	103	2,756	16.8	17.5	92	5,783	18.8	36.7	103	4,186	20.2	26.6	111
Graduated high school	36,201	29,187	43.0	80.6	103	7,548	44.0	20.9	110	13,183	42.9	36.4	102	8,456	40.9	23.4	98
Did not graduate high school	19,944	13,897	20.5	69.7	89	3,949	24.1	19.8	104	6,508	21.2	32.6	92	3,440	16.6	17.2	72
Employed	49,122	39,592	58.4	80.6	103	9,505	58.0	19.3	102	17,176	55.8	35.0	98	12,911	62.4	26.3	110
Employed full-time	41,357	33,319	49.1	80.6	103	7,816	47.7	18.9	100	14,403	46.8	34.8	98	11,100	53.7	26.8	112
Employed part-time	7,765	6,273	9.2	80.8	103	1,689	10.3	21.8	115	2,773	9.0	35.7	100	1,811	8.8	23.3	97
Not employed	37,238	28,245	41.6	75.8	97	6,886	42.0	18.5	97	13,387	44.2	36.5	102	7,772	37.6	20.9	87
Professional/manager	13,838	11,663	17.2	84.3	107	2,252	13.7	16.3	86	5,015	16.3	36.2	102	4,396	21.3	31.8	133
Tech/clerical/sales	22,113	17,935	26.4	81.1	103	4,302	26.2	19.5	103	7,896	25.7	35.7	100	5,736	27.7	25.9	108
Precision/craft	1,208	1,028	1.5	85.1	108	**191	1.2	15.8	83	*504	1.6	41.7	117	**333	1.6	27.6	115
Other employed	11,963	8,967	13.2	75.0	95	2,760	16.8	23.1	122	3,760	12.2	31.4	88	2,446	11.8	20.4	85

Exhibit 12.12 (*continued*)

	Total US '000	All users				Heavy users (four or more)				Medium users (two–three)				Light users (one or less)			
		A '000	B % Down	C Across %	D Index	A '000	B % Down	C Across %	D Index	A '000	B % Down	C Across %	D Index	A '000	B % Down	C Across %	D Index
Single	11,628	8,587	12.7	73.8	94	1,820	11.1	15.7	82	3,569	11.6	30.7	86	3,198	15.5	27.5	115
Married	53,109	43,298	63.8	81.5	104	10,786	65.8	20.3	107	19,778	64.3	37.2	105	12,734	61.6	24.0	100
Divorced/separated/widowed	21,624	15,952	23.5	73.8	94	3,785	23.1	17.5	92	7,416	24.1	34.3	96	4,751	23.0	22.0	92
Parents	32,344	26,121	38.5	80.7	103	7,139	43.6	22.1	103	11,431	37.2	35.3	99	7,550	36.5	23.3	97
White	74,071	59,284	87.4	80.0	102	14,124	86.2	19.1	100	27,221	88.5	36.7	103	17,938	86.7	24.2	101
Black	10,120	6,898	10.2	68.2	87	1,933	11.8	19.1	101	2,861	9.3	28.3	79	2,105	10.2	20.8	87
Other	2,170	1,655	2.4	76.3	97	*334	2.0	15.4	81	*681	2.2	31.4	88	*641	3.1	29.5	123
Northeast-census	18,325	14,156	20.9	77.2	98	2,658	16.2	14.5	76	7,103	23.1	38.8	109	4,396	21.3	24.0	100
Midwest	21,483	18,070	26.6	84.1	107	4,958	30.2	23.1	122	7,892	25.7	36.7	103	5,220	25.2	24.3	101
South	29,926	22,266	32.8	74.4	95	5,854	35.7	19.6	103	9,772	31.8	32.7	92	6,640	32.1	22.2	93
West	16,626	13,345	19.7	80.3	102	2,921	17.8	17.6	93	5,996	19.5	36.1	101	4,428	21.4	26.6	111
Northeast-mktg.	18,809	14,417	21.3	76.6	98	2,686	16.4	14.3	75	7,239	23.5	38.5	108	4,492	21.7	23.9	100
East Central	12,604	10,533	15.5	83.6	106	3,416	20.8	27.1	143	4,327	14.1	34.3	96	2,790	13.5	22.1	92
West Central	14,704	12,409	18.3	84.4	107	2,920	17.8	19.9	105	5,592	18.2	38.0	107	3,897	18.8	26.5	111
South	25,698	19,053	28.1	74.1	94	4,914	30.0	19.1	100	8,466	27.5	32.9	92	5,673	27.4	22.1	92
Pacific	14,543	11,425	16.8	78.6	100	2,455	15.0	16.9	89	5,139	16.7	35.3	99	3,831	18.5	26.3	110
County size A	35,301	26,901	39.7	76.2	97	5,954	36.3	16.9	89	12,513	40.7	35.4	100	8,434	40.8	23.9	100
County size B	25,652	20,496	30.2	79.9	102	5,125	31.3	20.0	105	9,355	30.4	36.5	102	6,016	29.1	23.5	98
County size C	13,413	11,055	16.3	82.4	105	2,916	17.8	21.7	115	4,608	15.0	34.4	96	3,531	17.1	26.3	110
County size D	11,994	9,386	13.8	78.3	100	2,397	14.6	20.0	100	4,287	13.9	35.7	95	2,702	13.1	22.5	94
Metro central city	27,494	20,827	30.7	75.8	96	4,983	30.4	18.1	95	9,294	30.2	33.8	95	6,550	31.7	23.8	99
Metro suburban	39,058	31,297	46.1	80.1	102	7,054	43.0	18.1	95	14,469	47.0	37.0	104	9,773	47.3	25.0	104
Non metro	19,809	15,714	23.2	79.3	101	4,354	26.6	22.0	100	7,000	22.8	35.3	99	4,360	21.1	22.0	92

Top 5 ADI's	19,248	14,469	21.3	75.2	96	2,889	17.6	15.0	79	7,033	22.9	36.5	103	4,547	22.0	23.6	99
Top 10 ADI's	26,751	20,184	29.8	75.5	96	4,259	26.0	15.9	84	9,632	31.3	36.0	101	6,294	30.4	23.5	98
Top 20 ADI's	39,079	29,891	44.1	76.5	97	6,485	39.6	16.6	87	13,978	45.4	35.8	100	9,428	45.6	24.1	101
HSHLD Inc. $60,000 or more	12,765	10,484	15.5	82.1	105	2,054	12.5	16.1	85	5,178	16.8	40.6	114	3,252	15.7	25.5	106
$50,000 or more	19,492	16,230	23.9	83.3	106	3,233	19.7	16.6	87	7,720	25.1	39.6	111	5,274	25.5	27.1	113
$40,000 or more	28,802	24,295	35.8	84.4	107	4,935	30.1	17.1	90	11,546	37.5	40.1	113	7,814	37.8	27.1	113
$30,000 or more	41,434	34,478	50.8	83.2	106	7,427	45.3	17.9	94	16,062	52.2	38.8	109	10,989	53.1	26.5	111
$30,000–$39,999	12,633	10,183	15.0	80.6	103	2,492	15.2	19.7	104	4,516	14.7	35.7	100	3,175	15.4	25.1	105
$20,000–$29,999	14,613	11,429	16.8	78.2	100	2,974	18.1	20.4	107	4,922	16.0	33.7	95	3,533	17.1	24.2	101
$10,000–$19,999	16,772	12,621	18.6	75.3	96	3,517	21.5	21.0	110	5,451	17.7	32.5	91	3,654	17.7	21.8	91
Under $10,000	13,542	9,309	13.7	68.7	88	2,473	15.1	18.3	96	4,328	14.1	32.0	90	2,508	12.1	18.5	77
Household of 1 person	13,686	9,601	14.2	70.2	89	1,584	9.7	11.6	61	4,539	14.8	33.2	93	3,479	16.8	25.4	106
2 people	29,863	23,557	34.7	78.9	100	5,201	31.7	17.4	92	10,848	35.3	36.3	102	7,508	36.3	25.1	105
3 or 4 people	32,539	26,757	39.4	82.2	105	7,114	43.4	21.9	115	12,007	39.0	36.9	104	7,636	36.9	23.5	98
5 or more people	10,273	7,922	11.7	77.1	98	2,493	15.2	24.3	128	3,369	11.0	32.8	92	2,061	10.0	20.1	84
No child in HSHLD	51,214	39,379	58.0	76.9	98	8,516	52.0	16.6	88	18,271	59.4	35.7	100	12,592	60.9	24.6	103
Child(ren) under 2 yrs	7,771	6,178	9.1	79.5	101	1,658	10.1	21.3	112	2,521	8.2	32.4	91	1,999	9.7	25.7	107
2–5 years	12,431	9,974	14.7	80.2	102	2,711	16.5	21.8	115	4,026	13.1	32.4	91	3,238	15.7	26.0	109
6–11 years	16,564	13,381	19.7	80.8	103	3,768	23.0	22.7	120	5,581	18.1	33.7	95	4,032	19.5	24.3	102
12–17 years	14,864	11,931	17.6	80.3	102	3,637	22.2	24.5	129	5,480	17.8	36.9	103	2,815	13.6	18.9	79
Residence owned	58,684	47,813	70.5	81.5	104	11,363	69.3	19.4	102	21,840	71.0	37.2	104	14,610	70.6	24.9	104
Value: $70,000 or more	29,899	24,916	36.7	83.3	106	5,110	31.2	17.1	90	12,243	39.8	40.9	115	7,563	36.6	25.3	106
Value: under $70,000	28,785	22,898	33.8	79.5	101	6,253	38.1	21.7	114	9,598	31.2	33.3	94	7,047	34.1	24.5	102
Magazines Quintile 1	17,469	14,253	21.0	81.6	104	3,631	22.2	20.8	110	6,367	20.7	36.4	102	4,255	20.6	24.4	102
Quintile 2	20,537	16,377	24.1	79.7	102	3,982	24.3	19.4	102	7,206	23.4	35.1	99	5,189	25.1	25.3	105
Quintile 3	15,763	13,044	19.2	82.8	105	3,226	19.7	20.5	108	6,169	20.1	39.1	110	3,649	17.6	23.1	97
Quintile 4	17,033	13,042	19.2	76.6	97	2,888	17.6	17.0	89	6,260	20.3	36.8	103	3,894	18.8	22.9	95
Quintile 5	15,559	11,121	16.4	71.5	91	2,664	16.3	17.1	90	4,761	15.5	30.6	86	3,697	17.9	23.8	99
Newspapers Quintile 1	13,180	10,889	16.1	82.6	105	2,279	13.9	17.3	91	5,211	16.9	39.5	111	3,399	16.4	25.8	108
Quintile 2	22,904	18,775	27.7	82.0	104	3,850	23.5	16.8	89	8,945	29.1	39.1	110	5,980	28.9	26.1	109
Quintile 3	15,554	12,050	17.8	77.5	99	3,302	20.1	21.2	112	5,389	17.5	34.6	97	3,359	16.2	21.6	90
Quintile 4	14,504	11,293	16.6	77.9	99	3,100	18.9	21.4	113	4,867	15.8	33.6	94	3,326	16.1	22.9	96
Quintile 5	20,216	14,830	21.9	73.4	93	3,859	23.5	19.1	101	6,351	20.6	31.4	88	4,619	22.3	22.8	95

Exhibit 12.12 (continued)

	Total US '000	All users				Heavy users (four or more)				Medium users (two–three)				Light users (one or less)			
		A '000	B % Down	C Across %	D Index	A '000	B % Down	C Across %	D Index	A '000	B % Down	C Across %	D Index	A '000	B % Down	C Across %	D Index
Total	86,361	67,837	100.0	78.6	100	16,391	100.0	19.0	100	30,763	100.0	35.6	100	20,683	100.0	23.9	100
American baby	1,974	1,766	2.6	89.5	114	500	3.1	25.3	133	847	2.8	42.9	120	420	2.0	21.3	89
American health	1,420	1,157	1.7	81.5	104	300	1.8	21.1	111	499	1.6	35.1	99	359	1.7	25.3	106
Architectural digest	927	811	1.2	87.5	111	*140	0.9	15.1	80	398	1.3	42.9	121	273	1.3	29.4	123
Baby talk	1,405	1,128	1.7	80.3	102	310	1.9	22.1	116	496	1.6	35.3	99	323	1.6	23.0	96
Barron's	*250	*226	0.3	90.4	115	**9	0.1	3.6	19	**123	0.4	49.2	138	**95	0.5	38.0	159
Better homes & gardens	16,745	13,919	20.5	83.1	106	3,542	21.6	21.2	111	6,409	20.8	38.3	107	3,968	19.2	23.7	99
Bon appetit.	2,732	2,191	3.2	80.2	102	417	2.5	15.3	80	1,007	3.3	36.9	103	766	3.7	28.0	117
Bride's	2,565	2,058	3.0	80.2	102	497	3.0	19.4	102	882	2.9	34.4	97	678	3.3	26.4	110
Business week	1,786	1,462	2.2	81.9	104	*252	1.5	14.1	74	667	2.2	37.3	105	542	2.6	30.3	127
The cable guide	3,934	3,070	4.5	78.0	99	858	5.2	21.8	115	1,327	4.3	33.7	95	885	4.3	22.5	94
Capper's/grit (gross)	1,047	770	1.1	73.5	94	*171	1.0	16.3	86	380	1.2	36.3	102	*219	1.1	20.9	87
Car and driver	353	276	0.4	78.2	100	**47	0.3	13.3	70	*162	0.5	45.9	129	**67	0.3	19.0	79
Changing times	799	649	1.0	81.2	103	*112	0.7	14.0	74	333	1.1	41.7	117	*203	1.0	25.4	106
Colonial homes	1,279	1,087	1.6	85.0	108	*219	1.3	17.1	90	574	1.9	44.9	126	293	1.4	22.9	96
Conde nast limited (gross)	10,444	8,549	12.6	81.9	104	1,828	11.2	17.5	92	3,679	12.0	35.2	99	3,042	14.7	29.1	122
Conde nast pkg. women (GRS)	18,651	15,085	22.2	80.9	103	3,711	22.6	19.9	105	6,463	21.0	34.7	97	4,911	23.7	26.3	110
Conde nast traveler	636	562	0.8	88.4	112	**155	0.9	24.4	128	*263	0.9	41.4	116	*144	0.7	22.6	95
Consumers digest	1,480	1,254	1.8	84.7	108	*241	1.5	16.3	86	728	2.4	49.2	138	285	1.4	19.3	80
Cosmopolitan	8,433	6,507	9.6	77.2	98	1,477	9.0	17.5	92	2,807	9.1	33.3	93	2,223	10.7	26.4	110
Country home	2,069	1,820	2.7	88.0	112	397	2.4	19.2	101	892	2.9	43.1	121	531	2.6	25.7	107

Country living	4,753	3,972	5.9	83.6	106	989	6.0	20.8	110	1,871	6.1	39.4	111	1,111	5.4	23.4	98
Cycle	*103	**76	0.1	73.8	94	**31	0.2	30.1	159	**20	0.1	19.4	55	**25	0.1	24.3	101
Cycle world	*185	*125	0.2	67.6	86	**57	0.3	30.8	162	**26	0.1	14.1	39	**41	0.2	22.2	93
Diamandis mag network (GRS)	2,543	2,017	3.0	79.3	101	525	3.2	20.6	109	876	2.8	34.4	97	615	3.0	24.2	101
Diamandis MTRCYCL grp (GRS)	288	*201	0.3	69.8	89	**88	0.5	30.6	161	**46	0.1	16.0	45	**67	0.3	23.3	97
Discover	1,690	1,359	2.0	80.4	102	*251	1.5	14.9	78	831	2.7	49.2	138	278	1.3	16.4	69
Ebony	4,493	3,158	4.7	70.3	89	780	4.8	17.4	91	1,355	4.4	30.2	85	1,024	5.0	22.8	95
Elle	1,471	1,068	1.6	72.6	92	*261	1.6	17.7	93	432	1.4	29.4	82	375	1.8	25.5	106
Esquire	695	487	0.7	70.1	89	**110	0.7	15.8	83	253	0.8	36.4	102	**124	0.6	17.8	74
Essence	2,587	1,811	2.7	70.0	89	435	2.7	16.8	89	791	2.6	30.6	86	586	2.8	22.7	95
Family circle	14,728	11,960	17.6	81.2	103	3,140	19.2	21.3	112	5,621	18.3	38.2	107	3,200	15.5	21.7	91
Family circle/McCall's (GRS)	26,796	21,810	32.2	81.4	104	5,730	35.0	21.4	113	10,194	33.1	38.0	107	5,886	28.5	22.0	92
The family handyman	1,061	864	1.3	81.4	104	*283	1.7	26.7	141	417	1.4	39.3	110	*165	0.8	15.6	65
Field & stream	2,162	1,820	2.7	84.2	107	506	3.1	23.4	123	811	2.6	37.5	105	503	2.4	23.3	97
Financial world	310	*255	0.4	82.3	105	**35	0.2	11.3	59	**180	0.6	58.1	163	**40	0.2	12.9	54
Flower & garden	1,681	1,369	2.0	81.4	104	324	2.0	19.3	102	712	2.3	42.4	119	333	1.6	19.8	83
Food & wine	913	763	1.1	83.6	106	**123	0.8	13.5	71	425	1.4	46.5	131	*215	1.0	23.5	98
Forbes	936	770	1.1	82.3	105	**170	1.0	18.2	96	349	1.1	37.3	105	251	1.2	26.8	112
Fortune	1,147	929	1.4	81.0	103	**146	0.9	12.7	67	461	1.5	40.2	113	322	1.6	28.1	117
GQ/gentlemen's quarterly	701	574	0.8	81.9	104	*152	0.9	21.7	114	273	0.9	38.9	109	*150	0.7	21.4	89
Glamour	6,012	4,738	7.0	78.8	100	1,285	7.8	21.4	113	2,035	6.6	33.8	95	1,417	6.9	23.6	98
Golf	672	546	0.8	81.3	103	*232	1.4	34.5	182	*191	0.6	28.4	80	*123	0.6	18.3	76
Golf digest	792	662	1.0	83.6	106	*165	1.0	20.8	110	*289	0.9	36.5	102	*208	1.0	26.3	110
Golf digest/tennis (gross)	1,204	992	1.5	82.4	105	255	1.6	21.2	112	430	1.4	35.7	100	307	1.5	25.5	106
Good housekeeping	16,621	13,513	19.9	81.3	104	3,675	22.6	22.1	116	6,171	20.1	37.1	104	3,668	17.7	22.1	92

Exhibit 12.12 (*continued*)

	Total US '000	All users				Heavy users (four or more)				Medium users (two–three)				Light users (one or less)			
		A '000	B % Down	C Across %	D Index	A '000	B % Down	C Across %	D Index	A '000	B % Down	C Across %	D Index	A '000	B % Down	C Across %	D Index
Gourmet	1,892	1,570	2.3	83.0	106	*236	1.4	12.5	66	663	2.2	35.0	98	671	3.2	35.5	148
Harper's bazaar	1,964	1,575	2.3	80.2	102	380	2.3	19.3	102	693	2.3	35.3	99	502	2.4	25.6	107
Health	2,273	1,810	2.7	79.6	101	510	3.1	22.4	118	760	2.5	33.4	94	540	2.6	23.8	99
Hearst gold buy (gross)	8,047	6,499	9.6	80.8	103	1,411	8.6	17.5	92	3,285	10.7	40.8	115	1,804	8.7	22.4	94
Hearst home buy (gross)	9,167	7,625	11.2	83.2	106	1,755	10.7	19.1	101	3,819	12.4	41.7	117	2,050	9.9	22.4	93
Hearst man power (gross)	1,555	1,228	1.8	79.0	101	347	2.1	22.3	118	586	1.9	37.7	106	295	1.4	19.0	79
Hearst woman power (gross)	40,582	32,820	48.4	80.9	103	8,364	51.0	20.6	109	14,777	48.0	36.4	102	9,679	46.8	23.9	100
Home	1,593	1,345	2.0	84.4	107	*203	1.2	12.7	67	693	2.3	43.5	122	450	2.2	28.2	118
Home mechanix	439	*360	0.5	82.0	104	**51	0.3	11.6	61	**250	0.8	56.9	160	**60	0.3	13.7	57
Homeowner	758	680	1.0	89.7	114	*234	1.4	30.9	163	357	1.2	47.1	132	**89	0.4	11.7	49
HG/house & garden	2,068	1,689	2.5	81.7	104	405	2.5	19.6	103	750	2.4	36.3	102	584	2.6	25.8	108
House beautiful	3,135	2,566	3.8	81.9	104	547	3.3	17.4	92	1,374	4.5	43.8	123	645	3.1	20.6	86
Inc.	477	385	0.6	80.7	103	**28	0.2	5.9	31	*221	0.7	46.3	130	**136	0.7	28.5	119
Inside sports	525	375	0.6	71.4	91	**73	0.4	13.9	73	*208	0.7	39.6	111	**94	0.5	17.9	75
Jet	3,834	2,563	3.8	66.8	85	625	3.8	16.3	86	1,074	3.5	28.0	79	863	4.2	22.5	94
Knapp signature coll. (GRS)	5,252	4,347	6.4	82.8	105	760	4.6	14.5	76	2,097	6.8	39.9	112	1,490	7.2	28.4	118
Ladies home journal	13,006	10,544	15.5	81.1	103	2,702	16.5	20.8	109	4,859	15.8	37.4	105	2,983	14.4	22.9	96
Life	5,305	4,209	6.2	79.3	101	1,077	6.6	20.3	107	1,841	6.0	34.7	97	1,291	6.2	24.3	102
Los Angeles times magazine	1,863	1,441	2.1	77.3	98	364	2.2	19.5	103	586	1.9	31.5	88	491	2.4	26.4	110
Mademoiselle	3,464	2,817	4.2	81.3	104	664	4.1	19.2	101	1,331	4.3	38.4	108	822	4.0	23.7	99

McCall's	12,068	9,849	14.5	81.6	104	2,590	15.8	21.5	113	4,573	14.9	37.9	106	2,686	13.0	22.3	93
Honey	1,895	1,593	2.3	84.1	107	*266	1.6	14.0	74	879	2.9	46.4	130	448	2.2	23.6	99
Mother earth news	493	438	0.6	88.8	113	**84	0.5	17.0	90	*233	0.8	47.3	133	**121	0.6	24.5	102
Muscle & fitness	832	617	0.9	74.2	94	*162	1.0	19.5	103	*254	0.8	30.5	86	*201	1.0	24.2	101
National enquirer	11,215	8,648	12.7	77.1	98	2,383	14.5	21.2	112	3,947	12.8	35.2	99	2,318	11.2	20.7	86
National geographic	9,116	7,647	11.3	83.9	107	1,514	9.2	16.6	88	3,590	11.7	39.4	111	2,543	12.3	27.9	116
Natural history	551	420	0.6	76.2	97	**50	0.3	9.1	48	*226	0.7	41.0	115	*145	0.7	26.3	110
New woman	2,500	2,135	3.1	85.4	109	546	3.3	21.8	115	953	3.1	38.1	107	637	3.1	25.5	106
New York	916	673	1.0	73.5	94	**108	0.7	11.8	62	382	1.2	41.7	117	*183	0.9	20.0	83
The New Yorker	896	765	1.1	85.4	109	**109	0.7	12.2	64	394	1.3	44.0	123	262	1.3	29.2	122

SIMMONS MARKET RESEARCH BUREAU, INC. 1990

* Projection relatively unstable because of sample base — use with caution
** Number of cases too small for reliability — shown for consistency only

NEW YORK

former, minute-by-minute ratings can be used to evaluate TV programming, whereas, in the latter, 'raw data' is limited.[45]

Media research elsewhere

Outside of the USA, Canada, most Western European countries, and Japan, media research conditions have to be examined on a country-by-country basis.

The A.C. Nielsen Company, a Division of Dun & Bradstreet, is a highly respected marketing and media research firm which operates in twenty-seven countries that account for nearly 90 per cent of the gross domestic product for all free market economies.[46] Where Nielsen is providing media research services, accurate and reliable information can be obtained. Mexico is a case in point. Their services include:

- investment in TV, radio, newspapers, and magazines
- monitoring and verification of commercials on TV and radio
- national study of exposures to various media
- advertising penetration studies

New door in Guatemala, a McCann-Erickson Media Fact Book (1991) gives credit to one research service for providing TV and cable penetration information, average annual ratings by station, and reach and cost information by geography and programme type. Similar but somewhat less detailed information is available for radio. While the same service conducts annual studies on newspapers and magazines, information is limited to the Guatemala City area where one-fifth of the population and a large per cent of the wealth is concentrated. Print information is limited to the basics: circulation (rounded to the nearest 1,000 and, therefore, believed to be unaudited), space rates, and editorial content. In the *McCann-Erickson Fact Book*, all cinema and outdoor data appears to have been generated by that organization, indicating the lack of outside research services for those media.

Further south, information obtained in Costa Rica indicates that advertisers have to rely on their advertising agencies to provide media information for planning and evaluating purposes. For example, the Alberto H. Garnier Advertising Agency recently took on the responsibility of researching and publishing information on the viewing, listening, and reading habits of the inhabitants of the Central Valley where the majority of Costa Ricans live. The research was supported by media owners. Ratings, readership, and cost data, however, are not covered in these reports.[47]

In Latin America generally, reliable magazine media research is not available; what is available is sometimes conflicting.[48]

In the Eastern European countries such as Hungary where the process of creating a market economy is in progress and advertising is recognized as an important marketing tool, one of the main problems to be overcome is the lack of reliable media research. Apparently the start up of an Austrian research firm in Budapest will help solve this problem.[49] However, it will take time to develop accurate and reliable information for planning and evaluating purposes across the media spectrum. No doubt international advertising agencies located in Hungary like McCann-Erickson will be key catalysts in bringing about the improvements needed.

Summary

Planning and evaluating a media programme is a complex process. Many factors must be taken into account, particularly when the programme spans more than a single country. To begin with, the principles of media planning must be understood. This includes the essential strategy components — reach, frequency, and continuity — and their balance which is dependent on the predetermined media objectives. This understanding must be coupled with knowledge of the target audience, where they are located, and when they should be reached. Related planning considerations must take into account the characteristics of the product, media availability, and the need to involve intermediaries. The media mix and scheduling patterns must conform with the predetermined balance of reach, frequency, and continuity, and the budget constraints. While some information is available on print media rates across borders, cost information and media specifications for broadcast media needs to be obtained locally.

International media planning for consumer products from a home country base requires a knowledge of host countries' environments, including climate and season, language, demographics, religion, laws, and political orientation of the media.

Cross border business-to-business media planning can be sharpened by having a clear knowledge of the industry and functional targets.

In certain circumstances, the media planner is not only responsible for planning and evaluating but also buying. However, it is customary to separate but coordinate the planning and buying functions. In a large, full-service agency the overall media function is managed by generalists with support from specialists as needed. International media representatives play an important role between media owners and buyers of print (press) advertising, particularly the smaller, less widely circulated publications of all types. The trend in media buying and selling is becoming more concentrated and centralized. Nonetheless, buying remains largely a matter for in-country organizations, and advertisers still have considerable flexibility in selecting the manner in which they wish to organize the overall media function.

Evaluating media effectiveness is an important aspect of media planning at both the beginning and end of the cycle. The tools for evaluation will vary from country to country, but generally is more comprehensive and reliable in the more advanced industrial economies.

Questions

1   Explain the meaning of and relationship between reach, frequency, and continuity.
2   Name two marketing, copy and media factors that will affect effective frequency.
3   Describe ways in which it is possible to build reach in television and print.
4   Identify and briefly explain the three basic questions to be answered at the outset of the media planning process.
5   In what way(s) can indexing be used be used to determine the allocation of the media budget?
6   How can product features, price and quality influence media planning?
7   In what ways can television, radio, magazines and newspapers complement each other in a media plan?
8   Explain the difference among continuous, flighting, and pulsing media patterns.
9   Where can information be found for international media planning purposes?
10 What factors would you take into account in planning an international media programme?
11 Roth has explained a six-step system for developing international business-to-business media plans. List and briefly explain the six steps.
12 Briefly discuss the rules of the media planner, media buyer, and media representative.
13 Explain why centralization and negotiation have emerged as major themes in media buying and selling.
14 What major research services are available for evaluating media effectiveness:
    a   In the UK?
    b   Pan-regionally?
    c   In Mexico?
    d   In Guatemala?
    e   In Eastern Europe, e.g. Hungary?

Notes

1   Stein, Gail (1985) How do media buyers make decisions. *Advertising World*, June, 10.
2   Sissors, Jack Z. and Bumba, Lincoln (1990) *Advertising Media Planning*, 3rd edn, NTC Business Books, Lincolnwood, IL, chs. 6 and 9.
3   Naples, Michael J. (1979) *Effective Frequency*, Association of National Advertisers, Inc., New York.
4   *The BBDO Media Approach.* A presentation, BBDO, New York.
5   Manton, Michael (1984) Potent brew for planners. *Marketing*, 27 September, 37–42.
6   Manton, *op. cit.*
7   Sissors, *op. cit.*, 84.
8   Wells, William, Burnett, John and Moriarty, Sandra (1989) *Advertising*, Prentice Hall, Englewood Cliffs, NJ, p. 225.
9   Levine, Erika Engels (1990) Int'l media planning step by step. *International Advertiser*, September/October, 30, 32, 33, 42.
10 Hindustan Thompson Associates Limited, *Thompson Pocket Reference to Media in India 1991*, Hindustan Thompson, Bombay, 2.
11 McCann-Erickson Guatemala, *Media Fact Book (Information General de Medios) 1991*, McCann-Erickson, Guatemala City, 39.
12 The Advertising Association (1990) *Marketing Pocket Book 1991*, The Association, London, 8.
13 Comite Medios Mexico, (1990) *Mercado y Demografia*, Asociacion Mexicana de Agencias de Publicidad AMAP Mexico City.
14 Hindustan Thompson, *op. cit.*, 3.
15 Levine, *op. cit.*, 32.
16 Levine, *op. cit.*, 30.
17 Levine, *op. cit.*, 32.
18 Bernard, Andre (1990) *Planning and Buying Media in the New Europe.* A presentation, Lintas: Worldwide, Chicago, 2 October.
19 Roth, Robert F. (1982) *International Marketing Communications*, Crain Books, Chicago, pp. 265–267.
20 Sissors, *op. cit.*, 295.
21 BBDO Media Department presentation, New York.
22 Jarvis, Mike (1989) Centralized media buying: fact of life or passing fad?. *International Advertiser*, January/February, 14.
23 Grieb, Rosemary (1985) How do media buyers make decisions. *Advertising World*, June, 32.
24 Lhoest, Jo (1978) The media representative scene in Europe. *Advertising World*, Autumn, 22.
25 Stein, *op. cit.*, 32.

26   How do reps represent — and present — their media? (1985) *Advertising World*, April, 12—14, 22, 23.
27   Ourusoff, Sandra, in *ibid.*, 23.
28   Stewart, David W. and McAuliffe, Kevin J. (1988) Determinants of international media purchasing: a survey of media buyers. *Journal of Advertising*, **17**, (3), 22, 23.
29   Personeni, Jane (1990) *Reader's Digest* presentation, Pleasantville, New York, December.
30   Stewart, *op. cit.*, 22—26.
31   Bernard, *op. cit.*
32   Jarvis, *op. cit.*
33   Perriss, John (1989) Centralized media buying: fact of life or passing fad? International Advertiser, January—February, 12.
34   Bernard, *op. cit.*
35   Perriss, *op. cit.*, 12—14.
36   World Federation of Advertisers (1990) *The Advertiser and Media Buying*, pp. 4—9.
37   Wilmshurst, John (1985) *The Fundamentals of Advertising*, Heinemann, London, pp. 146—7.
38   Wilmshurst, *op. cit.*, 148—9.
39   Wilmshurst, *op. cit.*, 164.
40   The Advertising Association, *op. cit.*, 99.
41   *Ibid.*, 96, 97.
42   *Ibid.*, 112, 113.
43   German speaking Europe: an abundance of media research (1982) *Advertising World*, December, 12, 14, 16.
44   Research Services Ltd. (1988) *Pan European Survey 4*, Wembley, England.
45   Bernard, *op. cit.*
46   Nielsen Marketing Research (1987) *International Food and Drug Store Trends Annual Review, 1987*, A.C. Nielsen Company, Northbrook, IL, 3.
47   Direccion de Medios (1987) *Estudios Sobre Los Habitos de Exposicion a la Radio, Prensa, y Television*, Albert H. Garnier, S.A., San Jose.
48   Personeni, *op. cit.*
49   Serenyi, Janos (1991) Media scene in Hungary. Fax report, McCann-Erickson, Budapest, 2 January.

Part Five *Sales Promotion, Public Relations and Packaging Media*

The purpose of these next two chapters is to convey this thought: to be a complete marketing communicator it is necessary to have a working knowledge of the scope and application of all forms of message transmission, not just mass or mail media. While these chapters are by no means complete, the reader should be able to grasp the breadth of possibilities that exist and gain some insight as to how sales promotion media, public relations and packaging can be used to enhance the international marketing communication plan.

13 *Sales promotion*

Recall that in Chapter 2 the relative importance of different elements of the promotion mix was discussed. Trends in expenditures on advertising, consumer and trade promotion showed that advertising had lost its prominence to other forms of promotion in terms of monies spent in the consumer sector. In the business-to-business sector, it never had been preeminent; personal selling was and is the principal promotion budget item and will remain so into the foreseeable future. What is clear, however, is that in the consumer sector sales promotion activities have accounted for an increasing amount of the overall marketing promotion budget in the USA and elsewhere.

In the UK, 'there are no detailed estimates of expenditures on sales promotion because of the problem of definition and lack of authoritative measurement system'.[1] This sums up a global problem. However, in the UK one measure of promotion growth is the number of coupons distributed which rose from 3.0 million in 1984 to 4.9 million in 1989, a 63 per cent increase.[2] This vitality has also been encountered in Japan where expenditures on sales promotion increased more than 10 per cent in 1988 over 1987. There was expectation that the trend would continue, fuelled by strong economic growth and more intense competition, particularly in the durable consumer goods, service, and leisure sectors.[3]

The activities which are included under the heading sales promotion will vary considerably depending on where and who is asked to give an explanation. In Japan, for example, the Dentsu Yearbook chapter on sales promotion covers consumer incentives which are listed under these headings: premium, POP, printing-DM, exhibitions and PR events, commercial space-cultural facilities, outdoor advertising, transit advertising, and flyers.[4] (In this text (direct) mail, outdoor, and transit are considered advertising and treated elsewhere.)

In 1988, according to *Advertising Age*, a total of $370 million in service revenues of US sales promotion agencies were divided in this manner:

	Per cent		*Per cent*
Consulting	26.9	Incentives	3.4
Production	10.9	Audio, visual	3.1
POP	10.7	Events	3.0
Creative	8.6	Advertising	2.6
Direct mail	6.3	Premiums	2.5
Sweepstakes	5.6	Fulfillment	2.2
Graphics	3.7	Other	10.5

This will give the reader an idea of the variety and relative importance of the services offered by sales promotion agencies.

In reviewing the services of the eighty-two agencies that produced the information shown above, it was apparent that many specialized in a particular service such as POP (point-of-purchase advertising/display materials), sweepstakes, premiums, or incentives.[5]

General classification

Now that the scope of this activity has been presented, an attempt will be made to provide a general framework of reference for sales promotion before proceeding to explain the topic more fully. For this purpose, Robert Coen's working definition of (consumer) sales promotion provides a good foundation. It includes:

1 *Direct consumer promotions* — coupons, money-back offers, refunds, contests, sampling (and sweepstakes).
2 *In-store consumer promotions* — displays, point-of-sale material plus some couponing, sampling (and demonstrations).
3 *Trade and other promotions* — co-op contributions to retailers' price promotions and others — such as novelties, premiums, and trade contests.[6]

The communication aspects of all the activities mentioned in Coen's definition would be a responsibility for marketing communicators. Monetary incentives to middlemen and consumers are separate but related marketing programme matters. Incentives to middlemen include free goods (e.g. buy five cases, get one free), off-invoice allowances, and display allowances. (Incentives of this kind along with consumer incentives listed in point 1 above, account for the major portion of the monies that have been shifted from advertising to promotion in recent years.) These are marketing department matters to be worked out between product marketing and sales managers, subject to higher level approval.

However, it is the responsibility of marketing communicators to convey information in the appropriate form about these trade deals and incentives as well as all other activities previously mentioned as a part of complete promotion packages. This transmission requires communication to all participants in the channel of distribution from the organization's field sales force through to the ultimate consumer. Booklets, brochures, fact sheets, flip charts, demonstration kits, and other forms of audio-visual presentation are tools of the trade that call for the professional touch of marketing communicators.

Other forms of sales promotion to be added to the list are sponsorships of events, meetings and seminars, exhibits (temporary and permanent), and trade shows. It must also be recognized that public relations marketing activities are very much a form of sales promotion but are treated separately in the next chapter.

While it is obvious that business-to-business marketers will be less apt to engage in sales promotion to the same degree as consumer marketers, the activity does play an important role in most marketing plans. Activities may involve distributors, dealers, and customers, and include contests, incentive awards, premiums, novelties, sponsorships, and trade shows...and all the information necessary to communicate the promotions with freshness and excitement.

Organizational considerations

As communication plans become fully integrated, as they should be, conflict may arise as to who should perform what function. Rivalry may develop among advertising, sales promotion, public relations, and the marketing departments within the firm. Services offered by suppliers may overlap. Sales promotion agencies prepare advertising, public relations agencies develop trade and point-of-sale programmes. Direct response specialists prepare coupon promotions. And advertising agencies attempt to serve all of their clients' sales promotion needs. As evidence that these types of conflicts exist, *Advertising Age* ran an article in May 1989 on sales promotion shops (agencies) with the headline and caption, 'Shops increasingly crossing the line − as they handle more advertising-oriented material, sales promotion shops head to another confrontation with (advertising) agencies.'[7]

How can order be brought to this kind of chaos? It's easy, if corporate management is worth its salt. It is accomplished by first having the expertise to understand the role that each element of the marketing and promotion mix can play; then determining how the work will be divided within the company, establishing responsibilities, lines of authority, and means of communication internally. The selection of suppliers of services and the work they are to perform will be undertaken by those given responsibility for the various communication functions on consultation and approval by higher management.

Sales promotion planning

The sales promotion programme must be properly coordinated with all other elements of the marketing mix to perform its role in achieving the objectives of the overall plan. Product advertising campaigns have annual objectives and tend to be evaluated on a year-to-year basis. Sales promotion activities tend to be concentrated at special times of the year and be of a temporary nature.

Objectives are set and evaluation procedures are established with the specific time frame in mind.

Sometimes advertising 'asks for the order', and sometimes it doesn't. Sales promotion invariably does the former. Advertising is primarily an image building vehicle. It creates the environment for a sale. The primary purpose of sales promotion is to trigger buying action. Not only does a product have to be one of the three or four brands that consumers feel are suitable alternatives but must also be attractively presented and priced. This is where a sales promotion programme can make the difference.

When promotions are supported by advertising, the product's message should be the same and the visual elements should look alike, have the same 'feel'. (This is one potential point of conflict between advertising and sales promotion staff and/or suppliers...where management must draw the lines of authority and responsibility − clearly.)

This is a sampling of different sales promotion audience targets, objectives, strategies, and means of evaluation which would be key elements in the sales promotion plan:

Target	Objective	Strategy	Evaluation
Field sales personnel	Facilitate sales presentation	Provide sales brochure and audiovisual aids	Follow-up questionnaire to sale force
Field sales personnel	Increase sales during promotion period	Develop prize catalogue. Award points for prizes according to sales volume	Compare sales records before and after Promotion
Wholesalers and distributors	Stimulate interest in new product	Prepare product demonstration kit and material for sales meetings	Sales people report on effectiveness
Wholesalers and distributors	Open new retail accounts	Provide cash bonus for each account opened	Count new accounts
Retailers	Increase shelf space for product	Conduct and communicate results of research study showing most profitable shelf arrangement	Sales force reports on new space allocations
Retailers	Secure temporary off-shelf display space	Provide attractive display. (Offer display allowance.)	Count number used, length of use, product sold, and cost of deal

Retailers	Gain product features in retailers' ads	Offer co-op ad allowance	Count number and size of features, product sold, and cost of deal
Consumers	Stimulate product trial	Deliver samples with money-off coupons to target market	Count number of coupons redeemed and product sold; compare against cost of programme
Consumers	Induce repeat purchase	Place coupon in/on packages	Count coupons redeemed. Track sales
All intermediaries	Familiarize with full product line	Participate in annual industry trade show	Track visits to display booth, number of intermediaries followed up, new accounts opened.

In the foregoing schedule it can be observed that sales promotion involves a combination of communication activities and buying incentives to help move goods (push) and consumers (pull) at the point of purchase. This is also the reason why many marketers of goods and services make a special effort to design temporary and permanent displays and signs, for use at the point of sale. There is good reason for this special effort if a 1986 POPAI/Dupont study has validity. Among 4,000 shoppers in 100 stores the study revealed that two-thirds of the consumers' purchase decisions were made in the store.[8]

Just because many consumer purchase decisions are made after entrance into the retail store, it doesn't mean that promotional planning should begin and end at the point of sale. Repeated studies in the USA over the years have demonstrated that in-store displays, signs and retail advertising in combination produce greater results than any one device used by itself.

The essence of good promotion

What it takes to place signs and displays in a retail store or a distributor's showroom, to arouse consumer interest, to gain dealer/distributor cooperation, as with advertising, is a good idea or promotion concept in combination with a coordinated promotion effort. To support this contention, several concepts and programmes that worked for selected marketers will be explained. If it becomes clear that a promotion concept has merit as a result of research, judgment, or a combination of the two, then every effort should be expended to make sure that maximum funds available are put behind the promotion in a coordinated manner involving middlemen and end users. Promotion elements likely to be included are advertising; product/promotion publicity; wholesaler, retailer and consumer incentives to gain intermediary cooperation and stimulate end user action; point-of-sale promotion activities and retailer cooperative advertising.

Some six years ago, an expert in the field who cannot be located at this writing, in alluding to the switch in budget allocations for many soap and health and beauty aid products away from 'above-the-line' advertising to 'below-the-line' promotion, identified a trend to what he described as 'event oriented' promotional marketing. It is more than sales promotion...it is a fully integrated marketing effort of a short-term duration staged periodically and tied in with a brand's or organization's long-term image building investment in advertising. It is equally appropriate for companies that are vertically integrated from production to retail outlets like a well-known marketer of sewing machines and accessories. The company found itself owning retail stores that were once on 'high street' and now found themselves on 'second street'. Event-oriented promotional marketing programmes became essential for their survival and growth.

Several specific examples

'JIGGLERS'*

An idea for a promotion may come from any place...even right out of the recipe files, providing someone has the genius to recognize it. Take the case of JELL-O*, a ninety-three-year old gelatin dessert product of Kraft General Foods which had been in a long-term sales decline. In recent years, the brand's most requested recipe on the company's consumer hotline was one calling for four boxes of product that made 'finger food', perfect for an after school snack. A modest research project was instituted to determine what sizes and shapes consumers would prefer. Dinosaurs and geometric shapes won out. Dubbed 'JIGGLERS' and promoted with free moulds in dinosaur and geometric shapes, this new way to enjoy JELL-O has become a smash hit. The advertising put behind this promotion showed an eight-year old boy with a big smile holding up a JELL-O heart and star with the caption, 'Now Make JELL-O you can eat with your hands!' JIGGLERS (bold) was spelled out underneath. At the bottom beneath the illustration of the boy the words appeared: 'Make a handful of fun!' Sales during the initial promotion were 50 per cent ahead of the same four-week period during the previous year and up 10 per cent for the year as a whole.[9] Who says a promotion idea can't reverse a declining sales trend!

* JELL-O and JIGGLERS are registered trademarks of Kraft General Foods Inc. Reproduced with permission.

A bank promotion targeted to youth brings in adults and local business
A bank in the New York area established an objective to distinguish itself from
competition and bring in new customers at one of its shopping centre branches.
The central promotion idea to realize these goals was a bank-within-a-bank
for youths up to age seventeen. 'By focusing on customer market segments
instead of product lines, the bank hoped to demonstrate interest in its customers
and their financial concerns, build customer loyalty, and bring in new consumers
and commercial accounts.' The four-week promotion included a back-to-
school sweepstakes in the centre with twice weekly drawings and $25 gift
certificates for winners redeemable for merchandise at participating centre
shops. The bank-within-a-bank was a self-contained facility which required a
specially issued youth ATM card for admittance, a special teller, banking
games, and a computer with interactive video with a story on the value of
saving. The results of the promotion included regional and national press
coverage, the opening of 'thousands of Bank for Kids Accounts', 15 per cent of
which generated new parent accounts. In addition, one-quarter of the participating centre shopkeepers established commercial banking relationships with
the branch.[10]

Sales force promotion
To increase market share in a region of the country where the company's
performance was below par, a special sales promotion was designed by the
country's leading manufacturer of glass fibre shingles. The idea was to educate
the sales force about the product improvements and superiority over competitive
offerings at the company's research and development centre. At the conclusion
of the educational session, the sales people were equipped with 'eye-catching
presentation kits and video cassette to convert roofing contractors to Fibreglass
Singles'. As part of the promotion package, contractors were offered samples
for use on their next job. Funded by local field sales force budgets, the training
programme and promotion resulted in a regional share increase of 10 per
cent.[11]

Ingenious sampling programme halts a sales decline
Trend reversal is one of the most difficult assignments a marketer can tackle.
That was the situation facing the marketing group of Nescafe Soluble Coffee in
Belgium in the mid-1980s. The soluble form had lost much of its convenience
to ground coffee with the growth of easy-to-use automatic coffee makers and
the concentration of business in a few hands that put aggressive advertising
and promotion efforts behind their ground coffee brands. While attitudes
towards Nescafé had improved as a result of advertising, no improvement had
been experienced in sales.

   How to change behaviour in light of the situation was the question. New
freeze-dried soluble coffee technology produced a market research response

which indicated that new Nescafe in cup quality was comparable with regular fresh-brewed coffee. Sampling, if affordable, would be ideal means of stimulating trial, but more than one cup at a time was needed to convince consumers of the merits of the improved product. It turned out the production had the answer: a ten cup sample jar could be produced at a reasonable cost, and in Belgium, because couponing was permitted, this device could be used in conjunction with sampling as an added stimulus to purchase after trial. The programme included these objectives and strategies:

Objectives	*Strategies*
• Large-scale sampling	• Sample 1/10th Belgium at a time
• Provide more than one time trial	• Use ten-cup sample jar
• Sample under best circumstances	• Distribute Sunday morning at bakeries
• Develop programme at minimum cost	• Use cost-efficient sample jars and point of sale promotion

Many good ideas went into the creation of this programme. The key idea was the Sunday morning Bakery shop sampling. It is traditional in Belgium for residents to go to their local bakeries for a special Sunday type bread, then go home to enjoy a leisurely breakfast including a good cup of coffee.

The Nestlé sales organization obtained 95 per cent cooperation from the shop keepers who put up teaser posters ahead of time indicating that a special offer was coming. Customers who arrived on the Sunday morning of distribution thought they would get a cup of coffee in the bakery. Instead they were surprised and pleased to receive a special yellow sample bag with a free 200 g jar of Nescafe, an explanatory leaflet, a chance to enter a contest to win a free holiday and a coupon worth twenty francs off a regular-sized jar.

There was an immediate surge in sales resulting in a 10 per cent increase over the previous period.[12]

Pepsi-Cola character and premium promotions in Mexico

What do you do to upstage your rival when they are the leader? One way is to think of a series of clever promotions to boost your business. That is precisely what Pepsi-Cola did in Mexico at points in the year when industry sales are at the low end of the annual sales curve which correlates with the temperature. (If a successful promotion is run at the top of the sales curve, bottlers would run out of glass, the predominant form of packaging due to cost.)

Pepsi-Cola's first big promotion hit was built around the use of the Snoopy character and a Snoopy plastic drink cup premium which could be received free in exchange for forty bottle tops. This Snoopy promotion was supported by radio advertising (TV was not permitted) plus posters and an in-store display promotion programme.

Thirty-eight million Snoopy cups were made to fill the premium requests. . . that's nearly one-half the total Mexican population!

For the next promotion, the Batman character was selected. The premium this time was a thirty-two-ounce Batman cup that was made available for ten bottle tops and 1,000 pesos. The nine-week promotion coincided with the distribution of the Batman film in Mexico. The Batmobile car toured the country in support of the promotion. The Batman promotion was advertised on television (permission granted this time by the authorities) in conjunction with Pepsi-Cola's image commercials. Over 44 million Batman cups were distributed to fill consumer orders. The programme more than paid for itself.

The follow-up promotion was built around the Bugs Bunny character. Bugs gave the daily commentary on the World Cup football (soccer) matches in Italy which Pepsi-Cola sponsored in Mexico. (Mexicans love football even though their team was not represented.) Bugs was also available on the sides of a Pepsi-Lindro, a large plastic squeeze bottle with top and plastic straw, which was used as the premium offer. As in other promotions, support was provided at the point of sale. Thirty-five million lindros were distributed against this promotion.

The magnitude of response received for these promotions was extraordinarily large for Mexico or most countries of the world.[13]

Where contests and sweepstakes fit in

Both contests and sweepstakes have been used extensively in the USA for the purpose of attracting attention, increasing awareness, and helping stimulate demand for products of a company. These devices may or may not be permitted in other countries. In sweepstakes, winners are determined on the basis of chance and no product purchase is required. In contests respondents must solve a specific problem such as a puzzle and may have to show that they also purchased the product.[14]

Sweepstakes are used five times as often as contests in promoting products because they are easier to understand and administer, generate five to ten times as many entrants — everybody has a chance to win — are considerably less costly and do not pose the same legal complexities as contests.[15]

Sweepstakes are used by magazines and newsletters to solicit subscriptions and renewals, by retailers to generate store traffic, by manufacturers and marketers to raise the level of awareness and interest in branded merchandise, and by catalogue marketers to increase number and size of orders.[16]

In many instances, sweepstakes and contests are frequently employed as one component of an overall promotion effort, for example, combined with a price-off coupon offer and supported by consumer advertising and/or a point-of-sale display programme. As a stand-alone sales promotion activity, these techniques are not normally as effective as other forms of promotion.

The same approach is needed in planning a contest or sweepstakes as any other advertising or promotion effort. The plan should include target audience, objectives, duration, theme or central selling idea, visual presentation, budget, timetable, coordination with other promotion activities, and a means of evaluation. Special attention is needed with respect to rules, regulations, and legal considerations.[17]

It is customary for marketing communicators to seek assistance from experts in planning contests and sweepstakes.

Tie-in promotions

This is a form of promotion that is used by one manufacturer or two or more manufacturers in developing a joint promotion of compatible products. The promotion has to be based on an idea that is of interest to the target audience. For example, manufacturers of a pie crust dough mix and pie filling might team up to sponsor a tie-in promotion. Another possible combination could be a pasta and a canned meat sauce. The combination does not have to be food; it could be manufacturers of sporting equipment and clothes. Whatever the combination, the event should have a theme, e.g. 'new strawberry rhubarb surprise...made with Brand X Strawberry Rhubarb Pie Filling and Brand Y Pie Crust Mix'. Promotions of this type are normally supported by advertising, often containing a store-redeemable price-off coupon; retailer trade allowances for displays and/or advertising features; and point-of-sale material. Both 'push' and 'pull' are needed to create excitement and stimulate extra sales volume.

Sometimes retailers are the catalysts in sponsoring a multi-brand tie-in promotion. For example, a southern US supermarket organized an in-store tie-in promotion with the town's annual chilli cook-off contest. (Chilli is a popular dish in the USA made with a number of ingredients including kidney beans, and chopped meat.) The point-of-sale promotion brought together onions, mushrooms, tomatoes, and chilli seasoning, ingredients normally specified in a chilli recipe. As a result of the promotion volume on these items increased up to 200 per cent.[18]

Joint manufacturer and distributor/dealer promotion programmes

As a part of the total marketing effort, advertising programmes that involve manufacturer and middleman can be beneficial to both parties. Cooperative advertising is the most widely used type of programme. The manufacturer pays a portion of the retailer's advertising cost (usually 50 per cent) or provides a certain allowance per case on all cases sold to a retailer during a specified period. Exhibit 13.1 shows one type of cooperative advertising where different manufacturers participate with a retail chain store to have their products featured in the retailer's advertisement.

One of the problems encountered in cooperative advertising is control. In cases where the payment is made on the basis of a fixed percentage of sales or

Exhibit 13.1 *Cooperative advertising. Reproduced by permission of Caldor Inc., Norwalk, CT, USA*

on the basis of a specified allowance per case sold to the dealer during the promotion period, it is up to the sales organization in coordination with marketing headquarters to see that the money paid has been used for the intended purpose.[19] While this may not be the direct responsibility of the marketing communicator, the problem should be recognized and understood. One of this person's roles is to see that dealers receive creative materials to help in composing the advertisement in a way that will present the manufacturer's product in the best possible light.

An alternative approach is where the manufacturer prepares the advertisement, leaves space for the dealer's name, address, and 'phone, and makes reference to the dealer(s) as the place to buy the product. Advertising of this type is placed by the manufacturer. One advertisement can be prepared and used in many local or regional markets. Under these circumstances, the organization's sales force 'sells' the advertising campaign, explaining the benefits of participation. The dealer cost of participation may come from the manufacturer's cooperative advertising budget or a portion of the advertising cost may be billed to the dealer. In some cases, the manufacturer pays the total cost. (Peebles and Ryans give a more complete explanation how such a programme can be set up.[20]) As with any other programme, the pulling power in terms of stimulating interest, building customer traffic and/or creating sales should be tracked in order to evaluate the advertising's effectiveness.

One example of dealer participation advertising is the co-op programme conducted by Jaguar cars for its US dealers. While it may be utilized to reinforce national strategic product advertising, it can also be used for competitive 'tactical' messages or to promote short-lived leasing or other incentives to prospects. (See Exhibit 13.2.)

In another situation, a US manufacturer of printing presses that sold through dealers in seventeen countries found from experience it was more advantageous to conduct an attention and interest-building advertising campaign controlled from headquarters rather than leave it up to dealers in the company's network.

At the beginning of overseas advertising, the company, Harris Graphics, contributed advertising funds to individual dealer campaigns. For example, if a dealer spent $1,000 on 'co-op' advertising, Harris Graphics would match those funds. However, it was discovered that dealers tended to promote themselves and not Harris Graphics. This prompted the company to take control, plan campaigns centrally, produce quality advertising at headquarters with help of its advertising agency, have the copy translated with assistance from its dealers into local languages, and place the advertising in printing trade magazines in dealers' countries. The advertising was uniform in visual and verbal appeal and content. Each advertisement suggested that the reader contact the local agent for details, giving name and address of the dealer in each ad. An annual schedule of advertising was run in one or two trade publications in each of seventeen countries at a cost of $100,000. Other media alternatives such as international editions of news and business magazines were significantly more costly and would not reach the intended audience.[21]

Another form of joint manufacturer–dealer advertising is built around a sales promotion concept that will interest consumers and stimulate buying action as well as create product awareness and interest. Consumer advertising

Exhibit 13.2 *Jaguar dealer participation print advertisement. Reproduced by permission of Jaguar Cars Inc., Mahwah, NJ, USA*

is coordinated with dealer support and point-of-sale promotion. An example of this type of promotional advertising is demonstrated by the Goodyear Plus Campaign in the UK.[22] The purpose was to create extra sales during a spring promotion period. To create interest and stimulate buying action a contest was developed. Winners and their spouses would receive an all-expense paid six-day New York holiday including round-trip travel on a British Airways Concorde SST. One contest entry form was made available with the purchase of a Grand Prix-S Tyre. Four winners were selected; one from each region in which the contest promotion ran. The dealers who endorsed the winning entry forms also received the same holiday prize.

Dealer participation in the promotion was solicited by the Goodyear sales force. To be listed in the Goodyear consumer advertisements which ran twice during the promotion in thirty-three newspapers in the four regions, dealers needed to purchase at least fifty tyres. The consumer newspaper advertisement can be seen in Exhibit 13.3.

Dealers were also encouraged to run their own tie-in advertising, format for which was supplied by Goodyear, and set up in-store promotions. Sales during the promotion period were double sales the same period a year earlier.[23]

Will promotion concepts travel?

To conduct a successful international sales promotion effort, at least two elements are needed: 'a promotion of sufficiently general appeal to attract customers for a variety of cultures and a knowledge of national regulations'.[24]

Here is one example: Kodak 'Kolorkins Fantasy Creatures' promotion. It proved to be a great success in Canada where the idea was conceived. The promotion was then extended to the USA and Swiss markets with other markets such as Spain and Australia being considered. The Kolorkins 'were four colourful plush creatures designed to amplify the colour aspects of Kodak products and spur multiple purchases'. To receive a free Kolorkin consumers had to send in proofs of purchase from a combination of different Kodak products − film, cameras, processing, and papers. Life-sized Kolorkins made appearances for Kodak at various special events such as the opening of the Olympic games.[25]

International promotion and regulations

As previously stated, it is necessary to know local regulations when planning cross-border promotions. Among five of the most populated nations in Europe, regulations permit many forms of promotional techniques including in-pack premiums, extra or free product, cross promotions, contests, self-liquidating premiums and various types of couponing. West Germany, however, is the exception. All forms of promotions other than free product and in-store demonstrations are either not permitted or need prior clearance. Cash rebates are not permitted in Italy. Sweepstakes in all countries other than Germany where they are not allowed may or may not be permitted; prior clearance should be obtained.[26]

For no other reasons than regulations and cultural differences, when planning

Exhibit 13.3 *Newspaper advertisement − Goodyear promotion**

* The Goodyear campaign example and illustration are reproduced from Peebles, Dean M. and Ryans, John K. Jr (1984) *Management of International Advertising*, Allyn and Bacon, Inc., Boston, pp. 188−192 by permission.

cross-border sales promotion activities it would appear that in-country assistance from experts, in-house or from outside services, is essential.

Sponsorship

Sponsorship can be linked either directly or indirectly to the marketing of goods and services. When sponsorship is one of the marketing communication tools selected for an individual brand or service it comes under the direction and supervision of marketing management. When sponsorship becomes a project for a company overall, the responsibility for its overall planning and management would most likely lie in the corporate communications or public relations department.

Recent trends

Sponsorship for promotion purposes is associated with some type of event, often one that is repeated at a regular interval, every year or every four years as in the case of the Olympics. Sports are the most frequently used type of activity for commercial sponsorship. This is followed by arts sponsorships. Rapid growth of sponsorship was experienced in the 1980s. For example, in the UK, sports sponsorship increased nearly five-fold between 1980 and 1986, while art sponsorship increased nearly nine-fold.[27] By 1989, total expenditures on sports sponsorships in the UK were estimated at 2,000 million pounds, and art, 33 million pounds.[28] The same year 3,900 US companies expected to spend an estimated $2.1 billion on event sponsorship[29] as compared with 2,700 companies and $1.35 billion in 1987.[30]

A definition

The purpose of sponsorship, as a means of promoting goods and services, is to relate the company or brand to a social, cultural, or athletic event in order to benefit from the 'exploitable commercial potential associated with that activity'.[31]

Sponsorship as a sales promotion activity should not be confused with the sponsorship of a radio or television broadcast. The latter is a media matter and is the responsibility of those in charge of that function.

Sports, arts, and other events

In the UK, sports and arts events rank in the following order in terms of sponsorship expenditures:[32]

Sports	*Arts*
Horse racing	Classical music
Golf	Festivals

Football	Theatre
Athletics	Visual arts
Cricket	Opera
Equestrian	Dance
Snooker	
Tennis	

The significance of sponsorship to the major retailer in Spain and also the largest advertiser, El Corte Ingles, is indicated by the list of events, mostly sports and cultural, that this organization was involved with in the major cities in Spain as reported in their 1983 *Annual Report* and shown in Exhibit 13.4.[33]

These activities have been maintained as an integral part of El Corte Inglés promotional activities. For example, in 1989 this organization exclusively staged the first travelling exhibition to Madrid, Barcelona and Valencia of 128 art treasures from the Kremlin which represented works of great artistic and historical significance of the seventeenth century. In 1990, the 'El Corte Inglés sponsored Barcelona Footrace', attracted 60,000 competitors and proved to be the most popular run in Europe.[34]

Corporate versus product marketing support

The use of sponsorship for corporate and product marketing support can be one and the same or can be separate, and, as indicated earlier, indirectly linked. In the case of El Corte Ingles, a strong corporate identity related to the interests of people in a given market area will no doubt create the kind of good will that will stimulate store traffic and that, in turn, will produce sales. The sponsorship of tennis tournaments by Virginia Slims brand of cigarettes is designed to create awareness and brand recognition among the target market.

Corporate sponsorship that is aimed at shareholders, financial institutions, the company work force, the plant or office community, and/or the general public lies in the domain of public relations. The purpose in these instances is to maintain good relationships, and demonstrate good citizenship and social responsibility. These programmes should indirectly benefit product and company sales. Since this text is on marketing communications that directly benefit sales, the focus on sponsorship under these circumstances is on programmes that will have an effect on target market audiences.

Sponsorship objectives

By sponsoring events appropriately selected, brand or company awareness can be heightened, a personality or image can be shaped, positive attitudes can be formed.

Events will provide an audience in attendance and in certain cases a listening and/or viewing audience via electronic media. Sponsors are interested in the attending audience, in the media audience, in both, and/or in the event

Exhibit 13.4 *Activities EC Corte Ingles sponsored or cooperated in*

Madrid
— Somontes Pigeon Shooting Trophy.
— Bullfighting Exhibition
— IV & V Performances of Theater and Music at the University.
— I College Sport Trophy.
— XXIX San Isidro Pelota Prize.
— II Castilla Golf Trophy.
— Cooperation in Juvenalia 83 and the festivities of Madrid and villages within the Province.

Barcelona
— V Popular Run "City of Barcelona."
— VI Sardana Dancing School.
— IV Children's Fancy Dress Contest.
— Clavé Chorus Concerts.
— II Basketball TVE Contest in Catalogna.
— XVI Chess World Oscar.
— Contribution to festivities of Las Corts and La Merced.

Sevilla
— Handicrafts Fair.
— Spain Championship of Spanish pure bred horses.
— Exhibition of aircraft kits.
— Motocross for the youngers.
— Autumn painting exposition award.
— International Philatelic Exhibition.
— Contribution to April Fair.

Bilbao
— VII Basque Ball Provincial Tournament.
— VII Zarauz-Galdácano International Amateur Cycle Race.
— III City of Bilbao Pyrotechnic Contest.
— XIII El Corte Inglés Trawler Prize. IX Flag.
— VIII Bizcayan Contest for stone pulling by oxen.
— I Bizcayan Inter-clubs horse Tournament.
— Euskalerría at El Corte Inglés.

Valencia
— IV Show of old and young painters.
— Picture Contest "Valencia in Fallas."
— Homage to Maestro Serrano.
— VIII Galotxa Regional Contest.
— XII Edition of Declamation in Valencian Language.
— V Contest of Popular Carols.
— Contribution to festivities of La Magdalena in Castellón.

Murcia
— Children's Fancy Dress Contest.
— Francisco Salzillo's Workshop.
— The Alicante 500 km. by night Rallye.
— XXIII Edition of Miners' Folk Songs.
— Mediterranean Botanic Garden.
— III Women's Painting Exhibition Contest.
— Contribution to Septemper Fair and Murcian Cycle Race.

Vigo
— II Vigo Opera Festival.
— VII Children's Fancy Dress Contest.
— XIV Festival of the Muñeira Dance.
— El Corte Inglés Golf Award.
— II Urban Cycle Race.
— VII "Young Galician Painters" Exhibition Contest.
— II El Corte Inglés Trawler Prize.

Las Palmas
— V "Open" Chess Tournament.
— "Media" Tennis Tournament.
— IV Popular Run.
— VII Canarian Lateen Sail Race.
— Canarian Young Artists.
— VII International Rallye.
— Contribution to Carnival Celebrations.

Malaga
— Children's Fancy Dress Contest.
— Exhibition of the Holy Week in Malaga.
— IV Inter-school Chess Tournament.
— IV Painting & Design Contest "Young Malaga Painters."
— Exhibition "The Guitar and Its Cultural Influence."
— Children's & Juniors' Judo Contest.
— August Fair - Homage to Regions.

Zaragoza
— School of "jotas" (dance).
— I Week of Aragonese Cooking.
— II Spring Pigeon Shooting Contest.
— I Homage to traditional Sport.
— School Chess Tournament.
— Aragonese Yawl Race.
— Contribution to the "Virgen del Pilar" Celebrations.

as an entertainment for customers, dealers, and suppliers. For example, Rolex sponsored horse shows in the USA because of the characteristics of the audience in attendance and by the publicity which the participation in the event could create to reach other horse owners who had the affluence to buy an $8,500 watch. Budweiser sponsors baseball, football, and basketball, not so much for the audience in attendance, but for the millions of people watching the event on television. As a spokesperson for Budweiser was quoted as saying, 'events personalize a brand's image, and give it personality'. Suntory of Japan sponsored golf events in Scotland which were televised to Japan to create an aura of Scottish heritage for its whisky brand.[35]

What to sponsor

In developing marketing communication programmes whether at the corporate or brand level, whether international or country-specific, planning begins with the identification of target audiences and the setting of communication objectives. Once established, alternative means of attaining these objectives can be considered. Sponsorship could be one of these alternatives. For an event to qualify, its audience, costs, and its ability to be used as an entertainment medium for those a firm does business with must be scrutinized carefully. The extent of media coverage to be provided, if any, will be more important for mass-marketed products like razor blades and carbonated beverages than for class items like expensive watches and cars. Opportunities for guest entertainment will be more important to some than others. Companies may wish to entertain customers, prospects and intermediaries. For those that do, the possibilities and cost must be determined.

As for type of sponsorship, the alternatives may range from being the principal sponsor of the event itself such as the Buick (car) Golf Classic, to one of a number of sponsors as in the case of World Cup Football or the Olympics. Another possibility is to sponsor an individual or team that participates in the event such as a driver and/or a car in a Grand Prix or the Indianapolis 500. For those that sponsor participants, a strong emotional response on the part of consumers may turn into an intense relationship with the sponsor. However, this partisan approach can alienate opposition supporters, and when defeat is experienced instead of victory, the positive relationship may disappear.[36]

International sponsorships

When it comes to developing an international presence, the Olympics and World Cup are major possibilities. Kodak, for example, viewed its participation in the 1988 Olympic games as an opportunity to:

1 Use the Olympic theme to enhance the Kodak brand name in many nations.

2 Strengthen the company's relations with business and political leaders among the 154 nations which participated in the games.
3 Improve Kodak's image as a leader in the photographic industry on a global and also on a country basis wherever it conducted operations.

The programme was carried out by having corporate headquarters provide its marketing subsidiaries in each country promotional materials and tools on which in-country campaigns could be developed to capitalize on the Olympic sponsorship.[37]

This kind of sponsorship is reserved for those with large pocket books. Six US sponsors contributed over $80 million to the Olympic Organization over the four years that included the 1988 games.[38] The US Postal Service paid $10 million to become a worldwide sponsor of the 1992 Olympics games.[39]

Companies interested in expanding internationally 'see event and sports sponsorships as the best way to enter new markets'.[40] This may be the reason why Volkswagen, Sudmilch, Kraft-General Foods, and American Airlines all became sponsors of the first women's Grand Prix Tennis Tournament in Leipzig, East Germany with a prize of $225,000 and big names like Steffi Graff and Arantxa Sanchez.[41]

When it comes to global sponsorship, Philips involvement in the 1986 World Champion Football provides a good example of how corporate communications and national subsidiary companies can work together to maximize their investment in an event.[42]* The prime objectives to be realized as a result of the sponsorship included corporate and consumer product brand awareness and image building leading to product preference on the part of the trade and the public at large. In return for becoming a sponsor, Philips received the following:

1 Perimeter advertising boards: two behind the goals and two on the side opposite the television cameras at each of fifty-two World Cup matches in Mexico.
2 The designation of Official Supplier and Official Product (name) to the competition.
3 The right to use official World Cup emblems, trophy, and mascot.
4 Full page advertisements in each official programme or publication relating to the event.
5 Franchise and display rights at the competition sites and international press centre.

---

* The example and illustrations of Philips' participation in World Cup football is included by permission of Philips Corporate Marketing Communications, Eindhoven, The Netherlands.

Because Philips received an order for and delivered over 100 television cameras to the television network in Mexico for broadcasting purposes, this became an opportunity for further exploitation.

Event-generated TV and press coverage

The four-week event was televised in 161 countries with an estimated cumulative audience of nearly thirteen billion people. The final match was witnessed by nearly 600 million... extraordinary numbers by any standards. Approximately 5,400 minutes of television coverage was produced, and the average exposure time of the Philips perimeter advertising boards was eighteen out of every ninety minute match (i.e. 20 per cent of the broadcast time). Exhibit 13.5 shows how an advertising board would look on a television screen.

Because of the popularity of World Cup football and the location of the Philips advertising boards, an 'amazing' number of 'Philips photographs' appeared in newspapers and magazines the world over of the type shown in Exhibit 13.6

Exhibit 13.5 *How an advertising board would appear on a television screen*

Exhibit 13.6 *Philips advertising boards*

Sponsorship exploitation by corporate marketing communications and the
national organizations

With respect to the World Cup communication budget, approximately one-
half was spent on advertising and the other half spent on sponsorship activities.
Highlights of the joint headquarter-national company programme which
was initiated and coordinated by the corporate communications department
included these activities.

1   Information flow to national organizations (NOs).

  • An action manual was prepared by the headquarter's advertising agency
    and sent to all NOs containing advertising and promotion concepts,
    artwork, use of the logo and mascot along with dos and do nots regarding
    use of the official marks.
  • Premium and give-away information.
  • A colouring book for children in the form of a ball featuring Pique, the
    mascot, and using Philip's products (which a number of NOs used in
    their national promotions).

2   Corporate advertising ran in a list of fifty-two major national and inter-
    national newspapers and magazines in the May–June period with themes
    that included: 'Philips on the ball in Mexico', 'Mexican cup fever, World-
    wide by Philips', and 'Philips the team behind every scene in Mexico'.
3   'Good morning World Cup fans, for the next four weeks you'll be watching
    Philips'. . . This was an advertising concept for newspapers that was run
    by corporate communications in international media and by forty National
    Subsidiary Organizations (NOs) in all parts of the world on the day of the
    opening match in Mexico. See Exhibit 13.7 for the advertisements which
    appeared in newspapers in two different countries.
4   Newsflash tapes and publicity releases about the delivery of Philips broad-
    casting equipment to Televisa for coverage of the games was sent to all
    major television networks around the world. The video story received
    considerable pick-up.
5   National organizations not only took advantage of the 'Good Morning
    World Cup' kick-off advertising concept but also ran advertising and staged
    promotions throughout the four-week sports event. Philips Bangladesh was
    the sole sponsor for telecast of all fifty-two matches in that country. Philips
    Belgium ran a tie-in promotion with a sports magazine and Cinzano, a
    fellow World Cup sponsor, involving dealers and consumers in contests to
    win Philips and Cinzano prizes. This was in addition to a major print
    campaign on Philip's involvement in World Cup. Philips Germany took
    advantage of a corporate communications suggestion from their public
    relations agency to stage a promotion involving giant two-metre Philips

Exhibit 13.7   *Good morning World Cup newspaper advertisement*

footballs. These footballs were toured through seventeen cities for people to sign after making a donation to Mexican earthquake victims. This promotion which communicated the message that Philips was an official World Cup sponsor attracted a lot of attention, excitement, and press coverage. These are just a few of the many examples of the manner in which the NOs supported the World Cup sponsorship. A programme of this scope could not be conducted without the central planning, implementation, and coordination received from corporate communications and its advertising and public relations agencies.

Sponsorship can be a local affair

In contrast to such mammoth global enterprises such as the Olympics and the World Cup examples, companies can use sponsorship as a vehicle for achieving certain marketing communication objectives on a much smaller scale. Here is how Premier Bank of the State of Louisiana in the USA capitalized on the 1989 Louisiana Senior Olympics − 'a prestigious event' − to help differentiate itself from competition among the fifty- and -over bank customer. With over 100 branches, the bank used the sponsorship to promote their fify-plus 'premier partners' programme in every market. As a primary sponsor, the bank's logo was printed on the cover of every registration form and its branches became distribution points for local registrations. Additional name recognition was achieved by having the bank's name and logo appear on all press releases, billboards, posters, brochures, newsletters, and T-shirts worn by volunteers. To help promote the games, the bank ran newspaper advertisements in all markets prior to the start of the games. As a primary sponsor, Premier paid $18,000 in cash and provided $2,000 of in-kind services...well worth the attention and interest generated in the fifty-plus Premier Partners' programme and the goodwill created for the bank.[43]

Measuring effectiveness

The same kind of measurement should be used in evaluating sponsorship activities as any other marketing communication programme. Factors to evaluate include:

1 Actual versus estimated media exposure as a result of signage, and paid for advertising.
2 Press releases and feature stories disseminated and actually used by editors.
3 Number of attendees predicted and number actually counted (including method of counting).
4 Number of guests entertained.
5 Feedback from employees, dealers, and suppliers who attended.
6 Pre−post awareness and attitude measures if audience can be isolated.
7 Response to other related promotion activities staged as measured by participant feedback and press coverage.

In all instances where money was expended, the results achieved should be compared with the cost of the activity.

Trade shows and exhibitions

As the USA has been the centre for development of modern advertising up until recent years, West Germany has held that position with respect to trade shows or trade fairs. (The terms 'shows' and 'fairs' are used interchangeably.) Trade shows are a global phenomenon, however, with large and small events taking place in most if not all countries of the world. Paris is the site of the premier trade show for the aerospace industry.[44] The Tokyo Business Show attracted 465,900 visitors.[45] But West Germany is the centre for international fairs. Each year about 100 international trade fairs take place in that country. Approximately 87,000 companies participate, roughly 60 per cent of which are German and 40 per cent are foreign.[46]

A business-to-business marketer like Harris Graphics reported expenditures on international trade shows were three times greater than on print advertising. While the company participates in trade shows in Rio de Janeiro, Caracas, Shanghai, Djakarta, and elsewhere, the budget is primarily spent in Europe and Germany, not only to reach printers in that region but also those who visit from Nigeria, Zimbabwe, South Korea, Ecuador, and other countries.[47]

Anatomy of a trade fair facility

The Dusseldorfer Messen is one of the great trade fair sites of the world. It is located a short distance by public transportation from the centre of Dusseldorf and close to Germany's second largest airport. Dusseldorf itself is a metropolis of 1.5 million people and home of 25,000 companies including 3,000 branches or subsidiaries of foreign multinationals.

Physically, the fair grounds complex is comprised of fifteen exhibit buildings with nearly two million square feet of space. The Messe-Centre is a central facility for information, food, hospitality, an international telecommunications, fair management, and administration. The other major facility is a congress centre with space arrangements for 10 to 1,200, a total seating capacity of 4,400 in twenty rooms, and banquet accomodations to seat and serve up to 1,200. See Exhibit 13.8 for the fair grounds layout.

In 1986, thirty events were held, eight of them were the number one fairs worldwide in their respective industries which included boats, footwear, package production, medical equipment, industrial, safety and occupational health. A total of 20,300 exhibitors participated during the year, 3,700 of which were German and 6,600 foreign from sixty-one countries. The shows attracted 1.4 million visitors from 132 different countries.[48]

Exhibit 13.8 *NOWEA – Dusseldorfer Messen*

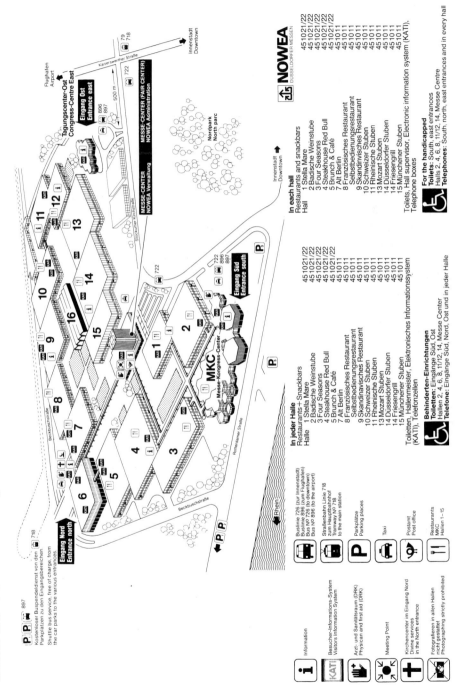

In jeder Halle

Restaurants + Snackbars

Halle
1 Stella Mare 45 10 21/22
2 Badische Weinstube 45 10 21/22
3 Four Seasons 45 10 21/22
4 Steakhouse Red Bull 45 10 21/22
5 Brunch & Café 45 10 21/22
7 Alt Berlin 45 10 11
8 Französisches Restaurant ... 45 10 11
Selbstbedienungsrestaurant . 45 10 11
9 Skandinavisches Restaurant . 45 10 11
10 Schweizer Stuben 45 10 11
11 Rheinische Stuben 45 10 11
13 Mozart Stuben 45 10 11
14 Dusseldorfer Stuben 45 10 11
14 Friesengrill 45 10 11
15 Münchener Stuben 45 10 11

Toiletten, Hallenmeister, Elektronisches Informationssystem (KAT), Telefonzellen

Behinderten-Einrichtungen
Toiletten: Eingänge Süd, Ost
Hallen 2, 4, 6, 8, 11/12, 14, Messe Center
Telefone: Eingänge Süd, Nord, Ost und in jeder Halle

In each hall

Restaurants and snackbars

Hall
1 Stella Mare 45 10 21/22
2 Badische Weinstube 45 10 21/22
3 Four Seasons 45 10 21/22
4 Steakhouse Red Bull 45 10 21/22
5 Brunch & Café 45 10 21/22
7 Alt Berlin 45 10 11
8 Französisches Restaurant ... 45 10 11
Selbstbedienungsrestaurant . 45 10 11
9 Skandinavisches Restaurant . 45 10 11
10 Schweizer Stuben 45 10 11
11 Rheinische Stuben 45 10 11
13 Mozart Stuben 45 10 11
14 Dusseldorfer Stuben 45 10 11
14 Friesengrill 45 10 11
15 Münchener Stuben 45 10 11

Toilets, Hall supervisor, Electronic information system (KAT), Telephone boxes

For the handicapped
Toilets: South, east entrances
Halls 2, 4, 6, 8, 11/12, 14, Messe Centre
Telephones: South, north, east entrances and in every hall

Information

Besucher-Informations-System
Visitors Information System

Arzt- und Sanitätsraum (DRK)
Physician and first aid (DRK)

Meeting Point

Kirchencenter im Eingang Nord
Divine services
in the North entrance

Fotografieren in allen Hallen
nicht gestattet
Photographing strictly prohibited

Busline 726 (zur Innenstadt)
Busline 896 (zum Flughafen)
Bus NO 726 (to downtown)
Bus NO 896 (to the airport)

Straßenbahn Linie 718
zum Hauptbahnhof
Tramway NO 718
to the main station

Parkplätze
Parking places

Taxi

Postamt
Post office

Restaurants
MKC
Hallen 1–15

Kostenloser Buspendeldienst von den
Parkplätzen zu den Eingangsbereichen
Shuttle bus service, free of charge, from
the car parks to the various entrances

Eingang Nord
Entrance north

Eingang Ost
Entrance east
Tagungscenter-Ost
Congress-Centre East

MESSE-CENTER
NOWEA Verwaltung
MESSE-CENTER (FAIR CENTER)
NOWEA Administration

Eingang Süd
Entrance south
MKC
Messe-Kongress-Center

Flughafen
Airport

Innenstadt
Downtown

Nordpark
North parc

Innenstadt
Downtown

Kaiserswerther Straße

Rhein

NOWEA
DÜSSELDORFER MESSEN

Choosing the right fair

Fairs may be classified as either horizontal or vertical. Horizontal fairs will involve many different product categories and therefore have a broad audience appeal. Where a firm's product requires public acceptance or approval, the large horizontal fair is a good choice. The vertical fair promotes a single or related industry category such as boats or printing and paper. In Europe the vertical type of fair is growing in popularity as a major marketing and promotion vehicle for many specific product categories.[49]

To obtain preliminary information on the existence, location, and timing of different shows a good place to start is by contacting an industry association office at home or abroad. International Chamber of Commerce offices are another good place to check. In the USA, the Department of Commerce will have information on most of the major trade shows of the world. *Business America*, a Commerce Department publication regularly lists a schedule of international trade fairs. Host country commercial officers at consulates should be able to provide country-specific information about such events.

After basic information is obtained on the fairs of interest, if time and money permit, a personal inspection is a good idea before a decision to participate is reached. It should be realized that the established major shows will have a large following. To participate, it may be necessary to get on a waiting list for two to three years before an exhibit space opening becomes available.

Objectives and strategies

Reasons for trade show participation in general and attendance at a particular show should be related to the firm's marketing objectives and plans. Among those objectives are:

- to create and maintain an image among prospects and customers
- to establish personal contact with prospects and customers
- to introduce a new product
- to demonstrate non-portable equipment
- to explain technical problems and offer solutions
- to gather intelligence for the design of new or improvement of existing products
- to learn of the latest developments of competitor and complementary products
- to recruit personnel and/or agents and distributors
- and to make sales[50]

A special note about sales at trade shows is needed. Some say that this is where many sales transactions occur. An official at NOWEA in Dusseldorf disagrees with this notion. The principal purpose of participation is to bring buyer and seller together. The visitor (buyer) wants to see what's going on in the field, and come in contact with those who are important in the industry and those who have products (services) of possible interest. However, the buying decision is more likely to be made at home after all the alternatives are considered.[51]

The decision to participate

When it has been determined that international trade show participation will help meet the marketing objectives of the firm, a number of factors should be considered before a decision is reached to participate in a particular show. Factors that should be checked are past attendance figures of customers and prospects, including the reliability of the information obtained: Were your customers there? Will they be there again next year? How many attendees are expected? What are their titles and functions? Where are they from? A common sense approach is to estimate the number of real prospects and customers that, realistically, can be met and talked with; then determine the cost per contact. For estimating costs, all items of expense should be taken into account except personal travel and normal entertainment. The expenses to include are display stand design and construction, shipping, setting up and dismantling, and storing if to be used again. In addition, all the communication materials to be used in advance, during, and for follow-up after the show is over should be estimated. When completed, the cost estimates can be matched up with the prospect and customer contact estimates to determine cost per contact. This is a means of evaluating the merits of the trade show approach against other forms of reaching prospects and customers.[52]

When marketing management determines that international trade fair participation is desirable and the fair or fairs in which to participate have been decided, the job becomes one of formulating communication strategies to support the selling effort in order to maximize the return on this promotion programme.

Communication techniques

Hans Hollander advises that competitors' activities at the trade show in prior years should be studied carefully. Under no circumstances should competitors' efforts be copied.[53]

With respect to the creation of an exhibit, Roth offers this advice:

- make your product the star
- demonstrate
- show product applications
- encourage participation
- hand out good technical literature, not advertising blurbs
- and don't clutter up your exhibit[54]

Another important consideration is a central theme for the exhibit which should relate to the basic communication strategy of the firm. With these factors in mind, booth specifications can be developed for approval by management. When approved, booth design and construction is usually undertaken by a firm which specializes in this type of work. Because a project of this nature can run into thousands of pounds, several design houses are usually asked to bid on the job. When the successful bidder is selected, this firm will need to know all of the requirements to which the exhibit must conform at the particular trade fair. When the design is approved and the construction is completed, shipping may be handled by the design firm, otherwise a freight forwarding company will have to be retained for this purpose. Adequate lead time — often a year or more — is necessary when participating in a trade fair across the ocean and a new exhibit is needed. A timetable should be established for each phase of the project including allowance for unexpected delays.

A determination should be made of all the promotion material which will be needed at the trade fair. This can include fact sheets, specifications, applications, case histories, and questions and answers about the product(s) and the company. The material should project the exhibit theme and be in keeping with the image that the company wishes to project. A timetable for the completion of this work should also be established.

Advanced invitations to visit the booth should be sent to all key customers and prospects. If the product(s) being displayed has a broad base of interest, pre-fair advertising should be considered. A listing and possibly a special feature in the trade show directory are important additional considerations.

Careful track should be kept of all customers and legitimate prospects who visited the booth during the show so that each can be followed up after the event. One of the worst mistakes made by industry on a day-in, day-out basis is the failure to develop a streamlined follow-up procedure regarding contacts made with potential buyers at a trade fair.[55]

Entertainment should be planned in conjunction with the needs of headquarters and any field sales offices. Individual arrangements are up to the sales people in attendance. Other than the entertaining that can be done at the exhibit booth, a hospitality suite at a nearby hotel or possibly a special breakfast or luncheon for key customers and prospects may be in order. It is customary for buyers to receive many invitations to be entertained. Therefore, the timing has to be good or the type of entertainment has to be out of the ordinary or both conditions must prevail. For example, one exhibitor at the Dusseldorfer Messen chartered a Rhine River tourist vessel to tie up alongside the fair grounds. The ship was not only used to house corporate staff but also VIP customers and to entertain other customers and prospects at different occasions during the trade fair.[56]

Evaluation

Various techniques can be used to evaluate the cost-effectiveness of participation. Visual impact and location of the display stand should be evaluated by company staff that attended the show along with the presentations made by competitive organizations.

Attendance records should be kept by means of counting requests for information and business cards received. Informal feedback can be obtained from customers and prospects in follow-up meetings by the field sales organization. Records on customers and prospects who visited the display booth can be compared against official attendance records. However, the number of post-show sales call follow-ups and resulting orders are the ultimate of the value of participation.

Summary

As explained at the beginning of this chapter, sales promotion activities have grown considerably in importance in recent years in various countries throughout the world. A classification framework was provided that not only included direct consumer promotions, instore consumer promotions, and trade promotions but also sponsorships, exhibits and trade shows.

Organizational matters, planning, characteristics and examples of different types of promotions were treated. The examples included food recipe, bank, sales force, sampling, and premium promotions; contests and sweepstakes; tie-in and manufacturer−dealer promotions; and cooperative advertising.

Differences in regulations among nations were pointed out. Sponsorship of both a global and local nature was described. Examples were used to illustrate both types of sponsorship.

The final section in the chapter explained the use of trade shows and exhibitions. This included the importance of researching alternatives in advance, setting objectives, developing strategies, formulating a communication programme, and devising a means of evaluation. In other words, it is necessary to perform all of the tasks called for in a marketing communication plan.

Questions

1 Describe the various types of sales promotion activities and a system for three-way classification.

2 Identify two targets for a manufacturer of branded tea and the objectives,

strategies and means of evaluation that could be included in a sales promotion plan aimed at these targets?

3   What made the JELL-O JIGGLERS promotion a success?

4   Do you think the Nescafé sampling programme could be used successfully in other countries? Why or why not?

5   Are characters like Snoopy, Batman, and Bugs Bunny appropriate for promotions to be conducted in Europe, the Middle East, and Africa?

6   Explain the difference between and merits of contests and sweepstakes.

7   Discuss the advantages and disadvantages of co-op advertising as compared with dealer participation advertising.

8   Explain what sponsorship is and point out what benefits sponsorship can bring to a manufacturer or retailer.

9   Describe the assortment of communication activities that Philips used during its sponsorship of World Cup football. If you were in charge of corporate communications for Philips, would you recommend similar involvement in the next World Cup? Give reasons.

10 List five possible objectives to be realized in participating in a trade fair.

11 Explain what questions should be asked before deciding whether or not entering a specific trade show makes sense.

12 Develop a check list for planning, implementing, and evaluating effectiveness of a programme to participate in a trade show of a product of your choice at a facility like the Dusseldorfer Messen.

Notes

1   The Advertising Association (1990) *Marketing Pocket Book 1991*, London, 81.

2   *Ibid.*

3   Dentsu, Inc. (1989) *Dentsu Japan Marketing/Advertising Yearbook 1990*, Tokyo, pp. 131, 205.

4   *Ibid.*, pp. 208–229.

5   Top services of sales promotion agencies (1989) *Advertising Age*, May S-2, 4, 19.

6   Coen, Robert F. (1989) *Getting Real about Spending Trends for US Advertising and Promotion*. A presentation, ARF 35th Annual Conference, New York, 10–12 April, 5.

7   Fahey, Allison (1989) Shops increasingly crossing the line. *Advertising Age*, 11 May S-11.

8   Berger, Karen (1990) *The Rising Importance of Point-of-Purchase Advertising in the Marketing Mix*. Paper delivered at the Point-of-Purchase Advertising Institute, Chicago, 2 October.

9   Philip Morris Companies, Inc. (1990) *Company News*, 14.

10 The reggie award winners (1989) *Potentials in Marketing*, April, 37−38.

11 Robinson, William (1989) The best promotions of 1988. *Marketing Communications*, May, 66.

12 Nestlé Belgilux (1987) Presentation, May.

13 Pepsi-Cola Mexicana (1991) Presentation, 15 January.

14 Shimp, Terence A. (1990) *Promotion Management and Marketing Communications*, 2nd edn, The Dryden Press, Chicago, p. 585.

15 Russell, Thomas and Verrill Glenn (1986) *Otto Kleppner's Advertising Procedures*, 9th edn, Prentice Hall, Englewood Cliffs, NJ, pp. 346−349.

16 Bachenheimer, Paula (1987) A look at a winning marketing tool. *Direct Marketing*, September, 30.

17 Russell, *op. cit.*, 349.

18 Berger, *op. cit.*, 18.

19 Peebles, Dean M. and Ryans, John K. Jr. (1984) *Management of International Advertising*, Allyn and Bacon, Inc., Boston, p. 185.

20 Peebles, *op. cit.*, 185−187.

21 Cudlipp, Edyth (1983) Reaching the international market on $100,000 a year. *Advertising World*, Oct/Nov 6, 8, 10, 12.

22 This example is from Dean M. Peebles and John K. Ryans Jr (1984) *Management of International Advertising*, Boston, Allyn and Bacon Inc, pp. 188−192 and is reproduced with permission of Allyn and Bacon.

23 Peebles, *op. cit.*, 188−192.

24 Hall, Dave and Bantick, Keith (1987) Sales promotion: learning the global language/hard sell kept simple. *Marketing*, 19 February, 40−45.

25 *Adweek* (1989) The awards of excellence, New York, p. 12.

26 International Marketing and Promotion, London.

27 The Global Media Commission (1988) *Sponsorship: Its Role and Effects*, International Advertising Association, New York September, p. 4.

28 The Advertising Association, *op. cit.*, 96.

29 Walley, Wayne and Donation, Scot (1989) That right hook: tie-ins are key to sports' value. *Advertising Age*, 12 June, 3, 75.

30 Shimp, *op. cit.*, 505.

31 Adapted from Shimp, *op. cit.*, 507, and The Global Media Commission, 2.

32 The Advertising Association, *op. cit.*, 96.

33 El Corte Ingles (1984) *Annual Report 1983*, Madrid, 34.

34 El Corte Ingles (1990) *Memoria 1989*, p. 25 and El Corte Ingles (1991) *1990 Annual Report*, p. 35.

35 The Global Media Commission, *op. cit.*, 8, 9.

36 The Global Media Commission, *op. cit.*, 4.

37 Olympic sponsorship: Kodak's global game plan (1989) Marketing Communications, January, 24−25.

38 Morrow, David, J. (1989) How to quit losing in the Olympics. *Fortune*,

24 April, 265–274.

39 Hackney, Holt (1991) Sports, Inc: changing image. *Financial World*, 22 January, 48–49.

40 Walley, *op. cit.*, 3, 75.

41 Hong, Peter and Phillips, Dennis (1990) Look out Wimbledon, here comes Leipzig. *Business Week*, 24 September, 54.

42 Corporate Marketing Communications, *World Cup Mexico' 86*, *General Sponsorship Review*, Philips, Eindhoven.

43 Single, Jennifer (1989) The mature market: sponsoring senior Olympics. *Bank Marketing*, August, 37, 39.

44 Humbert, Richard P. (1987) Trade fairs are an excellent way to take advantage of the growing opportunities in Western Europe. *Business America*, 21 December, 5.

45 Dentsu, *op. cit.*, 220.

46 Schafer, Joachim (1987) Foreign trade shows are a timely way to cut the trade deficit. *Marketing News*, 20 May, 12.

47 Cudlipp, *op. cit.*, 10, 12.

48 Düsseldorfer Messe Gesellschaft mbH (1991) *Annual Report*, Nowea, Dusseldorf.

49 Humbert, *op. cit.*, 3.

50 Roth, Robert F. (1982) *International Marketing Communications*, Crain Books, Chicago, pp. 214, 215.

51 Krumbiegel, Dieter W. (1987) Personal presentation at Dusseldorfer Messen, May.

52 Roth, *op. cit.*, 208–214.

53 Hollander, Hans (1985) Presentation on international trade shows, Rye Brook, New York, October.

54 Roth, *op. cit.*, 216–217.

55 Hollander, *op. cit.*

56 Krumbiegel, *op. cit.*

14 *Public relations and packaging*

Introduction

Along with sales promotion, certain public relations activities and packaging can contribute significantly to the effectiveness of a marketing communications programme. It is for this reason that these two topics are treated in this chapter.

Public relations

Public relations has gained importance over the years and today has become a function of major significance reporting directly to the office of the chief executive in many international businesses. It is or should be 'objective oriented' in nature, supporting 'the organization's business goals whether they be marketing, social responsibility, public policy, manufacturing, or human resources'.[1]

Before delving directly into the role of public relations in marketing it may be useful to reflect on the breadth and depth of the field today as viewed by US leaders and experts in the field.

Like advertising, the practice of modern day public relations appears to have its roots in the USA though the function is now performed at the same or higher level of sophistication in many countries in Europe, Japan, Canada, Mexico and elsewhere. Textbooks are replete with reasons why it is difficult to establish a universal definition. Without labouring the subject this definition, written by Dr Rex F. Harlow, which sets forth the principal components of the practice of public relations is useful:

> Public relations is a distinctive management function which helps establish and maintain mutual lines of communication, understanding, acceptance, and coop- eration between an organization and its publics; involves the management of problems or issues; helps management to keep informed on and responsive to public opinion; defines and emphasizes the responsibility of management to serve the public interest; helps management keep abreast of and effectively utilize change, serving as an early warning system to anticipate trends; and uses research and sound and ethical communication techniques as its principal tools.[2]

The term public relations is actually misleading because there are in fact many publics to be dealt with as indicated by this list:

1   Customers
2   General public
3   Stockholders
4   Government
5   Media
6   Suppliers
7   Employees
8   Activist groups
9   Financial community
10 Distributors

In compiling this list Terpstra and Sarathy point out that the 'importance of any particular group will vary from country to country', and that 'the firm's level of involvement in a market will also affect the publics (with which) it must deal.'[3]

In dealing with these diverse publics, public relations practitioners engage in such activities as policy planning, crisis management, corporate identity, employee communications and consumer affairs as well as community, investor and government relations and marketing support. (These are the ten chapter titles in Bill Cantor's book *Experts in Action*.)[4]

The major public relations functions (and tools) emphasized by corporate communications departments, outside agencies and counselling firms include:

- Opinion research
- Legislative and competitive intelligence
- Counselling top management
- Communication policies
- Liaison with public officials
- News releases and media relations
- House publications
- Speeches, scripts and interviews
- Graphics and films
- Shows, exhibits and special events
- Booklets and brochures
- Product/service publicity
- Financial reports[5]

Public relations, as revealed in this brief overview, has become an essential function for organizations of all sizes and types, domestic and international, vital for survival and growth. But rather than treat all aspects of public relations, because this text is about marketing communications, attention will be concentrated on the relationship and coordination of these two functions.

Organizing the public relations function

Public relations is considered first and foremost as a centralized, corporate function providing product publicity and related services to the firm's operating divisions and departments. Marketers may question the location of the function in the organization. There are three valid reasons for this approach:

1 By concentrating the function in a single corporate department, a more experienced and professional staff can be maintained to serve the needs of the organization.
2 Because public relations assignments and workloads will vary among departments their needs are better and more efficiently served by a central staff.
3 The press is too important an audience to remove from the control of a central department.

This same line of reasoning can be applied to organizations of all types including the multinational with subsidiary operations in different regions and/or nations of the world which have their own public relations units. In this case, there should be a linkage of all subsidiary public relations units with corporate headquarters for company-wide guidance and coordination.

Even if individual public relations practitioners are assigned to marketing units, they should report professionally through the public relations chain of command.

Inside or outside counsel

With respect to the question of inside staff or outside counsel, that is a decision for management. If the company is large and has international subsidiaries, an inside staff is a must. The size of the staff would be dependent on the nature and scope of assignments for marketing, other departments served, and the corporation as a whole. It is quite likely that the large organization will have internal staff and also retain outside counsel. For example, product publicity is handled internally while financial public relations is the responsibility of an outside firm under the supervision of the head of public relations for the company. In some cases, the internal staff may be held to a minimum and the actual public relations work is conducted by one or more agencies on the outside.

Counselling

It is possible that many business people will equate public relations with publicity and promotion as the primary roles in supporting the marketing effort. This is not the case, however, among enlightened managers. A critical role of public relations is to guide the business and its marketings programmes through 'the maze of difficult-to-understand, volatile, and decisive public opinions' that can 'result in public criticism. . .even cancellation of product or advertising'[6]. . .and possibly the survival of a business. There is good reason for this, in the USA anyway, because traditionally the relationship between business and government has been adversarial. Since the Second World War the growth of consumerism, environmentalism, and change in treatment of minorities has had a profound effect on the environment for business. These developments have led to new legislation and laws relating to air, water, women, blacks, packaging, lending, housing, and advertising. . .and the list is not complete. Business may operate by doing 'everything they can within existing laws to maximize profit'. . .and retain a large, costly legal staff to operate in this fashion. The alternative is to recognize that 'the spirit of the law, and even the spirit of public opinion, are at least as important to marketing as technical adherence to the law'. If top management adopts this view and is concerned with adjusting policy to the social, political, and environmental issues, public relations will have an important role to play in counselling on short- and long-range business and marketing plans. Here are some ways in which public relations counsel can help:

1 *Business development and acquisitions* Advising management of alcohol and cigarette companies 'on the advisability of getting into areas that are generally considered more socially useful'.
2 *Advertising* Counselling management on the type of television programming in terms of taste and appropriateness for the intended audience.
3 *Other marketing mix considerations* Counselling marketing management on such matters as 'price in relation to value, product proliferation without significant innovation, guarantees and warranties, ethnic sensitivities, and misleading promotions'.
4 *Consumer complaints* Give the public relations staff the responsibility for handling these matters.

With the potential of having public interest 'make or break virtually any marketing decision', a close working relationship is needed between marketing and public relations.

The ability of public relations to perform these critical counselling functions is dependent on the person or persons given this responsibility. Among the talents needed. . .which are not easy to come by. . .are:

• a high degree of contemporary awareness
• sophistication in government relations and affairs
• ability to use public opinion research effectively

- tough mindedness coupled with a high degree of social consciousness
- and enough intelligence to win the respect of some of the smartest people in the business, the marketing executives.[7]

Having found or developed this kind of talent, the public relations counsellor must have the support and backing of the chief executive officer to carry out the counselling function. (As the reader can surmise, the counselling function is not limited to marketing but encompasses the organization's interaction with many if not all of the publics previously identified.)

Social responsibility

In addition to the counselling function, public relations work can either have an indirect or direct effect on product and service marketing. Being a good neighbour, demonstrating corporate citizenship, sponsoring programmes that benefit some segment of society, speaking out forthrightly on issues that effect business operations all contribute to the stature and reputation of the firm which will indirectly aid the marketing effort... providing there is an effective programme of communications to inform constituent publics.

When it comes to programmes of social responsibility La Caixa deserves special mention. Isidro Faine Casas, Director General, A. Ejecutivo, provided this description:

> Caja de Ahorros y Pensiones de Barcelona, 'La Caixa', the institution, resulting from the merger undertaken on 27 July 1990, between Caja de Pensiones para la Vejez y de Ahorros de Cataluña y Baleares and Caja de Ahorros de Barcelona, is a Spanish financial institution that has a unique mission of social responsibility. The merger is now fully consolidated and, as a result of it, La Caixa is the first financial institution in Spain and the second savings bank in Europe. This responsibility emanates from its non-profit, beneficent and social nature, whose main purpose is to encourage savings and to finance economical activity, and also to return the profits to the society through community projects. The budget for 1992 community projects amounted to $72.4 million, and the breakdown of its operations is as follows:

Cultural programmes
- Libraries   120
- Cultural centres, exhibition halls and cultural houses   94
- Science museum (visitors)   356,779
- Science tent: travelling museum (visitors)   209,704
- Art, photography, science and literature exhibitions (visitors)   1,348,739
- Concerts, recitals, lectures and music courses   198

Educational programmes
- Participating students   675,637

Social programmes

- Attendance 146,237
- Own and associated recreation clubs for elderly 97

Fellowship programme to extend studies abroad (1982—1991) 450[8]

No wonder La Caixa is the first financial institution in Spain.

Corporate identity

One collective corporate effort that can have a direct benefit on the marketing programmes of a company concerns corporate identity. That's why companies like Canon, Coca-Cola, IBM, and Pepsi-Cola spend millions of dollars in the market places of the world on signage. The idea of presenting a uniform appearance everywhere a company operates and is seen by its publics is believed to have a synergistic effect on its overall communication programme. A case in point is the corporate identity programme of KLM Royal Dutch Airlines. With a network of 150 destinations or more in seventy nine countries and a moderate communications budget, KLM found itself with an array of signage, literature, and in-country advertising programmes that lacked a common identity. To obtain the maximum impact for the funds allocated for these purposes, it was decided that a single 'house style' or corporate identity should be created and that a corporate identity steering group should be formed to implement and monitor the corporate identity programme. The result was the adoption of a single logo, signature line, and colour scheme to be used in all forms of communication. This is shown in Exhibit 14.1. (The standard colours are white and blue for the logo: white on blue background or blue on white background.)

Visual standards were established for planes and offices (external and internal), dress for customer service personnel, printed matter, and mail and mass media campaigns. The concept was based on one approach, one face, one voice.[9]

Exhibit 14.1 *The KLM logo and signature line. Reproduced by permission of KLM*

In commenting on house style, Mr J.F.A. de Soet, President KLM, Amstelveen stated, 'One essential element in competition is a strong, immediately recognizable world-wide image.' He further defined (house style) design as:

> ...a strategic discipline of the first order and a primary marketing tool in a fiercely increasing global competition. For the outside world, design is the only visible definition of the corporation, its name, its face, its personality, its philosophy, its values, its products, and its people...[10]

The public relations/publicity plan

As for direct support of marketing, the public relations/publicity plan should be an integral part of the company's overall marketing programme. This plan should have its own set of objectives that are linked to the marketing goals. Other elements of the plan include the strategies and tactics to achieve the objectives along with the appropriate evaluative procedures. Here is an example of publicity objectives and strategies in support of the marketing effort, and the side-by-side manner in which to set them up.

	Objective	*Strategy*
1	To prepare the way for the sales call.	Provide information about the company and its products.
2	To generate sales leads.	Develop and place stories and case histories on product performance.
3	To become recognized as an industry leader.	Attain third party (editorial) endorsement. Maintain an open channel of communication on industry developments.
4	To 'humanize' the organization.	Obtain news coverage of key personnel.[11]

These strategies are implemented and objectives are realized by disseminating information, called publicity, about a company and its products or services. One authority described the work of a 'publicist' as matching newsworthy developments of a company to the 'media's mandate'. This simply means presenting information of interest to readers, viewers, or listeners.[12]

As pointed out by Jim Sill, 'Editorial space is solely dependent on the perceived interest of a given readership as interpreted by the editor.' Since editors select material based on its newsworthiness, it is important for the person in charge of publicity to tell the difference between genuine news and other types of communication such as promotional material. The bottom line is that (technical) publicity carries the implied endorsement of the publication which carries the article and is one of the most economical communication tools available to industrial equipment (and other) marketers.[13]

News sources

Where does news about a product or service come from? From research and development, quality control, manufacturing, sales representatives, distributors, dealers, customers of all types. It is not found at the advertising agency and it doesn't just come to the publicist; he or she must search it out.

Types of publicity

Publicity stories are called different names and written for different purposes. The *news release* for general circulation will run one to two pages and contain factual information. A summary lead is common, answering these questions: who, what, where, when, and why. Often the release will be accompanied by a black and white photograph with caption. The news may be about a special development, event, or change in a person's status, e.g. a promotion or new appointment. See Exhibit 14.2 for an example of a news release.

In contrast, the *feature story* is a detailed explanation about a product, process, trend, case history, or profile of a company which an editor either believes is newsworthy or of special interest to readers.[14] Other names for publicity stories are roundups, 'how to' stories, and forecasts.[15]

The press conference

The work of the publicist does not end with the written word. When a story breaks a *press conference* will be held. This event has to be carefully planned and executed in terms of who will be invited, who will speak, what will be said, where the event will take place, what amenities will be included (coffee, tea, food, etc.), and what information will be distributed at the end of the conference (photos, fact sheets, releases, special stories, etc.) This information is normally presented in a press kit for attendees. Press conferences are held to announce a merger or acquisition, introduce a new product or process, open a new plant, or impart information about some other major newsworthy event.

Timing

Publicity like other marketing communication activities require considerable lead time in order to maximize opportunities for placement of feature and news stories. One authority recommends working as much as six months back from the time a feature story might be run by a publication. For weeklies, stories should be prepared up to six weeks in advance and dailies prefer up to two weeks advanced notice.[16] For late breaking items, the lead time can be

Exhibit 14.2 *Example of the first page of a two-page news release. Reproduced by permission of Prodigy*

PRODIGY®

Interactive Personal Service

Prodigy Services Company
445 Hamilton Avenue
White Plains, NY 10601

For press information, call
Marti Griffin (914) 993-3412

It's All In There!

PRODIGY TO LAUNCH EXPANDED FINANCIAL NEWS DATABASE

NEW YORK, November 19 -- The PRODIGY service, the nation's most-popular home computer network, announced today that it will broadly expand its news content to include an in-depth financial news database. The database, which begins electronic "publication" on December 1, will contain thousands of articles and information from respected business news sources of the Dow Jones News Service, including Barron's and The Wall Street Journal. It will be available to all of the PRODIGY service's 1.1 million members at no additional charge.

The financial news database includes news on U.S. and Canadian companies, industries, U.S. government agencies, financial markets, the stock market and the economy. News stories will be updated continuously from 7:30 a.m. to 7:00 p.m. every business day. All stories and columns are easily reached through a variety of indexes, such as industry or news group. Members can also search for a particular company by name or stock symbol.

"This is great news for our members who are investors," said Prodigy Senior Vice President Henry Heilbrunn. "They now have access to much of the information available to professional money managers, but at a price affordable to almost every home."

The PRODIGY service costs $12.95 monthly (or less in an annual subscription) with no connect-time charges. More than a third of all PRODIGY service members regularly use its financial services. (There are hundreds of other information and transactional features.) "Our members asked for more in financial information, and we're giving it to them," said Heilbrunn.

(more)

shortened. If placing publicity across borders, the lead time would have to be extended.

Costing out the publicity programme

Just because publicity receiving placement in the media is 'free', does not preclude the need for a budget. It should be evident that there are a number of charges to be incurred in the process of developing a publicity programme. These include time and overhead charges for the person (people) working on the project, whether they are company personnel or suppliers of publicity services. Under the latter circumstances, time charges are usually multiplied by a factor of two to three to cover overhead, operating expenses and profit. If working with an independent contractor, a fee is usually negotiated. For example, the fee for a two-page article written by a technical specialist might range from US $2,000 to $4,000 depending on the number of rewrites needed. Out-of-pocket expenses may or may not be marked up when billed to a client. But the costs of camera-ready art, photos, graphs, schematics, etc. must be included when costing out a publicity programme.[17] In contrast, for advertising campaigns, in addition to the out-of-pocket charges mentioned above, there is the cost of space or time.

Examples

Here are three examples to demonstrate how a public relations programmes, including publicity, can produce results for product marketers.

The first is about a programme for a cookie, cracker, and snack manufacturer that responded to a major health concern in the USA which involved cholesterol raising ingredients in products, particularly highly saturated palm and coconut oils. (This is an issue — which a public relations counsellor could have been monitoring — that became sufficiently important among activists and consumers in general in order to prompt action on the part of the manufacturer.) The response to this consumer concern was the reformulation of all products to eliminate the potentially harmful oils and animal fats along with new labelling on packages that gave complete nutritional information.

To communicate these changes a comprehensive public relations programme was developed by the company personnel and its outside public relations counsel with four objectives:

1   To demonstrate the company's interest in a major health issue.
2   To heighten consumer awareness of the role of tropical oils and animal fats in raising cholesterol levels.
3   To communicate the benefits of using the company's reformulated products.

4   To make the company's initiatives known among health professionals, nutritionists and the medical community.

The public relations programme consisted of two phases. The first was to announce the reformulation of its products. The second was to sustain interest in the story as the company's reformulated products flowed into and through the channel of distribution to the grocers shelves all across the country.

The initial announcement was made on a popular and widely watched nationwide morning television show. This was followed by news coverage via wire service to all major print and broadcast media across the country. The effort generated many requests for additional information nationwide and prompted visits by representatives of major electronic media to company headquarters to interview executives and observe the new products being produced. The results of this initial campaign was coverage of the story on television news shows of three networks following the initial morning show announcement, and in newspapers by a number of major dailies and a syndicated column that ran in over 1,000 papers nationwide.

Following the initial announcement phase, a variety of public relations techniques were put to work to sustain interest among the general public and to reach the health professionals who influence consumer choice. For this purpose a press kit containing a booklet on cholesterol, fat intake, and tips on healthy snacking was produced with an accompanying release which offered copies to the public and instructions for ordering. Other elements of the press kit included a feature release on the reformulation story and a 'backgrounder' on the company itself. The booklet was also publicized in a mailing to food editors of 500 dailies across the country.

In addition to this material, a well-known health expert and author of a book on cholesterol was retained to discuss this health issue and present the company's programme on television interviews and to lifestyle editors of major consumer magazines.

Supplementing the work of the doctor in spreading the story were tours made to twenty-four cities in the USA on the part of two registered dieticians to give print and broadcast interviews on the subject of cholesterol and the major reformulation programme of the company.

To reach the healthcare community, information was disseminated to pub-lications that were read by nutritionists, nurses, and other professionals. A special mailing of the cholesterol booklet was made to the full membership of the dieticians association in the USA. This was supplemented by attendance at the annual pediatrics association conference in order to have doctors sample company products and be offered the booklet for distribution to patients.

The results, which were carefully monitored, included 7,500 requests for booklets from consumers, numerous letters and requests for booklets from health professionals, 680 articles or broadcasts in addition to the 1,000 features as a result of the syndicated column story. It was estimated that over 100 million people were exposed to the company's reformulated product programme, thereby developing broadscale goodwill and product differentiation from competitors.[18]

In this second example, a first-ever public relations programme for the leading manufacturer of shoe care products is explained.

Even though the company dominated the shoe care business in the US with 90 per cent share of market in the principal retail outlets, it had been 'hard pressed to find new avenues for significant sales growth'. A research study revealed a major problem in that people under forty were far less likely to shine their shoes than their elder counterparts. However, it was also found that this group was 'very concerned with making a good first impression, particularly in business situations'. This contradiction sparked the idea behind and objective for the public relations effort: to raise the level of awareness of the general public, particularly among younger people, of how well-polished shoes affected one's image.

With the help of an image consultant firm, a test was devised, (actually two, one for men and one for women) to test their potential for getting ahead. Polished shoes were only one of several criteria in the test that makes up a professional image. The purpose of the test was to establish a person's image index. The test was intended to attract interest in a light vein and at the same time get people thinking about their appearance.

A press kit was prepared that included the image indexes, male and female, along with an explanation including the use of experts in the field who developed the tests. Use of experts lent credibility to the programme. Kits were distributed to newspapers and feature editors throughout the USA.

In the first three-month period it was estimated that seventeen million impressions were generated. For a programme like this to be successful, the right idea is needed as evidenced by the initial response.

Follow-up efforts were planned for women's service magazines and for vertical publications in the shoe, apparel, and leather industries. Future efforts were planned for target groups like college students.

The payoff anticipated for this programme was increased sales which management felt would come about in time.

For a company that dominates an industry but is experiencing no growth in sales, a public relations programme like the one just explained can be infinitely more powerful in stimulating new business than a comparable effort for the same money in an advertising campaign.[19] In either case, the idea behind the campaign must be extraordinary!

The third example involves the launching of the Polaroid Spectra Camera. This was a major new product launch for a company whose instant cameras had experienced declining sales in the 1980s in the face of the increasing popularity of the 35 mm camera and the corner developing store. The Spectra represented the development of a complex new photographic system comprised of camera, film, accessories, and laser copy prints and enlargements for people 'who appreciate the difference between a photograph and snap shot'. The company wanted to make this new development as popular as Madonna. . . get it on covers of magazines. . . recreate the Polaroid 'take, see, share' experience. The introductory strategy was to create a newsworthy event, build activities around it, impress Wall Street analysts, and appeal to various audiences, industry opinion leaders, influencers, dealers, and employees.

The comprehensive campaign included a mixture of public relations, product publicity, special events, brochures, fact sheets, and a vigorous introductory and follow-up consumer and trade advertising effort. As for public relations, which took a leading role at the outset, these events and activities took place in the following order:

1 Pre-publicity. The concept was introduced to dealers at the photo industry's annual convention. The idea was to 'tease', not show, make a promise that the new development would not be a disappointment.
2 Advanced key media contact. Top executives of four key camera publications were flown to Puerto Rico to be entertained and introduced to the Spectra. The camera was demonstrated, after which the editors were given the opportunity to try the new system under a variety of conditions. Secrecy was pledged until the introductory date. Result — at the time of the introduction the camera received rave notices from all publications.
3 Press party introduction. The location selected was the Century Plaza in Los Angeles. Polaroid's CEO was the kick-off speaker to press representatives from all across the country. A roof-top luncheon followed with a true Polynesian Village motif. A giant three-storey model of the Spectra was unveiled. Media guests were invited to tour and observe a demonstration of the camera's new technology inside the giant camera. Glamorous press kits and cameras with all the features were distributed to the guests for trial in the Polynesian roof top village. The event was 'high tech, colourful, Hollywood all the way!'
4 Post launch. The giant model was shipped to New York to reside between the World Trade Towers over the Fourth of July and Statute of Liberty celebration in an exhibit built around a 'portraits of liberty' theme. The New York press party launch provided the facts in a surrounding with plenty of 'hoop-la' including a Dixieland jazz band.
5 Opinion leaders. One thousand opinion leaders. . . people with stature and visibility were identified and sent samples of the new Spectra Camera.

The multimillion dollar launch of the Spectra combined all forms of marketing communications. The introductory advertising campaign was spearheaded by minute television commercials which ran on all three major networks at the same time at 9pm in the evening. A six-page insert in weekly and monthly magazines appeared...high visibility advertising, all with the same look and feel. But much of the initial excitement for the new product was created by the public relations events just outlined.

The result was extraordinary press and television coverage from editors all across the country. One leading newspaper even published an article on (Polaroid's) 'manipulating the media'.[20]

A glimpse of the public relations practice around the world

Judging from the attendance at the International Public Relations Association World Congress in 1988 with 700 delegates from forty-five countries including China, the Soviet Union, and Hungary, interest in this field is truly of an international magnitude.

As for the state of the art, this varies considerably from country to country and from region to region. While at different stages of development, the 'situation, mission, and purpose of public relations is the same'. The sophistication of the profession is similar in Europe, Japan and the USA where managements have recognized its value and importance. In many countries in different Third World regions the economic and political conditions have not been conducive to sophisticated public relations.[21]

Japan

It is reported that in Japan, where the state of the art is well-advanced, the emphasis has switched away from 'fire fighting' or defensive public relations. Marketing and corporate public relations activities are now in the forefront with particular emphasis on information gathering, corporate and association activities, event and special facility sponsorship, and corporate identity.

Information gathering underlies any successful communication programme. It is of vital importance to obtain a reading on public opinions and attitudes toward the firm and its product and services, both for planning and evaluating purposes. Corporate publishing has attracted a considerable amount of attention by those companies who find it enhances their prestige and image. One example is the Dentsu book published in English on the advertising and marketing business which has been referred to in many instances in this text. In so doing, Dentsu becomes the 'voice of authority' on these functions which, of course, is their business as well. Similarly, the Johnson Corporation published a special book on combating household mould, a major problem that home-owners face each summer in Japan. Again, they become the voice of authority on the subject. This paves the way for the sale of the products they manufacture to combat this problem.

Industry associations have been stepping up their public relations efforts to 'promote sales and improve the public image'. For example, the National Milk Promotion Association sponsored a symposium on 'what to eat for victory' at the opening of the Olympic Games in Seoul.

Event sponsorship has been widely engaged in by Japanese companies. The Mitsui Group of thirty firms held a drama festival (Mitsui Festival 1988) in Tokyo by inviting foreign groups to perform modern dramas. Kirin established a 'Heartland Beer Jungle' which is a space in Tokyo decorated like a primitive jungle that became a 'trendy' location to enjoy the sponsor's product.

Corporate Identity (CI) has become a major programme for many Japanese companies. CI programmes were instigated not only to improve visual and mind images but also to improve image in terms of modernization and internationalization in response to 'changing and expanding business conditions'.[22]

Elsewhere in the world
In the UK, public relations has also realized substantial growth according to Seitel and is the location of the headquarters of the world's largest public relations agency, the Sandwick Group. This organization bills more than $71 million in public relations fees and has about 700 staff members.

On the Continent, the practice is not as fully developed except in possibly France, Germany, and the low countries. Seitel points to the complications of language, culture, and traditions when attempting to plan cross-border public relations campaigns.

In the Americas, the practice in Canada is on a par with the USA and is also well developed in Mexico. In other Latin American countries the practice can be inhibited by government control of media.

In Africa, the type of governments, many authoritarian, and general economic and cultural conditions have posed a constraint on all types of marketing communications including public relations.

Language barriers and government control of media are two of the biggest problems facing cross-border public relations' programming in many parts of the world.[23]

For companies that have the need for this function on an international scale, the options for suppliers of this service are essentially the same as with advertising. A firm may retain a single international agency to plan and execute public relations programmes in all markets served, employ a network of affiliated but independent agencies, use a regional agency to serve its needs in parts of the world, or hire separate agencies to perform the function in each country where needed. The argument against using a single multinational agency is that its offices in various countries may not possess the same level of expertise and proficiency. The argument for is based on the concept that through coordination and interaction of staff members in different offices, superior public relations services can be uniformly provided.

In terms of types of public relations services, environmental issues, crisis preparedness, executive training, financial information, and corporate developments involving acquisitions and mergers are matters that lend themselves to a global public relations approach. This can be dependent on the form of client organization, central or decentralized. However, when it comes to support of product marketing programmes, multinational clients are likely to let individual country subsidiaries manage their own public relations support activities.[24]

Packaging

Size, shape, protection, convenience, communication, and conformance are factors to consider in developing effective packaging.

Products destined for consumption in industry to provide other goods will call for packaging that will ensure satisfactory protection from the point of manufacture to the point of use. Information contained on the package (or crate) for industrial equipment should plainly show name, origin, net/gross weight, cube, content, and any cautionary information about the product and its handling. Products destined for personal consumption in the home and elsewhere and certain types of office products have more complex packaging requirements.

Before proceeding with a discussion of the variables mentioned at the outset, a brief explanation of the different aspects of packaging will be given. Labels consist of words, illustrations, and symbols (trademarks) that go on packages. Packages may be made of glass, plastic, metal, paperboard, or other flexible material such as cloth. Plastic and paperboard products can have overwraps or inner liners to enhance product protection and the appearance of the product. Sometimes the packaging material is a laminate of plastic, aluminum foil, and/or paper as in the case of individual servings of instant coffee. This form of packaging is also used to contain and protect a variety of liquid products such as apple juice. See Exhibit 14.3. Other products sold in these containers range from whole milk to wines and water. The milk is processed at very high temperatures before filling. This process in combination with the properties of the Tetra Brik Pak package eliminate the need for refrigeration until after the package is opened. The label can be printed directly on the surfaces of the package or printed on paper and then affixed to the sides and/or top of the container.

Size and shape

If the item to be marketed does not have a fixed size and shape as in the case of a particular model of computer or television set, size and shape of package

Exhibit 14.3   *Packaging to protect liquid product. Reproduced by permission of Apple & Eve, Roslyn, New York*

become important matters for consideration. For example, the most popular Fab detergent package size is a pouch for single usage. More than 60 per cent of the market in Guatemala is accounted for by sales in the 409 size.[25] See Exhibit 14.4.

Exhibit 14.4   *Fab detergent single usage pouch. Reproduced by permission of Colgate-Palmolive (Central America) SA, Guatemala City, Guatemala*

In the USA the most popular size of the same product is likely to be one pound (454 grams) or more. Washing habits and income levels in Guatemala and the USA are not the same. The majority of washing done in the USA is in automatic washing machines whereas much of the wash in Guatemala is still done by hand. As Terpstra points out, 'Low incomes usually mean low usage rates and small purchase amounts.'[26] The implication is that the package size(s) should be in keeping with the kind of usage, frequency of use, product acceptance, and ability to pay when developing packaging plans across borders. Another example of the difference in package sizes is with razor blades. In some countries they are sold individually; in others they are sold by the package.[27]

When considering shapes of package goods, there are at least two considerations. One concerns aesthetics. What shape is most pleasing to customers and prospects? While costs, filling and handling requirements, and source of supply are factors to be taken into account, within these constraints which shape is preferred? Tall and thin, short and broad, cylindrical, square? Many options are available, particularly when plastic is the packaging material.

Among other concerns to packaged goods marketers is the availability and dimensions of shelf space in stores where the product is to be sold. If the average shelf height is ten inches (25.4 centimetres), package height must conform to this constraint. Another matter of concern to retailers is lateral space. It is at a premium, particularly in the modern super or hypermarket; therefore, narrower packages are preferred to wider ones.

Habits and homes of shoppers should also be considered. Where consumers walk instead of drive to stores and shop daily instead of weekly, smaller packages are more acceptable than larger ones. The space available for storage in homes should also be taken into account.

Protection

With respect to protection, there are two aspects to consider: protection from breakage or damage as the product moves through the channel of distribution, and preserving the contents from possible harm such as flavour deterioration. In the former case, the protection is provided by outerwrap and the shipping case in which the product(s) is placed. In the latter case, protection is provided by the materials and technique by which the product is packed. Instant coffee (other than individual servings) is packed in glass. In addition the jar is likely to be filled with inert gas to displace the air (oxygen) in the jar before filled with product. This will prevent the oils in the coffee from going rancid and moisture pick-up before the jar is opened. This is also the reason where there is a foil seal at the top of the jar.

Another protection factor is climate. Different climates necessitate different forms of protection. For example, saltine crackers in a northern climate are usually packed in a paperboard carton with a plastic outer and inner wrap. In the tropics this product is normally found packed in tin to prevent moisture penetration and insect infestation.

Convenience

This is a factor with a number of dimensions. Among them are ease of opening and closing a package; also dispensing. Is a screw cap or flip top opening preferred? Should a metal can have a self-opening device? If so, what type is more convenient? If a glass container is large, consideration should be given to a shape that has a waist instead of straight sides so that it is easier to grip. If a liquid, should a squeeze bottle (tube) be used, or is a pump device preferred. Should the product be sold in bulk form to be measured out or should the product come in pre-measured packets? If the product is a liquid bath soap to be used in the shower, how would consumers respond to an attached plastic loop to hang the container on the hot or cold tap? Should the product's closure be a screw cap or would a flip top which can be actuated with one hand be preferred? For a single serving product, would there be an advantage in packing the ingredients in a container from which it can also be consumed? These are a sampling of questions which those involved in packaging should be asked and have answers for.

Conveniences of the type just introduced will add value to a product, help set it apart from competition. Marketing communicators should be particularly interested in these aspects of packaging for the differential advantages which can be realized through communications, purchase, and use. For example, Birkel (Germany) introduced an 'instant' noodle soup which is prepared by the addition of boiling water. To add convenience, it is packaged in a plastic container which becomes the cup from which the soup is consumed. When Henkel entered the toothpaste market in Europe the need was felt for more than a unique product formulation. It was the first company to use a package with a pump dispenser.[28] Most of the convenience features mentioned will add to the price of the product. For this reason, the costs and benefits of the alternatives must be thoroughly researched before decisions are reached.

Communications

When it comes to communication, the domain of the international marketing communicator, there are also many considerations to face. It becomes a multi-dimensional design problem involving size (dimensions), shape, colours, illustrations and words. Size(s) must conform to the conditions of the environment as previously discussed. As for shape, should the physical appearance be graceful and delicate, strong and sturdy, modern or old-fashioned, expensive or inexpensive?

Colours have important communication values. . .and also constraints when used on packaging in different countries. Colours can produce psychological reactions, both positive and negative, so should be selected with care. Colours are also used in packaging to differentiate different varieties in a product line such as drink mix flavours and types. For hot drinks, warm colours such as red may be appropriate. For cold products, blues and greens connoting coolness should be considered. To communicate richness for a coffee product, dark brown could be a good choice. Shades of a colour also have different communication values. Medium reds indicate strength and passion, whereas darker reds are more serious and lighter reds are happier.[29] The use and contrast of colours are also important for making certain elements stand out such as brand or product name. The Nescafé Brand for example, is printed white on dark brown. While the actual colours are not shown, the contrast can be observed in Exhibit 14.5. Coca-Cola appears as white lettering on a medium red background. Both of these brands achieve excellent visibility.

Exhibit 14.5   *The use and contrast of colours. Reproduced by permission of Nestlé Belgilux, Brussels, Belgium*

Care, however, must be taken with colours when considering the packaging of brands that will be sold in more than one country. Religious beliefs, patriotic feelings, and aesthetics of colours will make a difference. Yellow is associated with disease in Africa. Red is a lucky colour for the Chinese. As for specific product situations, it was reported that a manufacturer of medical scanning equipment lost business in a middle eastern country business because of the whiteness of the equipment. Parker's white pens were not well received in

China because white is the colour of mourning and the green pens didn't go over in India because that colour is associated with bad luck.[30] To avoid problems of this nature, some suggest that the colours of a country's flag should be used in packaging design. However, this approach could result in having a delicate, feminine cosmetic product look like an oil can.

Illustration as well as basic choice of colours and overall design is a job for the professional. Since package design is a special visual form of communication, it should be left to specialists in this field as opposed to art directors in an advertising agency. The latter work in a medium that normally calls for a softer, lighter touch, whereas package design is customarily harder and bolder. Regardless of who creates the design, the main front panel of a package and a print advertisement share one essential characteristic in common. Each is best when it is simple, bold and uncluttered. (In packaging, if needed, additional wording and illustrations can be left for the sides and/or back panel.) As examples, see Exhibit 14.6 which shows the front panel of a noodle package and the front face of a plastic container for an after bath lotion.

Wording and descriptive material

The relevant information for packaging include descriptive, usage, precaution-ary, service, and other information. (The legal requirements for labelling are treated in a subsequent section.) On the front panel it is customary to include brand and product name, net weight or volume, and product illustration. If the product is not visible, a brief description of the product is in order. If visible and the brand name is well known like Nescafé, it is not necessary to say 'instant coffee'. Other descriptive information can include number of servings, amount per serving, expiration or 'use by' date, ingredients and nutritional data.

Directions for preparation or use and storage and maintenance may be needed depending on product. Sometimes the words will be accompanied by pictures to aid understanding.

Precautionary information, if needed, can include poisonous or hazardous properties, antidotes, dosages, and health warnings.

Service information involving warranties, repair facilities, expiration dates, and returnability may be needed or required in many instances.[31]

As for writing package copy, the help of lawyers and technical people will most likely be needed. However, the actual writing should be undertaken by the communication specialist. This task should not be relgated to someone untrained in writing consumer copy.

Products that are developed to be sold across borders must be appropriately named and conform with international requirements. For example, the YES Brand Nestlé candy bar shown in Exhibit 14.7 was developed as a Pan-

Exhibit 14.6 *Front panels of packaging. Reproduced by permission of Birkel, BSB Nahrungsmittel GmbH, Weinstadt-Endersbach, Germany and Johnson & Johnson, Dusseldorf, Germany*

European candy bar. Its name had to be acceptable in all countries and its packaging had to conform with European Community standards. Inspection of the package will show that the product's description, ingredient listing and company address is printed in five languages.

Brand names must be carefully checked for meaning when attempting to market goods across borders. 'Yes' obviously received Pan-European acceptance. The classic example of mis-branding is the Chevrolet Nova when introduced in Spanish speaking countries. Nova when translated means 'no go'. Another auto manufacturer had planned to use the same name for a model to be introduced in Mexico that it was selling in the USA. However, it found that the name 'sable' had certain negative connotations in Spanish; therefore,

Exhibit 14.7 *A Pan-European candy bar. Reproduced by permission of Nestlé Belgilux, Brussels, Belgium*

it substituted the name of another model, Taurus, that was not being sold in Mexico.

Promotion

For promotional purposes, where permitted, one or more offers may be 'flagged' on the front panel and explained on the side or back panel of a package. Quaker Puffed Wheat cereal is an example of this. As shown in Exhibit 14.8 a special offer on Corning Ware Cookware was announced on the front panel and explained on the back panel. The consumer was asked to pay the special price of $15.95 plus $1.50 handling and include two UPC purchase seals to take advantage of the 60 per cent saving on the four-piece French White Cookware set offer.

In other instances, a package may be used to present more than one offer. As can be observed in Exhibit 14.9, Kellogg's Special K Waffles from Eggo package carried a 'personalized weight less diet offer' on the front panel and a 20 cent store coupon on a side panel. The personalized weight loss offer was a special inducement for consumers to buy that package. The 20 cent coupon was a money-off incentive for repeat purchase.

Where legal, a package of one product may also be used to carry a sample of another item. This provides a special incentive to buy one product and an inexpensive means of sampling for the other product. This was the case with Reach toothbrushes (German). Reach carried a foil sample of TheraMed toothpaste.

Another practice used by some marketers in the USA is to run a special pre-priced promotion pack for a limited period of time to stimulate sales as in the case of SOS steel wool soap pads. See Exhibit 14.10. (Pre-pricing is illegal in some countries.)

Testing packaging

The communication values of a package can be tested in ways that are similar to print advertising. For example, alternative designs can be exposed to focus groups for evaluation purposes. Tachistoscope testing, a projection device that flashes pictures on a screen, can be undertaken to test brand name recognition and other features of the package and its design. Surveys may be conducted among the target audience to determine attitudes towards the packaging. Two or more packages can be rated by respondents using a semantic-differential scaling technique. Opposite adjectives are given, e.g. strong-weak, feminine-masculine; respondents are asked to place a mark on the scale between the extremes which represent their opinion of the package with respect to each characteristic listed.[32]

Short of using the kind of research techniques just mentioned, there is one simple test that all packaged goods to be sold on retail or wholesale store shelves should be given. When evaluating the recommendations of the designer, this person and those responsible for giving approval should go to a local store and then place the new package design on the shelf alongside its competition where it is intended to appear. Then make judgments. In this way, and only in this way can the design be properly evaluated.

Conformance

Packaging requirements of local governments must be obtained, understood, and adhered to when marketing products across borders. Packaging and labelling laws in the USA, for example, include precautionary warnings for poisonous or hazardous properties of a product. Weight must be prominently displayed on the front panel of food and over-the-counter drug products. Ingredients must be listed in order of importance. All drug products must prominently display instructions for use and what to do in case of accidental overdose[33]

While labelling laws vary widely from country to country, commonly found are regulations covering these specifications: country of origin, weight, description of contents, name of producer, special information regarding additives and chemical content.[34]

Marketing communicators working on labelling and packing of hazardous

Exhibit 14.8 *(continued)*

Exhibit 14.9 *A package used to present more than one offer. Reproduced by permission of the Kellogg Company. Kellogg's®, Special K™ and Eggo® are registered trade marks of the Kellogg Company*

Exhibit 14.10 *A special pre-priced promotion pack. Reproduced by permission of Miles Inc., Bedford Park, Illinois*

materials should be knowledgeable of the United Nations recommendations on this subject. Measurement regulations should also be explored. Standard metric sizes will be encountered for liquid products in Germany and for alcohol in the USA. Bilingual labels are required in Canada and Belgium.[35] This is also true in Arab countries.

Laws may also preclude the use of wording which implies the existence of an unproven benefit. In France, for example, Henkel could not use the toothpaste brand name TheraMed because it had a medical connotation. The name was changed to Theraxyl.

Summary

At the beginning of this chapter public relations was defined in terms of function, scope, and position in the organization. Counselling on matters that relate to a firm's citizenship along with matters that relate to its marketing programmes were described as key functions of the public relations practitioner. The overall image of a firm, as well as the perceptions of its products and/or services will have a bearing on its ultimate success over time.

Public relations/publicity programmes are designed to enhance corporate image and improve awareness and understanding of the firm's offerings.

Research generated by writing and disseminating press releases, 'backgrounders', and feature stories are basic public relations communications techniques. However, any communication technique, including advertising, booklets and brochures, staging meetings and shows may become the tool of the public relations practitioner.

While the state of the art may differ, public relations activities are conducted by organizations in all parts of the world.

Packaging has significance to the marketing communicator because it delivers the ultimate product message at the point of purchase or rejection. For this reason, great care and sensitivity is needed in designing the package in terms of size, shape, handling, opening, pouring, closing, content protection, and storage convenience as well as communication value.

Because purchasing behaviour and cultural values involving aesthetics, language, customs, and beliefs will vary from country to country, these differences must be known and understood when developing packaging for use in host country environments. If on- or in-package promotion is being considered, accommodation must be made for this activity. Finally, the packaging laws of countries will vary and must be understood. All these elements were discussed in this chapter so that at least the fundamentals of this aspect of marketing communications could be understood.

Questions

1   Which of the publics of public relations mentioned are the prime targets for marketing communications?
2   Discuss the key role that public relations counselling can play in support of business and marketing programmes.

3 How important would you say corporate identity is for large multinational business organizations? Give reasons.

4 Explain why the public relations/publicity plan is similar or dissimilar to the normal marketing communication plan.

5 How can product publicity and other PR tools and techniques be used to augment the marketing communications plans?

6 Do cross border public relations programmes encounter the same or different problems as those experienced in advertising and sales promotion programmes? Explain.

7 Give reasons why the following factors should be given careful consideration when designing packaging:
   a size and shape
   b protection
   c convenience

8 Discuss the implications of shape, colour, and illustration in package design.

9 What written elements should go and what should not go on the front, side panels, and back of a paperboard package.

10 What is the ultimate test of a new package design?

11 Describe how packaging laws may vary from one country to the next.

Notes

1 Kelly, Robert A. (1981) How to plan and set objectives for public relations efforts. *Marketing News*, report on a talk, New York, 11 April, 11−17.

2 Cutlip, Scott M. and Center, Allen M. (1982) *Effective Public Relations*, 5th edn, Prentice-Hall Inc., Englewood Cliffs, NJ, Exhibit 1.1, p. 5.

3 Terpstra, Vern and Sarathy, Ravi (1991) *International Marketing*, 5th edn, The Dryden Press, Hinsdale, Illinois, p. 524.

4 Cantor, Bill (1984) *Experts in Action − Inside Public Relations*, Longman Inc., New York, table of contents.

5 Cutlip, *op. cit.*, 24−25.

6 Thurston, Robert N. (1983) In *Lesly's Public Relations Handbook*, 3rd edn, Prentice-Hall Inc., Englewood Cliffs, NJ, pp. 185−191.

7 *Ibid.*, 188.

8 Letter from Isidro Fainé Casas, Director General A. Ejecutivo, Caja de Ahorros y Pensiones de Barcelona, 27 March 1992.

9 Scholvinck, Lucas (1987) Presentation given to a Pace University study group at KLM Royal Dutch Airlines headquarters, Amstelveen, The Netherlands, 20 May.

10 KLM (1990) *The Image of a Company: History of the Future*, Amstelveen, The Netherlands.

11 Adapted from Reilly, Robert T. (1982) *Public Relations in Action*, Prentice Hall Inc., Englewood Cliffs, NJ, Chapter 12.

12 Levin, Donald M. (1986) How to publicize products and technology. *Chemical Engineering*, 13 October.

13 Sill, Jim (1982) How to make technical publicity work for you. *Industrial Marketing*, June, p. 95.

14 *Ibid.*, 96.

15 Levin, *op. cit.*

16 *Ibid.*

17 Sill, *op. cit.*, 95.

18 Philips Publishing Inc. (1990) Case study No. 2206. *PR News*, 12 March, Potomac, Maryland.

19 *Public Relations Journal* (1989) Kiwi's first-ever public relations effort shines. *Public Relations Journal*, pp. 5, 7. Reprinted by permission of *Public Relations Journal*, Public Relations Society of America, New York.

20 Wolf, Eelco, Verch, Allan, Venne, Greg, Schneider, Grant and Strum, Lonny (1986) Polaroid launches the Spectra. Presentation by Polaroid executives to area collegiate faculty and students sponsored by the Center for Communication, New York, 6 November.

21 Hiebert, Ray E. (1984) In Cantor, Bill, *Experts in Action — Inside Public Relations*, Longman Inc., New York, p. 5.

22 Dentsu Inc. (1989) *Dentsu Japan Marketing/Advertising Yearbook 1990*, Dentsu Inc., Tokyo, pp. 249–260.

23 Seitel, Fraser P. (1989) *The Practice of Public Relations*, 4th edn, Merril Publishing Co., Columbus, Ohio, pp. 504–505.

24 *Inside PR* (1990) A world of difference. September, pp. 9–15.

25 Gerichter, Peggy (1992) Letter from Peggy Gerichter, Marketing Manager, Colgate-Palmolive (Centro-America) SA, Guatemala City, April.

26 Terpstra, *op. cit.*, 277.

27 *Ibid.*

28 Jacobi, Arno and Fend, Ulrich (1987) Presentation by Henkel executives to a Pace University study group, Dusseldorf, 25 May.

29 Russell, Thomas and Verrill, Glenn (1986) *Otto Kleppner's Advertising Procedure*, Prentice Hall, Englewood Cliffs, NJ, p. 516.

30 Onkvisit, Sak and Shaw, John J. (1989) *International Marketing*, Merrill Publishing, Columbus, Ohio, pp. 491, 492.

31 Global Products and Services Commission (1987) *Labeling and Advertising: Their Functions in Consumer Information*, International Advertising Association, New York, p. 5.

32 Russell, *op. cit.*, 520, 521.

33 *Ibid.*, 524.

34 Terpstra, *op. cit.*, 277.

35 Onkvisit, *op. cit.*, 491, 492.

Part Six *The Road Ahead*

Having attempted to present the basic principles and practice of international marketing communications in some breadth and depth, this final section and chapter draws on the wisdom of observers and experts in order to depict a scenario for this business function in the years ahead.

15   *Current trends and future developments*

Introduction

In this final chapter a number of thoughts about the current and future state of the art of marketing and marketing communications will be intermingled with the concepts, principles and practices previously discussed.

The essence of good business practice

To begin with all students of marketing should be wary of material published on this subject in text books including this one. The principal reason is that these books are written for the most part by educators who have not had sufficient practical experience, are getting information second hand, and want to differentiate their work from other authors. However, their points of difference are frequently without empirical foundation that result in misinformation and a proliferation of meaningless labels. A case in point is the so-called paradigm shift in marketing from a 'transaction-oriented focus' involving a price-oriented, short-term sales mindset to a long-term, relationship-oriented point of view where internal team work becomes very important.[1] Nonsense! Surely, Drucker, McKitterick, GE, Henkel, Fokker, IBM, Coca-Cola and many other well-known multinational companies never had solely a 'transaction-oriented focus'. The essence of good business involves repeat purchase, serving customers and consumers, and developing long-term relationships.

As for marketing communications, when imaginatively conceived, and methodically planned and executed, programmes of this nature can play a vital role in creating and maintaining long-term relationships with all members in the channel of distribution from sales force to end user. This has been the successful way of the past, is of the present, and will be of the future. It does not mean, however, that all corporate managements necessarily have or will adhere to basic principles of good communications practice.

A business scenario for today and tomorrow

Corporate management is ultimately responsible for all acts of the enterprise, good and bad. Those organizations that will be in the forefront of their industries overtime will have a highly skilled top management team sensitive to the needs of the markets served, responsive to actual and potential inroads of competitors, knowledgeable of the ways in which resources should be allocated, and supportive of the middle managers and staff specialists that prepare, execute, and evaluate business plans.

The environment for business will become a more challenging arena. On the one hand, there will be more intense competition on the part of global participants in the established industrialized markets of the world such as North America, Western Europe, Japan and Australia. On the other hand, there will be competition for a place and position in the newly forming markets of Eastern Europe, where 370 million consumers reside,[2] China, India, and other developing economies in Latin America and elsewhere.

The kind of intelligence that apparently led some US car makers to believe that 'Honda will never be more than a motorcycle shop'[3] is obviously unacceptable.

Trend reversal is more fiction than reality if it is true that 'nine out of ten attempts to relaunch, restage, or turn around dying products and services fail to reverse share decline'.[4] 'Brands are/will become the most valuable assets of the company. It will be more important for companies to own markets than factories. What is needed is dominance of consumers' and retailers' minds at the point of consideration.'[5]

In Europe a few but growing number of global brands will be found and more Euro brands will exist. In addition, there will be continuing growth of strictly local brands, provided by multinational and local firms alike. While this group will comprise only a small portion of total consumption, they will be 'Extremely important pieces of decor, valued out of all proportion to their practical importance, badges.'[6]

For the large company, the trend in the West has been one of acquisition of late led by Philip Morris' purchase of Kraft General Foods and Jacobs Suchard, Nestlé's acquisitions of Carnation and Rowntree, and Procter & Gamble's purchases of Noxell, Max Factor and Betrix. As one observer has pointed out, 'It is accepted wisdom now that it is easier to buy brands than build them.'[7] While the Japanese have also been acquisition-minded in certain business sections such as real estate and finance, in the consumer product field their brands such as Toyota, Honda, Canon, Shiseido and Sony continue to gain share of world markets.

Whether a company owns all factors of production or chooses to source product from other organizations with the designated quality on time at the least cost either at home or abroad, the battle for brand leadership will be fought in markets of any consequence in all parts of the world. As Larry Light pointed out, one study of over 2,700 businesses revealed that market leaders average a pre-interest, pre-tax return on investment of 31 per cent whereas those brands that rank four or more only deliver a 12 per cent return. Thus he concluded that market dominance is the only way of building an 'enduring, profitable brand asset'.[8]

State-of-the-art technology is the underpinning for brand leadership in many types of businesses. In certain instances it may be more advantageous to enter into a partnership arrangement than purchase, acquire, or be acquired. This is the route that giant IBM and Apple Computer Inc. have chosen in an attempt 'to maintain their powerful yet threatened positions in the computer industry'. Despite its size, IBM launched a partnership approach in doing business based on the realization it couldn't go alone 'in developing technology and winning customer acceptance'.[9]

IBM, Apple, and processors of all types of goods and services will need to benefit from increased speed of operations. Time will become increasingly valuable at the expense of traditional factors of production such as raw materials and labour. This prediction led Alvin Toffler to conclude that it is apt to be more profitable to operate in a developed economy with a small group of highly educated and paid employees than in a backward factory in a less developed country with many poorly educated, low paid workers.[10]

If this scenario materializes, the gap between what has been called the north and south (developed and developing countries) and what Toffler now calls the 'fast and slow' will widen. Participation in the 'fast-moving global economy' by the 'slow' will call for major investment in technology and informational systems accompanied by the appropriate education and training and 'global network' linkages.[11]

Consumer targets

What are the implications for consumer products and services? In the 'slow' countries, demand will be confined largely to pockets of more affluent consumers located in the major metropolitan markets.

In the USA, consumers are described as being older, wiser, more pragmatic, conservative, selective, demanding of diversity, and critical of political and advertising claims. There will be a greater respect for individuality. A higher value will be placed on quality and convenience. Home will be the focus of life.[12] Niche marketing will become increasingly important, targeting any demographic group from senior citizens to babies, and localizing marketing activities to recognize the long standing differences in tastes and preferences between such groups as New Yorkers and Californians.[13] Blacks and Hispanics have also become special targets of marketing programmes for many types of products ranging from cognac to vitamin and mineral-fortified orange juice. The universal cry for marketers has become 'Be global. Compete locally.'[14] As suggested earlier, there will be some global brands, more Euro brands, and a number of strictly local brands as well. Traditions and cultures in Europe bring about different consumption patterns. (Change if it occurs, will be gradual.) Take for example, beer and wine consumption in selected European countries shown side-by-side in Exhibit 15.1.

As observed in the bar charts in Exhibit 15.1, marked differences exist in the consumption of these two beverages among the five countries. Beer consumption is significantly greater in the UK, Belgium, and West Germany while wine drinking in Spain and particularly France outdistances the consumption of that beverage in the other three.[15]

In Europe, there is no such thing as a single audience. Instead grouping by 'language clusters' is a distinct possibility: German-speaking countries...Latin countries...and English-speaking countries (the UK, Scandinavia and possibly Holland).[16]

As for change (in Europe and elsewhere), as Barry Day stated, 'we face change by hanging on to what we *are* and what we *know*. And then inching forward.'[17]

When projecting one's thinking to 2020, the consumers, at least in 'fast' countries, will have more choices. This means smaller market segments and more niche positioning. Consumers as always will respond with at least as much emotion as reason, but will have a problem of cutting through the clutter to sort out the product and service offerings.[18]

Technology, information, organization and speed will be important factors to be reckoned with as marketing communication programmes are carried out in home and host countries.

Exhibit 15.1   *Beer and wine consumption in selected European countries*
Source: *HPM Putenux, France*

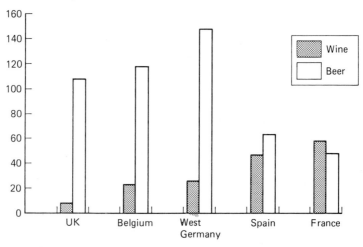

Communications research

Communications researchers have attempted for years and continue to attempt to link advertising exposure to sales. Called 'single source research', some organizations such as Nielsen, measure not only advertising but also other media exposure, retail displays, feature advertising, retail pricing, and couponing stimuli along with sales and behavioural response. This research involves 'the measurement, integration, and interpretation of all factors influencing consumer behaviour and the resulting sales effect'. The technology used in this system include optical check-out and in-home scanners, hand-held terminals, television monitors, and personal computers.[19] Some researchers are pessimistic about the possibilities of single source research doing the intended job. Measurement, reliability, and predictive value problems are reasons cited. One research authority has indicated that the industry to date has not been able to demonstrate that single source information is reliable and being used to assist decision making.[20] Other researchers are optimistic. One states that 'although single source data research has not yet been perfected, ultimately it will revolutionize our ability to study marketing input-output relationships'.[21]

Other current areas of concern for researchers included syndicated research, survey response rates, adequate numbers of personnel trained in quantitative methods, research methodology, and management's role in the process. Syndicated research services of the Simmons, MRI, TGI type have been accused of 'just throwing out information' which, in most cases, isn't meaningful but in which unknowing marketers place 'blind' reliance. Response rates are so low that projection is not possible and in some cases the results are not even helpful. English majors who lack training in statistics and mathematics and are influenced more by the needs of marketing than good research techniques are found in marketing research assignments. Conversely those researchers with the proper training are burdened by a lack of concern for the marketing problem. To correct these personnel imbalances and improve research methodology there is a need for improved management understanding and greater involvement.[22]

Today's problems can be readily solved if they are recognized and treated. In syndicated research, for example, an open and forthright dialogue between clients and suppliers of research with a focus on weaknesses of any given service can lead to improvement as in the case of Nielsen Broadcast Studies.[23]

However, the field of research is by no means static. The technique of 'message maximization modelling' has evolved from conjoint analysis, advertising concept testing, and simulated test marketing according to Kevin Clancy.[24] Clancy also envisions that psychophysiologic measures such as galvanic skin response and brainwave testing, response measures of the 1960s, will be used again in the future to evaluate copy, and other communication elements. Other techniques which will be used to develop and evaluate marketing programmes including computer-based decision support systems and thinking machines called 'expert systems'.[25]

The field for marketing and communications research is rich with concepts and techniques to be perfected so that marketing communication planning and evaluation can be enhanced. This will be possible with management backing, trained personnel, and a reasonable deployment of resources.

Organizational changes in the firm

If the ideas expressed about speed of operations and information processing, brand leadership, ownership of markets, and heightened competition have validity, the importance of marketing and marketing communications will increase in the years ahead. This means that more CEOs will have marketing backgrounds. It will not necessarily mean that more people will be working in marketing jobs; instead those managing the function will be more experienced and better trained. Organizational shifts are apt to bring practitioners in closer contact with the markets they serve. Companies like Campbell Soup, Frito-Lay and Pepsi-Cola are reported to have adopted a more regional approach. Procter & Gamble has converted assistant product managers to assignments that involve responsibility for implementing regional marketing programmes.[26] As research techniques, aided by the latest technology, improve in facilitating decision making and evaluating marketing communications effectiveness, managers of this function will gain stature within the marketing organization, but not, as some propose, be elevated to the status of chief research officer reporting directly to the president. Marketing managements that cannot accept or convey a 'straight unfiltered view of what's happening in the market place' will not be welcome in the business organization of the future.

The status of advertising agencies

Advertising agencies have come under attack recently in the USA for several reasons. The latest criticism has been levelled by author, Martin Mayer, who believes that ad executives have gone from 'Gurus to Vendors' simply writing and drawing ads that 'fulfill a strategy created by the product's maker...' An ad praised by Mayer in his new book, *Whatever Happened to Madison Avenue?*, wasn't created by an ad agency because the client couldn't find one which shared their marketing vision! The public is being bombarded with '6,000 Network ads per week' which are 'slicker, prettier and more expensive' but 'tell viewers more about what the manufacturers think of the product than what the client wants'. At least part of the blame for ad agency malaise in the large agency can be attributed to takeovers and public ownership. Profits and stock prices have become the preoccupation in place of investment in technology and new techniques. 'Agency heads who used to write advertising now worry about leveraged buy out debt.'[27] Mayer's sentiments are reinforced by John Hartman who describes 'one-stop agencies, offering clients under one roof a smorgasbord of related and unrelated consulting services, acquired in waves of acquisitions' as a 'marketing non-trend'. Divestiture now is the remedy sought by these 'hot trend agencies' to cope with the debt incurred by their 'acquisition binges'.[28]

In another vein, Larry Light characterizes the classic agency structure as 'too large, inefficient, and unproductive'. He made a number of points which deserve reflection, including:

- The idea of having the agency organization parallel the client brand-management structure is a waste of money.
- Account planning and the planner will replace that old-fashioned account executive. . . . a senior advertising manager and advertising planner are all that's needed to administer the creative process.
- The obsolete account executive filter will give way to direct contact with the client on the part of creative and media people, researchers and planners.
- As with clients, agencies need to budget for and establish research and development (R & D) departments to explore new techniques and methodology to cover all aspects of the communication function.
- 'The total communications agency is an idea whose time has gone.' Convenience is no substitute for quality. Evidence does not exist that one-step communications service will maximize quality. Most marketers prefer to select marketing services supplies on 'the strength of their specific expertise'.
- Agencies of the future will concentrate all its efforts on the task of creating and producing superior quality advertising.[29]

Mayer, Hartman and Light provide students of advertising and marketing communications with plenty to think about. No doubt the better managed full-service, multinational advertising agencies (or whatever name of the future they decide to use) will not only survive but also prosper over time, but not necessarily with the same organizational structure. The multinationals have always had a mix of domestic and international business. Host countries offices in many instances were formed through acquisition of local agencies, and are staffed for the most part by the host country nationals. The big advantage of the multinational agencies serving the multinational account is the potential ability of better coordination coupled with the ability to call on worldwide talent to solve a client problem. The problem remains, however, of producing uniform high-quality advertising across an agency network. This problem is compounded when multinational agencies attempt to provide their clients with other services such as (direct) mail, sales promotion, and public relations. They will be perpetually plagued by competition from smaller, aggressive, flexible creative shops and suppliers of single services (e.g. PR or sales promotion).

On a more optimistic note, Munson sees the advertising agency of the future as becoming a vertical network that can handle multinational client relationships and a series of horizontal networks that can deliver integrated marketing communications programmes in the principal markets that clients do business.[30]

The real squeeze is placed on the medium-sized advertising agency operating in a single environment who may be forced to expand, be acquired or become part of a network of independently owned agencies in different countries. This dilemma was expressed in an article on UK mid-size agencies who faced 'tough choices about forging European networks — or selling out to one' in light of the impending realization of a single European market place.[31]

Retailer's clout

Trade concentration and power, particularly in the grocery field, is a well-established phenomenon. In the majority of European countries, Australia, Canada, and New Zealand 60 per cent or more (as high as 94 per cent in Australia) of the trade buying is concentrated in ten organizations. And if the trend in the hypermarket and supermarkets share of grocery business is an indicator of concentration and power, the USA and Japan would have to be added to the list.[32] These outlets have put considerable pressure on manufacturers to increase payments of promotional allowances of various types. In Europe, Day calls it a 'local stranglehold' on the part some retailers but believes it won't be as easy for retailers to achieve on a pan-regional basis.[33] Nonetheless, product marketers and their agencies in many countries of the world need to establish and maintain close working relationships with those who have the final say as to whether or not, where and how much product of a manufacturers will be stocked on their shelves.

One of the reasons for retailer strength is the information they have at their fingertips on all brands of merchandise stocked as a result of universal product codes and retail check-out scanners. Nielsen marketing research reported on the rapid growth of scanners in all parts of its universe of twenty-seven countries which account for almost 90 per cent of the gross domestic product of free market economies.[34] Another trend that is unsettling to marketers is the growth of retailer brands. For example, Duncan Bain reported that some big retailers have more than 50 per cent of certain category sales in their own branded merchandise which has come to be 'synonymous with good value and quality'.[35]

Plight of manufacturers' brands

Where will this leave the marketer of branded products? Essentially, in the same position as the marketer has been all along. It is and always has been mandatory for manufacturers to build substantial and sustainable relationships with retailers so that each party may achieve their objectives. While this relationship is created and maintained in the name of a company by its sales organization, the business that is transacted is on a brand-to-brand, not company basis, regardless of company. The major marketers may gain some leverage in so far as gaining distribution goes, but ultimately the brand will be judged on its ability to sell at a rate which will satisfy the retailers.

This is where sales promotion comes in.

Promotional needs

Retailers look for promotional concepts that not only boost sales of the sponsoring brand but also will increase store traffic and, depending on the nature of the promotion, build related item sales as well. Too often the manufacturer repeats the same promotion from one period or one year to the next. In the USA it's all too likely to be another coupon in a free-standing insert. As James Mack reports, 'the manufacturer is saying, "I need to do something else besides couponing. It's costly. I'm not really sure how effective it is." And the retailer's saying, "why are you just delivering another coupon? I want something that is going to bring people into my store"...'[36] And so the marketing communicators have their work cut out: to develop concepts and programmes that will stimulate consumer interest and buying action, and achieve retailer objectives of generating increased store traffic which, in turn, will induce related item and/or total store sales.

To begin with, any promotion should have a theme, e.g. 'the gleam of stainless steel' for a store-wide department store promotion to merchandise all stainless steel items in the store: pots, pans, coffee makers, cutlery, flatware, furniture, etc. All manufacturers of these items can get behind this promotion and support it with cooperative advertising, displays and point-of-sale materials. The store will benefit from the sale of the various items promoted, not just a single item, and the increased traffic and total sales that such a promotion will generate. (This was the actual theme and concept for a highly successful nationwide promotion, implemented on a market-by-market basis that was sponsored by the supplier of one of the essential ingredients for stainless steel in the late 1950s. The theme selected was suitable for consumer as well as retailer advertising.)

Coordinated marketing communication services

What this type of effort leads up to is a very close coordination between consumer advertising and trade promotion. While there is disagreement as to whether the advertiser or suppliers of communication services should provide the leadership in developing these programmes, right now it appears that goods and service marketers are at the helm. The question is whether or not the advertiser is properly coordinating the total communication effort. If that is the case, then the firm can orchestrate the total communication programme. If not, there is an opening for suppliers of all types of communication services including the advertising agency. Whether or not the agency can or should provide the leadership is problematical. If attempted, 'the tools by which that advertising man will (have to) build his client's business will change dramatically. Those tools will be integrated marketing communications where a unified message is provided not just by media advertising but also by those important so-called below-the-line disciplines of sales promotion, public relations, direct marketing, package design, etc.'.[37]

The role of advertising and other forms of marketing communications

Larry Light, as stated earlier, perceives that the role of the full service advertising agency's will diminish and then disappear.[38]

This view would not be shared by all the full service, worldwide organizations, such as McCann-Erickson, Ogilvy & Mather, Dentsu, Saachi and Saachi, and J. Walter Thompson. However, it does point to a distinction between the role of advertising and other forms of marketing communication, such as sales promotion. The former is an image-based vehicle designed to create awareness and build loyalties based on an understanding and special feeling for a product or service. The latter is a 'doing' vehicle used to encourage immediate purchase of a product.[39]

Duncan Bain envisions the emergence of marketing service groups which combine advertising and all the other communication tools discussed in this book.[40] The successful groups will be those whose management and personnel can bridge the cultural gap between creators of advertising campaigns and other forms of marketing communications. To provide total marketing communication services, advertising cannot be viewed as being a first-class citizen and other services, such as sales promotion, second-class.[41] Operating in the system will be a combination of multidisciplinary managers and functional specialists, with, to quote Muson, 'A passion for using all the tools at their disposal to build clients' businesses and clients' brands.'[42]

Communication channels and tools

Fractionation of target audiences, decisions of media owners, planning practices of communicators, the desire of marketers to reach prospects and customers at the point of consideration, and new technology will bring about change in the channel of communication. Changes, however, will be influenced by countries' and regions' regulatory bodies.

In nations of the world where television viewing opportunities, household penetration, and commercial use of the medium have been inhibited for economic, social, or political reasons, such as in China, India, Indonesia and Eastern Europe, significant growth will come in years to come. As the number of television channels increase and the use of the medium for transmitting advertising messages is approved in countries where it is not yet permitted in Europe, the medium's importance as a medium for advertising will continue to grow. In countries like the USA and possibly in Japan where the networks and major stations have been cluttered with commercials and the quality of programming is no longer satisfactory to many people, the dominant broadcasters will continue to lose audience in absolute numbers and share.

The idea of Pan-European satellite television communication is either premature or has passed its peak. With respect to programming, the major media entrepreneurs have already retreated from emphasis on Euro coverage to either 'an extended local base or a thematic base like sports, pop music and so on'.[43]

As one US expert, Gale Metzger, views the media scene, the term 'massed' media will become more appropriate than *mass*. In other words if an advertiser wishes to reach a large number of people it will be done by using air shows, football games, other special events, etc., but not by means of a specific vehicle such as television.[44] Another view is that use of mass media to reach a mass market has become outmoded in the USA. In the future the emphasis will be on designing media and marketing plans to reach selective targets. This will be made possible by technology and more precise tools of management.[45] More ways will be found to interact directly with consumers and prospects. Computers and telecommunications will be channels for this communication.

One method gaining popularity among personal computer owners is the Prodigy service, a joint venture of IBM and Sears department stores. Household members can now save time and money by shopping, banking, trading securities, and obtaining a broad range of information, education, and entertainment at home. The software is user friendly and the array of services are available at low cost. Households connect to the Prodigy Service through a regular 'phone line attached to a home computer with an inexpensive modem. For the product or service marketer, Prodigy can be used to advertise and make sales direct to the consumer. In return, Prodigy takes a commission on each transaction.

Other interactive systems being developed and tested include television and kiosk communication stations located in stores and shopping centres. One of these is ACTV system being developed by Massachusetts Institute of Technology's Media Lab. Testing has been conducted in a regional cable TV system which permits viewers by means of special controls to personalize TV programming around their individual tastes. For example, if watching a sports event like the Olympics, the viewer would have the option of selecting one of four concurrent events and specific camera angles. The ACTV system is able to remember the demographics of each viewer and therefore deliver a commercial to a predetermined target group. For example, a woman is watching an exercise show and wants a particular type of aerobic workout. The system can give that exercise regimen and also remember it. This information can be used for purposes of commercial targeting. Other capabilities of ACTV being developed are an in-home printing system to permit delivery of coupons and a telephone modem device to permit information gathering that will link commercial and coupon to store purchase.[46]

Different manufacturers are experimenting with free-standing, interactive kiosks. One nationwide truck renter conducted a six-month test of kiosks in major shopping in Dade County, Florida. The Kiosks were called 'Ryder Touch-TV moving centres' which provided prospective movers with housing information, mortgage payment calculations, and guidelines on finding the right neighbourhoods in selected areas. The idea was not to make a direct sales but project a favourable image for Ryder on the part of those who used the system.[47]

Some advertising agencies are taking an active role in these developments like McCann-Erickson with ACTV. Ogilvy & Mather's Interactive Media Group is pioneering kiosk development for clients like Ryder. Other agencies have elected not to adopt a pro-active position; rather let others do the development and selling work for the reason that little immediate return is seen and the potential may never be realized.[48]

In the magazine field, technology now permits selective binding so that different editorial content and different advertisements can be delivered to different target groups. Using laser jet printing, magazines can now be addressed and delivered to selected people.

This is just a sampling of the new techniques and tools of communication that may have a major impact on the manner in which commercial messages are delivered in the future.

But what appears evident is that weight of advertising as measured by reach and frequency will have to be expanded to include home video, home computers, direct marketing vehicles, catalogues, etc.[49]

One constraint that all marketing communicators must be concerned with is 'intrusiveness'... intrusiveness of measurement techniques and the communication itself. In one meeting of 300 advertising industry leaders, virtually all hands in the room were raised in answer to a question a speaker asked: 'Is there too much advertising today?' Lynn Upshaw's response to this is that future planning by media professionals will have to take into consideration such factors as:

- Is the audience expecting to see a commercial message?
- Are the viewers or readers likely to resent such a message?
- Does the risk or irritation offset the positive effect of a media exposure?
- Is there anything that can be done with the creative execution to lessen the possible backlash to the intrusiveness?[50]

A related constraint, but broader in scope is brought about by the fact marketing communicators are getting closer and closer to the ideal situation: 'The ability to target our consumers, to be able to talk to them virtually one-on-one.' This prompted Barry Day to ask, 'Are we smart enough, sensitive enough to talk one-on-one with people we have traditionally referred to as "all housewives", "under 35", "former users"?'[51]

The social-political climate

As brought out in Chapter 5, there has been a worldwide increase in restrictions imposed on advertising over the past ten years. Threats to advertising have become a persistent and growing phenomenon. The problem has become particularly acute in the European community. Dr John Gray, eminent political philosopher, put the situation in a very clear perspective in his article on 'The Case For Freedom in Advertising', first published in *The Daily Telegraph*, London, 24 September 1991 which reappeared in the *International Advertiser*, New York, December 1991, vol. 4, no. 4. The major portion of Dr Gray's article, with his permission, is reproduced below. It is worthy of serious study and reflection.

One of the most characteristic paradoxes of our age is that, as freedom of artistic and cultural expression has waxed, freedom of commercial expression has been on the wane. Often, the same people who demand that literature and the arts be untramelled by traditional moral standards have been in the forefront of movements calling for paternalistic curbs on advertising.

Conventional liberal wisdom seems not to perceive the threat to diversity in the media posed by advertising bans and curbs which would inevitably entail huge revenue losses. Nor does it seem capable of grasping that bans on the advertising of tobacco and alcohol products are as much an authoritarian interference in freedom of lifestyle — and thereby as illiberal — as censorship in the arts. The fact is that restrictive codes on the advertising of medicines, or financial services, or the ways in which women may be represented in advertisements, differ in no fundamental way from the kinds of curbs which they would at once reject elsewhere.

In its hostility to market institutions, liberal opinion neglects the vital truth that, though freedom of expression can nowhere be entirely unlimited, there is nothing in advertising that should deny it the protection rightly given to other modes of expression. Like political discourse, advertising is not purely informative, but aims to influence behaviour. It makes an appeal to our interests and it has a practical objective.

Like religious discourse, advertising seeks to have an effect on the lives of those to whom it is directed, in politics and religion alike, we recognise the risks of demagogy and error but choose to run them because the dangers of censorship are greater. Increasingly, on the other hand, we impose on advertising bans and controls undreamt of in other areas of life — and which, if they were imposed on political and religious life, would have consequences that are barely imaginable.

It is as if commercial expression has been singled out as being peculiarly invidious and so in need of special justification and particularly stringent regulation.

The truth is that advertising is like other modes of expression — they are all branches of a single tree, whose root is freedom of communication. Policies that prohibit the advertising of certain products, such as those currently proposed within the European Community, are policies that thwart and subvert individual freedom. Prohibitionism in advertising denies the individual responsibility for his own choices and shifts that responsibility to an authoritarian body. Like any form of state censorship, it aims to use the powers of government to mould and shape the beliefs of citizens on the model of the current orthodoxies — in this case, on the new puritanism that bases itself on considerations of health and prudence rather than of right and wrong. All such advertising bans violate freedom of expression — a fact acknowledged in a recent landmark judgment in Canada when Mr Justice Chabot ruled a ban on tobacco advertising unconstitutional for just this reason.

Prohibitions and overregulation in advertising can be defended, if at all, only by the liberal arguments used to justify authoritarianism in the past. Religious toleration was opposed because it would lead to the propagation of error by demagogues and would endanger civil peace. Democracy was rejected because most people were too gullible and manipulable to be trusted with the choice of their rulers.

Only if we accept the picture of ordinary human nature suggested by these arguments do advertising bans and restrictions of the sorts currently proposed make sense. But if we view ordinary people in this way — as weak, stupid and unfit to make their own choices — what justification is there for democracy, or for any sort of individual freedom?

Advertising plays an indispensable role in the market economy. It gives us information about products beyond what is expressed in their price, and supports a degree of variety in the media that would otherwise be unsustainable. Even so, the fundamental argument for freedom in advertising is not in the end an economic argument, it is an ethical argument. In making available to us information we could acquire in no other way, and in making us aware of products of which we would otherwise be ignorant, advertising enhances our powers of choice and thereby our freedom.

The case for freedom in advertising is all of a piece with the case for freedom of expression itself. Nothing in it turns on the status of advertising as commercial expression. It turns on whether we look on ordinary men and women with respect as trustworthy reasoners and choosers, or whether − in reactionary and illiberal fashion − as incorrigibly infantile, fit only for authoritarian administration. If we think the latter, then we will go along with current proposals for advertising bans and restrictions − proposals whose end-result can only be, not the abolition of advertising, but its effective monopoly by the state.

When critics of advertising portray freedom of commercial expression as a small thing, not entitled to the protections afforded other modes of communication, they reveal their animus towards the practical freedoms of commerce rather than anything in the logic of the argument. It is time we recognised that supporters of advertising bans and restrictions are showing themselves to be enemies of freedom of expression itself.*

To promote a better understanding of advertising's role in society, the International Advertising Association is launching a global campaign for advertising aimed at every level of society which will communicate 'the benefits of advertising through simple concepts which are comprehensible to all'.†

Final thoughts on medium and message

Many factors will contribute to the changes which will take place in marketing communications in the years to come...A more highly fragmented market place, greater difficulty in getting viewer and reader attention, increased media fractionation, more advanced measurement techniques. This will occur in a world that is likely to see rapid economic growth and social and political change in some parts and declines in mature economies and in lesser developed societies where change is not able to overcome tradition. 'Green issues will continue to flourish', and continued emphasis will be needed on effective self-regulation to avoid further damage to the image of the ad (marketing communication) industry.[52] As for the process by which marketing communications decisions are reached, the questions will remain the same:

* Gray, John (1991) The case for freedom in advertising. *International Advertiser*, December, **4**, (4), 3−4.
† IAA News (1991) *International Advertiser*, December, **4**, (4), 4.

- Who is the target?
- What weight is needed to reach them?
- Where should marketing communications run?
- What should the message be?
- How effective is the marketing communications?

As for the message, it will still be the result of a creative process, not a scientific process. 'How to talk to whom' will become one of the most critical steps in the advertising decision-making process.[53]

For this reason, in concluding this text, these 'All world imperatives' of Paul Harper seem to be particularly appropriate:

- Be sure you have something to say. Say it simply, clearly.
- Surround your message with friendliness and warmth:

  - The approach should involve an extended open hand — not a fist that pounds the desk.
  - Wrap a good natured smile around the words.

- Use words to punctuate strong images, not to preempt them:

  - Finesse language barriers by messages that only need to be seen.
  - Accent with music.
  - Enhance with the kind of humour known to be universal.

- At all cost, mind manners...observe simple good taste.
- Speak to the hopes and dreams of people, not merely to their needs:

  - People every where have legitimate yearnings for romance, love recognition and advancement.
  - To a degree that what we have to offer can promote these dreams we owe it to our customers to show them so.
  - No sale is ever made totally in the mind; the heart is also a worthy target.[54]

Questions

1 Discuss your point of view of the current state of international marketing communications. Give reasons for your position.
2 Why will it be more important for companies of the future to own markets rather than factories?

3   What is needed to build profitable brands of today and tomorrow? How do you go about it?
4   Explain why it may be better in the future to source products from a more rather than less developed economy.
5   What do you think the prospects will be for slower economies to close the gap with faster economies? Give reasons.
6   Do you think communication research will improve in the future? Explain.
7   In what ways will the advertising agency of tomorrow differ from today's agency?
8   What are the implications of growing retailer strength on manufacturers of branded merchandise? How can marketing communicators help?
9   Describe what you believe the marketing communication service company will be like in the future.
10 In what ways will communication techniques and tools differ tomorrow from today?

Notes

1   Kotler, Philip (1991) Philip Kotler explores the new marketing paradigm. *Review*, Marketing Science Institute, Spring, 1, 4, 5.
2   Vale, Norman (1990) Eastern Europe...new land of opportunity. *International Advertiser*, **3**, (5), 7.
3   Hartman, John W. (1991) Trends without a future. *Business Marketing*, March, 64.
4   Clancy, Kevin J. (1990) The coming revolution in advertising: ten developments which will separate winners from losers. *Journal of Advertising Research*, Feb/Mar, 47.
5   Light, Larry (1990) The changing advertising world. *Journal of Advertising Research*, Feb/Mar, 31.
6   Day, Barry (1990) 1992, and the USA. Presentation at Lintas Future Day, Chicago, 2 October, 25.
7   Munson, Shipley J. (1988) Speech to the New York chapter of the International Advertising Association, 9 November, 4.
8   Light, *op. cit.*, 31.
9   Pollack, Andrew (1991) IBM, APPLE join up in historic deal. *The News and Observer*, Raleigh, North Carolina, 4 July, 1.
10 Toffler, Alvin (1990) Toffler's next shock. *World Monitor*, November, 34−38, 41, 42, 44.
11 *Ibid.*, 44.
12 Light, *op. cit.*, 30, 31.
13 Munson, *op. cit.*, 7−9.

14　Light, *op. cit.*, 32.
15　HDM (1990) Presentation of HDM to a group from Pace University, Paris, 30 May.
16　Day, *op. cit.*, 28.
17　*Ibid.*
18　Morgan, Anthony I. and Cameroon, Patricia A. (1990) How will decisions be made in 2020? *Journal of Advertising Research*, Feb/Mar, 39−41.
19　Nielsen Marketing Research (1988) *Marketing Trends*, Northbrook, ILL, (2), 3, 4.
20　Metzger, Gale (1990) In *Roundtable Discussion: A Creative Exploration of the Future* (moderated by Bill Cook). *Journal of Advertising Research*, February, 16.
21　Clancy, *op. cit.*, 51.
22　Dunn, Ted and Rubens, Bill (1990) In *Roundtable Discussion: A Creative Exploration of the Future* (moderated by Bill Cook). *Journal of Advertising Research*, February, 17−18.
23　Rubens, Bill and Metzger, Gale (1990) In *Roundtable Discussion: A Creative Exploration of the Future* (moderated by Bill Cook). *Journal of Advertising Research*, February, 22.
24　Clancy, *op. cit.*, 49−50.
25　*Ibid.*, 50, 51.
26　Munson, *op. cit.*, 8.
27　Moore, Martha T. (1991) Ad agencies losing clout, author says. *USA Today*, 10 July, Section B, 1, 2.
28　Hartman, *op. cit.*
29　Light, *op. cit.*, 33−34.
30　Munson, *op. cit.*, 17.
31　Murrow, David and Wentz, Laurel (1989) UK shops face 1992 pressures. *Advertising Age*, 8 May, 48.
32　Nielsen Marketing Research (1987) *International Food and Drug Store Trends 1987*, A.C. Nielsen Company, Northbrook, ILL, 36, 53.
33　Day, *op. cit.*, 29.
34　Nielsen Marketing Research, *op. cit.*, 3, 36.
35　Fahey, Alison (1989) British invasion settles in for long run. *Advertising Age*, 1 May, 5−10.
36　*Advertising Age* Roundtable (1989) Sales promotion: what's ahead. *Advertising Age*, 8 May, 39.
37　Munson, *op. cit.*, 14.
38　Light, *op. cit.*, 34−35.
39　*Advertising Age* Roundtable, 38 and Berger, Karen (1990) The rising importance of point-of-purchase advertising in the marketing mix. Point-of-purchase Advertising Institute, Chicago, 2 October, 1.
40　Fahey, *op. cit.*, 5−8.

41   *Advertising Age* Roundtable, *op. cit.*, 39.
42   Munson, *op. cit.*, 20.
43   Day, *op. cit.*, 27.
44   Metzger, *op. cit.*, 21.
45   Light, *op. cit.*, 33.
46   Mandese, Joe (1990) McCann's bet. *Marketing and Media Decision*, February, 30.
47   *Ibid.*, 32.
48   *Ibid.*
49   Morgan, *op. cit.*, 40.
50   Upshaw, Lynn (1990) As they see it. *Marketing and Media Decisions*, December, 101, 102.
51   Day, *op. cit.*, 27, 28.
52   Neill, Roger (1991) The age of the big idea. *International Advertiser*, **3**, (5), 11.
53   Morgan, *op. cit.*, 40.
54   Harper, Paul C, Jr. (1981) Advertising's international opportunity. Presentation, IAA luncheon meeting, New York, 10 March.

Index